ADAMS
COVER
LETTER
ALMANAC

SECOND EDITION

Adams Media
Avon, Massachusetts

Published by Adams Media, an F+W Publications Company
57 Littlefield Street, Avon, MA 02322 U.S.A.
www.adamsmedia.com

ISBN 10: 1-59337-600-6
ISBN 13: 978-1-59337-600-0
Printed in Canada.

J I H G F E D C B

Library of Congress Cataloging-in-Publication Data
Adams cover letter almanac / Richard Wallace, editor.—2nd ed.
p.   cm.
ISBN 1-59337-600-6
1. Cover letters. 2. Job hunting. I. Wallace, Richard.- II. Adams Publishing (Avon, Mass.)

HF5383.A26 2006
650.14'2--dc22
2005034593

This publication is designed to provide accurate and authoritative information with regard to the subject matter covered. It is sold with the understanding that the publisher is not engaged in rendering legal, accounting, or other professional advice. If legal advice or other expert assistance is required, the services of a competent professional person should be sought.

— From a *Declaration of Principles* jointly adopted by a Committee of the American Bar Association and a Committee of Publishers and Associations

Many of the designations used by manufacturers and sellers to distinguish their products are claimed as trademarks. Where those designations appear in this book and Adams Media was aware of a trademark claim, the designations have been printed with initial capital letters.

This book is available at quantity discounts for bulk purchases.
For information, call 1-800-289-0963

CONTENTS

HOW TO USE THIS BOOK

The Adams Cover Letter Almanac, Second Edition, is a comprehensive guide packed full of helpful tips for crafting a job-winning cover letter. Since the previous edition was published, computers, e-mail, and the Internet have markedly changed the way we search for, and respond to, job opportunities. To reflect those changes, this new edition has been expanded to include the latest information about electronic cover letters, online classifieds, and career Web sites.

To get the most from this book, we recommend that you begin by looking over Part I: "All about Cover Letters." Here you will find everything you need to know about writing hard copy and electronic cover letters, from piecing together an introduction to choosing the right format. Are you wondering how to personalize each letter? Should you mention personal preferences, like a salary range? What are the common blunders you should avoid? Part I will answer all your cover letter questions, and more!

Part II: "All about Job Hunting" addresses more general job-search issues such as how to network effectively and how to determine the best companies to contact. If you're having trouble designing an effective strategy for finding employment in today's tough job market, look no further. Part II provides a step-by-step guide for job hunters.

Once you're ready to begin writing, we suggest you turn to Part III: "Sample Cover Letters." This section contains more than six hundred examples of cover letters used by real people to win real jobs. The letters address twenty-five types of situations including responses to classified advertisements (print and Web postings), information requests, and thank-you letters. Choose the chapters that are applicable to your special circumstances and start writing your letters, using the samples as guidelines.

Remember, there is no one "right" way to write a cover letter. The advantage of having so many different styles and formats is that you can pick and choose elements from numerous samples and custom-design each cover letter to fit your needs.

PART I

All about Cover Letters

CHAPTER 1

INTRODUCTION TO COVER LETTERS

Purpose of the Cover Letter

Your cover letter is more than likely the first contact you will have with a potential employer. If it is well written, your letter will lead the reader to the other part of your application—your resume. If your letter is poorly written, however, the employer may not even take the time to review your resume, and your application has a good chance of ending up in the trash.

Put yourself in the boss's shoes. If you were doing the hiring, what attributes would the ideal candidate for employment possess? You probably would prefer that the person have work experience similar to, or at least applicable to, the position for which he or she is applying. You would want the candidate to be ambitious and anxious to contribute his or her energy and skills to the success of your company. The perfect candidate would demonstrate interest in, and knowledge about, your industry *and* your specific organization. (An applicant's prior knowledge of an industry or a particular company suggests that he or she has a compelling interest in the firm, and is not looking at the current opening as "just another job.") In short, if you were doing the hiring, you probably would want to hear from an energetic, dedicated, and skilled candidate.

Your cover letter affords you the opportunity to present yourself as *the* perfect candidate. You can begin by learning how to create an effective sales pitch.

The Sales Pitch

Imagine your cover letter as a marketing tool, much like a television or radio commercial. Effective commercials catch your attention by highlighting only the most attractive features of a product.

Your cover letter should be your commercial, the place where you highlight your most attractive features as a potential employee. Remember, employers typically receive hundreds of applications for each job opening. No one is going to waste time reading through a long letter crammed with text. Be brief and succinct. You should avoid detailing your entire work history in your cover letter—save that information for your resume. The best way to distinguish yourself is to highlight one or two of your accomplishments or abilities that show you are an above-average candidate for the position. Stressing only one or two unique attributes increases your chances of being remembered by the recruiter and getting to the interview stage, where you can elaborate on the rest of your accomplishments.

In addition, the cover letter allows you to carefully select one or two accomplishments or special skills that reflect your suitability for the desired position. If you are applying for a job that doesn't fit directly into your experience, make sure you explain how your background and qualifications match the position's requirements. For example, imagine you are a bank accountant seeking an applications programmer position in a computer software development company. A well-crafted cover letter would emphasize your relevant computer experience, and de-emphasize your accounting background.

Personalize Each Letter

The success of your job-hunting campaign relies on the *quality* of your contacts and how well you maintain them, not on the *quantity* of applications you send out. Taking time to research each employer promises to be much more effective than sending out hundreds of form letters and resumes. In effect, you are saying to an employer, "This is where I want to work. I have done my research and I am confident about my decision." Also, the employer will view your interest as an indication that you are likely to stay with the company for a substantial period of time if hired. (For more information on researching a potential employer, see Chapter 7.)

First, try to determine the appropriate person to whom you should address your cover letter. In general, the more influential your contact is, the better. Try to contact the head of the department in which you are interested. If you are applying to a larger corporation, it is likely that your application will be screened by a human resources or personnel department. If you are instructed to direct your inquiry to this division, attempt to find out the name of the senior manager. This way, you may be able to cut down on the number of people your resume passes through on its way to the final decision-maker. In any event, be sure to include your contact's name and title on both your letter and envelope. This will ensure that your letter will get through to the proper person, even if there's been a recent change in staffing and a new person occupies this position.

When to Send a Cover Letter

Every time you make contact with a potential employer, send a cover letter. Whether your resume is sent as an initial inquiry, or whether you are following up on a phone conversation, job interview, or position offering, write a carefully composed, polished letter. If you have recently contacted a hiring manager, sending another copy of your resume may not be necessary. In general, a resume does not have to accompany every cover letter you send, but a cover letter must be enclosed every time you send a resume. Even if you are following up on an advertisement that reads simply "send resume," be sure to include a cover letter. It is considered unprofessional to send out a resume without one.

CHAPTER 2

THE ANATOMY OF A COVER LETTER

Even before a potential employer reads a word of your cover letter, he or she has probably already made an assessment of your organizational skills and attention to detail simply by observing its appearance. How your hard copy correspondence looks to a reader—its format, length, even the size, color, and quality of the paper on which your letter is printed—can mean the difference between serious consideration and automatic rejection. The same goes for electronic submissions, which have their own set of unique rules and standards. Whether you are making your bid for consideration by "snail mail" or online, you simply cannot afford to offer a less than perfect presentation of your credentials. This chapter not only outlines the basic formats you should follow when writing hard copy and electronic cover letters, it shows you how to put the finishing touches on a top-notch product that will improve your chances of getting to the next step—the interview.

Hard Copy Cover Letters

Length

Rule number 1: Keep it brief! Four short paragraphs on one page is the ideal length for a hard copy cover letter. Anything longer is unlikely to be read.

Paper Size

Use standard 8½-by-11-inch paper for your cover letter. If you use a smaller size, the correspondence will appear more personal than professional; a larger size simply looks awkward. Keep in mind, too, that paper other than the standard size can easily get lost in an employer's files if too small or, if too large, discarded altogether because it doesn't fit neatly with other documents inside a standard manila file folder.

Paper Color

White and ivory are the only acceptable paper colors for a cover letter. The same goes for resumes. If you think neon pink or lime green paper will make a prospective employer more likely to notice your letter, you're right. In all likelihood, he or she will pay attention just long enough to toss it into the circular file.

Paper Quality

As with resumes, standard, inexpensive office paper (20# bond) is generally acceptable for most positions. If you are applying for an executive or top-level position, however, you may want to invest in heavier, more expensive stationery, such as ivory laid.

Preprinted Stationery

Unless you're a top-level executive with years of experience, you should avoid using preprinted stationery. And never, never print your cover letter on the stationery of your current employer!

Typing and Printing

Even if you have perfect penmanship, a cover letter is no place to show it off. Your letter should never be handwritten; it should always be typed. And this is no time to experiment with odd typefaces, either. Conventional wisdom says that serif fonts are easier to read than sans serif (serifs are those little "feet" on the edges of the letters). Times New Roman is the most popular serif choice, but you might also consider Bookman, Century, Garamond, or Palatino. Use a letter-quality printer and make sure that your toner cartridge has plenty of ink. Paragraphs should be aligned flush left with a ragged right margin for greater readability. Double space between paragraphs; do not indent the first line. And be sure to proofread your letter before sending it out. Nothing screams "poor prospect" like a spelling error.

The Envelope

Your cover letter and resume should always be mailed in a standard, business-size (#10) envelope. The only exception to this rule is when you are enclosing an attachment, such as a writing or graphic arts sample or photographs, that cannot be folded to fit inside a #10 envelope. The address on the outside of your envelope should match the address on your cover letter; include the recipient's full name and title preceded by Mr. or Ms. Always type your envelopes using the same font as your cover letter; handwritten addresses are unprofessional.

Ten Key Ingredients of Successful Hard Copy Cover Letters

Looks do count, but only up to a point. Even if your cover letter is printed on the highest quality paper and typed on a state-of-the-art computer, if it isn't arranged according to the proper format or does not contain the necessary information, you may not come across as the best candidate for the position you are seeking. Certain basic guidelines should be followed when composing the actual contents of your letter.

1. **The return address.** Type your return address and phone number in the top right-hand corner of your letter; do not include your name. As a general rule, avoid using abbreviations (St., Ave., Blvd., etc.) in the addresses of your

cover letters. You may, however, abbreviate the state, using U.S. Postal Service guidelines—i.e., FL, not Fla., for Florida; MI, not Mich., for Michigan, etc.

2. **The date.** The date should appear two lines beneath your return address on the right-hand side of the page. Write out the date in full; do not use abbreviations.

   Example: January 12, 20—

3. **The addressee.** Always try to find out the name and correct title of the addressee before you send out a cover letter. Flush left and two lines beneath the date, state the full name of the addressee. On the next line, state the individual's formal business title; then on the subsequent line, give the name of the company. This is followed by the company's address, which generally takes two lines. Occasionally, the individual's full title or the company name and address will be very long, and can appear awkward if you try to stick to the usual number of lines allocated. In such cases, feel free to use an extra line or two as needed.

4. **The salutation.** Your salutation should be typed two lines beneath the address. It should begin with "Dear Mr." or "Dear Ms.," followed by the individual's last name and a colon. Even if you have previously spoken with an addressee who has asked to be called by his or her first name, you should never be so informal in the salutation.

   In cases where you do not know the name of your addressee, such as when you are responding to "blind" advertisements, it may be necessary to use a general salutation. In these circumstances, salutations such as "Dear Hiring Manager" or "Good Morning" may be stronger choices than "Dear Sir or Madam" or "To whom it may concern." In any case, avoid gender-specific salutations like "Dear Gentlemen," or "Dear Sirs."

5. **First paragraph.** State immediately and concisely the position for which you wish to be considered and what makes you the best candidate to fill this particular job opening. If you are responding to a classified ad, be sure to reference the name of the publication and the date on which the ad appeared. Keep the first paragraph short and hard-hitting.

   Example: Having majored in mathematics at Boston University, where I also worked as a Research Assistant, I am confident that I would make a very successful Research Trainee in your economics research department.

6. **Second paragraph.** Briefly expound on the contributions you might make to this company, and show how your qualifications will benefit this firm. If you are responding to a classified ad, specifically discuss how your skills relate to the job's requirements. Remember, keep it brief and to the point. This is not a time to ramble.

Example: In addition to my strong background in mathematics, I offer significant business experience, having worked in a data processing firm, a bookstore, and a restaurant. I am sure that my courses in statistics and computer programming would prove particularly useful in the position of Trainee.

7. **Third paragraph.** Describe your interest in the corporation. Subtly emphasize your knowledge about this firm (the result of your own research efforts) and your familiarity with the industry. You should present yourself as eager to work for any company to which you may apply.

Example: I am attracted to City Bank by your recent rapid growth and the superior reputation of your economic research department. After studying several different commercial banks, I have concluded that City Bank will be in a strong competitive position to benefit from upcoming changes in the industry.

8. **Final paragraph.** In the closing paragraph, specifically request an interview. Include your phone number and the hours you can be reached, or indicate that you will follow up with a phone call within a few days to arrange an interview at a mutually convenient time.

Example: I would like to interview with you at your earliest convenience. I am best reached between 3 P.M. and 5 P.M. Monday through Friday at (617) 555-5555.

9. **The closing.** The closing should appear two lines below the body of the letter and should be aligned with your return address and the date (toward the right-hand side of the page). Keep your closing simple—"Sincerely" usually suffices. Space down four lines (enough to allow for your signature) and type your full name as it appears on your resume. Your typed name should align with the closing.

     Sign above your typed name in blue or black ink. Remember to always sign your letters! As silly as it sounds, people often forget this seemingly obvious point. A simple oversight such as this suggests that you are inattentive to details.

10. **The enclosure line.** If you are enclosing a resume or other materials with your letter, include an enclosure line, flush left, at the bottom of the letter.

Example: Enc. Resume
           Writing sample

GENERAL MODEL FOR A HARD COPY COVER LETTER

Your Address
Your City/State
Your Phone

Date

Contact Person Name
Title
Company
Address
City/State

Dear Mr./Ms._____:

    Immediately explain why your background makes you the best candidate for this particular position. Keep the first paragraph short and hard-hitting.

    Briefly expound on the contributions you might make to this company. Show how your qualifications will benefit this firm. Remember, however, to keep the letter short; few employers will read a cover letter that is longer than one page.

    Describe your interest in the corporation. Subtly emphasize your knowledge about this firm (the result of your own research efforts) and your familiarity with the industry. You should present yourself as eager to work for any company to which you may apply.

    In the closing paragraph, you should specifically request an interview. Include your phone number and the hours when you can be reached. Alternatively, you might prefer to mention that you will follow up with a phone call (to arrange an interview at a mutually convenient time within several days).

Sincerely,

Your full name as it appears on your resume
(typed)

Enc. Resume

GENERAL MODEL FOR A HARD COPY FOLLOW-UP LETTER

Your Address
Your City/State
Your Phone

Date

Contact Person
Title
Company
Address
City/State

Dear Mr./Ms._____:

Remind the interviewer of the position for which you were interviewed, as well as the date of your meeting. Thank him or her for the opportunity to interview.

Confirm your interest in the opening and the organization. Use specifics to emphasize both that you have researched the firm in detail and considered how you would fit into the company and meet the requirements for the position.

As in your cover letter, emphasize one or two of your strongest qualifications and slant them toward the various points that the interviewer cited as the most important for the position. Keep the letter brief; a half-page is plenty.

If appropriate, close with a suggestion for further action, such as a desire for a second interview. Mention your phone number and the hours you can best be reached. Alternatively, you may prefer to indicate that you will follow up with a phone call within the next few days.

Sincerely,

Your full name as it appears on your resume
(typed)

Enc. Resume

Electronic Cover Letters

The majority of job opportunities posted on the Web, and even many that appear in traditional classified ads these days, ask for resumes by e-mail. When making your application electronically, you may be tempted to simply shoot off your resume and leave it at that. Don't. Just like a hard copy resume, which should never go in the mail without a cover letter, your electronic resume shouldn't travel solo either. And while the rules for electronic submissions are fewer—you don't have to worry about paper size, color, or quality, for example—there are still a few guidelines you should keep in mind.

Length

The primary purpose of e-mail is to communicate quickly and concisely. This is not the place to be verbose. Keep your sentences short and limit your letter to no more than a paragraph or two. And by all means, do not even be tempted to use the abbreviations (LOL, IMHO, etc.), funky spellings, or smiley face emoticons everyone seems to slip into their e-mail messages these days. Remember that the purpose of your letter is to land an interview and ultimately a job. If you want to appear serious and professional, save the "cutesy" stuff for e-mail messages to friends.

Typing

E-mail messages tend to be less formal than hard copy correspondence, so you have a little more leeway with regard to selecting a font. Keep in mind that your recipient will be reading this letter on a screen, so the simpler the type style, the better. Sans serif fonts like Arial and Univers work well online. Courier New, a serif font that mimics the old pica typewriters, or Times New Roman may also be good choices. The body of your letter should be aligned flush left. Double space between paragraphs and do not indent the first line. Be sure to proofread your letter, but do not rely solely on your spellchecker to do so. Computer spell-checkers can't distinguish between different spellings of the same word. To the computer, "their" and "there" or "two" and "to" are correct regardless of the context in which they are used. Remember to reread your message carefully before you hit "send." Believe it or not, your attention to grammatical details, or lack thereof, makes a strong statement to a prospective employer about your job worthiness.

To Attach or Not to Attach?

There are two schools of thought with regard to e-mail attachments. Some employers want to receive resumes as attachments; others, fearing viruses perhaps, prefer that you paste your resume into the actual e-mail message. The employer's preference will sometimes be stated in the ad or job posting, but when in doubt, paste. Cover letters are another matter altogether. They should never be sent as attachments. Why? Because, for the sake of simplicity and to avoid file corruption in downloading on the other end, you should attach only one file per e-mail. Make your cover letter the e-mail message and attach the resume to it.

Six Key Ingredients of Successful Electronic Cover Letters

The format for electronic cover letters is less formal than hard copy correspondence. Since you'll be working within a framework dictated by your e-mail provider, you need not worry about typing in a return address or date at the top of the page. You do, however, need to be concerned about creating the best possible first impression. Here are a few basic guidelines you should follow.

1. **Your e-mail address.** Even before a prospective employer reads your electronic cover letter, he or she has the chance to form a first impression. Make it a good one by selecting an appropriate e-mail address. If the screen name on your e-mail account is something like "sexychick" or "borrn2Bwild," the chances are good a prospective employer won't even open your message. Keep the cutesy names for personal e-mails, and come up with something that sounds more professional for your job search. Some combination of first and last name or initials is probably your best bet.

2. **Subject line.** Every e-mail message you write gives you an opportunity to spell out the subject of your message. With regard to electronic cover letters, the subject line is the place where you can let your recipient know that you are applying for a particular position, answering a specific ad, or updating information you may have sent previously. Do not be tempted to leave the subject line blank. That's what "spammers" do, so often in fact, that many people never open any messages they receive that do not specify a subject, especially if they don't recognize the sender; they simply delete them. If you want your cover letter to be read, fill out the subject line.

3. **The salutation.** Your salutation should be the first line of your actual e-mail message. You may begin with "Dear Mr." or "Dear Ms.," followed by the individual's last name and a colon. In cases where you do not know the name of your addressee, such as when you are responding to "blind" advertisements, it is perfectly acceptable to open with a generic salutation. "Dear Sir or Madam" or "To whom it may concern" may be a little formal for this medium; however, "Dear Hiring Manager" or "Good Morning" are perfectly acceptable. Beware of using salutations that are gender-specific. "Dear Gentlemen" or "Dear Sirs" might be offensive to some.

4. **First paragraph.** State immediately and concisely the position for which you wish to be considered and why you are the best candidate to fill this particular job opening. If you are responding to a classified ad or Web-based job posting, be sure to reference the name of the publication or the number assigned to the posting. Keep your first paragraph short and hard-hitting.

   Example: I am responding to your posting for an advertising account executive (Job #45678), which recently appeared on Monster.com. I am a seasoned advertising professional with more than eight years of experience in creative development, account supervision, and sales. Most recently, as the primary liaison between three key accounts and the creative team at a midsize advertising agency in Madison, Wisconsin, I have repeatedly demonstrated my ability to manage multiple priorities in a deadline-sensitive environment.

5. **Second paragraph.** In an electronic cover letter, the second paragraph is your close. This is where you reference your resume (either pasted below or attached) and suggest an interview, if appropriate.

Example: The resume pasted below spells out the details of my educational background and professional experience. I would welcome the opportunity to meet with you personally to discuss my qualifications and how I might put them to work for your clients. I look forward to hearing from you soon.

6. **The closing.** The closing should appear two lines below the body of your message. Keep it simple—"Sincerely" is usually enough. Space down a line or two and type your full name as it appears on your resume. If you are attaching your resume as a separate document, you may also wish to type your physical address, phone number, and e-mail address at the bottom of your e-mail message.

GENERAL MODEL FOR AN ELECTRONIC COVER LETTER

To: contact person's e-mail address
From: your e-mail address
Subj: use this line to let your recipient know that you are applying for a particular position, answering a specific ad, or updating information you may have sent previously.

Dear Mr./Ms._____:

　　Immediately and concisely state the position for which you wish to be considered and why you are the best candidate for the job. Reference the specific classified ad or Web posting, if applicable. Keep the first paragraph short and hard-hitting.

　　Reference your resume (either pasted below or attached) and suggest a face-to-face meeting, if appropriate.

Sincerely,

Your name

Your address
Your city/state
Your phone
Your e-mail address

CHAPTER 3

A QUESTION OF STYLE

After you have chosen a career path, written your resume, and researched prospective employers, you are ready to begin composing your cover letter. Unlike a resume, a cover letter shouldn't just summarize your credentials. Think of it, instead, as a sales tool, a vehicle you can use to demonstrate why your skills and background make you *the* perfect candidate for the specific position you seek. Choosing the best writing style will help your cover letter stand out from other job seekers in a positive way. This chapter covers everything you need to know before and after you begin writing. Late-breaking information on related topics is available online at *www.truecareers.com*.

What Writing Style Is Appropriate?

In general, your cover letter should adopt a polite, formal style that balances your confidence in yourself with a sense of respect for the potential employer. Keep the style clear, objective, and persuasive rather than narrative. In other words, don't waste precious space boasting about personal accomplishments; use the space instead to describe the qualifications you possess that are particularly relevant to the job you are seeking. To illustrate this point, consider these approaches from two marketing directors who responded to the same classified advertisement:

Candidate A: "In 1998, I graduated from college, and moved to Boston because my sister lived there. When I couldn't find a job, I ended up back in graduate school in New York, where I stayed until 2000. Once graduated, I flew back to my favorite city, Boston, and have been successful in marketing ever since."

Candidate B: "In addition to a Bachelor of Arts degree in Business Administration, I recently received a Master's degree, cum laude, in International Marketing from Brown University. This educational experience is supported by two years of part-time experience with J&D Products, where my marketing efforts resulted in increased annual product sales of 25 percent."

Can you guess who landed the job? Candidate B, of course. Candidate A may be equally qualified, but she chooses to focus on irrelevant information, and fails to relate her qualifications to the desired position. Candidate B, on the other hand, successfully highlights only pertinent data, including educational training and specific accomplishments. The result is a targeted and cohesive statement that easily grabs the attention of a prospective employer.

Tone

Before you sit down to write, take some time to think about how you would sell your qualifications in a job interview. You probably would (or should) think harder about what to say and how to say it than you would if you were sitting down to talk to a friend. Above all, you would want to sound polite, confident, and professional. The tone of your cover letter should be no different. You should immediately communicate your eagerness to join the firm and confidence in your ability to handle the job. The trick, of course, is to sound enthusiastic without becoming melodramatic. Take, for example, the candidate who expressed his desire to enter the advertising field as "the single, most important thing I have ever wanted in my entire twenty-three years of existence." Yikes! That's a bit over the top. Now consider what the candidate who was actually offered the position had to say: "My extensive research into the industry, coupled with my internship and educational training, have confirmed my desires to pursue an entry-level position in advertising."

Your tone may vary somewhat depending on your profession: A comedian and a chemist, for example, probably would choose dissimilar tones. While it would be perfectly fitting for a comedian to adopt a light-hearted, familiar tone that showcases his or her sense of humor, the chemist would be better served by a more formal voice. Remember, always, to use your best judgment when establishing tone, and to err on the side of caution. Put yourself in the employer's place: Is there the slightest chance that he or she might be turned off by your tone? If so, adopt a more moderate voice.

The tone of your letter may also vary depending on where you are in your career path. A recent college graduate might focus on his or her eagerness to enter the workplace, whereas a seasoned executive would probably choose to display a reserved confidence in his or her extensive experience.

If you are accustomed to the tone used for online instant messaging and e-mail chats with your friends, you might assume that electronic cover letters should incorporate the same easy informality and quirky shortcuts (i.e., 2 for "to," and RU for "are you"). Not so. The tone used in electronic cover letters must sound every bit as professional as that of their hard copy counterparts. The only real difference between the two is length. While a hard copy cover letter typically encompasses four paragraphs, the electronic version rarely takes up more than two. You still need to encapsulate your relevant qualifications, of course; you just have less space in which to do so.

If you are planning to job search online or to post your resume to the Web, you should also be aware of the importance of key words. The people looking to hire new employees with specific skills search the Web using certain key words. If your resume does not contain the right ones, your materials may just drift forever in cyberspace, pretty much inaccessible to the people who could potentially offer you a job. See Chapter 9 for more information about key words.

State Your Purpose

Don't make the employer guess your purpose for writing. Open your letter by explaining your intent, whether it is to request an informational interview or to respond to an advertisement for an actual job opening. Your reader does not have the time or desire to search for an explanation, so spell out your purpose up front.

Bear in mind that your cover letter is an advertisement, not an affidavit. Do not feel compelled to describe every job you've ever had or every responsibility with which you have been entrusted. If you are applying for an entry-level bank teller position, it is not advantageous to include detailed descriptions of your summers as a camp counselor or lifeguard. The hiring manager doesn't need to know the entire course of your career; what matters is your pertinent experience.

Present Yourself as an Industry Insider

No matter where you are in your career path, you can easily sell yourself as an industry insider and a desirable employee. Bone up on the industry you're targeting in your job search, then use the knowledge you have gathered to cite industry-wide trends or recent achievements by the company to which you are applying. Not only will you appear well prepared, but your letter will rise above those who have neglected to do their homework!

Emphasize Concrete Examples

Your resume details the duties you have performed in previous jobs. In contrast, your cover letter should highlight your most significant accomplishments. Instead of stating something like, "My career is highlighted by several major achievements," cite concrete examples:

- "While Sales Manager at Corpco, I supervised a team which increased revenues by 35 percent in eighteen months."
- "I published four articles in the *New England Journal of Medicine*."
- "At EarthFriends, I advanced from telephone fund raiser, to Field Manager, to Canvas Director within two years."

List tangible, relevant skills rather than personal attributes. A sentence such as "I am fluent in C+, Pascal, and COBOL programming languages" is a better description of your capabilities than a vague statement like "I am a goal-oriented, highly skilled Computer Programmer."

Use Powerful Language

Your language should be hard-hitting and easy to understand. Make your letters "pop" by using action verbs such as "accelerated," "designed," "implemented," and "increased," rather than passive verbs like "was" and "did." Don't make the mistake of thinking that the bigger the word the more intelligent you will sound. For maximum impact, use simple, everyday language and avoid abbreviations and slang. And do steer clear of language that is too specialized or jargon-heavy, even if you are applying for a job that requires technical expertise. Keep in mind that the first person who reads your cover letter is often a human resources manager who may not possess the same breadth of knowledge as your future boss.

In the course of a job search, it is tempting to use catchphrases that you may have picked up from various job-search reference materials, phrases that sound as though they *should* go in a cover letter. Be assured that almost every person who applies for a position presents him- or herself as a "self-starter" with "excellent interpersonal skills." Improve upon these pompous-sounding self-descriptions whenever possible by listing actual projects and goals. "I am a determined achiever with proven leadership skills" can be rephrased to read "While at MoneyWorks, I successfully increased the number of projects completed ahead of deadline, while supervising a staff of fifteen." It says the same thing, but in specific, quantifiable terms. Once you begin working, employers will discover your personal attributes for themselves. While still under consideration for a position, however, concrete experiences carry more weight than vague phrases and obscure promises.

Action verbs make a cover letter come alive. Which of the following might you substitute for weaker verbs in yours?

accelerated	evaluated	prepared
accomplished	examined	presented
achieved	executed	prioritized
administered	expanded	processed
advised	expedited	produced
analyzed	extracted	programmed
appointed	facilitated	promoted
arranged	formulated	proposed
assisted	founded	provided
attained	generated	published
balanced	headed	recruited
budgeted	helped	regulated
built	identified	reorganized
calculated	illustrated	represented
catalogued	implemented	researched
chaired	improved	resolved
collaborated	increased	restored
compiled	initiated	restructured
composed	innovated	retrieved
computed	instructed	reviewed
conducted	integrated	revised
constructed	interpreted	scheduled
consulted	launched	shaped
created	maintained	sold
delegated	managed	solved
demonstrated	marketed	streamlined
designed	mediated	summarized
developed	monitored	supervised
devised	negotiated	taught
directed	operated	trained
edited	organized	upgraded
educated	performed	utilized
encouraged	persuaded	worked
established	planned	wrote

Vary Your Sentence Length

Initially, the recipient of your letter will probably just scan it rather than read it closely. If, at first glance, your sentences look unwieldy, he or she may never get around to reading it at all. Short, concise sentences are much more effective than long-winded ones. Ideally, a hard copy cover letter should be no longer than four paragraphs, an electronic submission no longer than two. In either case, paragraphs should consist of no more than three sentences. If you find yourself writing more, you should probably take an editing pencil to your copy or, at the very least, break up that single long paragraph into two or more shorter ones.

Including Personal Preferences

Candidates often worry if, and how, they should incorporate their preferences for working environment, availability to travel and/or relocate, and salary demands into a cover letter. As a rule of thumb, mention work preferences only if you are confident they match the job description your potential employer offers. For instance, don't state that you work best independently in a formal office setting if you are applying for a position that you suspect may require group interaction or extensive travel. If you are applying to an out-of-state firm, indicate your willingness to relocate; otherwise, a hiring manager may question your purpose for writing and may not take the initiative to inquire.

Refrain from discussing salary requirements in your letter unless the advertisement you are responding to specifically requests that you do so. If you must include salary information, offer it as a range rather than lock yourself into a specific figure. Another option is to simply indicate in your letter that salary is negotiable.

Don't Forget to Proofread!

The cover letter is your first impression before a prospective employer and you can't afford to make it a bad one. As with your resume, mistakes in cover letters cannot only be embarrassing, particularly when something as critical and obvious as your name is misspelled, they can sometimes even cost you the opportunity to progress to the next step in your job search. Always proofread your cover letter and resume as carefully as possible. Get a friend to help you—read your draft aloud as your friend proofs the final copy. Then switch places; have your friend read it aloud while you check the letter. Finally, sit down and read your letter word for word, checking for spelling and punctuation as you go. You may be tempted to leave the proofreading entirely up to your computer's built-in spellchecker. Don't. Spellcheckers cannot distinguish between words that sound alike, but have vastly different meanings. For example, if you inadvertently type "My experience includes *to* years as a customer service representative at . . . ," your spellchecker won't flag the error because every word in the sentence is spelled correctly; the computer doesn't know you meant to write *two*. By trusting too heavily on your spellchecker, you can easily miss obvious errors.

CHAPTER 4

TWENTY COVER LETTER BLUNDERS TO AVOID

So far, we've seen what makes a successful cover letter. Now it's time to consider what doesn't. Even seemingly small errors, like misspelling or misplacing a word, can diminish your hard work. From typographical mishaps to erroneous employer information, all mistakes have a negative impact on the application process and ultimately your chances of landing the job. Serious errors will send your application directly into the wastebasket. Be forewarned: Carefully read and reread your cover letter several times before hitting the "send" button or dropping it into the mailbox. For additional tips online, go to *www.truecareers.com*.

The following list outlines some of the most common cover letter mistakes and, more importantly, suggests ways to correct them. These examples have been adapted from real-life cover letters gathered during the course of our research. Although some of these blunders may seem obvious, they occur far more often than you might think. Needless to say, none of the inquiries that included these mistakes met with positive results.

1. **Unrelated career goals:** Tailor your cover letter to the specific position you wish to apply for. A hiring manager is only interested in what you can do for the company, not what you hope to accomplish for yourself. He or she certainly doesn't want to know that you'll be taking this job only until a better opportunity comes along. Your letter should convey a genuine interest in the position and a long-term pledge to fulfilling its duties. Consider the difference between these two real-life examples:

   Example A (wrong way): "While my true goal is to become a Professional Dancer, I am exploring the option of taking on proofreading work while continuing to train for the Boston Ballet's next audition."

   Example B (right way): "I am very interested in this proofreading position, and I am confident of my ability to make a long-term contribution to your capable staff."

2. **Comparisons and clichés:** Avoid obvious comparisons and overused clichés; such expressions distract from your letter's purpose, which is to highlight your most impressive skills and accomplishments.

Here are a few real-life blunders we encountered in this category: "My word processor runs like the wind," "I am a people person," "Teamwork is my middle name," "Your company is known as the crème de la crème of accounting firms," "I am as smart as a whip," "Among the responses you receive for this position, I hope my qualifications make me leader of the pack." If you find yourself peppering your copy with phrases like these, hit the delete key and start over. Your goal is to land a job, not to demonstrate your facility for recalling hackneyed expressions.

3. **Wasted space:** Since cover letters are generally no more than four paragraphs long (just two for electronic submissions), every word of every sentence should be directly related to your purpose for writing. In other words, if you are applying for a position as a chemist, include only those skills and experiences most applicable to that field. Any other information weakens your message. Some real-life blunders we've run across include:

Example: "As my enclosed resume reveals, I possess the technical experience and educational background to succeed as your newest Civil Engineer. In addition, I am a certified Gymnastics Instructor who has won several local competitions."

Example: "I am writing in response to your advertisement for an Accounting Clerk. Currently, I am finishing an Associate degree at Fisher Junior College. My courses have included Medieval Architecture, Film Theory, American History before 1900, and Nutrition."

4. **Form letters:** Mass mailings, in which you send the same general letter to a large number of employers, are not a good idea. This approach does not allow for any personal touch. Every cover letter that you write should be tailored to the position you are seeking and should demonstrate both your commitment to a specific industry and your familiarity with each particular employer. Mass mailings indicate to a hiring manager that you are not truly interested in joining his or her organization. They also suggest that you're just plain lazy. Look at it from the employer's perspective: if you aren't willing to exert the energy to draft an individualized letter in order to search for a job, where might you cut corners once you land one?

    Savvy hiring managers can recognize mass mailings in a heartbeat. Certain formats and phrases just tend to stick out. In one real-life mass-mailing mishap, the candidate created a form letter in which he left blank spaces for penning in the employer's name and the position applied for. Another applicant who was indecisive about her field of interest created in her letter a list of possible positions for which she might apply. Before sending out each letter, she circled the most appropriate one depending on the company she was targeting.

5. **Inappropriate stationery:** As we mentioned in Chapter 2, white and ivory are the only acceptable paper colors for a cover letter. We've seen letters in every shade from hot pink to electric blue and, to be honest, the color was the *only* thing we noticed. Also, we recommend standard weight (20#) plain paper; steer clear of onion skin or personalized stationery.

As a general rule of thumb, the stationery you choose should not distract from the contents of your cover letter. A cat enthusiast who applied to our company "enhanced" her letter with several images of her favorite felines. A musician applying for an office position sent a letter decorated with a border of musical notes and instruments. We remember the paper all right, but, sadly, nothing else about either applicant. Remember, never rely on graphics to "improve" your cover letter; let your qualifications speak for themselves.

6. **"Amusing" anecdotes:** Generally speaking, if you desire serious consideration, your cover letter should adopt a serious, professional tone. Imagine yourself in an interview setting. Since you do not know your interviewer, you're not likely to joke with him or her until you have determined what demeanor is appropriate. Likewise, when writing to a potential employer you have never met, you should remain polite and professional. Avoid blunders like the one this job seeker made:

Example: "I feel I am especially qualified to join your staff, as my name, Chris Smith, almost rhymes with your company, **Christmas**, company."

7. **Erroneous company information:** If you were the employer, would you want to hire a candidate who confuses your company's products and services with those of another company or who misquotes information about recent goings-on? To avoid such errors, be sure to verify the accuracy of any company information that you mention in your cover letter., By the same token, if you haven't researched the company, don't pretend that you have. Vague statements like "I know something about your company" or "I am familiar with your products" signal to an employer that you haven't done your homework; you're just bluffing.

   When citing information about a company, be specific. The following is an example of an effective way to use company information in your cover letter: "I have been following Any Corporation's growth for many months and I was excited to learn of your recent acquisition of C&M, Inc. Congratulations on successfully entering the international market!"

8. **Desperation:** In your cover letter, you should sound determined, not desperate. While an employer appreciates enthusiasm, he or she may be turned off by a desperate plea for work. A fine line often separates the two, so the best advice we can give you is to follow your instincts. Here are a few blunders to avoid: "I am desperately eager to start, as I have been out of work for six months," "Please call today! I'll be waiting by the phone," "I really, really need this job to pay off medical bills." In one letter we came across, the candidate even dramatically enlarged the type for his closing statement, which read, "I AM VERY BADLY IN NEED OF MONEY!"

9. **Personal photos:** During the course of our research for this book, we came across instances in which candidates enclosed actual photographs in their job applications. We opened one letter to find an 8-by-10-inch glossy of a doctor surrounded by her patients. Another candidate used his computer to electronically scan his image onto the cover letter stationery. A third enlarged a

picture of his face to cover an 8-½-by-11-inch sheet of paper, then handwrote his letter on top of it!

Unless you are seeking employment in modeling, acting, or some other industry where your looks may help get you the job, it is not appropriate to send a photograph. An employer will see what you look like soon enough should you make it to the interview stage. Until then, even the cutest dimples and whitest smile won't help you get a foot in the door!

10. **Confessed shortcomings:** In an attempt to head off an employer's possible objections to some aspect of their application, job-hunters will sometimes call attention to their weaknesses in their cover letters. This is a mistake because the letter ends up emphasizing your flaws rather than your strengths. For example, avoid statements such as: "Although I have no related experience, I remain very interested in the Management Consultant position," and "I may not be well qualified for this position but it has always been my dream to work in the publishing field." Concentrate instead on promoting your strengths, by drawing the employer's attention to the valuable skills, related experience, and industry knowledge you *can* bring to the position.

11. **Misrepresentation:** In any stage of the job-search process, never, *ever*, misrepresent yourself. In many companies, erroneous information contained in a cover letter or resume will be grounds for dismissal as soon as the inaccuracy is discovered. Protect yourself by sticking to the facts. You are selling your skills and accomplishments in your cover letter. If you have achieved something, say so, and put it in the best possible light. Don't hold back or be modest—you can bet your competition won't. At the same time, however, don't exaggerate to the point of misrepresentation, as these examples demonstrate:

Example: "In June, I graduated with honors from the American University. In the course of my studies, I played two varsity sports while concurrently holding down five jobs."

Example: "Since beginning my career four years ago, I have won hundreds of competitions and awards, and am considered by many to be the best Hair Stylist on the East Coast."

12. **Demanding statements:** Keep in mind that your cover letter should demonstrate what you can do for an employer, not what he or she can do for you. For example, instead of stating, "I am looking for a unique opportunity in which I will be adequately challenged and compensated," say "I am confident that I could make a significant contribution to your organization, specifically by expanding your customer base in the Northwest region and instituting a discount offer for new accounts."

Also, since you are requesting an employer's consideration, your letter shouldn't include personal preferences or demands. Statements such as, "It would be an overwhelmingly smart idea for you to hire me," or "Let's meet next Wednesday at 4 P.M., when I will be available to discuss my candidacy further," may put a potential employer on the defensive. Job candidates' demands are rarely met with enthusiasm.

13. **Missing resume:** Have you ever forgotten to enclose all the materials you refer to in your cover letter? On numerous occasions, we've received letters with no resumes. Writing samples have been promised but not delivered. Not only is this a disappointment, it can be a fatal oversight. It shows a lack of attention to detail. And no employer is going to take the time to inform you of your mistake; he or she has already moved on to the next application.

14. **Personal information:** Do not include your age, weight, height, marital status, race, religion, or any other personal information in your cover letter or resume unless you feel that it directly pertains to the position you are seeking. For instance, age might be relevant if you are seeking a job at a seniors' organization and height and weight may be important if you are applying to an athletic team or for a position at a weight management clinic.

    Similarly, you should list your personal interests and hobbies only if they are directly relevant to the type of job you are seeking. If you are applying to a company that greatly values teamwork, for instance, citing that you organized a community fundraiser or played on a basketball team will probably be advantageous. When in doubt about whether to include information concerning non-job-related activities, however, leave it out.

15. **Choice of pronouns:** Your cover letter necessarily requires a thorough discussion of your qualifications. Although some applicants might choose the third person ("he or she") as a creative approach to presenting their qualifications, potential employers sometimes find this point of view disconcerting; it sounds like someone other than the job applicant wrote the letter. Using the first person ("I") point of view is generally preferred.

    Example A *(wrong way):* "Chris Smith is a highly qualified Public Relations Executive with more than seven years of relevant experience in the field. She possesses strong verbal and written communication skills and her client base is extensive."

    Example B *(right way):* "I am a highly qualified Public Relations Executive with more than seven years of relevant experience in the field. I possess strong verbal and written communication skills and my client base is extensive."

16. **Tone trouble:** Tone problems are subtle, and may be hard to detect. When you are reading your cover letter back to yourself, patrol for tone problems by asking yourself after each sentence: Does that statement enhance my candidacy? Could a hiring manager interpret that last statement in an unfavorable way? Have a second reader review your letter. If the letter's wording is questionable, by all means rewrite it. Always phrase your statements in a positive way!

17. **Gimmicks:** Gimmicks such as sending a home video or a singing telegram to replace the conventional cover letter may seem like a clever way to set yourself apart. But no matter how creative such ideas might seem on the surface, the majority of employers will be more impressed with a simple, well-crafted letter. In the worst-case scenario, gimmicks may even work against you, eliminating you from consideration. Examples we've seen include sending a poster-size cover letter by courier service and mailing a baseball hat with a

note attached that reads, "I'm throwing my hat into the ring!" Big risks like these are not only expensive, they can backfire and blow your name right out of the running. Save your money; most hiring decisions are based on qualifications not gimmicks.

18. **Typographical errors:** It is very easy to make mistakes in your letters, particularly when you are writing many in succession. But it is equally easy for a hiring manager to reject out of hand any cover letter that contains errors, even those that seem minor at first glance. Don't make the mistake that one job-hunting editor recently made, citing his attention to detail in a cover letter in which he misspelled his own name!

Here are a few common technical mistakes to watch out for when proofreading your letter:

- Misspelling the hiring contact's name or title in the address, in the greeting, or on the envelope.
- Forgetting to change the name of the organization you're applying to each time it appears in your letter. There's nothing wrong with using the same basic letter to target several employers within a specific industry. Just remember, if you are applying to Boots and Bags this time around, in your closing don't express enthusiasm for a position at Shoe City.
- Submitting your application for a particular position, then mentioning a different position in the body of your letter. For instance, one candidate applying for a telemarketing position included the following statement, "I possess fifteen years of experience related to the Marketing Analyst availability."

19. **Messy corrections:** Your cover letter should contain *all* pertinent information. If you realize after completing your letter that you have forgotten to communicate something to your addressee, retype the letter. Simply jotting a note in the margin is at best, unprofessional, and at worst, just plain lazy. For example, on one letter we received, the candidate had attached a "post-it" note stating his willingness to travel and/or relocate. This, and all other information, must be included in your final draft.

Also, try to avoid using correction fluid or penning in any corrections. Thanks to computers, it only takes a few minutes to pull up the file, make the correction, and print another copy.

20. **Omitted signature:** However obvious this might sound, don't forget to sign your name at the close of your cover letter. Far too many letters that we've seen had a typed name, but no signature. An employer might interpret this oversight as carelessness.

Also, your signature allows you the chance to personalize your letter. Don't blow it by using a script font or a draw program on your word processor. And although there is a rainbow of ink colors out there to choose from, always sign your name neatly in blue or black ink.

PART II

All about Job Hunting

CHAPTER 5

PLANNING YOUR
JOB-SEARCH CAMPAIGN

No matter how terrific they may be, your resume and cover letter alone will not land you a job. In order to be successful in your quest for employment, you will need a comprehensive and well-defined plan. A plan will help you maintain the vigorous pace your job search requires and keep you from becoming frustrated or losing motivation. It will also enable you to pace yourself and monitor your progress against predetermined goals. If your plan does not yield positive results within a specified period of time, you will be able to quickly spot the problems and correct them so that you do not continue to spend precious time and resources on techniques that won't help you land a job.

Your job-search plan should incorporate a number of different job-finding methods. Decide which of the strategies described in Chapter 6 you want to try first. If you plan to pursue classified ads, decide which publications and/or Web sites are worth monitoring. If you want to contact companies directly, find out which sources of company listings will best suit your needs. If you plan on networking (which experts strongly recommend), make a list of people you want to contact first.

Predict how much time you are going to spend pursuing these various avenues, then set up a detailed weekly schedule and stick to it. It's important not to overlook this step; it will help you be more productive and make it less likely that you will fall behind. More helpful tips for job searching are available online at *www.truecareers.com*.

Getting Organized

Organization will make your job search more efficient and less stressful. It goes without saying that you should try to keep your desk or work area free of clutter. Make a to-do list at the beginning of each day and try to accomplish each of your goals by the end of that day. Use your personal digital assistant (PDA) device or daily planner to record appointments. Be sure to carry your PDA or planner with you to interviews so that if you're asked to make a return visit, you can immediately check your schedule for a mutually convenient time.

It's also important to create a chart or similar system that shows where and to whom you've sent your resume. Use it to track whether or not companies have responded and when and if you need to follow up with a phone call.

Although PDAs and computerized spread sheets can be useful for organizing your job search, you may find good old-fashioned oversize index cards a better option. Keep each contact's name, position, company, address, telephone number, contact method, follow-up date, status, and other important details on individual cards for quick and easy reference. If you are responding to an advertisement in a newspaper, clip the ad and paste it onto the card, along with the name of the newspaper and the date. If an employer or networking contact gives you his or her business card, you can staple it to an index card, and jot down any other pertinent information as well. Keep all of your cards in an index card box in alphabetical order for easy reference.

How Long Should Your Job Search Take?

As you may have already discovered, finding a job is not easy. It takes a lot of energy and a tremendous amount of effort. Statistics show that the average job search lasts approximately one week for every $2,000 of income sought. So for example, if your goal is a position that pays in the $40,000 range, your search will take approximately twenty weeks. However, this statistic and others like it obscure one very important fact: You are the only one who ultimately controls what kind of job you end up with and how long it takes to find it.

If you are like most job-hunters, you will have to contact several hundred companies before you land the right job. If you put tremendous effort into your job search and contact many companies each week, you will probably get a job much sooner than someone who is only searching casually and sending out one or two resumes a week.

Job Hunting Full-Time

Ideally, for the first few months of your job search, you should make looking for a job your full-time job. If you're able to afford this luxury, be sure to work from a vigorous, intense job-search plan that allows you to invest a minimum of forty hours per week.

Vary your activities a little bit from day to day—otherwise your job search may quickly become tedious. For example, every Sunday you could look through the classified ads and surf the Web to determine which of the advertised jobs are appropriate for you. On Monday, follow up on these ads by sending out your resume and cover letter and making some phone calls. For the rest of the week, you may want to spend your time doing other things besides following up on specific job openings. On Tuesday, for instance, you might decide to focus on contacting companies directly. On Wednesday, you could do more research to find listings of other companies to contact. Thursday and Friday might be spent networking, as you try to set up appointments for the following week to meet with people and develop more contacts.

Every few weeks you should evaluate your progress and fine-tune your search accordingly. If you find that, after putting in a great deal of effort over a period of several weeks, you aren't even close to getting a job, then it's probably time to reconsider your options. Are the job-search methods you've chosen working well for you? Are you spending too much time responding to newspaper ads and not enough time networking and "cold" contacting? Could you be more aggressive in your job search? How?

The key to an effective job-search campaign is knowing when to persist in the current direction that your job hunt is taking and when to give up what you're doing and start over. It isn't easy. Often, talking with other job hunters and knowing the current state of the job market in your industry of interest will help you to draw this fine line.

Job Hunting While You're Still Employed

Looking for a new job while you're still employed can be a sticky situation. Time, or the lack thereof, can be a major problem and you may find yourself feeling more than a bit overwhelmed. Also, there is the very real concern that your current employer will find out that you're looking for a new job before you're ready to tell him or her. Despite these seeming obstacles, however, there are ways to maximize time and minimize stress during your job search.

First, set aside blocks of your days and/or evenings specifically for your job search. You may choose to "brown bag" your lunch so you can spend your lunch hour at your desk making networking calls or following up on resumes you've sent out. Plan to spend several hours on weeknights and on Saturdays mailing out resumes and tracking down job leads. Whatever schedule you decide upon, try to stick to it.

Executive recruiters and employment agencies that don't charge job hunters a fee may be particularly helpful to the employed job seeker. Not only will they do the footwork for you, but they can help you uncover job leads you might not be able to find on your own.

You also may want to consider the wide range of available services that can help you save time by handling some of the more mundane job-searching tasks while you're at work, such as a telephone-answering service or a resume service that mails out your resume to job leads you supply. These services can be extremely useful to the harried job hunter, but beware—some are not what they seem. Be an informed consumer and shop wisely.

Organization will play a key role in both the success and length of your job search. If you find yourself becoming overwhelmed, it may be worth your while to occasionally reread the section on getting organized at the beginning of this chapter.

Of course, time management and organization are probably not your only concerns. You may worry that you'll be found out by your current employer or wonder about the ethical issues involved in job hunting while you are still employed. To dispel any concerns you may have, know that you are under no obligation to inform your current employer that you are job searching until you are ready to give your notice. Revealing this information too soon may very well cost you your job. Remember, employers would rather lose you at their convenience than at your own.

To ensure that your job hunt remains under wraps, you should never tell any of your co-workers or colleagues of your plans. As obvious as this may sound, too many job seekers seem eager to "spill the beans"—and sadly, sometimes at their own expense. Also, you may choose to head your resume with a phrase like "Confidential Resume of . . ." or make a mention of confidentiality in your cover letter. Most recruiters will understand and honor this request for discretion. Ask hiring managers not to contact you at work but instead leave a message on your home answering machine, which you can check regularly during the day. However, despite your best efforts, hiring managers will sometimes overlook such a request and contact you at work anyway. If you find this happening to you, you may choose to route your calls to voicemail rather than through the receptionist.

It's important for job hunters to view their situation realistically. The days when employees dedicated their entire careers to a single employer are long gone. It is expected that people will change jobs several times during their career, and it would be foolish to leave a current position without having something else lined up. So if you have a misdirected sense of guilt, you shouldn't. Channel that energy into your job-search efforts instead.

Long-Distance Job Hunting

As if finding a job isn't tough enough, long-distance job hunting has its own set of challenges. There are several steps you can take to make this transition as smooth as possible. First, call or write your new city's Chamber of Commerce to get information on the city's major employers. Subscribe to a local newspaper and sign up with local employment agencies. Inform your networking contacts of your plans and ask them for any leads or suggestions they can give you concerning this new location. Do they know of anyone who works in that area who can offer suggestions or leads? Also, be sure to check with your national trade or professional association. Most large associations offer members access to a national network. Contact the national office for a list of chapters in your new metropolitan area.

If you are relocating to a new city because your spouse has been transferred, be sure to ask your spouse's company about spouse relocation assistance. Some larger companies may offer free career counseling and other job-hunting services to you. If your spouse's employer does not offer this service, consider contacting a career counseling center in your destination city for guidance. You may be able to negotiate with your future employer to pay the center's fees.

Planning Your Finances

In addition to being stressful, looking for a new job can be costly. Expenses relating to your job hunt can add up quickly, especially if you are currently unemployed and shouldering everyday living expenses without a regular income. The following are some guidelines to help you make this aspect of your job search somewhat smoother.

For starters, if you are laid off, you should know that most companies offer one week's to one month's severance pay for every year of service. Get a written copy of your company's policy. Immediately file for unemployment benefits and, if you can afford to, extend your health insurance. Some larger companies offer outplacement services to help employees make their transition to another job. Find out if your company makes available any such assistance.

Next, assess your financial fitness. Make a detailed list of all your expenses, separating them into three categories: priority one, priority two, and priority three. Priority one expenses should include the bare essentials such as rent/mortgage, utilities, groceries, gasoline, and car payment. Be sure to include job-search expenses in your priority one list, too. Priority two expenses should include important but not necessarily essential items, such as credit card payments (which can be put off until a later date), home repairs, and automotive maintenance. Priority three expenses should include more frivolous items that can be sacrificed temporarily, such as cable television, magazine subscriptions, leisure activities, and miscellaneous luxury purchases. Total your estimated expenses in each of these three categories.

Now, make a detailed list of your income and assets. This should include any income from part-time, temporary, and freelance work, as well as unemployment insurance, severance pay, savings, investments, spouse's income, and alimony.

If you estimate that it will take you six months to find a new job (not an unreasonable expectation in today's market), multiply the total of your priority one expenses by six and subtract it from your current income and/or savings for that same period of time. You may find that some budgeting is in order. Perhaps you can cut down on or eliminate some of those priority two and three expenses. Determine what is absolutely essential and what can be sacrificed for the time being; consider nothing sacred. Leave your credit cards at home when you go to the mall. Resolve to pay for everything with cash and before you pull out your wallet, ask yourself: Do I really need those shoes or that shirt right now?

You may also decide to write your creditors to request a reduced payment schedule in light of your employment situation. This may not always be possible, and it can affect your credit rating. However, when given a choice between receiving a partial payment or no payment at all, many creditors will agree to work out a plan that is acceptable to both of you. Be sure to ask your creditors to help preserve your good credit rating if possible.

Know too that some job-hunting expenses are tax deductible if you are looking for a new position in your current line of work. (Unfortunately, no tax relief is available if you switch careers or if you are a first-time job seeker.) All expenses associated with your job-hunting campaign are generally deductible, including resume preparation, printing, postage, telephone costs, travel costs, and employment agency fees. If your new job is at least fifty miles further from your home than your old job was, you may also be able to deduct up to $3,000 of your total moving expenses. Consult your accountant or tax professional to determine which deductions apply to your particular situation. And by all means, be prepared to document your expenses. Save those receipts! To generate additional income for yourself during this time, consider taking on part-time, freelance, or temporary work. You may also choose to borrow against your life insurance or retirement policy, if you have one, or accept a loan from a friend or relative.

Now that you've determined how much money you have and how much you'll need, establish a realistic budget. It should be very detailed and laid out on paper. Be sure to monitor your budget on a regular basis so you don't suddenly find yourself in a financial predicament that could have been avoided with better planning.

CHAPTER 6

THE BEST AND WORST WAYS TO FIND JOBS

You may be surprised to learn that some of the most popular job-search methods are, in reality, quite unsuccessful for most of the people who use them. In this chapter you'll have a chance to take a look at the real value of the many services and techniques at your disposal.

Employment Agencies

Employment agencies are commissioned by employers to find qualified candidates for job openings. As a job seeker, however, you should know that the agency's main responsibility is to meet the needs of the employer—not to find a suitable job for you.

This is not to say that you should rule them out altogether. There are employment agencies that specialize in specific industries or industry functions that can be useful for experienced professionals. However, employment agencies are typically not a good choice for entry-level job seekers. They often try to steer inexperienced candidates in directions they're not interested in going, and which often lead directly to clerical positions.

If you decide to register with an agency, your best bet is to find one that is recommended by a friend or associate. Barring that, you may be able to find the names of agencies in your area in directories, which can be found in your local public library, or by contacting:

National Association of Personnel Services (NAPS)
P.O. Box 2128
The Village at Banner Elk, Suite 108
Banner Elk, NC 28604
(828) 898-4929
www.recruitinglife.com.

Be aware that an increasing number of bogus employment service firms regularly advertise in newspapers, magazines, and online. These companies promise even inexperienced job seekers top salaries in exciting careers, all for a sizable fee. Others use expensive 900 numbers that job seekers are encouraged to call, for a hefty price per call, of course. Unfortunately, most people find out too late that the jobs they are promised—and probably paid the firm up front to find—don't exist.

As a general rule, most legitimate employment agencies will never guarantee you a job, nor will they seek payment until after you've been placed. Even so, you should check every agency you're interested in with your local chapter of the Better Business Bureau (BBB). Find out if it is licensed and how long it's been in business. Have any valid complaints been registered against the agency recently? And if so, has the firm been responsive to those complaints?

If everything checks out with the BBB, call the firm to ask if it specializes in your area of expertise and how it will go about marketing you. Before you sign any contract, have your attorney look it over. Find out up front who will pay the agency's fee. You should avoid any firms that are not "fee paid" by the employer.

After you have narrowed your selection down to a few agencies (three to five is best), send each one your resume with a cover letter. Make a follow-up phone call a week or two later, and try to schedule an interview. Be prepared to be asked to take a battery of tests on the day of your interview.

Above all, do not expect too much. Only a small percentage of all professional, managerial, and executive-level jobs are listed with these agencies, so they are not a good source of opportunities. Consider them just one more piece of your total job-search campaign, but focus your efforts on other, more promising methods.

Executive Search Firms

Also known as headhunters, executive search firms operate in much the same way as professional employment agencies. They seek out and screen candidates for high-paying executive and managerial positions and are paid by the employer. Unlike employment agencies, however, they typically approach viable candidates directly, rather than waiting for the candidates to approach them. Many prefer to deal with candidates who are already employed and will not accept "blind" inquires from job hunters.

These organizations are not licensed, so if you decide to go with an executive search firm, make sure it has a solid reputation. You can find names of search firms by contacting the following:

Association of Executive Search Consultants (AESC)
230 Park Avenue, Suite 1549
New York, NY 10169
(212) 949-9556
www.aesc.org

American Management Association (AMA)
Management Services Department
1601 Broadway
New York, NY 10013
(212) 586-8100
www.amanet.org

As with employment agencies, do not let an executive search firm become a critical element of your job-search campaign—no matter how encouraging it may sound. Continue to actively seek out your own opportunities and keep all of your options open.

Temporary Agencies

Temporary or "temp" agencies (such as Kelly Services and Manpower) can be a viable option, especially if you are currently unemployed and looking for a way to generate income while you search for a full-time position. Traditionally, these agencies have specialized in clerical and support work, but it's becoming increasingly common to find temporary assignments in other areas such as accounting, computer programming, and management consulting. Working on temporary assignments can provide you with a steady income during your job search and will add experience to your resume. It may also provide valuable business contacts or lead to job opportunities.

You can find temporary agencies listed in the *Yellow Pages*. Send your resume and cover letter and later call to schedule an interview. Be prepared to be asked to take a battery of tests on the day of your interview.

Newspaper Classified Ads

Contrary to popular belief, newspaper classified ads are not a good source of opportunities for job hunters. Few people find jobs through the classifieds, although many spend a tremendous amount of time and effort pouring through newspaper after newspaper.

According to career development consultant Charles Logue, less than 3 percent of all job openings are advertised in classified ads. Worse, so many applicants respond to these ads that the competition is extremely fierce. Even if your qualifications are strong, your chances of getting an interview are not. If you plan on using classified ads as a source for seeking employment, be sure to focus only a small portion of your job-search efforts in this direction.

"Blind" Ads

"Blind" ads are newspaper advertisements that do not identify the employer. Job seekers are usually instructed to send their resumes to a post office box number. Although this may sound suspicious, blind ads can be a source of legitimate job opportunities. A firm may choose to run a blind advertisement because it does not wish to be deluged with phone calls, or it may be trying to replace an employee who hasn't been officially terminated yet.

You should be aware, however, that blind ads are sometimes used for deceitful purposes, such as selling employment marketing services and to sexually harass unsuspecting job hunters. The best advice is to trust your instincts; don't allow yourself to be put in any situation that makes you feel uncomfortable.

Public Employment Service

Your state employment service, sometimes referred to as Job Service, maintains approximately 1,700 local offices (also called employment service centers) nationwide, which provide job placement assistance and career counseling. With so many white-collar workers out of work these days, state employment agencies are offering more and more services to accommodate professional and managerial personnel. Check your local phone book for the office nearest you.

Job Counseling Services

The job counseling services offered by your city or town may be another useful option. You can find them listed in your local phone book or by writing:

National Board for Certified Counselors
Terrace Way, Suite D
Greensboro, NC 27403
(336) 547-0607
www.nbcc.org

Nonprofit Agencies

It may be worthwhile to find out what services nonprofit agencies in your local community provide. Many of these organizations offer counseling, career development, and job placement services to specific groups such as women and minorities. You might also try contacting the national organizations below for information on career planning, job training, and public policy support.

For Women:
U.S. Department of Labor
Women's Bureau
200 Constitution Avenue NW
Washington, DC 20210
(202) 219-6606, (800) 827-5335
www.dol.gov/wb/

Wider Opportunities for Women
1001 Connecticut Avenue, S.W. Suite 930
Washington, DC 20036
(202) 464-1596
www.wowonline.org

For Minorities:
National Association for the Advancement of Colored People (NAACP)
4805 Mount Hope Drive
Baltimore, MD 21215-3197
(410) 521-4939, (877) NAACP-98
www.naacp.org

National Urban League
Employment Department
120 Wall Street, 8th Floor
New York, NY 10005
(212) 538-5300
www.nul.org

For the Blind:
Job Opportunities for the Blind Program
National Federation for the Blind
1800 Johnson Street
Baltimore, MD 21230
(410) 659-9314
www.nfb.org

For the Physically Challenged:
President's Committee on Employment of People with Disabilities
1331 F Street N.W., Suite 300
Washington, D.C. 20004
(202) 376-6200
www.pcepd.gov

College Career Centers

If you're a recent college grad, your school's career center is a great place to begin your job search. Your college career center can help you identify and evaluate your interests, work values, and skills. Most offer workshops on topics like job-search strategy, resume writing, cover letter writing, and effective interviewing, as well as job fairs where you can link up with prospective employers. The career center at your college should also have a career resource library where you can find job leads and an alumni network to help you get started on networking.

Even if you've long since graduated, the career center at your college may be able to provide you with valuable networking contacts. You should call to find out if your alma mater offers this or other services to alumni.

Web-Based Resources

Little more than ten years ago, only a handful of college students and recent grads were using the Internet to search for a job. Today, job seekers of all ages and experience levels say they couldn't get along without it.

Job hunting via the World Wide Web works two ways. You can either post your resume to the Web and wait for hiring managers with job openings to contact you, or you can respond to the online classified ads employers post for specific positions. If you elect to use the Web as part of your job search, you'll probably want to do both. In either case, your first step will be to find an appropriate career Web site, and there are dozens to choose from.

Thanks to an aggressive marketing campaign, Monster.com is perhaps the best known. But there are many others, including CareerBuilder.com, TrueCareers.com, Jobs.com, Jobs.net, BestJobsUSA.com, and HotJobsYahoo.com to name a few. For a comprehensive list of career Web sites, go to *www.google.com* and type in the word "jobs." You'll be amazed at the number and variety of Web sites that pop up. Some are general—offering a wide range of services for job seekers in broad categories, such as banking and finance, health care, manufacturing, retail, sales and marketing, etc. But there are specialized sites, too, where you can browse job availabilities in narrower fields such as higher education, aerospace, or entertainment. You can refine your search even further by accessing sites dedicated to jobs in a specific location. For example, we spotted Web sites listed on Google that are dedicated to job opportunities in Oregon and California, as well as in the United Kingdom, Canada, and Japan.

Putting together a resume for posting to the web can be tricky business (we've outlined some of the basics in Chapter 9), but it's really not all that difficult. Most of the career Web sites will walk you through the process, step-by-step. They also provide a wealth of information on cover letters, resumes, interviews, and other topics of interest to job seekers.

Posting your resume one day doesn't mean you can expect to be fielding dozens of calls inviting you to interviews the next. While it is true that thousands of hiring managers now have 24-hour access to your credentials, not many of them will actually ever offer you a job. Statistics show that fewer than 4 percent of new hires originate from resumes posted to career Web sites.

Conversely, your chances of landing a job from an online classified ad you answer are about the same or maybe a little worse than the chances of securing a position from a classified ad in the newspaper. And if you think the competition was fierce in the print advertising realm, you're in for a major rude awakening here. Now instead of a few hundred applicants in your metropolitan area, you're up against thousands from all over the world! We're not saying it's impossible to find a job through an online classified; we're just saying it will be tough. If you choose to use this medium, be aware that the odds are stacked against you, and make it only a small component of your overall job search efforts.

Direct Contact

One of the best ways to find a job is by direct contact. Direct contact means introducing yourself to potential employers, usually by way of a resume and cover letter, without a prior referral. This type of "cold contact" can be very effective if done correctly. Refer to Chapter 7 for additional information.

Networking

Networking is perhaps the most effective job-hunting tool of all. It can be used by anyone, even those job-hunters who don't already have an "insider network" of professional contacts in place. Networking takes many forms; with a little skill and a whole lot of effort, it can be a very productive tool. Chapter 8 takes you through the networking process step-by-step.

CHAPTER 7

CONTACTING COMPANIES DIRECTLY

Direct contact (also called "cold contact") may be defined as making a professional, personal approach to a select group of companies. Done well, it can be an excellent method for most job seekers, leading to many opportunities, and possibly, job offers. However, if you're an experienced professional looking for a high-level managerial or executive position, direct contact may not work so well for you. Your many years in the work force have afforded you the opportunity to make important "connections" within your particular industry, and as a result, you'll probably have greater success with networking (see Chapter 8).

The Best Companies to Contact

One of the most common mistakes job-hunters make is limiting their search to large, *Fortune* 500–type companies. Despite the fact that most of these giants have dramatically downsized their work forces in recent years, big corporations still look attractive to many job seekers, who flood their human resources departments with resumes. IBM alone receives close to a million resumes a year! As you might surmise, the odds of snaring a job with Big Blue aren't too terrific. But don't give up hope! At countless numbers of midsize companies with anywhere from one hundred to one thousand employees, the competition is much less fierce and job openings abound. Yet even though experts predict that as many as one-third of all new jobs in the coming years will be created by midsize firms, the majority of job hunters continue to overlook them, which may be good news for you. Fewer applicants means less competition for the positions available.

You may be surprised to learn that small companies—those with fewer than one hundred employees—are the best source of job opportunities today. While job growth in some other sectors of the U.S. economy is stagnant, small business hiring continues at a steady pace. Among those small companies polled recently for a survey by the National Federation of Independent Businesses, more than half reported that they had hired or tried to hire at least one new employee in the first three months of 2005. A whopping 87 percent said their positions went unfilled because they had few or no applicants. What does this mean for you, the inveterate job seeker? If you target carefully, taking care to apply only for those positions which directly match your qualifications, you should have a better than average chance of landing a job. On the downside, small companies do tend to provide less job security than midsize firms and offer fewer employee benefits.

Do Your Homework

If you are trying to enter a new field, your first order of business is to do a little background research. Find out the current trends in the industry and become familiar with the names of the major and up-and-coming players. Thanks to the Internet, the information you are looking for is as close as your fingertips. Spend an evening surfing the Web and you may be amazed at the things you can learn without ever leaving home. Industry trade journals and informational interviews are two more terrific ways to uncover the kind of "insider" information you need to know. Check your local library for a copy of *The Encyclopedia of Business Information Sources* or *Predicasts F&S Index* to identify publications in your field of interest.

If you are seeking a new position in a field in which you are a veteran, you'll want to be sure to stay abreast of the latest industry trends. Surf the Web on a regular basis, talk with associates, attend meetings of your professional association's local chapter, and read the trade journals that serve your industry.

What to Look For

Once you've done your homework about the industry in general, you are ready to look for more specific information about individual employers. At this point in your job search, what you should be looking for are the basics about many different companies, including:

- Company name, address, phone and fax numbers.
- Names and job titles of key contacts.
- Is the company privately or publicly held?
- Products the company manufactures and/or services it provides.
- Year of incorporation.
- Number of employees.

As your job search progresses and you narrow your prospects, you'll want to dig deeper, refining your research so that you are prepared to field questions and make insightful comments when you finally get the chance to meet face-to-face with a potential employer in your chosen field.

Where to Find It

Where do you find this kind of in-depth information about potential employers? Start with your computer. These days, even small and midsize firms have their own Web sites. But if the ones you're interested in don't, you may still be able to find the information you need online. Try "Google-ing" the name of the company or its principals and see what happens. Be sure to check the Web sites for local media, too. You may find articles about the firm in the online archives of local daily newspapers or weekly business journals serving the area where the company of interest is located.

Another great source of information are the *JobBank* books, a series of employment directories listing companies with fifty or more employees in larger cities and metropolitan areas throughout the U.S. Each *JobBank* book provides such vital information as key contacts, positions the company commonly hires for, types of educational backgrounds sought, and fringe benefits offered.

JobBank books are available in many libraries and most bookstores for the following cities and states: Atlanta; Austin/San Antonio; Boston; Carolinas; Chicago; Connecticut; Colorado; Dallas/Fort Worth; Florida; Houston; Los Angeles; New York; New Jersey; Ohio; Philadelphia; Phoenix; San Francisco; Seattle; Virginia; and Washington, D.C.

There are many other resources you can use to find listings of companies, most of which are probably on the reference shelves at your local library. Reference librarians are eager to assist patrons, so if you get stuck, don't be afraid to ask for help. Describe the kind of information you're looking for and the librarian will point you in the right direction. In the meantime, here's a list of our favorite directories to get you started:

- Dun and Bradstreet's *Million Dollar Directory* is a good place to begin your research. It lists approximately 160,000 companies that are both publicly and privately held and is updated annually.
- *Standard & Poor's Register of Corporations, Directors, and Executives* lists fewer companies than the *Million Dollar Directory* (about 45,000), but provides valuable biographical information on thousands of company officials.
- *Corporate Technology Directory* (Corporate Technology Information Services) focuses on the products produced by approximately 35,000 companies. This is a great resource for job seekers interested in high-tech industries, including computers, biotechnology, environmental engineering, chemicals and pharmaceuticals, and transportation.
- *Personnel Executives Contactbook* (Gale Research) lists key personnel and other contacts at 30,000 publicly and privately held companies and government agencies.
- *The National JobBank* (Adams Media) lists key contacts at more than 17,000 small and large companies. It includes information on common positions filled and educational backgrounds desired; it is updated annually.
- *Directory of Human Resources Executives* (Hunt-Scanlon) names human resource executives and provides information on the number of employees and areas of specialization of 5,000 public and private companies.
- *Directory of Corporate Affiliations* (National Register) is one of the few places where you can find information on a company's divisions and subsidiaries. This particular book lists information on approximately 4,000 parent companies.

Many of these resources can also be found on CD-ROM at your library. These "books on disk" are easy to use and, because you "read" them on a computer, they can save you a lot of time leafing through page after page. You won't be able to take the CD-ROM home, of course, but that's okay. The computer you'll be using is probably linked to a printer; you can make hard copies of the information as needed.

Be sure not to overlook the countless industry-specific directories that are available, too, such as *Dun's Directory of Service Companies, Martindale-Hubbell Law Directory*, and *Standard Directory of Advertisers*. These are terrific places to find potential employers and often include information on professional associations and industry trends. Ask your reference librarian for help in identifying the directories that specialize in your field of interest.

Think Big

As a rule of thumb, you should begin your job quest at the top. Try first to contact a department head or the president of the company you'd like to work for. This will probably be easier to do at smaller companies where the top executive may be directly involved in the hiring process. As you apply to larger and larger companies, you may find yourself bumped back to the human resources office. Don't become frustrated if this happens to you; try instead to at least contact the key decision-maker in human resources or personnel.

Your first step in contacting a company directly is to mail your resume, accompanied by a personalized cover letter, and, if appropriate, a self-addressed stamped envelope. Part I of this book offers pointers for writing an attention-grabbing cover letter; in Part III, you'll find actual samples of "cold" letters that worked for other job seekers.

The 60-Second Pitch

Approximately one week after mailing your letter to a key decision-maker, follow up with a phone call. Don't simply ask if your inquiry was received—employers are inundated with hundreds of resumes and it's unlikely that the man or woman on the other end of the line will remember yours. A better approach would be to state that you've sent your resume and then explain, in 60 seconds or less, why you think you're the best candidate for the position. We call this the "60-second pitch."

Your 60-second pitch should be a clear, concise summary about yourself. It should include three important elements:

1. The kind of work you do (or want to do);
2. Your strongest skills and accomplishments;
3. The specific position you are seeking.

Use your resume as the basis for addressing each of these elements in putting together your pitch. Think about how you want to phrase your words ahead of making your call. Write your pitch down and read it aloud until it flows easily and naturally. The last thing you want to be is tongue-tied when it comes time to pick up that phone, so practice, practice, practice.

Here's how one communications professional created a 60-second pitch from her resume:

"Hello. My name is Elaine O'Connor. I'm a production assistant with a Bachelor of Arts in Communications and three years of solid broadcasting and public relations experience. I have extensive practice developing and researching topics, pre-interviewing guests, and producing on-location video tapings.

"I've been watching your station for some time now and I've been impressed with your innovative approach and fast growth. I recently sent you my resume and was wondering if you anticipate any openings that might be appropriate for someone with my background?"

Mike, a stay-at-home dad who was returning to a full-time position when his daughter entered the first grade, also had a terrific 60-second pitch:

"My name is Mike Johnson. I sent you my resume last week and I'd like to take a moment to introduce myself. I've been working part-time as an accounts receivable supervisor for the past five years and have expertise in payables, receivables, and credit. I'm looking for a full-time accounting position.

"I read the article about your firm's recent expansion in last Sunday's business section and think that we might make a great match. Do you have a few minutes?"

As you can see, tailoring your pitch to the needs of each particular employer will make your 60-second statement just that much stronger. At the same time, you should memorize the "core" of your pitch—the part about your qualifications that you will recite to every potential employer—so that you feel more confident and sound more natural. You'll probably be nervous the first few times you make a pitch, just be sure to always speak slowly and clearly.

If you are invited to an interview after you've "pitched" yourself to the employer, great! If not, don't let the conversation end there. Don't be afraid to ask your contact a few questions: Are there any particular qualifications you are looking for in a candidate? Is there anything else I can do or any additional information I can send (writing samples, clippings, a portfolio) to help you make your decision? Even if the employer says no, that your initial application is sufficient, you may still have earned a few points with your interest and enthusiasm.

Then, if you have not already done so, specifically ask the employer if he/she would have a few minutes to meet with you. If that doesn't work, ask if he or she knows anyone else in the industry who might be interested in speaking to someone with your qualifications. If you are unable to arrange an interview or get a referral, ask the employer if he/she would mind if you called back in three to four weeks. Your goal is to elicit a positive result from the phone call—whether it's an appointment for an interview or simply a scrap of job-hunting advice. Don't give up too easily, but don't nag, either. Be professional and courteous at all times.

Getting Past Gatekeepers

Gatekeepers are those receptionists, assistants, and other staff members who screen calls for their executive bosses, making sure that only the most important ones get put through to the top. You should expect to encounter many gatekeepers throughout your job search. How you handle them can have a major impact on the success of your campaign.

If you run up against a gatekeeper, don't request a call in return unless the contact will recognize your name. Simply give your name and ask when it's best to call back. Call again the next day at the time suggested. Keep calling once a day for at least five days. If you are still unable to reach your contact, change tactics.

As an alternative, try asking for your contact by his or her first name. You could say, for example, "This is Susan Thomas. Is Sharon in?" If you speak with an air of confidence and authority, you just might get through.

If you're asked what the call is about, try saying that you've been in correspondence with Sharon and she's expecting your call (it's true—you sent your resume and cover letter, mentioning that you'd be calling, didn't you?). If you're pressed to be more specific, you can say, "I would like Sharon's expertise on a sales and marketing issue." Or use an implied referral, "I was just talking with John Barker at ACME Industries about something that might interest Sharon. Would you put me through, please?"

Whatever approach you choose to take, never say that your call is personal—this sends up a red flag to most gatekeepers and will hurt your chances of getting through. And don't say you're calling about a job, either. The gatekeeper may have been specifically instructed to block calls from job seekers.

If none of these approaches work, try calling when the gatekeeper is least likely to be there—before or after office hours and during lunch. When gatekeepers aren't around, employers will often answer their own phones.

Another technique that works well is to call the office of the company president and say something like, "Hi. I don't think I really need to speak with the president—I'm just trying to find out who's in charge of sales and marketing. Could you help me with that?" Then be sure to thank the person and jot down his or her full name. Then you can get past that person's gatekeeper by saying something like, "Bill Warner in the president's office suggested I speak with Sharon Rice. Is she in?"

If none of these suggestions works for you, as a last resort you should ask for the gatekeeper's help. You could say, "Joe, I've been trying to reach your boss for some time now and I haven't had much luck. Do you have any suggestions on how I might be more effective?" A sincere and polite request for help will often get you through to your contact, or, at the very least, it win you a useful bit of advice.

If you've exhausted all of these techniques and feel as if you'll never get through, don't waste any more of your time. Simply chalk it up to experience and move on to other, more promising contacts and opportunities on your list.

Contacting the Same Firm Twice

One approach that can be very effective is to re-call some of the companies you contacted a few months previously. This shows that you are genuinely interested in the firm and it will certainly make you stand out in your contact's mind. You might say something like:

> *"My name is Robert Shustak and I contacted your firm several months ago about an entry-level position in advertising. I've been talking with other firms and I'm very much committed to this industry. I recently saw your firm mentioned in the local newspaper, and I'm more convinced than ever that your company would be a terrific place to work.*
>
> *"I feel I have a lot to offer you and I'd like for you to reconsider my application."*

The technique works especially well when you contact firms with whom you actually interviewed. Only a fraction of those applying for a position get to the interview stage; if you were one of them, the firm was obviously impressed with your qualifications. Chances are good that you might still be considered for another position at that company.

You don't have to make your subsequent contact by telephone, of course; you can also write a letter. Part III of this book contains several samples of "resurrection" letters you can use as examples for the letter you might send to a company that interviewed you but did not make an offer.

Don't Give Up!

Cold contact can be both challenging and time-consuming. But no matter how frustrated you may become during the process, it's important that you remain polite to your contacts (and their gatekeepers!) at all times. Like anyone else, they appreciate courtesy and they'll be more willing to help out a professional, friendly caller than someone who sounds frustrated or unpleasant.

Job searching is not an easy task for anyone. If you go into the process expecting some rejection, the turndowns will be easier to swallow when they happen. This is a time when attitude becomes crucial. If you're optimistic and continue to believe in yourself, you already have the most important quality you need for a successful job search.

CHAPTER 8

NETWORKING YOUR WAY TO A JOB

Networking is the most effective of all job-hunting tools. In fact, experts report that close to 90 percent of all jobs are found through networking. This chapter is designed to dispel the mystery and confusion that often surrounds this job-search method. As you read on, you will see that networking is not just for people with lots of professional experience. It can work for anyone—even people with few or no contacts in the business world. To learn more online, go to *www.truecareers.com*.

Overcoming Hesitation

If you feel hesitant about networking, you're not alone. Many job seekers mistakenly think that networking is somehow degrading or manipulative. They suspect that networking really means pestering strangers for a job and begging for scraps of help and sympathy. They opt not to use this important tool and end up needlessly limiting their opportunities.

The problem is these people don't understand what networking really is all about. Networking means letting people you know—personally and professionally—that you are looking for a job. Nothing difficult or shady about that. You simply ask your friends and acquaintances to keep you in mind if they hear of any appropriate openings or know anyone who might need someone with your skills.

You'll probably feel a little awkward at first, especially if you're not used to asking for help, but with practice you'll grow more comfortable and gain greater confidence about making calls. Keep in mind that networking is a time-honored practice—in fact, it's how most job seekers get jobs. And, once you find the right job for yourself, you can "give something back" by lending a hand to another networking job seeker.

Present Yourself as an Industry "Insider"

One of the secrets of networking is knowing what you want—or at least appearing to know what you want. For instance, if you are trying to break into a field where you don't have any experience, tell your networking contacts that you are interested in the industry they work in and show them that you are knowledgeable about that industry. This way, you will be perceived more or less as an "industry insider." Better yet, if you can cite some work experience in that industry and a referral, people will be interested in talking with you.

So—how do you start? First, keep up-to-date with your industry of choice by reading its trade journals. Check your local library for *The Encyclopedia of Business Information Sources* or *Predicasts F&S Index* to identify publications in your field of interest. Once you have identified the appropriate publications, make reading them a regular habit.

In addition, keep an eye out for information about your chosen industry that appears in the mainstream media: your daily newspaper, publications like *The Wall Street Journal, Time,* and *Business Week,* local business journals, television and radio news broadcasts, books, and other sources.

Tracking Down Leads

Who should you contact? Obviously, if you have experience in your industry of choice, you need only leaf through your Rolodex or pull out your Palm Pilot for a ready-made list of people with whom you have already established contact. But how do you network if you don't have prior experience and contacts?

The answer is simple: Start with the people you already know. Friends, relatives, neighbors, your doctor, your hairdresser—even your plumber—can be a source of important business contacts. These people might not work in the industry you're interested in, but they may know someone you should contact. Someone who knows someone who . . . well, you get the idea.

At first, you might not think you have many contacts at your disposal—but if you stop to think carefully you'll realize that in fact you do. Let's say there are thirty people you can initially contact, but none of them works in the industry you're interested in. As a group, however, they may know sixty people, some of whom do work in that industry, a portion of whom work in a related industry, and still more who are in a position to know someone who works in the industry. That's a lot of people…and a lot of connections.

Now don't stop there. Contact people you know on a professional or academic basis, such as former teachers, past employers and co-workers, and established business contacts. Find out if your college, graduate school, or prep school offers networking services for alumni; if not, they may have an alumni directory you can use.

Consider joining a professional organization in your field of choice. If you don't know the associations in your field or their locations and publications, consult the *Encyclopedia of Associations* or *National Trade and Professional Associations of the United States.* Your local library should have these books on hand.

Lastly, you should make a point of getting out and talking to people in your industry through informational interviews, at seminars, even at social events—anywhere you might expect to find "insiders." Before too long, you'll have established a whole network of important contacts. And don't overlook those broad-based networking events you may have seen advertised around town either. Whole businesses are devoted these days to setting up seminars on the subject of networking and to hosting regular events where people can get together for a couple of hours and, for a small fee, exchange ideas and business cards. There's probably at least one such opportunity near you. Ask around or check online to see when networking events might be held in your metropolitan area, then give one a try. You never know what might come from a quick ten-minute conversation with a complete stranger!

What Should I Say and Do?

When approaching a contact for the first time, start out by telling him or her a little bit about your qualifications and what kind of job you're looking for. If the contact is not someone who already knows you well, you should cite the name of the person who referred you and then introduce yourself with your 60-second pitch (as described in Chapter 7). While it's easy to get distracted as you meet and greet people, always try to stay focused on the real purpose of your call. Be sure at some point to ask the contact if he or she knows of anyone who might be looking for someone with your qualifications. Then take it one step further by asking for the names of anyone who might know anyone looking for someone with your qualifications.

If the conversation is going well, you may decide to ask your contact if he or she would have a few minutes to meet with you. If you are unable to arrange an interview or get a referral, ask the employer if it would be all right to call back in three or four weeks.

> *"Anthony Barrett? Hello, my name is Leslie Pellham. Jason Randall at Computing Associates was telling me yesterday about your company's recent innovations in applications and recommended that I speak with you. Do you have a minute to talk with me? Great.*
>
> *"I've been a programmer for eleven years at PC Systems and I'm looking for a change of pace. I was hoping you could tell me a little more about your firm and the qualities you look for in job candidates.*
>
> *"I see. Well, I have a thorough knowledge of COBOL, Pascal, Fortran, and C++ in both Windows and Unix environments. I also have experience in information mapping. It sounds as if we might make a good match. Could I come in and meet with you for a few minutes at your convenience?"*

Now, if Anthony agrees, Leslie should schedule an appointment and thank him for his time. If Anthony declines, however, Leslie should politely persist:

> *"Oh, I understand—you don't have any openings right now. Is there someone you can think of who might be looking for somebody with my qualifications? Also, I'd like to send you my resume anyway, in case a position opens up in the near future."*

If Anthony says he can't think of anyone, Leslie should ask him for a referral. Chances are that her polite persistence will pay off and she'll come away with the name of at least one new contact.

Networking for Those Entering a New Field

If you are trying to enter a new field, it's a good idea to ask your contacts for information about the industry in general and about their particular position within it. Are there any specific qualifications or training that would make some candidates more competitive than others? Tell each of your contacts a little bit about your situation and ask for advice.

This is how Jim, a recent college graduate, "pitched" himself to a potential employer:

"Ms. Silva, my name is Jim Philipps and my uncle, Joe Adams, suggested that I call you. I've just graduated from City University with a degree in English. I've been working part-time as a bank teller for two years and I very much want to pursue a career as a loan officer. I realize that you may not have any openings at this time but I was hoping that you would be able to meet with me for a few minutes to discuss the banking industry."

Ms. Silva then says she's very busy and she doesn't have the time to meet with Jim. Jim politely persists:

"I understand that you're busy—that's why I'll only ask for one more minute of your time. As you know, I have some part-time work experience in banking. Are there any other specific qualifications or training you could recommend that would help me get a job as a loan officer?"

Ms. Silva then gives Jim some advice on how to get a job in the banking industry.

"Thank you for that suggestion—I'm sure it will be very helpful. Now, would you be able to refer me to someone who might be looking for someone with my qualifications?"

If Ms. Silva says no, Jim should ask if she knows anyone who might know anyone in the banking industry who *is* looking for an employee. The point is to get at least one referral or job lead from each contact.

"Thank you for referring me to Ms. Lehman at Center Bank—I'll be sure to call her today. In the meantime, though, could I send you my resume for your files? Great. Thank you again for all your help. By the way, Uncle Joe says 'hello!'"

The Informational Interview

Informational interviews are an important way of building your network and can lead to valuable information and opportunities. If you tell a contact that all you want is advice, make sure you mean it. Never approach an informational interview as though it were a job interview—just stick to gathering information and leads and see what happens.

Tell your contact right away that all you would like from him or her is to learn more about the industry or company in question, and that you'll be the one asking all the questions. Also, unless it's specifically requested, sending your resume to someone you'd like to meet for an informational interview in advance of your meeting will probably give the wrong impression.

"My name is Jim Philipps and David Silva suggested I call you. I've just graduated from City University with a degree in English and I'm interested in beginning a career as a loan officer.

"I know that you may not have any openings at this time, but I would like to come by and talk with you for a couple of minutes about the opportunities that might be available in banking."

Sometimes an employer will mistake your intentions and tell you up front that he or she has no jobs available. If this happens, you can say something like:

"I understand that you might not have any openings right now, but I'd like to have a chance to meet with you for a couple of minutes anyway, just to discuss the banking industry in this city and the opportunities one might expect at those places that might be hiring. Would that be possible?"

You might find that the straightforward approach sometimes works better:

"My name is Jim Philipps and David Silva suggested I call you. I've just graduated from City University with a degree in English and I'm interested in beginning a career as a loan officer. I assure you I won't ask you for a job, but I was hoping that you would be able to meet with me briefly to discuss the banking industry."

Now that you've scheduled an informational interview, make sure that you're prepared to take the lead. After all, you're the one who asked for this appointment and you'll be doing the interviewing—not vice versa. Have some specific questions ready, such as:

- How did you get started in this business?
- What do you like most about your job, your company, and your industry?
- What do you dislike most about your job, your company, and your industry?
- What would you say are the current career opportunities for someone with my qualifications in the industry?
- What are the basic requirements for an entry-level position in the industry?
- Is there a trade association or a trade publication that might aid me in my job search?
- Where do you see the industry heading in the near future?

- What advice would you give to someone looking for a job in this industry?
- Can you think of anything else I should know about the industry?
- Do you know of anyone who might be looking for someone with my qualifications?
- Do you know of anyone who might know of anyone looking for someone with my qualifications?

Send a Thank-You Letter

If a networking contact has been particularly helpful to you, by all means send a thank-you note. And even if you didn't get everything you hoped to get from your meeting, still drop your contact a line. Not only is this courteous, it keeps your contacts current. Part III provides a complete "how-to" for creating outstanding thank-you letters, as well as several examples.

More Networking?

Networking is, in many respects, a never-ending process. You need to continually "work" your network in order for it to be effective. For example, go back and call once again those people you already contacted for leads several months ago. You could say something like:

> *"As you may remember, we spoke several months ago about my interest in a career in banking. I was hoping that you might know of some other people who might be looking for someone with my qualifications."*

You may be pleasantly surprised. It's not uncommon to catch a contact in a different frame of mind and learn of someone new. Nor is out of the realm of possibility that since the two of you last spoke, your contact has met someone in your industry of interest. After all, he or she is probably networking too.

Networking Online

If you're one of those people who fears networking—you'd rather have a root canal than make a cold call, for instance—we have good news. You can build a network without ever even picking up the phone. The technique is called online networking, or "e-networking," for short. Anyone with a computer keyboard, Internet access, and an e-mail address can do it.

E-networking has lots of advantages, not the least of which are anonymity and immediacy. You have time to think about what you're going to say and how you'll respond, so there's no chance you'll get tongue-tied as you might during a first phone call or face-to-face meeting. Nor do you have to worry about taking notes during the encounter. You can simply print out the reply. And since everyone with an e-mail address is accessible by Internet, you won't have to work your way around gatekeepers or play telephone tag to get to the person you really want to talk to. While e-mail doesn't have quite the immediacy of a phone call, it comes in a close second. Most people check their e-mail pretty regularly throughout the day, so you're likely to get a swift reply to your requests for information and additional contacts.

The downside, of course, is that e-mail doesn't give you quite the give-and-take of conversation; you may have to send messages back and forth a few times as you get answers to questions that prompt more questions. Be careful how you phrase things, too. The tone of most e-mail messages is less like formal correspondence than a chat between friends, but without voice inflections and facial expressions. Consequently, a biting little quip that would sound clever face-to-face can sometimes come across in an e-mail as downright angry and sarcastic. Reread what you've written carefully before you click "send."

Building an e-Network: The First Step

Building a network online is a lot like building a network in the traditional way. You start from where you are…in this case, with e-mail. You probably already have a list of contacts with whom you regularly exchange e-mail. Start using it to gather industry information and to increase your contact base. Dash off a message to close friends, relatives, business associates, teachers, and past employers—in short, anyone you know who might know someone who might know someone—asking for their help in your quest for new career opportunities. Then stay in touch on a regular basis. Make it a habit to send a congratulatory note when one of your contacts makes a big sale or gets a promotion. When you come across an article you think might be of interest to a friend or business associate, pass it on. But be selective! Don't forward every funny joke that lands in your e-mail in box, or pretty soon, you may discover that your contacts are so overwhelmed with the number of messages originating from your e-mail address, they've just quit opening them altogether. It does you no good if even the messages for which you'd like a response aren't getting through.

E-mailing a new contact for the first time is much like making a cold call—but without the fear and trepidation. You will need to introduce yourself to the new contact, tell how you found him or her, briefly describe your background and the purpose of your message, then ask for what you need—information, advice, a referral, and/or the names of additional contacts. Watch the tone of your message and always be courteous. Since you are approaching someone you don't know, be especially careful about the subject line. Many people won't even open an e-mail if they don't recognize the sender. Instead of something vague like "Seeking your help re: career opportunities," try mentioning the name of the person who referred you in the first place. That should catch your contact's attention.

Going Beyond E-Mail

There's more to building a network online than just beefing up your e-mail address book, of course. Consider the following options for tapping into informational resources and establishing helpful contacts you might otherwise miss:

- **Newsgroups.** Newsgroups are components of the huge worldwide discussion forum known as Usenet. Remember the old office bulletin board? You'd post a note, then someone walking by would add a note to your note or post a note of their own. Pretty soon the board would be littered with all kinds of articles, notes, and notices. That's how newsgroups work. People with common interests come together in a newsgroup to post articles pertaining to a particular subject and to comment on the articles others have posted. There are thousands of newsgroups in operation, each devoted to a specific topic. You can join newsgroups about everything from the serious to the sublime to the just downright silly. There's undoubtedly at least one newsgroup devoted to your industry where you can glean interesting information and possibly make useful contacts. Be aware, however, that newsgroups are not regulated and most aren't even moderated. Whatever someone wants to post, they can. Don't accept everything you see as the truth. For information and instructions on using newsgroups, as well as lists of Usenet groups, go to Usenet Info Center Launch Pad at *http://metalab.unc. edu/usenet-i/*.

- **Chat rooms.** If you're computer savvy at all, you know how chat rooms work and you probably already participate in one or two for personal information and social interaction. Now, consider joining chats for the purpose of advancing your job search. Many career Web sites offer the opportunity for real-time chats with other job seekers and sometimes even with hiring managers. You'll probably be able to pick up some job-hunting tips as well as information about new developments and trends in your industry; you may even learn about job openings before they're widely advertised.
- **Networking Web sites.** Just as there are locally based networking events designed to bring people together for a little face-to-face conversation and the exchange of business cards, so too are there Web sites devoted to networking. Some have been established for the purpose of making professional contacts; others are socially focused. Most are open to all, but, in some cases, you will have to pay a fee to participate. Monster.com operates a networking Web site (*www.network.monster.com*). Others include *www. linkedin.com*, *www.tribe.net*, and *www.friendster.com*.

CHAPTER 9

RESUMES AND COVER LETTERS IN THE ELECTRONIC AGE

My, how times have changed. Twenty years ago, applicants in search of a job read the newspaper classifieds with a vengeance, typed each cover letter individually, sent their resumes to a copy shop to be printed in bulk on pretty paper, and, after slapping a stamp on the envelope, relied solely on the U.S. Postal Service to deliver the goods—hard copies all—to the desks of prospective employers. Today, we "shop" for job openings online, print personalized cover letters and resumes from our home computers, post our qualifications to online databases, and send cover letters by e-mail with resumes attached—no stamps required.

Welcome to the wonderful world of job-hunting in the age of technology! It's fast-paced and fiercely competitive. And though your educational background and experience may be top-notch, unless you're savvy about the latest techniques for getting noticed by the right people at the right time, your job search just might lead you nowhere.

No doubt about it, technology plays an integral role in today's recruitment and hiring process. For you, the modern-day job seeker, that's both good news and bad. On the upside, word processing software makes it easier to draft and revise resumes and cover letters and, thanks to online databases, thousands of prospective employers can have access to your credentials 24/7. But herein lies the rub: your application materials—and most specifically your resume—must stand up to the challenges of various technological environments. If you don't recognize terms like ASCII and scannability, or why they matter as you put together your resume, then you better start boning up. We're here to help you get started.

It is not our intention in this chapter to teach you how to write a resume; whole books have been devoted to that subject. What we're going to discuss, instead, are the steps you need to take to ensure that your resume has the best possible chance of being read by the people who are doing the hiring for the kinds of jobs you seek. These days, it's not so much what you say, but how you say it and show it off. When it comes to creating a resume for the electronic era, the presentation and format are as important as the content.

And while we're on the subject of content, you can get by in most technological environments with just one resume, if it's done right. But to cover your bases with regard to delivery, you will need to be able to generate that resume in two basic formats: one that is e-mailable and one that is scannable. Since your scannable resume will become the prototype for all formats—the hard copies you mail with your cover letter to prospects and carry to interviews, the documents you attach to e-mails, and the electronic resumes you post yourself to online databases—let's start there.

The Scannable Resume

It's a dog-eat-dog world out there—especially if you're hunting for a job. In some sectors of the economy, the job market is so tight that a single newspaper classified ad or online job posting is likely to generate hundreds, even thousands of applications. At the same time, more and more companies are slashing their recruiting budgets and trimming their hiring staffs to the bone. You do the math. There just aren't enough people to read all of the resumes that arrive on a weekly basis. Consequently, many hiring managers, especially those in large companies that receive thousands of resumes each month, have turned to computerized scanning systems to speed the sorting and processing of job applications.

When a resume arrives in the human resources department by mail or fax these days, the only human being who's likely to touch it is the clerk who feeds it through the scanner. From that point on, machines pretty much take over. If your hard copy resume is in a stack to be processed, here's what happens: the scanner sends an image of your document to a computer. The computer "reads" it, looking for key words, then files it accordingly in a database. When the employer has an opening to fill, he or she searches that database for resumes containing key words associated with the requirements for a particular position. If your resume contains key words that match those requirements, it will pop up and a human being will have the opportunity to finally read it, and possibly give you a call to schedule an interview. But if there are no key-word matches, your resume remains tucked deep inside the database doing absolutely nothing but sitting there until another opening with another set of key words comes along and the whole process begins again.

Not every company uses this scanning technology. Small and midsize firms still employ the human touch, and many companies with Internet presence and online databases prefer to receive resumes by e-mail. Still, enough large corporations rely on scanners so that you will definitely want to make "scannability" a consideration in finalizing your resume. If the chances are better than average that your document will be read by more computers than people, then you must make sure it exists in a format that is easy for a computer to recognize, read, and understand.

Your ultimate goal is to get your resume out of the database and into the hands of the hiring manager. The trick for doing this is twofold: 1) you must choose the right key words to describe your educational background and experience and, 2) you must format your resume so a scanner can read it. If it's incorrectly formatted, it will scan poorly or not at all and you've probably lost your shot at a job with this company.

How do you make your resume scannable? Read on.

Content
- **Name.** Your name should appear at the top of your resume, with your address following underneath.

- **Abbreviations.** Most resume-scanning systems will recognize a few common abbreviations like B.A./B.S., M.B.A., and state names. Widely used acronyms for industry jargon, such as A/R and A/P, which might appear in an accounting resume, are also generally accepted. If you are in doubt as to whether the abbreviation you want to use is a standard one, play it safe and spell the words out.
- **Key Words.** Using the right key words or key phrases in your resume is absolutely critical to its ultimate success—or lack thereof. We cannot stress this enough. Key words are the nouns or short phrases that the computer searches for when scanning your resume and deciding whether to select it for further consideration. Key words usually refer to experience, training, skills, and abilities. For example, an employer searching an employment database for a sales representative might use the following key word criteria:

> sales representative
> B.S./B.A.
> exceeded quota
> cold calls
> high energy
> willing to travel

If your resume contains all of these key words and phrases, it will be among the first resumes selected. If it lacks just one key word, it will be in the next bunch, and so forth. Sadly, however, even if you have the right qualifications for the position of sales representative and years of experience in a similar job, if none of these key words appears in your resume, the computer will pass right over your document and the employer will never see it.

To complicate matters even further, different employers search for different key words, sometimes even for the same positions. Whenever possible, use the buzzwords common to your field or industry to describe your experience, education, skills, and abilities. Though there is no way to know for sure which key words employers are most likely to search for, you can make educated guesses. Check the classified ads for job openings in your field. What terms do employers commonly use to describe their requirements? Executive recruiters who specialize in your field are also a good source of this kind of information. To maximize your resume's chances of being selected in the search, use as many key words as possible. Remember, you only have to use a key word once in your document for it to be selected; to cover all bases and improve your chances, use synonyms wherever possible.

- **Key-Word Summary.** This is a compendium of your qualifications, usually written in a series of succinct key-word phrases, that immediately follows your name and address.
- **Experience and Achievements.** Your professional experience should immediately follow the key-word summary, beginning with your most recent position. (If you are a recent college graduate, however, you should list your education ahead of your experience.) Be sure that your job title, employer, location, and dates of employment are all clearly displayed. Highlight your accomplishments and key responsibilities with bullets.

- **Education.** This section immediately follows the experience section. List your degrees, licenses, certifications, relevant coursework, and academic awards or honors. Be sure to clearly display the name of the schools and their locations, and your years of graduation.
- **References.** Don't waste valuable space with statements like "References available upon request." Though this statement was standard fare for resumes of old, it won't win you any points on a scannable resume.

Format

- **Length.** The conventional wisdom used to be that a resume should never be longer than one page. With scannable resumes you have a little more leeway. The more key words you use, the better the chances your resume will be selected in a key word search. This is no time to conserve space. If you need two pages to list all of your skills and qualifications, use two pages. Better a long resume with the right key words than a short one that is missing important information. If you go over one page, do make sure that your name appears on the top of each subsequent page. Do not staple your resume.
- **Paper.** Don't bother with expensive papers or fancy colors; they don't scan well. Use standard twenty pound, 8½-by-11-inch paper. To ensure a clear scan, your resume needs to be as sharp and legible as possible,; black ink on white paper works best.
- **Font.** Choose a no-decorative font with clear, distinct characters, such as Arial (Helvetica) or Times New Roman. Stay away from script-like fonts and never use a reverse box to print white type on a black or gray shaded background. Scanners can't read reverse type.
- **Font Size.** A font size of 12 points is ideal. Don't go below 10 or above 14 points for body text, as type that is too small or too large is difficult for the scanner to read. Your name should be larger than the largest font in the text of your resume, but no larger than 20 points.
- **Font Style.** Most scanners will accept boldface, but if an employer specifically tells you to avoid it, substitute capital letters instead for emphasis. Boldfacing and all caps should be reserved for your name or major section headings, such as "Experience" and "Education."
- **Graphics, Lines, and Shading.** A resume scanner will try to "read" graphics, lines, and shading as text, but the end result will be computer chaos. Avoid these elements. And do stick to traditional layouts for your resume. Scanners read from left to write and are easily confused by two-column formats.
- **Printing.** Whatever type of printing process you use, make sure the end result is letter quality. For best results have your resume printed at your local copy shop. Otherwise, a laser printer is perfectly acceptable. Do not use typewriters or dot matrix printers; the quality of type they produce is inadequate for most scanners. Your resume needs to be as sharp and legible as possible, so you should always send originals, not photocopies. For the same reason, you should always mail, not fax, your resume.

Should You Include a Cover Letter with Your Scannable Resume?

Yes. A resume should never go out by itself. Though cover letters are generally not scanned, some systems will take a "photograph" of your letter, and store it electronically with your resume. And while your cover letter will not help you in the initial selection process, it might set you apart from the competition in the final rounds of elimination. If you've taken the time to craft a letter that reiterates your strongest qualifications, you'll have the edge over other contenders who skipped this step.

As with your resume, your cover letter should contain key words reflecting your strongest qualifications. If you're responding to a classified ad, you'll want to echo as many of the key words mentioned in the ad as possible. And if you're sending your resume to a new networking contact, be sure to mention the name of the person who referred you. .

The E-mailable Resume

A resume that is scannable is also e-mailable. But if want to add some special touches, like italics or boldfacing to a resume you'll be e-mailing as an attachment, you need not be so worried about whether these formatting elements will survive their journey to another computer; your word processing software has implanted the appropriate codes to make that possible.

Suppose, for example, that you created your resume in Microsoft Word and saved it to your hard drive as a Word document (.doc). The minute you clicked "Save," your software automatically retained any special formatting codes, such as fonts, margins, tabs, etc., right along with the actual words you typed. To send your resume as e-mail, simply attach the .doc file to your e-mail message.

"But my recipient doesn't use Word. Now what do I do?"

You'll need to save a second copy of your resume, this time as a Rich Text File (.rtf). Rich Text Files are the universal donors of the computer world. When in doubt about the recipient computer's ability to read a particular word processing program, attach the .rtf version of your resume to your e-mail; now anyone should be able to read it in its original format regardless of the software they use.

From time to time you may run across prospective employers who ask for your resume by e-mail, but specifically request that you not send it as an attachment. In such cases, you will have to remove the formatting codes and paste your resume into your e-mail message. This is not as difficult as it sounds.

E-mail messages are typically sent in ASCII format, which stands for American Standard Code for Information Interchange. ASCII files are generic and because no special formatting codes are added, they can be read by pretty much any computer. The resume you paste into your e-mail message will need to be in ASCII form. Sorry, but all those codes that make your Word document look so inviting by telling your software when to center a line, indent a paragraph, or italicize a word, will have to go. But wait—you didn't put those codes there in the first place, so how do you take them out? By saving your resume a third time, as an ASCII file. To do so, select "Save As" from your File menu and, depending on which Word version you're using, choose "ASCII Text," "Plain Text," or "MS DOS Text" as your file type. The resulting resume won't be pretty, but it will be the right format for pasting into an e-mail message.

SCANNABLE COVER LETTER

47 Lake Shore Drive
Cambridge, MA 02138
(617) 555-5555
csmith@email.com

December 2, 20--

Ms. Pat Cummings
Controller
Any Corporation
1140 Main Street
Boston, MA 02215

Dear Ms. Cummings:

This letter is in response to your December 2 advertisement in the *Boston Globe* for the position of Assistant Controller. I am very interested in the position and believe I have the qualifications you are looking for. Please consider the following:

- More than twenty years of experience in Accounting and Systems Management, Budgeting, Forecasting, Cost Containment, Financial Reporting, and International Accounting.
- Implemented "team-oriented" cross-training program within accounting group, resulting in timely month-end closings and increased productivity of key accounting staff.
- Master in Business Administration degree in Management from Northeastern University.
- Results-oriented professional and proven team leader.

These are only a few of my credentials that may be of interest to you. I look forward to discussing them with you further in a personal interview. Thank you for your consideration.

Sincerely,

Chris Smith

Enc. Resume

▶ Letter echoes the key words used in the employment ad.

▶ Candidate uses bullets to emphasize his/her key credentials.

SCANNABLE RESUME

CHRIS SMITH
47 Lake Shore Drive
Cambridge, MA 02138
(617) 555-5555
csmith@email.com

KEY WORD SUMMARY

Senior financial manager with more than twenty years of experience in Accounting and Systems Management, Budgeting, Forecasting, Cost Containment, Financial Reporting, and International Accounting. M.B.A. in Management. Proficient in Lotus, Excel, Solomon, Real World, and Windows.

EXPERIENCE

COLWELL CORPORATION, Wellesley, MA
$100 Million division of Bancroft Corporation

Director of Accounting and Budgets, 20-- to present

Supervised Staff of 20 in General Ledger, Accounts Payable, Accounts Receivable, and International Accounting. Facilitated month-end closing process with parent company and auditors.

Implemented "team-oriented" cross-training program within accounting group, resulting in timely month-end closings and increased productivity of key accounting staff.

Developed and implemented a strategy for Sales and Use Tax Compliance in all 50 states with 100% compliance for both parent company and subsidiaries.

Prepared monthly financial statements and analyses for review by management executive board.

Accounting Manager, 20-- to 20--

Managed a staff of 6 in General Ledger and Accounts Payable. Responsible for the design and refinement of financial reporting package. Assisted in month-end closing.

Established guidelines for month-end closing procedures, thereby speeding up closing by 5 business days.

Promoted to Director of Accounting and Budgets.

FRANKLIN AND DELANY COMPANY, Melrose, MA

Senior Accountant, 20-- to 20--
    Managed A/P, G/L, transaction processing, and financial reporting. Supervised staff of two.
    Developed Management Reporting package, including variance reports and cash flow reporting.

Staff Accountant, 20-- to 20--
    Managed A/P, including vouchering, cash disbursements, and bank reconciliation. Wrote and issued policies. Maintained supporting schedules used during year-end audits. Trained new employees.

Junior Accountant, 20-- to 20--
    Assisted in general ledger closing. Monitored cash collections and accounts receivable.

EDUCATION
M.B.A. in Management, Northeastern University, Boston, MA, 20--
B.S. in Accounting, Boston College, Boston, MA, 20--

ASSOCIATIONS
National Association of Accountants

▶ Resume contains many key words such as Budgeting, Forecasting, and M.B.A..

▶ Format is "scanner-friendly": Nondecorative font, traditional layout, no italics or graphics.

PART III

Sample Cover Letters

CHAPTER 10

RESPONSE TO A CLASSIFIED ADVERTISEMENT (PRINT)

Response letters are written for job openings advertised in the classified ads, which appear in newspapers, magazines, trade journals, and professional publications. When writing your cover letter, you should keep the specifics of the advertisement in mind. If the job requires travel or relocation, make sure to specify your availability in your response. Only address salary preference if requested, phrasing it as a range so you don't limit your opportunities.

Be sure to tailor your letter to the specific requirements outlined in the ad. For instance, Marsha Z. recently reworked her cover letter to respond to an opening for a Computer Programmer. Although she had been working in retail, she de-emphasized her sales accomplishments to highlight computer courses she had taken, applications she is proficient in, and her experience working as an intern for an IBM computer design team. As a result, Marsha landed an interview!

It is important to keep in mind that classifieds demand a quick response. The faster your inquiry reaches an employer's desk, the more individual attention it will receive.

RESPONSE TO A CLASSIFIED ADVERTISEMENT (PRINT)
(Administrative Assistant)

178 Green Street
Ecru, MS 38842
(601) 555-5555
csmith@email.com

November 1, 20--

Pat Cummings
Office Manager
Any Corporation
1140 Main Street
Chicago, IL 60605

Dear Mr. Cummings:

Your October 30 advertisement in the *Jackson Review* calls for an Assistant with a background rich in a variety of administrative skills, such as mine.

As an organized and detail-oriented individual with five years' experience in administration, I believe my qualifications match your requirements. My strengths also include independent working habits and superb computer skills. As an Administrative Assistant at Lambert Hospital, I was in charge of all computer support, word processing and database, spreadsheet, and administrative functions. My duties included all purchasing, equipment maintenance, daily office operations, supervising of staff and volunteers, and coordinating various projects with staff and outside vendors.

I would appreciate the opportunity to discuss this position with you at your convenience, as it sounds like an exciting opportunity. If you have any questions, do not hesitate to contact me at the above-listed phone number or at *csmith@email.com*.

Sincerely,

Chris Smith

Enc. Resume

▶ Introduction is brief and attention-grabbing.   ▶ Candidate details applicable work experience.

RESPONSE TO A CLASSIFIED ADVERTISEMENT (PRINT)
(Administrative Judge)

178 Green Street
Fox, OR 97831
(503) 555-5555

May 23, 20--

Pat Cummings
Chairperson
Chicago Municipal Court
1140 Main Street
Chicago, IL 60605

Dear Ms. Cummings:

    Your advertisement in the May 30 issue of *Lawyers Monthly* is of great interest to me. I feel that I have the qualifications necessary to effectively handle the responsibilities of Administrative Judge.

    During the past four years as Assistant Attorney General, I have gained broad experience in the litigation of personal injury actions and workers' compensation claims. In this position, I made extensive use of my legal knowledge as well as my research, analytical, writing, and judgmental skills. I am confident of my ability to provide the expertise necessary for the professional representation of an Administrative Judge.

    The enclosed resume describes my qualifications for the position advertised. I would welcome the opportunity to personally discuss my qualifications with you at your convenience.

Sincerely,

Chris Smith

Enc. Resume

▶ Closing is brief and to the point.

▶ Letter cites advertisement's specific publication and date.

RESPONSE TO A CLASSIFIED ADVERTISEMENT (PRINT)
(Analyst)

178 Green Street
Henniker, NH 03242
(603) 555-5555

December 30, 20--

Pat Cummings
Director, Financial Planning
Any Corporation
1140 Main Street
Nashua, NH 03061

Dear Mr. Cummings:

I write in response to your advertisement for an Analyst in the December 28 edition of the *Telegraph*. During the past several years I have been actively involved, in both academic and workplace settings, with financial and business analysis as well as support activities involving corporate business and finance.

Although my present position has provided me with the opportunity for quality professional development as an Analyst and interesting challenges through diverse assignments, I am ready for a change. I am interested in joining a firm in which I can offer my analytical and qualitative skills toward making a substantial contribution to its overall success and reputation.

The enclosed employment profile is a summary of my experience. I would be glad to schedule an interview to discuss your requirements and my ability to handle the responsibilities of the position offered.

Should you require additional information prior to our meeting, please feel free to contact me at the above address and daytime number, or during the evenings at (603) 444-4444.

In the interim, I will look forward to your return response.

Yours sincerely,

Chris Smith

Enc. Employment profile

▶ Position applied for is clearly and immediately defined.

▶ Including an evening telephone number is optional in a cover letter.

RESPONSE TO A CLASSIFIED ADVERTISEMENT (PRINT)
(Assistant Curator)

178 Green Street
Bensonville, IL 60106
(708) 555-5555

June 21, 20--

Pat Cummings
Curator
Any Music Library
1140 Main Street
Evansville, IL 47713

Dear Ms. Cummings:

   I wish to be considered for the position of Assistant Curator of your music library as advertised in last Friday's *Evansville Courier*.

   My experience includes working as the Assistant Editor of *Classics Quarterly*, writing classical music reviews for the *Complete Record Guide*, conducting interviews and writing concert reviews for *Chicago Rock*, and writing rock and country album reviews for *Inside Edge*. I was also employed as the Classical Music Listings Coordinator for the *Complete Musical Almanac* summer and fall supplements. Currently, I am a part-time proofreader and copyeditor for *Art Illinois* and an evening announcer (two nights per week) at WKEM in Belleville.

   In addition, I offer a Bachelor of Fine Arts degree in Music from the University of Illinois, a Master's degree in Musicology from DePaul University, a year at Cambridge University (England) studying music and the arts, and doctoral studies at the University of Chicago.

   I am very interested in resuming regular, full-time employment with a facility in need of a skilled professional knowledgeable in all aspects of musicology. I have often visited and relied on the resources available at Any Music Library, and would welcome the opportunity to join your ranks. I am confident my experience could be applied to a successful career as your Assistant Curator.

   I would be happy to meet with you to further discuss the position and my ability to meet your needs. I will be in the Evansville area during the week of July 3, and will call your office to schedule a convenient interview time.

   Thank you for your consideration.

Sincerely,

Chris Smith
Enc. Resume

▶ Candidate includes all relevant experience to advertised position.

▶ Impressive educational background strengthens cover letter.

RESPONSE TO A CLASSIFIED ADVERTISEMENT (PRINT)
(Assistant Editor)

178 Green Street
Worcester, MA 01610
(508) 555-5555

June 28, 20--

Pat Cummings
Editor
Any Corporation
1140 Main Street
Boston, MA 02215

RE: Assistant Editor

Dear Mr. Cummings:

I recently read your advertisement in the *Boston Globe* for the position of Assistant Editor, and am highly interested in learning more about the job's specific requirements.

I possess strong written and verbal communication skills, as well as computer and desktop publishing experience. My accomplishments include:

- Winning the Columbia Scholastic Press Association's First Place Gold Circle Award for graphic art.
- Serving as feature editor, art editor, graphic artist, and reporter for various college publications.
- Completing a course in advertising art/desktop publishing, which focused on the use of PageMaker software.
- Proficiency in Microsoft Word and Excel software.

Please find my resume attached for your review. I would appreciate the opportunity to discuss my specific abilities in relation to your needs. I will call you next Monday to schedule a mutually convenient time to meet.

Thank you for your consideration.

Sincerely,

Chris Smith

Enc. Resume

▶ Setting desired position apart from body of letter may be advantageous when responding to classified advertisement.

▶ Letter uses bullets to highlight candidate's achievements related to advertised position.

RESPONSE TO A CLASSIFIED ADVERTISEMENT (PRINT)
(Assistant Hospital Supervisor)

178 Green Street
Stoughton, MA 02072
(617) 555-5555

July 27, 20--

Pat Cummings
Administrator
Any Corporation
1140 Main Street
Chicago, IL 60605

RE: Assistant Hospital Supervisor position

Dear Ms. Cummings:

I am writing in response to your advertisement in this past week's *Boston Phoenix*.

I recently took a sabbatical and finished my Bachelor of Arts degree in May at Emerson College. I am currently seeking full-time employment.

My employment background consists of twelve years at the Deaconess Hospital, where I provided a wide range of administrative, financial, and research support to the Chief Executive Officer. I have a strong aptitude for working with numbers and extensive experience with computer software applications.

I would be interested in speaking with you further regarding this position. I am hopeful that you will consider my background in administrative support, as well as my word processing, database, and spreadsheet skills, an asset to Any Corporation.

Thank you in advance for your consideration.

Sincerely,

Chris Smith

Enc. Resume

▶ Candidate expresses interest in returning to full-time employment.

▶ Candidate uses closing to suggest possibility of interview.

RESPONSE TO A CLASSIFIED ADVERTISEMENT (PRINT)
(Associate Desktop Publisher)

178 Green Street
Tacoma, WA 98447
(206) 555-5555

March 10, 20--

Pat Cummings
Managing Editor
Any Corporation
1140 Main Street
Richmond, VA 23225

Dear Mr. Cummings:

In response to your advertisement for an Associate Desktop Publisher, I am sending my resume for your review.

My ten years of computer experience include researching, developing, and documenting the operational procedures of a software seller. I was responsible for all aspects of the manual, from conceptualization to publication. I also coordinated and published the sales and marketing newsletter distributed to key accounts and sales representatives.

Successful completion of such projects requires skills in researching, organizing, writing, and editing. I am proficient in several desktop publishing and word processing applications, including WordPerfect, Microsoft Word, and Corel Ventura.

I will be moving to the Richmond area next week and would be happy to meet with you at your convenience. I will call your office during the week of March 17. Thank you for your consideration.

Sincerely,

Chris Smith

Enc. Resume

▶ Computer experience calls attention to candidate's technical knowledge.

▶ Candidate immediately specifies position being applied for.

RESPONSE TO A CLASSIFIED ADVERTISEMENT (PRINT)
(Athletic Director)

178 Green Street
La Crosse, WI 54601
(608) 555-5555

September 23, 20--

Pat Cummings
Headmaster
Any School
1140 Main Street
Brownsville, TX 78520

Dear Ms. Cummings:

I am writing to you regarding your opening for the position of Athletic Director, as advertised in the *Wisconsin State Journal*. I believe that, with my background in athletics and science, I have the technical knowledge, work ethic, and organizational skills to contribute to your team.

For the past nine years I have been coaching rowing. I feel strongly that the qualities embodied in rowing have made me successful in my various business and athletic endeavors. Goal setting, discipline, determination, and teamwork are applicable to any field.

I admire Any School's unique educational philosophy, which stresses the utility of athletics to instill discipline in young minds. I feel that I can contribute to your school's achievement-oriented environment.

Due to a change in the position of Head Crew Coach at Yale University, I was put in an interim position of responsibility for the smooth running of the boathouse. For the 20---20-- season, I dealt with all the ordering, budgeting, donation solicitation, spare parts inventory, and travel arrangements for the crews. I was, in effect, the administrative head of the boathouse.

I will call in approximately two weeks to discuss how I hope to contribute to your school. A resume is enclosed for your consideration.

Sincerely,

Chris Smith

Enc. Resume

▶ Candidate's most recent position is outlined in detail.

▶ Since company name and information is provided in advertisement, candidate promises to follow up inquiry.

RESPONSE TO A CLASSIFIED ADVERTISEMENT (PRINT)
(Business Consultant)

178 Green Street
Payne Gap, KY 41537
(606) 555-5555

June 3, 20--

Pat Cummings
Director of Recruiting
Any Corporation
1140 Main Street
Payne Gap, KY 41537

RE: Business Consultant; *Lexington Herald-Leader*; May 27, 20--

Dear Mr. Cummings:

I am a new M.B.A. graduate from Spain's premiere business school, la Universidad de Negocios. Although I have lived in Spain for most of my life, I am an American citizen and have just recently moved to Kentucky to seek permanent employment.

Your advertisement captured my attention because I am very interested in pursuing a career as a software consultant. Please allow me to highlight my qualifications as they relate to your stated requirements.

Your Requirements

- Experience consulting to small businesses
- Experience working in small businesses
- Marketing experience
- Enjoy using computers
- Assist in the development and implementation of new software products for small businesses

My Experience

- Graduated with an M.B.A. Immersed in case study method, in which students act as consultants, analyzing and solving business problems.
- Founded Widgetsoft, a software development business. Worked in small departments of larger companies. Enjoy handling multiple responsibilities and working closely with others.
- 4-½ years of progressive marketing experience. Possess strong writing, editing, and desktop publishing abilities.

- Fluency in Microsoft Excel, Microsoft Word, Windows XP, dBase. Programming experience in C+, Fortran, COBOL.
- At John Whitmore & Sons, I participated in the development of a new CD-ROM Atlas. Assisted with marketing, content, and user interface issues.

I believe my qualifications are commensurate with your requirements for this position. I would welcome the opportunity for an interview to discuss with you how I can help develop outstanding software products for Any Corporation.

Sincerely,

Chris Smith

Enc. Resume

▶ Unique format demonstrates candidate's ability to meet advertised job requirements.

▶ International work experience adds weight to candidate's qualifications.

RESPONSE TO A CLASSIFIED ADVERTISEMENT (PRINT)
(Campus Police Officer)

178 Green Street
Stanford, CA 94305
(415) 555-5555

February 23, 20--

Pat Cummings
Director of Security
Any College
1140 Main Street
Whittier, CA 92608

RE: Campus Police Officer

Dear Ms. Cummings:

My interest in pursuing and expanding my professional career in law enforcement and security management has prompted me to respond to your advertisement in the March issue of *Careers in Law Enforcement.*

For the past twelve years, my background has been concentrated in security and law enforcement. In my present position, I am responsible for maintaining the highest possible site and operations security for a key United States government defense contractor. From 20-- to 20--, I served in the United States Army where I was responsible for maintaining peak law enforcement/security alertness and the welfare of all personnel. In that capacity, I received numerous letters of commendation for superior job performance. I am a graduate of military police school, I have completed additional law enforcement seminars, and I am currently enrolled in a criminal justice degree program.

Through practical experience, I am well versed in military and international law as well as United States law and procedures. If we could meet in a personal interview, I could discuss further my qualifications and outline the potential contribution I could make to your security office.

I look forward to your response.

Sincerely,

Chris Smith

Enc. Resume

▶ Including a military record can be advantageous if it relates to candidate's job objective.

▶ Continuing education indicates candidate's ongoing commitment to his/her field.

RESPONSE TO A CLASSIFIED ADVERTISEMENT (PRINT)
(Canine Science Instructor)

178 Green Street
Winesburg, OH 44690
(614) 555-5555

February 25, 20--

Pat Cummings
Academic Administrator
Any College
1140 Main Street
Cincinnati, OH 45202

RE: Canine Science Instructor

Dear Mr. Cummings:

My interest in the position of part-time Instructor for courses in animal grooming and behavior training advertised in the February 24 edition of the *Cincinnati Post* has prompted me to forward my resume for your review.

In addition to a Bachelor of Arts degree in Behavioral Sciences, I hold certificates in Kennel Management, Dog Grooming, and Training, and continue to attend seminars in adult dog and puppy training. Beyond my academic pursuits, I have more than six years of hands-on experience teaching group obedience classes for dogs and puppies. I also provide private lessons, behavioral consultations, and training for AKC Titles.

After you have had the opportunity to review my qualifications, I would appreciate meeting with you to further discuss this position. I am well qualified to teach future instructors in courses on animal grooming and behavior training, and feel confident that I can provide the kind of student support expected of instructors at Any College.

Yours sincerely,

Chris Smith

Enc. Resume

▶ Including professional accreditation and licensure may be advantageous for certain kinds of work.

▶ Experience reinforces candidate's suitability for advertised position.

RESPONSE TO A CLASSIFIED ADVERTISEMENT (PRINT)
(Case Manager)

178 Green Street
White Plains, NY 10606
(914) 555-5555

December 17, 20--

Pat Cummings
Director of Social Services
Any Agency
1140 Main Street
Hoboken, NJ 07030

Dear Ms. Cummings:

I am responding to your advertisement in the *Star Ledger* for a Case Manager. My interest is in pursuing and expanding my professional career in the motivation and guidance of juveniles to achieve positive objectives and personal dignity. It is this goal that has prompted me to forward the attached resume for your review and consideration.

Please note that I have directed and dedicated my efforts, both academically and through the co-op program at Fordham University, to working with juveniles and prison inmates, guiding them through innovative programs in self-preservation. These programs required extensive communication and interaction with boards of trustees, agency personnel, and the Neighborhood Watch campaign. In addition, I have acquired excellent customer/client relations and communications skills, as well as sound knowledge of office procedures, in a variety of full-time and part-time positions.

I would welcome a meeting to learn more about your work at Any Agency and how I could contribute to your success. I will call next Monday to follow up on my inquiry.

Yours sincerely,

Chris Smith

Enc. Resume

▶ Activities highlight candidate's involvement in local community.

▶ Unrelated work experience is omitted from response letter.

RESPONSE TO A CLASSIFIED ADVERTISEMENT (PRINT)
(Chief Financial Officer)

178 Green Street
Rigby, ID 83442

June 25, 20--

Pat Cummings
Controller
Any Corporation
1140 Main Street
Boise, ID 83706

RE: Chief Financial Officer

Dear Mr. Cummings:

With reference to the above-advertised position, the attached resume is submitted for your evaluation.

I have a record of outstanding success in the management of corporate financial operations for fast-paced manufacturing companies and associated commercial operations in multilocation, multistate, and international environments.

My sixteen years of progressively responsible experience encompassed management of all aspects of the financial and treasury functions, in a range from Cost Accounting Manager to Chief Financial Officer and Vice-President, Finance. This experience has encompassed the successful management of corporate real estate, human resources, and general operations. In addition to holding an M.B.A. in Finance and a Bachelor of Arts degree in Accounting, I have been a Certified Public Accountant since 1978.

My resume is a good summary of my background and general experience. Please contact me at the above address or call (208) 555-5555 (home) or (208) 444-4444 (office), as I would like to arrange a mutually convenient time for a meeting, during which we can further discuss your current or anticipated openings. May I hear from you?

Yours sincerely,

Chris Smith

Enc. Resume

▶ Letter illustrates continual career progression.

▶ Candidate's highest educational achievement is shown before other less significant degrees.

RESPONSE TO A CLASSIFIED ADVERTISEMENT (PRINT)
(Child Care Director)

178 Green Street
Lime, OH 45804
(419) 555-5555

July 18, 20--

Pat Cummings
Director
Any Center
1140 Main Street
Toledo, OH 43660

RE: Assistant Center Director

Dear Ms. Cummings:

I am responding to your advertisement in the July 18 edition of the *Toledo Blade.*

I am a licensed Child Care Provider in the State of Ohio with three years' experience working in a private center facilitating the care of more than forty children. In this capacity, I have been solely responsible for the supervision of ten children, ranging in age from six months to five years. My duties include distributing meals and snacks, monitoring "playtime," and creating and instructing children in diverse educational activities.

In addition, I have experience working with children in various settings, and have held such positions as private nanny, tutor, camp counselor, and gymnastics instructor. I also wrote a children's book, which involved many hours of research and interaction with children of all ages.

I would appreciate the opportunity to provide you with several diverse and favorable references regarding my capabilities to fill this position. I will follow up on this inquiry in several days to schedule a meeting at your convenience.

With best regards,

Chris Smith

Enc. Resume

▶ Qualifications highlight candidate's leadership skills.

▶ Introduction immediately refers to publication where advertisement appeared.

RESPONSE TO A CLASSIFIED ADVERTISEMENT (PRINT)
(Claims Adjuster)

178 Green Street
Salisbury, NC 28145
(704) 555-5555

August 26, 20--
Pat Cummings
Claims Supervisor
Any Insurance Agency
1140 Main Street
Asheville, NC 28802

Dear Mr. Cummings:

Yesterday I read with interest your advertised opening for a Claims Adjuster in the *Citizen Times*. During the past fifteen years, I have been employed by a major insurance company where my primary area of concentration has been in workers' compensation claims handling.

Due to my company's consolidation, I am currently seeking to join an organization in need of a highly productive individual with a sound background in claims handling, cost containment, customer relations/service, employee training, and administrative support.

I am well organized and capable of researching and coordinating detailed data and can work effectively with professionals as well as corporate management to arrive at mutually favorable solutions.

Are you interested in filling your availability with an individual who, in previous positions, has cost-effectively negotiated more than 100 claims in a six-month period? If so, I would love to meet with you in a personal interview. I have enclosed my business profile for your review and am confident I can make an immediate and successful contribution to Any Insurance Agency.

Sincerely,

Chris Smith

Enc. Business profile

▶ Phrasing interview request in question form is a strong closing.

▶ Four short paragraphs is the ideal length for a cover letter.

RESPONSE TO A CLASSIFIED ADVERTISEMENT (PRINT)
(Clinical Research Nurse)

178 Green Street
Marietta, GA 30060

August 20, 20--

Pat Cummings, R.N.
Head Nurse
Any Hospital
1140 Main Street
Savannah, GA 31404

Dear Ms. Cummings:

I believe I have the combined clinical nursing and research skills that would qualify me as an ideal candidate for the Clinical Research Nurse opening you advertised in *Nursing Today*.

I am a dedicated professional capable of working with physicians and nursing, laboratory, and professional specialty groups, and can offer more than fourteen years of responsible experience ranging from Staff Nurse and Charge Nurse to Clinical Research Nurse with a major teaching hospital.

I hold a Bachelor of Science in Nursing, and my graduate studies have focused on epidemiology and international health. My experience encompasses sound knowledge of nursing quality assurance programs and in-service education programs. Throughout my career, I have worked both independently and as part of a team on studies involving psoriasis, cardiology, AIDS, sickle-cell anemia, amyloidosis, diabetes, and oncology.

Please contact me at the above address, or call (404) 555-5555 to arrange a mutually convenient time for a meeting. I am very interested in joining the nursing staff at Any Hospital and hope to speak with you soon.

Thank you for your consideration.

Sincerely,

Chris Smith, R.N., B.S.N.

Enc. Professional profile

▶ Valuable research experience is highlighted in detail.

▶ Introduction demonstrates candidate's suitability for advertised position.

RESPONSE TO A CLASSIFIED ADVERTISEMENT (PRINT)
(Conference Coordinator)

178 Green Street
Racine, WI 53406

December 22, 20--

Pat Cummings
Artistic Director
Any Deaf Theatre
1140 Main Street
De Forest, WI 53532

Dear Mr. Cummings:

The position of Conference Coordinator advertised in the January issue of *Deaf Today* is of great interest of me, and I have enclosed my professional profile for your review.

I am a deaf person who has had the opportunity to complete my undergraduate and graduate studies, and who has worked in responsible positions requiring strong leadership, planning, organizational, administrative, and communication skills. Throughout my career, I have worked with individuals and groups in diverse settings within public, private, artistic, and government sectors.

I am well versed in visual and performing arts as a student, performer, coordinator, instructor, and facilitator with concentration in providing services for, and instructing, the deaf community and the general public. I have the communications, public relations, and people skills necessary to establish an annual conference for Any Deaf Theatre that will meet the criteria of excellence you are looking for in a lasting international artistic exchange. It is a challenging undertaking that I feel I am capable of achieving.

Should you need additional information, please contact me at (414) 555-5555 TTY.

I look forward to your return response.

Sincerely,

Chris Smith

Enc. Professional profile

▶ Letter immediately states candidate's purpose.

▶ Candidate focuses on applying skills and experiences to advertised position.

RESPONSE TO A CLASSIFIED ADVERTISEMENT (PRINT)
(Contracted Typist)

178 Green Street
Baltimore, MD 21202
(301) 555-5555

February 14, 20--

Pat Cummings
Sales Manager
Any Corporation
1140 Main Street
Washington, DC 19180

Dear Ms. Cummings:

I am responding to your advertisement published in the *Washington Post* on February 13 concerning the position of Contracted Typist.

My primary qualification for this position is a typing speed of 90 wpm on a computer keyboard. In addition, I hold a Bachelor of Arts degree in English from Worcester State College with concentrations in writing and literary criticism.

I have a Pentium 4 machine with an HP LaserJet printer. I usually rely on Microsoft Word for Windows for documentation and manuscript work, but remain flexible concerning any custom requirements you might have. I use the integrated grammar and spell checker features of Word on all documents.

I would be glad to make myself available for an interview and typing test at your convenience. I look forward to learning more about Any Corporation.

With best regards,

Chris Smith

Enc. Resume

▶ Mentioning typing speed and word processing skills can be advantageous for administrative and office support positions.

▶ Candidate's functional skills are applicable to advertised position.

RESPONSE TO A CLASSIFIED ADVERTISEMENT (PRINT)
(Cosmetologist)

178 Green Street
Auburn, WA 98071
(206) 555-5555

August 13, 20--

Pat Cummings
Owner
Any Boutique
1140 Main Street
Seattle, WA 98134

Dear Mr. Cummings:

Enclosed please find my resume. I am very interested in applying for the position of Cosmetologist that was advertised in the *Seattle Post Intelligencer* on August 13, and am confident that you will find my skills ideally applicable to your needs.

Thank you in advance for your anticipated consideration. I look forward to meeting with you to discuss this opportunity.

Sincerely,

Chris Smith

Enc. Resume

▶ Letter is short and to the point.

▶ Enclosure line suggests candidate is a meticulous, detail-orientated professional.

RESPONSE TO A CLASSIFIED ADVERTISEMENT (PRINT)
(Customer Service Representative)

178 Green Street
Decorah, IA 51201
(319) 555-5555

September 6, 20--

Pat Cummings
Director of Public Relations
Any Corporation
1140 Main Street
Northampton, MA 01060

RE: Customer Service Representative

Dear Ms. Cummings:

My interest in the above position has incited me to forward my resume as requested in your advertisement published in the *Boston Sunday Globe.*

During the past several years at Fortmiller, Inc., my experience has been concentrated in the areas of billing, credit, collection, and customer service. In my current position as Customer Service Supervisor, I maintain the efficiency and accuracy of complex billing systems. This position also requires generating detailed reports for management. My position has given me the opportunity to set policies and procedures, implement systems, and participate in staffing and training personnel. During my tenure, 55 percent of the entry-level staff I trained advanced to managerial positions within Fortmiller, Inc.

Reading your requirements for the position advertised, I am confident of my ability to provide you with the experience and quality of performance you expect.

Once you have had a chance to review my qualifications, I would appreciate meeting with you for further discussion. I will call within the week to schedule an interview at your convenience.

Yours sincerely,

Chris Smith

Enc. Resume

▶ Qualifications highlight candidate's leadership skills.

▶ Candidate details applicable work experience.

RESPONSE TO A CLASSIFIED ADVERTISEMENT (PRINT)
(Dental Hygienist)

178 Green Street
Deer Park, NY 11729
(516) 555-5555

March 3, 20--

Pat Cummings, D.D.S
1140 Main Street
Lynbrook, NY 11563

Dear Dr. Cummings:

I would like to offer the attached confidential resume as an application for the Dental Hygienist position you advertised in the *Times-Union*.

I am confident that my training and experience could be effectively applied to the requirements of the position as described. If you would like any additional information, please do not hesitate to contact me. I look forward to meeting with you and further discussing the mutual benefit of our joining forces.

Thank you in advance for your consideration.

Sincerely,

Chris Smith

Enc. Resume

▶ Letter suggests discretion.

▶ Closing invites addressee to inquire about additional information.

RESPONSE TO A CLASSIFIED ADVERTISEMENT (PRINT)
(Dentistry Department Manager)

178 Green Street
Gaithersburg, MD 20879

February 10, 20--

Pat Cummings
Chief Administrator
Any Hospital
1140 Main Street
Chapel Hill, NC 27514

RE: Manager—Department of Dentistry

Dear Ms. Cummings:

The position you advertised is of great interest to me, and I hope to convince you of my capability to cost-effectively execute the responsibilities of Dentistry Department Manager.

My experience with Johns Hopkins Medical School's Department of Ophthalmology, Maryland Eye & Ear Infirmary, and Blue Cross/Blue Shield has involved interfacing and dealing with all operations and administrative departments on matters pertaining to fiscal and business reporting. I have extensive experience with MIS and firsthand experience with sophisticated programs designed to accommodate and control the rapid and profitable growth of business.

My business management, staff training and supervision, and administrative experience are essential requirements for maintaining equitable controls for a highly complex business. I can provide cost-effective fiscal management to maintain and increase profitability. Through efficient tracking and control systems, budget planning, and administration, I am able to generate cost savings and greater profit margins.

Should you require additional information, I will be glad to meet with you for further discussion. I can be reached at (301) 555-5555. In the interim, I look forward to meeting with you and joining your management team in the near future.

Sincerely,

Chris Smith

Enc. Resume

▶ Letter highlights candidate's management skills.

▶ Including telephone number is necessary in a cover letter.

RESPONSE TO A CLASSIFIED ADVERTISEMENT (PRINT)
(Director of Public Works)

178 Green Street
Liberty, SC 29657
(803) 555-5555

September 22, 20--

Pat Cummings
District Supervisor
Any Office
1140 Main Street
Charleston, SC 29403

Dear Mr. Cummings:

I am very interested in the position of Director of Public Works for the town of Liberty, as advertised in the September 20 edition of the *Post and Courier*.

During the past thirteen years, I have been actively involved in the management of diverse projects which require the ability to work with engineering, architectural, and construction professionals on public and private rehabilitation, restoration, and construction programs. My experience ranges from concept to signoff as well as the supervision of in-house and field crews on both privately and city/federally funded building and highway contracts.

I am an effective manager and budget administrator, and have the ability to work in harmony with individuals and groups in a busy construction/public works environment where concentration is on community services, safety, and the environment. As a longtime resident of Liberty, I believe I could reflect both personal and local interests in providing quality DPW services. I am confident of my ability to direct an efficient, cost-effective, and productive department.

Enclosed is my business profile for your consideration. I would like to learn more about the position, and will call your office early next week to see if we can schedule a meeting.

Thank you for your time.

Sincerely,

Chris Smith

Enc. Business profile

▶ Candidate matches his/her qualifications with potential employer's needs.

▶ Offering to phone the addressee rather than wait for a follow-up call shows initiative.

RESPONSE TO A CLASSIFIED ADVERTISEMENT (PRINT)
(Editorial Assistant)

178 Green Street
Austin, TX 78746
(512) 555-5555

June 4, 20--

Pat Cummings
Vice-President
Any Corporation
1140 Main Street
Dallas, TX 75275

Dear Ms. Cummings:

I am very interested in the Editorial Assistant position listed recently in the *Dallas Morning News*, and have enclosed my resume and a writing sample as an application. I am familiar with Any Corporation's publications, and would love the opportunity to contribute to your efforts.

My accomplishments include:

- Experience editing books and other materials for a wide variety of clients, including Reiling Press, Wilson Smith, and numerous corporate clients.
- Experience writing consumer materials, including chapters for fiction books published by Hollis Press, and a complete nonfiction book entitled *Easy Do It Resumes* (O'Leary Press).

Should you need additional information or writing samples, please feel free to contact me at the above-listed number. I look forward to joining the editorial team at Any Corporation, and will call your office next week to discuss this opportunity further.

Thank you.

Sincerely,

Chris Smith

Enc. Resume, Writing Samples

▶ Publications are impressive and add weight to cover letter.

▶ Job descriptions emphasize candidate's accomplishments.

RESPONSE TO A CLASSIFIED ADVERTISEMENT (PRINT)
(Events Planner)

---

178 Green Street
Tiverton, RI 02878
(401) 555-5555

August 21, 20--

Pat Cummings
Vice-President of Public Relations
Any Corporation
1140 Main Street
Chicago, IL 60605

Dear Mr. Cummings:

Please accept this letter as an application for the Events Planner position advertised in the *Providence Journal* on August 20. My confidential resume is enclosed for your review.

The position described is exactly the opportunity I am looking for. I am confident my six years' experience in public relations, coupled with my drive and enthusiasm, would enable me to make a significant contribution to your organization.

I believe the most important qualification of an Events Planner is the ability to plan well and soundly, and then to imbue a staff with the spirit of teamwork—in other words, to provide leadership and effective administration. I would describe myself as a well-organized, results-oriented, and effective problem-solver.

I welcome the opportunity to meet with you to further discuss my qualifications and your needs. Thank you for your time and consideration.

Sincerely,

Chris Smith

Enc. Resume

▶ Beyond matching qualifications with requirements, candidate highlights personal attributes applicable to advertised position.

▶ Closing thanks addressee in advance for attention.

RESPONSE TO A CLASSIFIED ADVERTISEMENT (PRINT)
(Features Reporter)

178 Green Street
Emmitsburg, MD 21727

July 20, 20--

Pat Cummings
Senior Reporter
Any Newspaper
1140 Main Street
Largo, MD 20772

Dear Ms. Cummings:

I am interested in the Features Reporter position advertised in the *Baltimore Sun*. As a recent graduate of Mount St. Mary's College with a Bachelor of Arts degree in Journalism, I am eager to begin a long-term association with a newspaper as a reporter.

As detailed in the enclosed resume, I possess broad experience in various fields of journalism. My internship with the *Emmitsburg News* provided me the opportunity to sharpen my writing and researching skills. My duties included field reporting, writing copy, and editing a variety of articles, all demanding strict deadlines. My skills in photography made me a greater asset to the *Emmitsburg News*, as I was able to photograph the subjects of stories as well. In addition, while completing my degree at Mount St. Mary's, I worked as Editor of the yearbook and Layout Editor of the student newspaper, where I became proficient in desktop publishing.

I currently have a flexible schedule and am available for an interview at almost any time, given advance notice. I can be reached at (301) 555-5555. I am very interested in reporting for *Any Newspaper* and hope to hear from you soon.

Sincerely,

Chris Smith

Enc. Resume

▶ Internship experience demonstrates candidate's familiarity with field of work.

▶ For recent graduates, extracurricular activities demonstrate potential for productivity.

RESPONSE TO A CLASSIFIED ADVERTISEMENT (PRINT)
(Field Finance Manager)

178 Green Street
Richmond, VA 23220
January 17, 20--

Pat Cummings
Chief Financial Officer
Any Corporation
1140 Main Street
Washington, DC 20002

Dear Mr. Cummings:

I am applying for the Central Area Field Finance Manager position advertised in the *Richmond Times-Dispatch*.

Enclosed you will find my resume, which details the skills necessary to enhance the central area's performance:

- Experience advising *Fortune* 100 and small company senior management on strategy, planning, and budgeting.
- Strong academic preparation and significant work experience in accounting and finance.
- Excellent working knowledge of microcomputer technology.

Finally, one item not on my resume is my desire to enter a high-growth industry with a leader. The Field Finance Manager position offers such an opportunity.

Please feel free to contact me at (804) 555-5555 if you have any questions and would like to meet to further discuss my interest in, and qualifications for, this challenging position.

Sincerely yours,

Chris Smith

Enc. Resume

▶ Bullets provide a clear and crisp presentation.

▶ Letter outlines candidate's skills relevant to advertised position.

RESPONSE TO A CLASSIFIED ADVERTISEMENT (PRINT)
(Film Archivist)

178 Green Street
New Castle, DE 19270
(302) 555-5555

July 22, 20--

Pat Cummings
Curator
Any Library
1140 Main Street
Macon, GA 31201

RE: Film Archivist Position; *Moving Picture Pictorial*, July 19, 20--

Dear Ms. Cummings:

I am interested in your advertised position for a Film Archivist. My passion for film and my applicable skills make me confident that I am a qualified candidate.

Currently, I am a reporter for the *Vertov Film Journal*, a monthly entertainment magazine. In addition, I am capable of shooting, printing, and developing 35-mm, black-and-white film. I also have proficiency in digital photography. During my last year at Brandeis University, I researched, wrote, and edited a 100-page senior honors thesis on the filmmaker Sergei Eisenstein. I enjoyed that project immensely, and would enjoy researching film and film-related literature on a daily basis.

I am aware that your library's film archive is the largest in the South. I would welcome the opportunity to employ my talents at Any Library, and am willing to relocate if offered the position.

I have enclosed a resume and a few writing samples for you to look over at your convenience. Thank you for your time, and I hope to meet with you soon to discuss your Film Archivist position even further.

Sincerely,

Chris Smith

Enc. Resume, Writing samples

▶ Research projects illustrate candidate's initiative.   ▶ Willingness to relocate can be advantageous.

RESPONSE TO A CLASSIFIED ADVERTISEMENT (PRINT)
(Fund Raiser)

178 Green Street
Roswell, NM 88202

June 2, 20--

Pat Cummings
Director
Any Organization
1140 Main Street
Alamogordo, NM 88311

Dear Mr. Cummings:

I am writing in response to your advertisement for a fund raiser appearing in this month's *Not-for-Profit Now!* Your organization strikes me as particularly dynamic, and I know that my energy, enthusiasm, and skills can only complement the success of your fiscal campaigns.

After graduating from the University of New Mexico (UNM) last June, I have been working in the University's development office at the Office of Public Programs. UNM is in its second year of a $450 million capital campaign—$25 million of which was raised this fall in a single record-breaking donation. My role in this stimulating and exciting time at the University has been as the Campaign Registration Coordinator. This position has afforded me many valuable experiences, not the least of which has been working for the University's expert fund raisers. Observant to detail and acutely aware of my surroundings, I have had the opportunity to become appreciative of the techniques of my colleagues, responsive to the interests of a variety of personalities, and proactive in the fulfillment of our goals. My job demands efficiency, precision, and the ability to juggle several different projects simultaneously. I feel confident that I can apply my skills in your organization.

Capable and eager, I look forward to the challenge I believe a position with your organization would afford me. I have enclosed my resume for your consideration. I look forward to speaking with you soon about my qualifications, and can be reached easily at (505) 555-5555.

Sincerely,

Chris Smith

Enc. Resume

▶ Letter focuses on filling employer's needs, not the job candidate's.

▶ Discussion of experience clearly spells out candidate's area of expertise.

RESPONSE TO A CLASSIFIED ADVERTISEMENT (PRINT)
(Gemologist)

178 Green Street
Gainesville, FL 36608
(904) 555-5555

June 2, 20--

Pat Cummings
Vice-President
Any Institute
1140 Main Street
Tampa, FL 33611

Dear Ms. Cummings:

I was very excited to read about the opening for a Gemologist in the latest edition of your company newsletter. I would like to submit my credentials as an application for this opportunity.

I became interested in the import/export of precious gems several years ago while living in Nepal. Upon my return to the United States, I enrolled in what my research revealed to be the best gemology school, the Gemologist Institute of America, in Santa Monica, California. This year I graduated with honors, and hold the title of Graduate Gemologist.

The enclosed resume summarizes my background, most of which has an emphasis in public relations, sales, promotions, and dealing with people of all socioeconomic levels and cultures. I am presently searching for an opportunity with an institute such as yours, where I might apply my training, skills, and knowledge in the technical and business facets of gemology to our mutual benefit.

After you have reviewed my qualifications, I would appreciate interviewing with you for this position. I am very interested in the opportunity that it provides, and am confident that my training and experience fit your requirements. Please note that I plan to follow up with a call in a few days. In the meantime, should you need additional information, please don't hesitate to call me at the phone number cited above.

Sincerely,

Chris Smith

Enc. Resume

▶ Educational credentials strengthen cover letter.

▶ Closing refers addressee to telephone number in return address.

RESPONSE TO A CLASSIFIED ADVERTISEMENT (PRINT)
(Home Economist/Coordinator)

178 Green Street
Reno, NV 89520
(702) 555-5555

July 25, 20--

Pat Cummings
Director, Home Economics Program
Any University
1140 Main Street
Seattle, WA 98109

Dear Mr. Cummings:

My interest in the position of Home Economist/Coordinator described in your advertisement in the *Seattle Times* has prompted me to forward the attached resume for your evaluation.

In addition to earning a Bachelor of Science degree in Home Economics and Nutrition Education, I have completed coursework in psychology and learning development, and have undergone supplemental training at the professional level with each employer since graduation, including a teaching hospital.

I possess excellent verbal, written, and interpersonal skills. In addition, I hold extensive experience with the development and training-related duties of seminars in my areas of expertise, and relate easily to all age groups and socioeconomic levels. As an alumnus of the University of Washington at Seattle and a native of the State of Washington, I am well acquainted with the overall family/business environment in which I would be working.

I will be in Washington on Friday, August 5. I would like to arrange to meet with you at this time to convince you of my ability to successfully fill your position. I will call your office on July 27 to schedule an interview.

Thank you very much for your consideration.

Sincerely,

Chris Smith

Enc. Resume

▶ Continuing education indicates candidate's ongoing commitment to his/her field.

▶ Closing provides specific time frame to allow for meeting.

RESPONSE TO A CLASSIFIED ADVERTISEMENT (PRINT)
(Hospital Administrator)

178 Green Street
Lapeer, MI 48446
(313) 555-5555

June 17, 20--

Pat Cummings
District Vice-President
Any Health Resource Corporation
1140 Main Street
Flint, MI 48502

RE: Hospital Administrator

Dear Ms. Cummings:

After reading your advertisement in the *Flint Journal,* I believe that Keller Memorial Hospital is in need of an Administrator who can provide direction, as well as strong marketing and financial expertise, to develop and implement its purpose. I am that person.

During my sixteen years as President/Treasurer of a multibranch, multi-state prosthetics, orthodontics, DME business, I directed all phases of operations from the construction of headquarter and manufacturing facilities to the sales and marketing of custom and durable medical products. Also, I have a strong background in the preparation of business plans and strategies, financial and budget analysis, financial package design, and forecasts and projections. All of my motivation has been directed toward new business development and expanding services in the health care field.

In addition, I am a strong organizer, enthusiastic speaker, capable leader, and team player who can interface effectively with medical professionals as well as support staff. In the role of Hospital Administrator, I am confident that I can provide you with the energy and experience necessary to achieve results, and would welcome the opportunity to reiterate this in a personal interview. I will contact your office next Monday to schedule a mutually convenient time to meet.

Thank you for your time.

Sincerely,

Chris Smith

Enc. Resume

▶ Introduction demonstrates candidate's suitability for advertised position.

▶ Setting desired position apart from body of letter may be advantageous.

RESPONSE TO A CLASSIFIED ADVERTISEMENT (PRINT)
(Hotel Manager)

178 Green Street
Traverse City, MI 49684

January 23, 20--

Pat Cummings
District Manager
Any Corporation
1140 Main Street
Marquette, MI 49855

Dear Mr. Cummings:

Enclosed is my resume, which I submit as a candidate for the Hotel Manager position advertised in the *Detroit Free Press* on January 23.

My experience in the hospitality industry is broadly based, and my accomplishments reflect a proven ability to perform in diverse and varied functions. My positions have ranged from Front Desk Clerk and Director of Sales and Marketing, to my current position as Assistant General Manager of a prestigious 3,000-room hotel. In this capacity I am responsible for all operational aspects of the rooms division, including front office, housekeeping, maintenance, reservations, quality control, and communications. In addition, as a member of the executive committee, I am involved in all budgetary and policy decision-making.

I have been involved in hospitality management for ten years, and while my present position is satisfying, the position of Hotel Manager you offer seems to provide the ideal next step, and an opportunity for a long-term association with a new organization.

I would greatly appreciate the opportunity to discuss your requirements, and how I might fulfill them. Please telephone me at your convenience. During the day, I can be reached at (616) 555-5555.

Thank you for your consideration.

Sincerely,

Chris Smith

Enc. Resume

▶ Discussion of experience indicates a series of promotions.

▶ Candidate includes all relevant experience to advertised position.

RESPONSE TO A CLASSIFIED ADVERTISEMENT (PRINT)
(International Buyer)

178 Green Street
Knoke, IA 50553
(515) 555-5555

February 3, 20--

Pat Cummings
Senior Marketing Manager
Any Corporation
1140 Main Street
Chicago, IL 60605

Dear Ms. Cummings:

In response to your advertisement for an International Buyer in the February 1 edition of the *Chicago Sun-Times*, I would like to submit my application for your consideration.

As you can see, my qualifications match those you seek:

YOU REQUIRE:

- A college degree
- Fluency in Italian and French
- Office experience
- Typing skills
- Willingness to travel

I OFFER:

- A Bachelor's degree in English from Long Island University
- Fluency in Italian, German, and French
- Experience as a receptionist at a busy accounting firm
- Accurate typing at 60 wpm
- A willingness to travel

I feel that I am well qualified for this position and can make a lasting contribution to Any Corporation. My salary requirement is negotiable.

I would welcome the opportunity for a personal interview with you at your convenience.

Sincerely,

Chris Smith

Enc. Resume

▶ Format is organized and visually appealing.   ▶ Discussion details how candidate's qualifications will benefit potential employer.

RESPONSE TO A CLASSIFIED ADVERTISEMENT (PRINT)
(Legal Assistant)

178 Green Street
Shoshoni, WY 82649
(307) 555-5555

September 18, 20--

Pat Cummings
Partner
Any Corporation
1140 Main Street
Chicago, IL 60605

Dear Mr. Cummings:

    I am writing in response to the Legal Assistant position advertised in the September 17 edition of the *New York Times*. Having recently graduated from New England School of Law, it is my intention to relocate to Chicago. I have enclosed my resume for your consideration.

    My work experience and scholastic endeavors have thoroughly prepared me for employment in a firm that specializes in various segments of law. Over the past summer and fall, I have been interning with a small general practice firm where I am entrusted with a great deal of responsibility. I write appellate briefs and memoranda in corporate, contract, and criminal law, and I draft complaints and answers. I also actively participate in attorney-client conferences by questioning clients and by describing how the law affects the clients' suits.

    I would appreciate the opportunity to meet with you and discuss how my qualifications could be guided to meet your needs.

    Thank you for your time and consideration. I look forward to meeting with you at your convenience.

With best regards,

Chris Smith, Esq.

Enc. Resume

▶ Internship experience demonstrates candidate's familiarity with field of work.

▶ Response letter immediately states candidate's purpose for writing.

RESPONSE TO A CLASSIFIED ADVERTISEMENT (PRINT)
(Librarian)

178 Green Street
Stanford, CA 94305
(415) 555-5555

January 24, 20--

Pat Cummings
Head Librarian
Any Library
1140 Main Street
Havre, MT 59501

Dear Ms. Cummings:

I was very excited to discover the availability of the Librarian position with Any Library. The job description as printed in the *Billings Gazette* suggests an "on-your-feet-and-running"-styled position, which would be a welcome extension of my present work.

My experience at the Stanford Law School for the past two years has focused mostly on editorial, research, and administrative work with book manuscripts, journals, and dissertations. I am confident this experience qualifies me for the position.

With that in mind, I enclose my resume and appreciate your consideration of me as a serious candidate. I am moving to Montana permanently next month, but would be happy to meet with you earlier for a personal interview.

Sincerely,

Chris Smith

Enc. Resume

▶ Candidate clearly expresses eagerness to work for specific employer.

▶ Direct quote suggests candidate is a meticulous, detail-oriented professional.

RESPONSE TO A CLASSIFIED ADVERTISEMENT (PRINT)
(Loan Officer)

178 Green Street
Owensboro, KY 42302

March 2, 20--
Pat Cummings
Branch Manager
Any Bank
1140 Main Street
Lexington, KY 40506

RE: Loan Officer Position

Dear Mr. Cummings:

In response to last Friday's advertisement in the *Lexington Herald-Leader*, I have enclosed my resume for your review. As you can see, my qualifications are an ideal match for your requirements.

You require:

- More than five years' experience.
- Skill in personnel and customer service relations.
- Extensive lending knowledge.
- A willingness to travel.

I offer:

- Nine years of rapidly progressive and responsible experience with a service-oriented commercial bank.
- Five years of full responsibility for the management of branch banking operations, training, directing, and coordinating activities of personnel, and establishing and implementing relationship banking programs for quality customer service and satisfaction.
- Skill in the implementation of institution policies, procedures, and practices concerning lending and new business development, and the granting or extending of lines of credit as well as commercial, real estate, and consumer loans.
- A willingness to travel.

I would welcome the opportunity for a personal interview to discuss the details of the position available and my capability to achieve mutual goals. I am well qualified to handle the position, and confident I will make a valuable contribution to your staff. Please contact me at the above address or by phone at (502) 555-5555.

I look forward to hearing from you.

Sincerely,
Chris Smith
Enc. Resume

▶ Unique format demonstrates candidate's ability to meet advertised job requirements.

▶ Closing encourages reader to respond to letter.

RESPONSE TO A CLASSIFIED ADVERTISEMENT (PRINT)
(Masonry Supply Manager)

178 Green Street
Waterbury, CT 06708

December 5, 20--

Pat Cummings
General Manager
Any Corporation
1140 Main Street
Hartford, CT 06115

Dear Ms. Cummings:

My interest in the position of Masonry Supply Manager (*Hartford Courant*, November 30) has prompted me to forward my resume for your review and consideration.

During the past ten years, my experience has been concentrated in the masonry and plastering products supply industry with a building materials firm. During my six years as General Manager, I took an old line business, which had undergone several years of poor management, and reversed the trend. I upgraded the firm's image and customer and vendor relations, which subsequently increased the dollar volume and bottom-line profits by 300 percent.

I am presently looking for a position where my experience will make a positive contribution to the start-up or continuing profitable operation of a business in which I am so well experienced.

I will contact you in a few days to arrange a meeting for further discussion. In the interim, should you require additional information, I may be reached at (203) 555-5555 between 9:00 A.M. and 5:00 P.M.

Sincerely,

Chris Smith

Enc. Resume

▶ Letter cites advertisement's specific publication and date.

▶ Use of concrete examples highlights candidate's achievements.

RESPONSE TO A CLASSIFIED ADVERTISEMENT (PRINT)
(Meeting Planner)

178 Green Street
Rohnert Park, CA 94928
(707) 555-5555

May 11, 20--

Pat Cummings
Vice-President, Marketing
Any Corporation
1140 Main Street
San Francisco, CA 94132

RE: Meeting Planner Position

Dear Mr. Cummings:

After reading your advertisement in the *San Francisco Chronicle*, I believe my qualifications match your requirements for a Meeting Planner.

During the past seven years, I have held positions requiring communications, sales, marketing, and supervisory skills in people-oriented, retailing, media, and educational environments. I am currently seeking a career opportunity offering a new scope of responsibility and more permanent challenge requiring creative skills as well as follow-through capability as an individual or member of a production team.

I am a quick study and have good presentation and communications training. I pride myself on the fact that I can readily take direction, and provide organization, creative imput, and an enthusiastic approach to the various segments of a position.

I believe I am the right candidate for the position of Meeting Planner and would like the opportunity to discuss your requirements and my ability to handle the responsibilities of the position offered. I will call your office next Monday to schedule an interview at your convenience.

I appreciate your time and consideration.

Sincerely,

Chris Smith

Enc. Resume

▶ Letter outlines candidate's skills relevant to advertised position.

▶ Powerful adjectives, when used sparingly, ensure maximum impact.

RESPONSE TO A CLASSIFIED ADVERTISEMENT (PRINT)
(Multimedia Specialist)

178 Green Street
Sparkill, NY 10976
(914) 555-5555

April 18, 20--

Pat Cummings
Director, Human Resources
Any Corporation
1140 Main Street
Staten Island, NY 10301

Dear Ms. Cummings:

This is in reply to your advertisement for a Multimedia Specialist published in the April 16 edition of the *New York Daily News*. In addition to a strong interest in catching the multimedia wave, I was attracted to the inviting tone of your advertisement. I would love a chance to meet and talk with you about this opportunity.

Toward this end, I have composed the following comparison demonstrating how my background and experience directly match the requirements listed for the position.

Your requirements:
- Lots of experience working in and consulting to small businesses.
- Enjoy using computers (but don't necessarily have any programming experience).
- Responsible for working with business writers, editors, and programmers to help design software packages for small businesses.

My qualifications:
- Was considered the "guru" of the small business market during my six years at Lotus.
- Generated more than 50 percent of my consulting income in the past year from small business clients.
- Confess to a rather strong attachment to computers; I've made my livelihood as a result of their existence for the past thirteen years.
- Walked in their shoes. Conceived of and authored an OS/2 *Tips and Techniques* software training tool for IBM.

- Led Lotus' entry into the small business market segment through managing product development and the launch of the 1-2-3 Small Business Kit and the Lotus spreadsheet for DeskMate. By designing innovative marketing programs leveraging the strengths of Tandy and small business administration, I enhanced product visibility that eventually led to an increase in sales by 75 percent.

I look forward to hearing from you, and for the chance to "get in on the fun."

Sincerely,

Chris Smith

Enc. Resume

▶ Letter responds to specific requirements outlined in classified advertisement.

▶ Candidate conveys a large amount of information in quick and easy-to-read format.

RESPONSE TO A CLASSIFIED ADVERTISEMENT (PRINT)
(Newspaper Intern)

178 Green Street
Charlotsville, VA 22906

April 7, 20--

Pat Cummings
Managing Editor
Any Newspaper
1140 Main Street
Lexington, VA 24450

Dear Mr. Cummings:

I enclose my resume in response to your listing in the University of Virginia's (UVA) career services office for a internship position with your newspaper. I am currently a junior majoring in English at UVA, and am seeking valuable career experience for the months of June through mid-September. I am hoping to use this summer to explore possible opportunities within the field of newspaper publishing.

The position you outline is one I feel I could enhance with my writing, editing, and expressive skills gained as an English major, as well as my past work experience, which has involved a great deal of organization, discipline, and responsibility. My active leadership and service roles have also helped me develop strong interpersonal and communication skills which I feel would make me a worthy addition to your staff.

I would greatly appreciate the opportunity to discuss with you how I might best meet your needs. I will call your office next week to confirm receipt of my resume and inquire about the publicized opening. In the interim, if you have any questions, please do not hesitate to call me at (804) 555-5555.

Thank you for your consideration in this matter.

Sincerely yours,

Chris Smith

Enc. Resume

▶ Personal interests and activities are relevant to candidate's field of interest.

▶ Letter clarifies candidate's career goals.

RESPONSE TO A CLASSIFIED ADVERTISEMENT (PRINT)
(Occupational Health Manager)

178 Green Street
Des Plaines, IL 60016
(708) 555-5555

July 26, 20--

Pat Cummings
Vice-President, Managerial
Any Corporation
1140 Main Street
Indianapolis, IN 46206

RE: Occupational Health Manager Position

Dear Ms. Cummings:

My interest in the position of Occupational Health Manager recently advertised in the *Indianapolis Star* has prompted me to forward my resume for your consideration.

In addition to my experience as a certified occupational health nurse and hands-on clinical expertise, I have twenty-one years of experience in positions that involved autonomous responsibility for the development and implementation of occupational health programs. All of these positions required sound knowledge of OSHA and general occupational health issues in critical work areas.

I received several commendations for my dedication and professionalism, and continually receive recognition for my communication skills and leadership excellence. Based on my qualifications, I believe I am the right person to oversee the delivery of occupational health services for one or more of your clients.

The enclosed resume is a brief summary of my qualifications. I would be delighted to meet with you in a personal interview and will call your office during the week of August 5.

Sincerely,

Chris Smith, R.N.

Enc. Resume

▶ Response letter emphasizes candidate's supervisory skills.

▶ After name, candidate includes professional title.

RESPONSE TO A CLASSIFIED ADVERTISEMENT (PRINT)
(Office Receptionist)

178 Green Street
Gastonia, NC 28054
(704) 555-5555

January 16, 20--

Pat Cummings
Personnel Supervisor
Any Corporation
1140 Main Street
Mt. Olive, NC 28465

Dear Mr. Cummings:

I am interested in applying for the Office Receptionist position as advertised in the *Herald Sun*, dated January 16. Attached please find my resume.

My areas of expertise lie in administration, organization, documentation, communications, and cost control. I am a detail-oriented individual and enjoy customer/client interaction. Additionally, I believe that an organization's client relationships are a tangible asset in a world where individualized service and assistance is rapidly declining. My administrative skills include a 70 wpm typing speed and proficiency on multiple word processing programs and spreadsheet applications.

I look forward to hearing from you and learning more about Any Corporation.

Sincerely,

Chris Smith

Enc. Resume

▶ Experience reinforces candidate's suitability for advertised position.

▶ Including a telephone number is essential in a cover letter.

RESPONSE TO A CLASSIFIED ADVERTISEMENT (PRINT)
(Park Maintenance Supervisor)

178 Green Street
Zanesville, OH 43701
(614) 555-5555

August 28, 20--

Pat Cummings
Chairperson
Any Reservation
1140 Main Street
Youngstown, OH 44501

RE: Park Maintenance Supervisor

Dear Ms. Cummings:

Please accept the enclosed resume as my expressed interest in applying for the Park Maintenance Supervisor position you advertised in the August 26 edition of the *Vindicator*. For the past twelve years, I have held a senior-level position as Fire Chief of the Zanesville Fire Department.

Although my position is secure, it is strictly administrative and does not allow me to physically participate, as I have in the past, in actual fire fighting or other hands-on activities that provide the outdoor work environment I most enjoy. For some time, I have realized that I must make a change, and the position described in your advertisement is what I have been looking for.

I have worked on a family farm, attended a degree program in agriculture, and, by choice, always worked full-time or part-time with tree and excavation services. I am thoroughly familiar with the operation, maintenance, and repair of equipment, and with safety practices for its operation; I also have the necessary background to train and supervise work crews using this equipment. Because my prime interest is job satisfaction, the salary is secondary and negotiable.

I feel confident that I can provide Any Reservation with reliability, dedication, and quality of work performance that will maintain the forested properties in the condition in which parks should be kept and enjoyed.

Since the department is not aware of my interest in making a change, your confidence is appreciated. I look forward to your return response.

Yours sincerely,

Chris Smith
Enc. Resume

▶ Letter focuses on filling employer's needs, not the job candidate's.

▶ Closing informs addressee of need for confidentiality.

RESPONSE TO A CLASSIFIED ADVERTISEMENT (PRINT)
(Photographer/Writer)

178 Green Street
Poughkeepsie, NY 12601

July 22, 20--

Pat Cummings
Human Resources Director
Any Corporation
1140 Main Street
Bellingham, WA 98225

Dear Mr. Cummings:

I am responding to the ad placed in the July 18 edition of the *Seattle Times* for the position of Photographer/Writer.

I am an accomplished photographer with more than ten years of experience in the industry. My career has provided me with the opportunity to work in the areas of commercial and industrial photography, portraiture, and wedding photography. I hold a Bachelor of Arts degree in English from Clark College where relevant coursework included Feature Writing, Photojournalism, and News Reporting.

I have attended seminars and workshops with the Fred Jones Workshop and the Winona School of Professional Photography. My photos have appeared in the Winona course catalog, BBI Printing Company's catalog, and numerous Smithco publications (including annual reports and newsletters).

My published writings include *A Shutterbug's Notes* and *Picture Your Pet.*

I would welcome the opportunity to discuss with you how my qualifications may suit your company's needs. Please contact me at the above address or by phone at (601) 555-5555. Thank you.

Sincerely,

Chris Smith

Enc. Resume

► Candidate succinctly outlines his/her relevant qualifications.

► Applicable coursework, workshops, and seminars are highlighted.

RESPONSE TO A CLASSIFIED ADVERTISEMENT (PRINT)
(Political Staffer)

178 Green Street
Bristol, RI 02809
(401) 555-5555

January 25, 20--

Pat Cummings
Director
Any Organization
1140 Main Street
Providence, RI 02908

Dear Ms. Cummings:

I am responding to the Political Staffer position advertised in the January 24 edition of the *Providence Evening Bulletin*.

Currently, I am employed as an Administrative Assistant at the State House in Providence. My primary responsibilities include writing press releases, researching and drafting legislation, and consistent constituent contact. I have also worked with various committees and legislators regarding an array of legislative issues.

I hold a Bachelor of Arts degree from Boston University (BU) in Political Science with a concentration in Public Policy. In addition to my coursework at BU, I worked as an intern at the Lieutenant Governor's office during the spring of 2004 and actively worked for several political and social causes on campus and in the Boston area. I also organized and managed my own successful campaign for Secretary of Student Affairs.

I am eager to continue my political career in the position of Political Staffer for your organization. I have the commitment, energy, and drive necessary to contribute successfully to your cause. I will call your office on January 29 to schedule an interview time that is convenient for you.

Thank you for your consideration.

Sincerely,

Chris Smith

Enc. Resume

▶ Educational credentials relate specifically to advertised position.

▶ Activities highlight candidate's involvement in local community.

RESPONSE TO A CLASSIFIED ADVERTISEMENT (PRINT)
(Preschool Director)

178 Green Street
St. Paul, MN 55105

July 10, 20--

Pat Cummings
Principal
Any High School
1140 Main Street
Minneapolis, MN 55404

RE: Preschool Director Position

Dear Mr. Cummings:

As a Speech/Language Clinician with extensive experience in the management and administration of programs dealing with special needs in education, I feel I have the qualifications necessary to succeed in the position of Preschool Director as advertised in the *Star Tribune*.

During the past eleven years, my experience with a professional, private agency has been concentrated in the area of special needs programs for multiple school districts. Prior to that, my work as a Speech Language Clinician involved the development and implementation of programs directed toward special education for preschoolers through twelfth grade in a public school system.

Although my positions were diverse and my achievements provided professional satisfaction, I am interested in making a new association with a large, highly recognized institution such as Any High School. As Part-Time Preschool Director, I hope to utilize my broad-based experience in special education to make a meaningful contribution to your professional management staff.

The enclosed resume summarizes my background and experience. I would appreciate the opportunity to meet with you to further discuss my qualifications and how I can best contribute to your needs. Please contact me at the above address or by phone at (612) 555-5555.

I look forward to hearing from you.

Yours sincerely,

Chris Smith

Enc. Resume

▶ Response letter immediately introduces candidate's qualifications.

▶ Candidate explains how extensive experience will benefit potential employer.

RESPONSE TO A CLASSIFIED ADVERTISEMENT (PRINT)
(Product Developer)

178 Green Street
Bismarck, ND 58501
(701) 555-5555

February 15, 20--

Pat Cummings
Chief Executive Officer
Any Technology
1140 Main Street
Bismarck, ND 58501

Dear Ms. Cummings:

I read with much excitement in your company newsletter the announce-ment of openings within your new products development department.

Please note that I have more than ten years of experience in manufacturing R&D, management of new product development, and existing product redevel-opment/upgrade. I am especially experienced with complex composite materials, precision metal castings, and PC board industries. In addition, I have extensive experience both as teacher and lecturer at several well-known universities. This expertise is supported by a Ph.D. in Materials Science/Engineering.

I am eager to join the Any Technology team, as its reputation for innovation is unparalleled. I will call to schedule an interview so that we may discuss further my qualifications and your requirements. Thank you for your consideration.

Sincerely,

Chris Smith

Enc. Resume

▶ Advanced degrees add weight to cover letter.   ▶ Closing reiterates candidate's interest in specific corporation.

RESPONSE TO A CLASSIFIED ADVERTISEMENT (PRINT)
(Production Assistant)

178 Green Street
Birmingham, AL 35294
(205) 555-5555

October 2, 20--

Pat Cummings
Vice-President, Production
Any Corporation
1146 Main Street
Mobile, AL 36630

RE: Production Assistant Position

Dear Mr. Cummings:

Your recent advertisement in the *Mobile Register* interests me, as my experience matches your requirements.

I would appreciate the opportunity to discuss how I might contribute to your organization. I will call your office the week of October 10 to schedule an interview at your convenience. In the meantime, I may be reached at the above listed daytime phone number or in the evenings at (205) 555-5555.

Thank you for your consideration.

Sincerely,

Chris Smith

Enc. Resume

▶ Format is neat and professional.

▶ Including an evening telephone number is optional in a cover letter.

RESPONSE TO A CLASSIFIED ADVERTISEMENT (PRINT)
(Production Controller)

178 Green Street
Pittsburgh, PA 15217
(412) 555-5555

February 23, 20--

Pat Cummings
Hiring Manager
Any Corporation
1140 Main Street
Boston, MA 02215

RE: Production Controller

Dear Ms. Cummings:

After seven years of progressively responsible experience in production, electromechanical assembly, soldering, testing, total quality management, and shipping and receiving in a precision manufacturing operation, I feel I have all the qualifications you require for the above advertised position.

During the past several years, my responsibilities as Group Leader necessitated that I provide a harmonious work atmosphere. While accomplishing this objective, I developed training procedures that allowed for cross-training, multi-ethnic/multicultural production personnel to work at ten assembly stations. This assured that all stations could be covered despite employee absences. In addition, I implemented TQM, which resulted in a 40 percent increase in productivity, a 20 percent decrease in production costs, and a flurry of letters from satisfied clients.

I am aware of Any Corporation's innovative approach to TQM, which has been used as an example across the country. I desire the opportunity to apply manufacturing know-how to the smooth running of your production operations.

Thank you for reviewing my credentials. I will contact you to arrange an interview.

Yours sincerely,

Chris Smith

Enc. Resume

▶ Percentages accentuate candidate's achievements.

▶ Candidate immediately expresses suitability for desired position.

RESPONSE TO A CLASSIFIED ADVERTISEMENT (PRINT)
(Program Coordinator)

178 Green Street
Holland, MI 49423
(616) 555-5555

September 30, 20--

Pat Cummings
Language Coordinator
Any Institute
1140 Main Street
Detroit, MI 48226

Dear Mr. Cummings:

I discovered your advertisement for a Program Coordinator, English as a Second Language in the *Detroit Free Press*. I was very much intrigued and am enclosing my resume detailing my relevant experience.

I feel I am particularly qualified for this job as a result of my double language major in college as well as my current enrollment in two language proficiency certificate programs. I am a person who deeply believes in the importance of language enrichment. I would like the chance to work for an organization that reflects both my interests and my personal commitment.

Having grown up in a bilingual (Spanish/English-speaking) environment and having studied abroad in both Spain and Mexico, I am well aware of the demands and technical challenges involved in the translation business. Language is forever evolving and new expression and technology breed new linguistic mutations daily. To meet these challenges and maintain my skills, I work on my languages weekly, both by continuing to take language classes and tutoring children in the fundamentals.

Given the opportunity, I am confident that my skills and language experience could make an immediate and long-term contribution to Any Institute. I would be delighted to discuss my qualifications with you. I will call your office on October 7 to schedule a convenient interview time.

Sincerely,

Chris Smith

Enc. Resume

▶ Foreign language skills and international exposure strengthen applicant's candidacy.

▶ Position applied for is clearly and immediately defined.

RESPONSE TO A CLASSIFIED ADVERTISEMENT (PRINT)
(Project Manager)

178 Green Street
Charleston, SC 29411
(803) 555-5555

April 10, 20--

Pat Cummings
Director of Human Resources
Any Corporation
1140 Main Street
Charleston, SC 29411

Dear Ms. Cummings:

In response to your ad for Project Manager in the April 9 edition of the *Post and Courier*, I have enclosed my resume for your review and consideration.

With more than twenty years of construction experience, I am familiar with project management in the role of owner's representative as well as general contractor/manager. I have managed projects regionally and nationally.

I will contact you the week of April 17 so that we may schedule an interview. I look forward to discussing my credentials and the requirements of the position with you.

Sincerely,

Chris Smith

Enc. Resume

▶ Letter highlights candidate's management skills.

▶ Letter is brief and concise.

RESPONSE TO A CLASSIFIED ADVERTISEMENT (PRINT)
(Public Relations Associate)

---

178 Green Street
Keuka Park, NY 14478
(315) 555-5555

May 2, 20--

Pat Cummings
Vice-President
Any Firm
1140 Main Street
Riverdale, NJ 10471

Dear Mr. Cummings:

In response to your advertisement in the *New York Times* for the Public Relations Associate position, I would like to touch on particular aspects of my background that should be of interest to you.

Between 20-- and 20--, I supervised (as a civilian employee) the internal formation and public relations programs for the U.S. Army in Frankfurt, Germany. As Director of Information Services, I was responsible for writing and publishing internal publications, brochures, and other communications. I also edited a community newspaper and magazine during this time.

For two years prior to that association, I edited a variety of military publications, both newspapers and magazines, while serving as a member of the uniformed services in Germany. During this period, I wrote news, sports, and feature articles as well as press releases. I conducted media events, prepared slide presentations, gave briefings, and designed other internal and external promotional materials in support of the 7th Infantry Division and its 30,000 American soldiers and family members in four German communities.

In 20--, I returned to the United States and completed work for my Master of Arts degree in Communications at Rutgers University. Prior to my relocation, I managed an annual budget of $500,000 while supervising a staff of eight in the Connecticut gaming industry. I also wrote promotional articles for the casino in the local newspaper and am adept at PageMaker, Microsoft Word, and Ventura desktop publishing programs.

I look forward to discussing my background and experience in detail with you and would be glad to make myself available for an interview at your convenience.

Sincerely yours,

Chris Smith

Enc. Resume

▶ Including a military record can be advantageous if it relates to candidate's job objective.

▶ Specifically citing number of personnel supervised draws attention to candidate's leadership abilities.

RESPONSE TO A CLASSIFIED ADVERTISEMENT (PRINT)
(Publicist)

178 Green Street
East Point, GA 30344
(404) 555-5555

February 4, 20--

Pat Cummings
Publicity Director
Any Corporation
1140 Main Street
Rome, GA 30162

Dear Ms. Cummings:

I am responding to your advertisement in the *Atlanta Constitution* for a Publicist.

I am confident that I have the skills and experience necessary to successfully meet the requirements of this position. As an Advertising and Promotions Assistant for a major newspaper, I have acquired strong interpersonal and communication skills. In addition, I have extensive experience with a number of computer systems and applications.

As the newest member of your publicity department, I would prove to be a diligent, organized, and enthusiastic employee. Could we meet for further discussion? I would be available at your convenience.

I look forward to your response.

Sincerely,

Chris Smith

Enc. Resume

► Candidate expresses willingness to meet at addressee's convenience in closing.

► Candidate immediately specifies position being applied for.

RESPONSE TO A CLASSIFIED ADVERTISEMENT (PRINT)
(Publisher's Assistant)

178 Green Street
Topeka, KS 66621
(913) 555-5555

January 18, 20--

Pat Cummings
Vice-President of Editorial
Any Corporation
1140 Main Street
Topeka, KS 66621

Dear Mr. Cummings:

I am writing in response to your advertisement in the *Topeka Capital-Journal* for the Publisher's Assistant position. Please consider me an applicant for the position.

I believe you will find that my training and varied experience are well suited to this position. My background as an administrative assistant, magazine production assistant, and teacher demonstrate my capacity to handle the challenges of providing superior executive support.

As a current temporary assignment worker with Alltemps in Topeka, I have become highly computer literate in both Macintosh and PC environments and accompanying software programs. I am organized and accurate, master new information rapidly, communicate effectively, and work well with other people.

Thank you for reviewing my credentials. I will call in a week to schedule a convenient time to discuss my qualifications and your expectations.

Sincerely,

Chris Smith

Enc. Resume

▶ Temporary experience is relevant to full-time employment.

▶ Candidate's functional skills are applicable to advertised position.

RESPONSE TO A CLASSIFIED ADVERTISEMENT (PRINT)
(Purchasing Agent)

178 Green Street
Grove Village, IL 60007
(708) 555-5555
Fax (708) 444-4444

February 4, 20--

Employment Manager
Any Corporation
1140 Main Street
Chicago, IL 60628

RE: Purchasing Agent

Dear Ms. Cummings:

Please accept this letter and resume as an initial application for the position you advertised in the January 18 edition of the *Macon Telegraph*. I am a self-motivated individual who can work well with people, grasp and expand on new ideas, tackle and follow through on difficult projects, and achieve or exceed objectives.

Please note that I have six years of experience ranging from Purchasing Clerk to Senior Buyer for multisite operations with purchases in excess of $1.5 million. I have been a key contributor to the successful setup and startup of new branch locations, from bare wall facility to fully trained and operating activity. In addition, my experience has encompassed sales support and telemarketing.

I have a proven track record because I am strongly motivated, well organized, and have excellent communication skills. I am confident of my ability to make an immediate as well as long-term contribution to Any Corporation, and feel that a personal interview would give us the opportunity to expand upon your requirements and my ability to meet them.

I appreciate your consideration of my application and look forward to your reply.

Sincerely,

Chris Smith

Enc. Resume

▶ Candidate matches his/her qualifications with potential employer's needs.

▶ Including a fax number is optional in a cover letter.

RESPONSE TO A CLASSIFIED ADVERTISEMENT (PRINT)
(Real Estate Sales Associate)

178 Green Street
Milwaukee, WI 53201
(414) 555-5555

December 20, 20--

Pat Cummings
Vice-President
Any Properties
1140 Main Street
Milwaukee, WI 53201

RE: Real Estate Sales Associate

Dear Mr. Cummings:

I am writing to apply for the above-listed position advertised in *Real Estate Weekly*, December 20, 20--. I am interested in contributing my real estate expertise to Any Properties.

I offer nearly twenty years of intensive experience involving the most sophisticated aspects of commercial and residential real estate sales and leasing, as well as associated areas of real estate development, property management, and rehabilitation. In addition to a current broker's license, I am very well grounded in real estate and business law.

I am considered a highly organized team player, with excellent verbal and written communication skills, an eye for detail, and the necessary persistence to conceive, package, and bring the big deals home.

My resume is a quick summary of my background and professional experience, but I feel that during the course of a personal interview my potential to contribute to Any Properties could be more effectively demonstrated. I will call to establish a mutually convenient time for such a meeting.

Thank you for your consideration.

Sincerely,

Chris Smith

Enc. Resume

▶ Setting desired position apart from body of letter may be advantageous when responding to classified advertisement.

▶ Candidate includes licensure relevant to his/her field.

RESPONSE TO A CLASSIFIED ADVERTISEMENT (PRINT)
(Regional Manager)

178 Green Street
Dubuque, IA 52001

August 7, 20--

Pat Cummings
Management Supervisor
Any Corporation
1140 Main Street
Peosta, IA 52068

Dear Ms. Cummings:

Please accept this inquiry as my expressed interest in the Regional Manager position advertised in the August issue of *Automotive Monthly*.

During the past twenty-two years, I have developed a successful track record as a professional with internationally recognized expertise in the automotive industries. In the last twelve years, I have specialized in customer satisfaction program development and strategic implementation consulting.

My extensive management experience has encompassed the design and evaluation of corporate marketing strategies and involved the evaluation of policies, projects, and new products. This experience is supported by a B.A. in Economics, an M.A. in Economics, M.B.A. coursework, a D.Sc., and a D.E.S. in Applied Mathematics.

Although my present position provides interesting diversity and challenge, I feel that it is time to move on to other opportunities. The enclosed professional profile provides only a portion of my qualifications and activities which I will be glad to expand on during a personal meeting. I will call your office on Monday, August 14, to schedule a mutually convenient meeting time.

Thank you for your consideration.

Sincerely,

Chris Smith

Enc. Professional profile

▶ Educational credentials accentuate candidate's qualifications.

▶ Candidate quantifies extensive experience.

RESPONSE TO A CLASSIFIED ADVERTISEMENT (PRINT)
(Researcher)

178 Green Street
Washington, DC 20057
(202) 555-5555

October 31, 20--

Pat Cummings
Human Resources Director
Any Newspaper
1140 Main Street
Chicago, IL 60605

Dear Mr. Cummings:

I am writing in response to the Researcher position advertised in the *Washington Post* on October 30. Please allow me to outline my skills as they apply to your stated requirements:

Writing Experience: I have authored or coauthored five books on sports and communications. In addition, I have been a reporter for both magazines and newspapers for many years. I have written more than 3,500 articles for publication, on topics ranging from crime and sports to medicine and humor. I know how to conceive of and research topics, and I am comfortable writing on almost any subject and in a range of styles. I am confident I would have no trouble matching the established style of your book series.

Editing Experience: I have copyedited a number of books on business topics and worked as an editor for several newspapers. I am capable of both minor polishing and major rewriting and, more importantly, of being able to tell which level of editing is needed. In addition, I taught English Composition and Writing for the Print Media at the high school level for five years.

I have enclosed a resume as well as a brief sample of my writing for your review. I look forward to meeting with you to discuss further how I could contribute to your organization.

Sincerely,

Chris Smith

Enc. Resume, Writing Samples

▶ Categorizing qualifications adds strength to cover letter.

▶ Unique format demonstrates candidate's ability to meet advertised job requirements.

RESPONSE TO A CLASSIFIED ADVERTISEMENT (PRINT)
(Restaurant Manager Trainee)

178 Green Street
Grand Junction, CO 81502
(303) 555-5555

November 15, 20--

Pat Cummings
Manager
Any Restaurant
1140 Main Street
Denver Post, CO 80202

RE: Restaurant Manager Trainee

Dear Ms. Cummings:

Please accept the enclosed resume as an application for your position advertised in the November 14 edition of the *Denver Post*.

During the past seven years, I have held positions of responsibility in banquet/special events catering, function management, and restaurant food service operations.

Currently, I am seeking a new association with a firm that can benefit from my experience in the above areas. I have additional experience in front desk operation; possess good organizational, leadership, training, and supervisory skills; and can provide quality service and performance in a high-volume setting. As my resume indicates, the vast diversity of food service settings with which I have been associated has made me extensively experienced in the management of virtually any type of food, beverage, and kitchen staff.

I have continually heard and read many favorable reviews of Any Restaurant, and I have always enjoyed my own dining experiences there. I would love to join your management team after completing the requisite training program. I will call you next Monday to arrange a mutually convenient time to discuss this opportunity further.

Sincerely,

Chris Smith

Enc. Resume

▶ Unrelated work experience is omitted from response letter.

▶ Closing emphasizes candidate's enthusiasm for desired position.

RESPONSE TO A CLASSIFIED ADVERTISEMENT (PRINT)
(Sales Representative)

178 Green Street
Northridge, CA 91324
(818) 555-5555

April 17, 20--

Ms. Pat Cummings
Vice-President
Any Corporation
1140 Main Street
Pittsburgh, PA 15217

Dear Mr. Cummings:

Please accept the enclosed resume as an expressed interest in contributing relevant experience to the position of Sales Representative, as advertised in the *Pittsburgh Post-Gazette*, on Wednesday, April 11.

I have accumulated several years of experience in the development of sales and marketing strategies. I have been involved in a number of diverse employment situations, including a self-owned business, in which I successfully utilized various sales techniques, such as cold calling, telemarketing, and prospecting. In my first two years at FloSoft, I increased our client base by 25 percent. While at the Brian Agency, I was part of a sales team that generated a record-breaking $10 million in one year. In addition, I have held numerous positions where I supervised and developed personnel and assisted in the facilitation of daily operations.

I would welcome the opportunity to meet with you and discuss ways in which my capabilities could be directed to suit your needs. I await your call to arrange a mutually convenient time to meet.

I look forward to talking with you in the near future. Thank you for your time and consideration.

With best regards,

Chris Smith

Enc. Resume

▶ Dollar amounts quantify candidate's accomplishments.

▶ Introduction immediately refers to publication where advertisement appeared.

RESPONSE TO A CLASSIFIED ADVERTISEMENT (PRINT)
(Senior HVAC Technician)

178 Green Street
New Martinsville, WV 26155
(304) 555-5555

November 12, 20--

Pat Cummings
Human Resources Director
Any Corporation
1140 Main Street
Charlestown, WV 25301

Dear Ms. Cummings:

At the request of Donald Lee of your department, I am enclosing my resume in response to the advertisement in last Friday's *Charleston Gazette* for an experienced Senior HVAC Technician.

I possess nine years of experience in after-warranty maintenance, preventive maintenance programs, and complete overhaul of major systems within a multibuilding, mixed-use industrial complex. I have also completed extensive and continuous education and training on the latest and most cost-efficient energy systems and control.

Presently, I am seeking a new association with an institution such as Any Corporation, where I can apply my technical as well as supervisory skills to provide high-quality, cost-efficient energy control system maintenance at a time when energy prices are at an all-time high.

I would welcome the opportunity to discuss your requirements and my ability to handle the responsibilities of the position offered. Could we meet for a personal interview? I can make myself readily available whenever you are free.

Thank you for your time, Ms. Cummings.

Sincerely,

Chris Smith

Enc. Resume

▶ Basis for referral is immediately established.

▶ Candidate thanks addressee for time extended.

RESPONSE TO A CLASSIFIED ADVERTISEMENT (PRINT)
(Site Location Supervisor)

178 Green Street
Smithfield, RI 02917

April 16, 20--

Pat Cummings
General Manager, Properties
Any Corporation
1140 Main Street
Bridgeville, PA 15017

RE: Site Location Supervisor

Dear Mr. Cummings:

    I am confident that I am the person you seek in your advertisement in the April 15 edition of the *Providence Evening Bulletin*. My interest is in joining a firm which has a need for a representative capable of working effectively with clients in real estate development, property management, and finance. Because of a broad and diverse background, I am well qualified to provide consulting and/or management services to clients with problems involving planning, financing, budgeting, scheduling, and monitoring any phase of development-related activity.

    During the past fifteen years, my experience as a developer, general manager, owner, and manager of residential, commercial, and industrial projects has been extensive. In conjunction with these projects, I was actively involved in investment analysis, whole loans and structured transactions, and financial control to assure quality completion within schedules and budgets.

    I relate well to individuals and groups at all levels of responsibility and can fulfill management responsibilities while expediting project completions from inception to final inspection.

    Although my resume is enclosed, I would be able to provide you with additional pertinent information as to my capabilities and goals during a personal interview. I am free to relocate and/or travel and the compensation package is negotiable. I can be reached at the above address or by phone at (401) 555-5555.

Sincerely,

Chris Smith

Enc. Resume

▶ Experience reinforces candidate's professional objective.

▶ Candidate emphasizes how past business experience is relevant.

RESPONSE TO A CLASSIFIED ADVERTISEMENT (PRINT)
(Social Worker)

178 Green Street
Northridge, CA 91324
(818) 555-5555

July 19, 20--

Pat Cummings
Director
Any Agency
1140 Main Street
Northridge, CA 91324

Dear Ms. Cummings:

In response to your advertisement in the summer edition of the *Social Justice Journal*, I would like to offer my services to fill the vacancy in the Social Worker position. I am confident you will find my experience and abilities qualify me for the position.

I possess extensive diverse and applicable experience. As stated in my resume, I received a Bachelor's degree in Dance Therapy, an interdisciplinary major, which involved extensive research into child psychology as well as artistic ability. While in college, I worked with children in a volunteer program called P.A.L.S., in which we visited and recreated with children in housing projects. I also visited a day-care program to study the psychology behind children's drawings for my senior research project. In addition, in high school, I worked with mentally disturbed adults.

As you can see, my background corresponds to your requirements. I look forward to hearing from you to discuss this job further.

Sincerely,

Chris Smith

Enc. Resume

▶ Volunteer experience gives candidate a competitive edge.

▶ Research projects illustrate candidate's initiative.

RESPONSE TO A CLASSIFIED ADVERTISEMENT (PRINT)
(State Administrator)

178 Green Street
Riverside, CA 92521
(909) 555-5555

December 23, 20--

Pat Cummings
President, New England Offices
Any Organization
1140 Main Street
Sacramento, CA 95821

Dear Mr. Cummings:

In response to your advertisement in the December 20 edition of the *Sacramento Bee*, please find my resume enclosed for your review. I am very interested in securing the position of State Administrator available at Any Organization.

During the past twelve years, I have held diverse and progressively responsible positions in development for nonprofit service organizations, universities, and educational institutions. These responsibilities have ranged from Secretary to Director of Development.

Throughout this period, I have been heavily involved in development strategies, annual fund campaigns, marketing and mailing programs, and media and public relations. Although these positions have been challenging and broad in scope, I feel that my expertise may be utilized to a better advantage by your organization.

I hope that, after reviewing my qualifications, you will consider me as the right candidate for State Administrator. I am confident of my abilities, and would like to schedule an interview to reiterate my desire for the position. I will call you on December 27 to follow up on my inquiry.

I appreciate your time and look forward to speaking with you.

Sincerely,

Chris Smith

Enc. Resume

▶ Since company name and information is provided in advertisement, candidate promises to follow up inquiry.

▶ Candidate focuses on relevant functional skills.

RESPONSE TO A CLASSIFIED ADVERTISEMENT (PRINT)
(Store Manager)

178 Green Street
New Haven, CT 06520
(203) 555-5555

December 22, 20--

Pat Cummings
District Supervisor
Any Corporation
1140 Main Street
Jacksonville, FL 32231

Dear Ms. Cummings:

In response to your advertisement for a Store Manager in the December 15 edition of the Sarasota *Herald-Tribune*, I am forwarding my resume. As detailed below, my experience qualifies me for the position.

You require:
- Managerial experience
- Superior written and verbal skills
- Budget management abilities

I offer:
- Five years as senior manager in a chain bookstore with an annual volume in excess of $2 million. Ability to manage inventory, personnel, cash flow.
- Accreditation as a high school teacher. Recognition for "Where We're At," a lighthearted historical essay.
- At University Towers, decreased outstanding rents by $5,000. Reorganized Sturtevant's retail promotions, effecting a 50 percent budget reduction.

May we discuss how I may contribute to your organization? I am available at your convenience to discuss employment opportunities, and the possibility of relocation.

Thank you for reviewing my credentials. I look forward to our initial conversation.

Sincerely,

Chris Smith

Enc. Resume

▶ Candidate focuses on applying skills and experiences to advertised position.

▶ Format is organized and visually appealing.

RESPONSE TO A CLASSIFIED ADVERTISEMENT (PRINT)
(Systems Trainer)

178 Green Street
Natchitoches, LA 71497
(318) 555-5555

July 16, 20--

Pat Cummings
Director
Any Corporation
1140 Main Street
Lafayette, LA 70504

Dear Mr. Cummings:

In response to your advertisement in the July 13 edition of the *Times*, I would like to apply for the position of Systems Trainer.

I am a skilled professional with extensive experience in the management of in-house and client-training services on state-of-the-art systems using technical and business applications. Although my current position has been challenging and provides a real sense of achievement, I feel it is time for a change to a firm such as Any Corporation where I can use my skills to establish meaningful changes in system automation and train personnel to a high level of performance.

In addition to a Bachelor of Science degree in Education and postgraduate study in computer science and business, I offer nine years of project and senior management experience with concentration in training, documentation, and related companywide services for business and technical environments. I have hands-on experience with many software and hardware systems, and believe that I can initiate and implement cost-effective, efficient breakthroughs in systems and training for Any Corporation just as I have for my previous employer.

I am confident in my ability to handle the responsibilities of the position offered. Could we meet in a personal interview?

I look forward to your reply.

Sincerely,

Chris Smith

Enc. Resume

▶ Closing is straightforward and concise.

▶ Job descriptions indicate how candidate contributed to his/her previous employers.

RESPONSE TO A CLASSIFIED ADVERTISEMENT (PRINT)
(Technical Writer)

178 Green Street
Santa Fe, NM 87501

July 22, 20--

Pat Cummings
Publicity Director
Any Tech
1140 Main Street
Santa Fe, NE 87501

Dear Ms. Cummings:

I am applying for the Technical Writer position advertised in July's *Engineering World*. My relevant experience is diverse and establishes me as a first-class candidate for this opportunity.

My writing experience is extensive. I am currently employed as a Technical Writer at Computer Systems International. My past work experience includes newspaper and freelance writing. At Computer Systems, I document software for use by manufacturers on IBM mainframes. We release three documentation sets: user guides, references, and batch operations and sample reports.

Since graduating from the University of Maine with a Journalism/English degree, my editorial experience has been diverse and rewarding. I edited medical manuscripts for medical and scientific publications and Henderson Medical Center. Specific duties included editing text for content, style considerations, grammar, and spelling. I also verified resources, coordinated artwork, and acted as liaison between physicians and journal editors.

At the *Albuquerque Journal*, as a sports editor and general assignment/photographer, I wrote sports and news articles and features. I also shot and processed photographs and designed pages. At MediaCorps, as a staff writer, I prepared press packages on new products.

I am available for an interview scheduled at your convenience. I may be reached at (505) 555-5555 (days) and (505) 444-4444 (evenings). Thank you for your consideration.

Sincerely,

Chris Smith

Enc. Resume

▶ Introduction is brief and attention-grabbing.　　▶ Educational credentials relate specifically to advertised position.

RESPONSE TO A CLASSIFIED ADVERTISEMENT (PRINT)
(Telemarketer)

178 Green Street
Omaha, NE 68182
(402) 555-5555

January 22, 20--

Pat Cummings
Director of Marketing and Sales
Any Corporation
1140 Main Street
Lincoln, NE 68522

Dear Mr. Cummings:

I am responding to your advertisement in search of a telemarketing professional in the *Lincoln Journal* dated January 16.

The enclosed resume provides details of my solid career experience in marketing and sales. My accomplishments include:

- Managing and directing sales of a national publication to business decision-makers and chief executive officers of major financial, educational, and municipal organizations that resulted in sales of $175,000 over a four-month period.
- Creating and implementing marketing strategy for a family-owned retail establishment that produced a substantial increase in sales.
- Establishing a marketing and public relations plan for a consulting firm that increased client base and significantly enhanced public recognition of the firm.
- Writing, editing, directing, and producing public service television program that involved timely legal and medical issues.

I would be pleased to discuss this matter with you in a personal interview and look forward to hearing from you.

Sincerely,

Chris Smith

Enc. Resume

▶ Letter uses bullets to highlight candidate's achievements related to advertised position.

▶ Response letter immediately states candidate's purpose for writing.

RESPONSE TO A CLASSIFIED ADVERTISEMENT (PRINT)
(Television Camera Operator)

178 Green Street
Pineville, LA 71359
(318) 555-5555

January 18, 20--

Pat Cummings
Production Manager
Any Television Station
1140 Main Street
New Orleans, LA 70018

Dear Ms. Cummings:

I aspire to find a challenging position where I am able to apply my technical and production talents. When I read your job description for a Television Camera Operator in the Sunday *Times-Picayune*, I felt that my background and skills would be a wonderful match for your requirements.

During the past three years, I have worked as a Production Assistant and Technical Operator in a television studio involved in all aspects of video production. I also have written, directed, produced, and edited three short 8 mm films and a music video that was shot using ENG equipment. These projects allowed me to sharpen many skills, such as conceptualization, camera work, and editing. In addition, I have received a Bachelor of Science degree and gained additional experience in video and camera operation from Ellis Technical Training School.

Once given the opportunity to demonstrate my talents, I am sure that I will prove to be a worthwhile addition to your station. Also, I am confident of my ability to quickly move through a training program and soon begin taping. I look forward to the opportunity for an interview and to meet with you in person.

Sincerely,

Chris Smith

Enc. Resume

▶ Candidate's practical experience outweighs his/her education.

▶ Response letter immediately introduces candidate's qualifications.

RESPONSE TO A CLASSIFIED ADVERTISEMENT (PRINT)
(Translator)

178 Green Street
Lawrenceville, GA 30246
(404) 555-5555

June 2, 20--

Pat Cummings
Head Translator
Any Organization
1140 Main Street
Atlanta, GA 30318

Dear Mr. Cummings:

I am writing in response to your May 30 advertisement in the *Atlanta Constitution* for a Translator. I was immediately intrigued by this position and would like to be considered in your search.

I am convinced that my interest, combined with my experience, could be well utilized by your organization. While completing my Bachelor of Science degree at Emory University, I worked as a Translating Assistant in the translation center on campus. My duties included translating documents from both Spanish and Russian into English and vice versa, verbally communicating with international contacts, and entering and editing articles and poetry for publication. It should be noted that several of the articles were in foreign languages I do not speak, which, as I'm sure you know, required strong attention to detail as part of the translation.

While at Emory, I spent a semester studying abroad in St. Petersburg, Russia. As a personal tutor, I developed lessons for English instruction to foreign students. This unique opportunity, as well as my extensive travel throughout Latin America, allowed me to sharpen my verbal and written Russian and Spanish translation skills.

I believe my experience and knowledge could successfully be applied to the Translator position you are seeking to fill. I would like to speak with you further in a personal interview and will call your office to schedule a convenient time. Thank you for your time and I look forward to meeting with you.

Sincerely,

Chris Smith

Enc. Resume

▶ Foreign language skills strengthen candidate's qualifications.

▶ College activities are related to candidate's field of study and career objective.

RESPONSE TO A CLASSIFIED ADVERTISEMENT (PRINT)
(Travel Agent)

178 Green Street
New Britain, CT 06050
(203) 555-5555

January 29, 20--

Pat Cummings
Owner
Any Travel Agency
1140 Main Street
New London, CT 06320

Dear Ms. Cummings:

I am responding to your advertisement in the *Wichita Eagle* for the position of Travel Agent.

As my enclosed resume indicates, I possess eleven years of extensive experience in the travel and tourism fields. As sole owner of a tourism-related business for four years, I oversaw and advised thirty host homes and inns operating in the New England area. I was independently responsible for maintaining accurate business records, purchasing supplies, and writing and editing all public relations materials, contracts, and policy guidelines. I enjoy writing and promoting New England as a premier business and leisure destination, and would welcome the opportunity to broaden my local attention to include the rest of the nation.

In addition, my association with the Greater Hartford Convention and Visitor's Bureau and the Southern Connecticut Bureau, as well as the Connecticut Chamber of Commerce, has considerably heightened my awareness of visitor markets and related disposable income. I believe my knowledge of current visitor trends coupled with my affinity for customer travel make me a qualified candidate for a position as a Travel Agent.

Thank you in advance for your generous consideration. I may be reached at my home phone number indicated above should you desire to contact me. I would be happy to make myself available for a personal interview at your convenience.

Sincerely,

Chris Smith

Enc. Resume

▶ Job-related affiliations demonstrate candidate's active participation in his/her field.

▶ Candidate expresses knowledge in his/her field of interest.

RESPONSE TO A CLASSIFIED ADVERTISEMENT (PRINT)
(*Writing Instructor*)

178 Green Street
Richmond, VA 23219
(804) 555-5555

June 1, 20--

Pat Cummings
Dean
Any College
1140 Main Street
Winston-Salem, NC 27108

Dear Mr. Cummings:

Please consider this letter and the enclosed resume as an application for the position of Writing Instructor as advertised in the *Richmond Times-Dispatch* last Wednesday.

I have been a college-level teacher of writing for the past eleven years and offer strong writing, editing, and proofreading skills. I am also a writer; my published works include short stories, essays, and poems. Last February, a one-act play of mine was produced in New York City. I also have experience ghostwriting, editing for the *Chapel Hill Review*, and publicity writing for a Raleigh rock group.

I am confident that the above-listed experience distinguishes me as a qualified candidate for your opening. I would be delighted to discuss further how my abilities match your requirements.

I have enclosed a writing sample and can provide letters of recommendation if needed.

Thank you for your attention to this matter.

Sincerely,

Chris Smith

Enc. Resume, Writing sample

▶ Enclosure line refers to all attached materials.

▶ Qualifications are geared to candidate's field of interest.

RESPONSE TO A CLASSIFIED ADVERTISEMENT (PRINT)
(Yacht Salesperson)

178 Green Street
San Francisco, CA 94132
(415) 555-5555

June 6, 20--

Pat Cummings
Vice-President, Sales
Any Corporation
1140 Main Street
Modesto, CA 95354

Dear Ms. Cummings:

If you are looking for an energetic, dedicated representative for the position in yacht sales you advertised in the *Modesto Bee*, I believe we have good reason to meet.

In addition to a Bachelor of Arts degree in Business Administration and Marketing, I have several years of successful experience in advertising, promoting, and selling high-priced properties to clients in the upper-income bracket. My experience and extensive travel as a co-host at international and domestic conferences, attended by government and business leaders, required refined communication skills and the ability to effectively negotiate with high-level decision-makers.

I would like to utilize these skills within Any Corporation to penetrate markets and increase sales of big-ticket items such as yachts. I am willing to travel, and believe that I will, through my persistent efforts, meet, and even exceed, mutual sales objectives.

Enclosed please find my resume. I will follow up this inquiry with a phone call in several days. I am very interested in learning more about the position and how my qualifications might suit you.

Sincerely,

Chris Smith

Enc. Resume

▶ Willingness to travel can be advantageous.　　▶ Educational credentials accentuate candidate's qualifications.

RESPONSE TO A CLASSIFIED ADVERTISEMENT (PRINT)
(Youth Center Director)

178 Green Street
Tuscaloosa, AL 35401
(205) 555-5555

August 20, 20--

Pat Cummings
Regional Director
Any Youth Center
1140 Main Street
Palo Alto, CA 94203

Dear Mr. Cummings:

Please accept the enclosed resume for the Executive Director position at Any Youth Center as advertised in the *Los Angeles Times*. I am excited to learn about this position and the opportunity to work with a progressive youth services organization.

As my resume indicates, during the past two years I have been researching and developing a new youth center in the Tuscaloosa County area. To date, I have developed programs serving more than 1,500 individuals and families, with a budget size almost doubling in one year. As I have learned, starting a youth center from scratch is a process that involves a great deal of planning on all levels. Much of my experience includes grant and proposal writing, public relations, and board and committee development. Community and corporate presentations are also part of my monthly schedule.

My present responsibilities and past experience have thoroughly prepared me for a branch executive position. As Director of Any Youth Center, I would make an immediate contribution to your staff through my ability to effectively manage personnel and create positive customer relations. I am eager to accept new challenges, and look forward to meeting with you regarding this position.

I appreciate your time and consideration.

Sincerely,

Chris Smith

Enc. Resume

▶ Letter immediately refers addressee to attached resume.

▶ Candidate clearly indicates type of position desired.

CHAPTER 11

RESPONSE TO A CLASSIFIED ADVERTISEMENT (WEB POSTING)

If, as a job hunter, your favorite day of the week is Sunday because that's when the biggest classified section arrives on your doorstep, we've got some good news. You no longer have to wait for the weekend to scan the best classifieds for a job. As long as you have a computer and access to the Internet, you can "shop" the help wanted ads around the clock any day of the week. Thanks to the proliferation of career Web sites like Monster.com, TrueCareers.com, and CareerBuilder.com, to name a few, you now have 24/7 access to thousands of job opportunities.

You can search the postings on those career Web sites in any number of different ways. Pick a broad category, like accounting, engineering, health care, or sales. Or search by location (city, state, foreign country) or by type of job (entry-level, supervisory, executive). Not interested in a salary below $40,000? You can sort the jobs by income bracket. There are always thousands to choose from and new jobs are added almost everyday, so if you didn't come across one that appealed to you yesterday, wait until tomorrow. There'll be a bunch more to check out. And once you've told the Web site's database exactly what you're looking for, you don't even have to log on to search. Whenever a position that matches your criteria becomes available, you'll be notified automatically by e-mail. After you've read the particulars and decide the position sounds right, click a button and voila! An e-mail screen pops up with the employer's name and the posting ID number already inserted. All you have to do is write the cover letter and attach your resume.

What could be simpler? Or more difficult. The bad news about online job postings is that you're not the only one who's looking at them. In case you thought the competition from a few hundred of your neighbors who read the same newspaper in hopes of finding a job was bad, now you're up against several million job seekers from around the globe who want the same position you do! Your chances of snagging it aren't that great.

This not to say you can never get a job through an online posting. Somebody must or else those career Web sites wouldn't be so popular. Let's just say it's not a good idea to put all your job-searcher apples into this one basket. By all means, peruse the Web postings on a regular basis. Just don't make them your only source of information about positions available. When you see one you like, go ahead and apply, and make sure your resume includes those all-important key words (see Chapter 9)! Who knows? You might get lucky. The worst that can happen is you get some good practice writing electronic cover letters.

RESPONSE TO A CLASSIFIED ADVERTISEMENT (WEB POSTING)
(Administrative Assistant)

To: *patcummings@anyfitnessclub.com*
From: *chrissmith@jobsearch.com*
Subj: Job #ABC004687

Dear Mr. Cummings:

I am pleased to submit my application for the position of Administrative Assistant with Any Fitness Club. I believe my positive attitude and exceptional people skills, combined with my willingness to work both independently and as part of a team, make me an ideal candidate for this job. As my attached resume indicates, I have more than six years of experience providing administrative and support services to the professional staff of a golf and tennis club in suburban San Diego, where my responsibilities included word processing and data entry, purchasing, inventory control, office equipment maintenance, and assistance with special events and promotions as needed. In addition, I hold an Associate degree in recreation management and, as a volunteer for the local chapter of the American Cancer Society, have served on the steering committee for the 20-- and 20-- "Run for the Cure" mini-marathon run/walk events, which drew more than 10,000 participants each.

I would appreciate the opportunity to meet with you to further discuss my qualifications and how I might utilize them to the benefit of your facility and club members. I look forward to hearing from you.

Yours sincerely,

Chris Smith

178 Green Street
La Jolla, CA 92037
(619) 555-5555
chrissmith@jobsearch.com

▶ Letter highlights skills and personal attributes that would be important for this job.

▶ Including volunteer activities is appropriate if they are applicable to the position.

RESPONSE TO A CLASSIFIED ADVERTISEMENT (WEB POSTING)
(Advertising Account Executive)

To: *patcummings@anyfirm.com*
From: *chrissmith@jobsearch.com*
Subj: Job #45678

Dear Ms. Cummings:

This is in response to your posting for an Advertising Account Executive (Job #45678), which recently appeared at Monster.com. I am a seasoned advertising professional with more than eight years of experience in creative development, account supervision, and new account development and sales. Most recently, as the primary liaison between three key accounts and the creative team at a midsize advertising agency in Madison, Wisconsin, I have repeatedly demonstrated my ability to manage multiple priorities in a deadline-sensitive environment.

The details of my educational background and professional experience are spelled out in my resume which, per your request, I have pasted below. I would welcome the opportunity to meet with you personally to discuss my qualifications and how I might put them to work for your clients. I look forward to hearing from you soon.

Sincerely,

Chris Smith

178 Green Street
Madison, WI 53703
(608) 555-555
chrissmith@jobsearch.com

(Note: ASCII version of resume would be pasted here)

▶ Candidate defers to employer's request that resumes be pasted, not attached.

▶ Letter is brief and concise.

RESPONSE TO A CLASSIFIED ADVERTISEMENT (WEB POSTING)
(Business Operations Manager)

To: *patcummings@anyfirm.com*
From: *chrissmith@jobsearch.com*
Subj: Job #999888ZYWX

Dear Mr. Cummings:

I believe I am ideally suited to the position of Business Operations Manager which you posted recently on Careerbuilder.com. I am a seasoned professional with more than eighteen years of business and corporate experience in the areas of cost accounting and financial analysis, procurement and contract administration, negotiations and contract procurement, budget oversight and forecasting, and business impact analysis. Supported by a Master in Business Administration degree in Finance and a Bachelor of Arts degree in Economics, my strengths include the ability to manage multiple projects of a diverse nature and a proven ability to analyze operational units in order to arrive at alternative methods of service delivery. I am equally adept at working with supervisors, colleagues, and subordinates, and have "hands-on" knowledge of computer programs for rigorous analysis, financial reporting, and high-quality presentations.

My goal is to join a firm that requires immediate use of these skills to either increase a rate of established growth, or to effect a turnaround situation. The attached resume describes my qualifications in greater detail. I will call you within the week to determine when your calendar might permit time for a personal interview. Thank you for your consideration.

Sincerely,

Chris Smith

178 Green Street
St. Louis, MO 63110
(314) 555-4444
chrissmith@jobsearch.com

▶ Background summary cites candidate's acquired professional skills and impressive track record.

▶ Closing indicates a time frame for follow-up activity.

RESPONSE TO A CLASSIFIED ADVERTISEMENT (WEB POSTING)
(Concierge)

To: *patcummings@anyhotel.com*
From: *chrissmith@jobsearch.com*
Subj: Job #XYZ007800

Dear Ms. Cummings:

    I was delighted to read your advertisement on truecareers.com for the position of Concierge for two reasons: 1) I share your philosophy concerning the role of a concierge in maximizing the overall guest experience, and 2) I believe I am the ideal candidate to fulfill this role at your hotel. My dedication to providing exemplary customer service is evidenced by more than six years of progressively responsible positions in upscale retail establishments and luxury hotel properties. My professional demeanor, organizational abilities, and exceptional attention to detail and follow-through, have garnered accolades from clients and employers alike. I know my way around the Internet and I am especially adept at securing whatever arrangements are necessary to ensure that every guest feels welcomed and well cared for during their stay, and that each one leaves, looking forward to his or her next return.

    I would greatly appreciate the opportunity to learn more about this position and to discuss in greater detail how we might work together for the benefit of your guests. I hope we can get together soon, as I am anxious to share my ideas. In the interim, I attach my resume for your additional information about my qualifications. Thank you for your consideration.

Sincerely,

Chris Smith

178 Green Street
Charlottesville, VA 22906
(804) 444-5555
chrissmith@jobsearch.com

▶ Letter opens with an unusual, attention-getting statement.

▶ Personal attributes are relevant to the position desired.

RESPONSE TO A CLASSIFIED ADVERTISEMENT (WEB POSTING)
(Pharmacist)

To: *patcummings@anydrugstore.com*
From: *chrissmith@jobsearch.com*
Subj: Job #345678JKLM

Dear Mr. Cummings:

Please accept the attached resume as my application for the Pharmacist position you recently posted to monster.com. I am a graduate of the College of Pharmacy, University of Illinois-Chicago, with more than eight years of professional experience, four of which have taken place in a retail setting. In addition, I hold PCAA certification in compounding and have attended continuing education seminars with regard to management of such chronic conditions as arthritis, diabetes, and pediatric asthma, At present I am one of five Registered Pharmacists who work rotating shifts at a pharmacy located inside a large discount retail establishment; our hours are 8 A.M. to 10 P.M. seven days a week. While I am well-compensated for my work and enjoy the challenge of a busy environment, I regret that, due to the high volume of prescriptions to be filled on a daily basis, I am unable to engage in the level of one-on-one patient counseling I enjoy and for which I am trained. I would welcome the opportunity to interact more directly with patients/customers and to oversee the "Medication and Disease Management" clinical programs you describe.

Can we sit down together soon to discuss my qualifications as they relate to your needs in greater detail? I will call you next week to set a mutually convenient time for our meeting. Thank you for your consideration.

Sincerely,

Chris Smith, R.P.

178 Green Street
Hoffman Estates, IL 60195
(847) 555-5555
chrissmith@jobsearch.com

▶ Candidate stresses interest in particular aspects of position described.

▶ Continuing education demonstrates candidate's commitment to the field.

CHAPTER 12

RESPONSE TO A "BLIND" ADVERTISEMENT

"Blind" advertisements do not list employer information, and generally direct inquiries to a post office box rather than to a company address. Since you're not provided with the company's name in a blind ad, your cover letter should sharply define your knowledge of the industry, position (if mentioned), and how your qualifications specifically match up to the stated job requirements. In other words, tailor your letter to whatever information is given. For example, consider a blind ad that reads:

> Large-size law firm in need of Paralegal with experience in legal research, writing briefs, and office administration.

Your response should highlight: what you know about the operations of large-size law firms; why you became and continue to be a Paralegal; how much experience you have in legal research and writing; and the specific office skills you can bring to this job. Avoid long-winded passages that do not follow these guidelines. Keep your response brief and to the point. By focusing on how your background and skills match the specific requirements of the job, you will have caught the attention of your readers without even knowing who they are. As a result, they're more likely to invite you for an interview, and suddenly you're one step closer to getting the job.

One caveat about replying to "blind" ads: If you are currently employed and looking for a new position because you sense that your boss is unhappy with your work performance, beware of responding to ads for jobs that sound similar to the one you already have. You could actually be applying for your own job!

RESPONSE TO A "BLIND" ADVERTISEMENT
(Administrator: Parks and Recreation Department)

178 Green Street
Jaffrey, NH 03452
(603) 555-5555

April 16, 20--

Personnel Manager
P.O. Box 7777
Hanover, NH 03755

Dear Personnel Manager:

The April 13 edition of the *Union Leader* ran an advertisement for a Parks and Recreation Department Administrator. I am very interested in making a significant contribution to convention planning, special event planning, and/or recreation products and services.

As my resume indicates, I offer twelve years of solid experience ranging from Waterfront Director to my most recent position as Program Administrator for all recreational aspects of a municipal parks and recreation department. Currently, I am seeking a new association with an organization that can benefit from my management and administrative expertise. I welcome the opportunity for a meeting.

Thank you for your consideration.

Sincerely,

Chris Smith

Enc. Resume

▶ Letter is brief and concise.

▶ Candidate matches his/her qualifications with potential employer's needs.

RESPONSE TO A "BLIND" ADVERTISEMENT
(Applications Programmer)

178 Green Street
Harrisburg, PA 17101

February 20, 20--

P.O. Box 7777
Harrisburg, PA 17101

RE: Applications Programmer

To whom it may concern:

If you have a need for a competent Applications Programmer with expertise in application development, maintenance, and enhancement of programs in purchasing, inventory control, contracts management, and related logistics applications, then we have good reason to meet.

During the past thirteen years, I have handled projects for Agtech and CompWare that require the ability to work effectively with large systems as well as PC-based software environments. My experience with the maintenance, development, and enhancement of programs is extensive and has required interaction with all departments and users to provide guidance and assistance in developing programs for procurement and logistics applications.

Although my present position has provided diversity and challenge, I am ready for a change and would like to join an organization in the public or private sector which has a need for my ability to cost-effectively handle the position of Applications Programmer.

The enclosed professional profile outlines my experience. I would like to meet for an interview, during which I can find out more about your company and will expand on the mutual benefits of my joining your ranks.

Since my present employer is not aware of my intent to make a change, I would appreciate your handling this inquiry in the strictest confidence. Should you require additional information prior to our meeting, please contact me at the above address or by phone at (717) 555-5555. I look forward to your return response.

Yours sincerely,

Chris Smith

Enc. Professional profile

▶ Letter outlines candidate's skills relevant to advertised position.

▶ Qualifications highlight candidate's problem-solving ability.

RESPONSE TO A "BLIND" ADVERTISEMENT
(Assistant Personnel Officer)

178 Green Street
Vienna, VA 22211

June 1, 20--

Human Resources Director
P.O. Box 7777
Arlington, VA 22203

Dear Human Resources Director:

I am writing to express my interest in the Assistant Personnel Officer position as advertised in the May 30 edition of the *Washington Post*.

As the enclosed resume indicates, I offer extensive experience, including my most recent position as Assistant Staff Manager at Virginia General Hospital. In this capacity I have recruited and trained administrative and clerical staffs, ancillary and works department staffs, and professional and technical staffs. I have also evaluated personnel, conducted disciplinary and grievance interviews, signed employees to contracts, and advised staff on conditions of employment, entitlements, and maternity leave.

Should my qualifications be of interest to you, please contact me at the above address or by phone at (703) 555-5555. I look forward to hearing from you.

Sincerely,

Chris Smith

Enc. Resume

▶ Candidate's most relevant work experience is prioritized.

▶ Qualifications call attention to candidate's relevant supervisory and administrative experience.

RESPONSE TO A "BLIND" ADVERTISEMENT
(Business Consultant)

178 Green Street
Dedham, MA 02026
(617) 555-5555
csmith@email.com

March 29, 20--

Human Resources Director
P.O. Box 7777
Cincinnati, OH 45221

Dear Human Resources Director:

I am responding to your advertisement for a Business Consultant in today's *Wall Street Journal*; it is likely that my consulting and executive experience with small businesses would be an excellent match for this position.

In 20--, while General Manager of Kimcorp, I developed an extension to the company's core production services business: a fast-turnaround, low-cost (and high-margin) circuit prototyping service. In addition, I conceived the functional specifications of a software package that would help designers execute board layout on their PCs. I have continued to work with computers throughout my career and to look for ways they can be better and more fully utilized in my business and consulting activities.

Enclosed is a copy of my resume. I look forward to speaking with you in more detail about this opportunity.

Sincerely,

Chris Smith

Enc. Resume

▶ Technical language is acceptable when it relates to candidate's field.

▶ Including an e-mail address may be advantageous, especially for certain fields of work.

RESPONSE TO A "BLIND" ADVERTISEMENT
(Case Manager)

178 Green Street
Golden, CO 80301
(303) 555-5555

May 27, 20--

Hiring Coordinator
P.O. Box 7777
Aurora, CO 80014

Dear Hiring Coordinator:

Please accept this letter and my accompanying resume as expressed interest in the Case Manager position advertised in the May 20-- issue of *Sociology Today*.

With a successful record of diverse social work experience, an eager desire to learn, and the determination to get the job done, I am confident that you will profit from my assistance. Most recently, I served as Case Manager for Dylan High School where I worked closely with at-risk students, coordinated outreach and referral services, supervised staff, and assisted community-based agencies and educational institutions in all activities involving students. In addition, my experience is supported by a Bachelor of Science degree in Social Work.

I would welcome the opportunity to discuss the position in detail. I can be reached between 5 P.M. and 10 P.M., Monday through Friday, at the above phone number. I look forward to your reply.

Sincerely,

Chris Smith

Enc. Resume

▶ Closing cites specific times candidate may be reached.

▶ Candidate includes all relevant experience to advertised position.

RESPONSE TO A "BLIND" ADVERTISEMENT
(Catering Manager)

178 Green Street
Mobile, AL 36608

October 13, 20--

P.O. Box 7777
Gainesville, GA 30503

RE: Catering Manager

Dear Sir/Madam:

    I write in response to your recent advertisement for a Catering Manager in the *Southern States Service Weekly*. Currently, I am seeking a new position with a firm than can benefit from my ten years of professional experience in the food service industry. Allow me to elaborate.

    I have held positions of responsibility in banquet/special event catering, functions management, and restaurant food service operations. I have additional experience in front desk operations, and I possess good organizational, leadership, training, and supervisory skills. I can also provide quality service and performance in a high-volume setting, and manage food, beverage, and kitchen staff with ease.

    The enclosed resume summarizes my experience. I would like the chance to expand on my qualifications in a personal interview. I am anxious to learn more about your firm and the available position, and to show you how I can meet your requirements.

    Please contact me at the above address or at (205) 555-5555 so that we may schedule a meeting time. I thank you for your time.

Sincerely,

Chris Smith

Enc. Resume

▶ Candidate quantifies extensive experience.

▶ Setting desired position apart from body of letter may be advantageous when responding to a "blind" advertisement.

RESPONSE TO A "BLIND" ADVERTISEMENT
(Chief Executive Officer)

178 Green Street
Madison, WI 53706
(608) 555-5555

July 24, 20--

P.O. Box 7777
River Falls, WI 54022

RE: Chief Executive Officer position

Dear Sir or Madam:

Selecting the right CEO for a $100 million U.S.–based operation can be a grueling process. I would like to take the stress out of that process by suggesting that you review my qualifications and the experience I can bring to your company.

As Corporate Vice-President of Sales, with an established record for the development of approximately $100 million in sales, my responsibilities have covered the gamut of successful strategies and techniques for growth and profitability. My involvement in sales, marketing, staff development, and production interface has been extensive, and my ability to organize and manage is well documented in the goals I have achieved with my present and past employers.

My resume is enclosed. If it is bottom-line results you are looking for, then we have good reason to meet for further discussion and mutual gain. Should you require additional information prior to our meeting, please do not hesitate to contact me.

I look forward to your return response.

Sincerely,

Chris Smith

Enc. Resume

▶ Introduction captures addressee's attention.　　▶ Experience reinforces candidate's suitability for advertised position.

RESPONSE TO A "BLIND" ADVERTISEMENT
(Editorial/Computer Production Manager)

178 Green Street
Beloit, WI 53511
(608) 555-5555

August 8, 20--

Hiring Director
P.O. Box 7777
South Milwaukee, WI 53172

Dear Hiring Director:

I am interested in the Editorial/Computer Production Manager position that you advertised in the *Milwaukee Journal*. Let me briefly match your needs, as I understand them, to my background.

Your requirements:
- Proofreading, researching, and writing skills.
- Knowledge of PC-oriented desktop publishing.
- Knowledge of computer online programs.

My relevant skills:
- Proficiency in proofreading and copyediting attained during seven years with a typesetting company. Completed freelance project in keying and copyediting for an IMIS Research reference book.
- Computerized a pre-PC typesetting system. Set up a WordPerfect-based newsletter system and completed initial work for a PageMaker-based hardware/software setup. Familiar with typesetting and page layout issues both from pre-PC and PC eras.
- Utilized PC communications for more than ten years. Independently set up an e-mail system using CompuServe. Expanded knowledge of online systems as a library and information sciences student.

I hope you agree that my qualifications make me an ideal candidate for this position. May we schedule a personal interview?

I look forward to hearing from you.

Sincerely,

Chris Smith

Enc. Resume

▶ Computer skills relate specifically to requirements outlined in advertisement.

▶ Format is organized and visually appealing.

RESPONSE TO A "BLIND" ADVERTISEMENT
(Executive Sous Chef)

178 Green Street
Austin, TX 78704
(512) 555-5555

July 7, 20--

P.O. Box 7777
Roanoke, VA 24001

RE: Executive Sous Chef

Dear Sir or Madam:

I am enclosing a copy of my resume for your review and hope it will convince you that I am the right choice for the position of Executive Sous Chef at your facility.

My experience in the restaurant industry goes back to my high school days and has taken me through all phases of the culinary arts in progressively responsible positions. During the past fifteen years, I have had the opportunity to work with Leisuretyme Properties. In my present position as Sous Chef at the Naturne Hotel in Austin, I have responsibility for both the brasserie and Charles Fisheries, which generate combined food revenues of $6 million, and have direct supervision of a staff of thirty.

My experience with Leisuretyme has included extensive work with banquet preparation and special themes for up to 2,500 guests in a facility generating $19 million in banquet business. Because of my ability to organize, train, and work effectively with personnel in quality, high-volume restaurants, I have been able to maintain a low-turnover, conscientious, highly productive work force in an industry notorious for personnel problems.

Based on my qualifications, I feel confident that I can handle the responsibilities of Executive Sous Chef and maintain high-quality food services at your facility. In addition, I am willing to relocate given a suitable opportunity.

Please contact me so that we can discuss how I may contribute my expertise to your organization. I look forward to our initial conversation.

Sincerely,

Chris Smith

Enc. Resume

▶ Letter incorporates industry knowledge into discussion of qualifications.

▶ Response letter emphasizes candidate's supervisory skills.

RESPONSE TO A "BLIND" ADVERTISEMENT
(Field Finance Manager)

178 Green Street
Presque Island, ME 04769
(207) 555-5555

February 6, 20--

Professional Staffing
P.O. Box 7777
Bangor, ME 04401

RE: Field Finance Manager

Dear Professional Staffing:

Please accept this letter and enclosed resume as an application for your Field Finance Manager opening advertised in the *Bangor Daily News*.

As a 20-- graduate of the University of Maine's Graduate School of Business, I have more than six years of business and financial analysis experience. This includes two years of domestic and international travel as an Internal Auditor for Manyfoods, Inc., two years of credit analysis at Millbury, and a treasury internship at Envirlab. Since my graduation, I have been working as a Business Analyst in the areas of banking, real estate, and restaurant management.

I have been recognized for my creative spirit and ability to identify practical solutions to current business problems. The following highlights some of my achievements:

- Participated in the due diligence and/or postacquisition reviews related to five acquisitions.
- Planned, coordinated, and/or participated in the compliance and productivity audits of forty-one independent business units.
- Participated in the fraud review of a major business unit.
- Researched, developed, and planned a cash collection reorganization that, when implemented, will save $120,000 per year.

Based on my job experience and educational qualifications, I am confident I can make an immediate contribution to your firm. I would appreciate the opportunity to further discuss my credentials with you in person. Thank you.

Sincerely,

Chris Smith

Enc. Resume

▶ Bulleted statements highlight candidate's on-the-job achievements.

▶ Candidate emphasizes how past business experience is relevant.

RESPONSE TO A "BLIND" ADVERTISEMENT
(Labor Relations Specialist)

178 Green Street
Worcester, MA 01610

April 8, 20--

Personnel Representative
P.O. Box 7777
Lowell, MA 01852

Dear Personnel Representative:

I am very interested in the Labor Relations Specialist position that appeared in the April 5 edition of the *Worcester Telegram & Gazette*. Enclosed is a copy of my resume for your review.

I offer more than fifteen years of human resource and labor relations experience which includes the following positions: Labor/Management Relations Analyst, Field Representative, and Legislative Assistant. I am fluent in Spanish, willing to travel, and anxious to put my skills to work for your organization.

Please call me at (508) 555-5555 with any further questions. I look forward to hearing from you.

Sincerely,

Chris Smith

Enc. Resume

▶ Letter cites advertisement's specific publication and date.

▶ Reference to bilingual ability may give an applicant the "edge" in certain professions.

RESPONSE TO A "BLIND" ADVERTISEMENT
(Legal Associate)

178 Green Street
Alfred, NY 14802
(607) 555-5555

October 28, 20--

P.O. Box 7777
Conway, SC 29526

RE: Legal Associate

Dear Sir/Madam:

In addition to a Juris Doctor degree, I recently received a Master of Law in Banks and Banking Law Studies with a concentration in International Law. I am looking for the opportunity to join the legal staff of a bank or corporation where I can put my experience in general legal practice and recent graduate degree to practical use as I further develop my legal capabilities.

My expertise is in the supervision of associate and support legal staff in all phases of research, document preparation, and coordination as required for all legal issues. I am well organized, accurate, and conscientious, interface well with individuals and groups, and feel confident that I can be a contributing asset to your firm.

I am most anxious to become a part of your firm and would appreciate meeting with you at your convenience. The enclosed resume is a brief summary of my academic accomplishments and work experience.

I look forward to your response.

Sincerely,

Chris Smith

Enc. Resume

▶ Educational credentials relate specifically to advertised position.

▶ Closing expresses candidate's interest in furthering candidacy through an interview.

RESPONSE TO A "BLIND" ADVERTISEMENT
(Librarian)

178 Green Street
Quincy, MA 02171

July 22, 20--

Personnel Director
P.O. Box 7777
Amherst, MA 01003

RE: Librarian

Dear Personnel Director:

In response to the July 21 advertisement in the *Boston Sunday Globe,* I have enclosed my resume for your review.

In addition to an M.L.S. degree and ALA accreditation, I have twelve years' experience as a Bibliographer and Acquisitions, Special Collections, and Reference Librarian with concentration in history and additional experience in philosophy and religion. In these positions, I provide general and specialized reference services, develop and manage collections, perform faculty liaison work, and conduct bibliographic instruction sessions at undergraduate and graduate levels. I am also experienced in assisting and training others in the use of electronic resources including CD-ROM, the World Wide Web, and other networked information resources for research.

Although my present position provides a challenging and rewarding atmosphere, I am interested in making a change where I can contribute my knowledge and experience in an academic setting. I have the ability to undertake a broad scope of responsibility and work effectively with a diverse population of students, faculty, and staff.

I am anxious to learn more about this position. Should you require additional information, please contact me at the above address or by phone at (617) 555-5555. I look forward to your response.

Sincerely,

Chris Smith

Enc. Resume

▶ Professional accreditation enhances candidate's qualifications.

▶ Unrelated work experience is omitted from response letter.

RESPONSE TO A "BLIND" ADVERTISEMENT
(Major Account Manager)

178 Green Street
Shreveport, LA 71101

November 14, 20--

Personnel Director
P.O. Box 7777
New Orleans, LA 70140

RE: Major Account Manager

Dear Personnel Director:

During the past fifteen years with an internationally recognized computer corporation, I have progressively advanced from such positions as Applications Maintenance Programmer and Regional Account Manager to my current position as National Account Manager. In this capacity, I am responsible for selling large computer systems to support from 30 to 250 users.

Although I have found these positions both fast-paced and challenging, I feel that my expertise in providing high visibility for increased sales can be more effectively utilized through working with upper management decision-makers on the development of pre- and postsales support programs. I am a high-energy, aggressive individual who enjoys a challenge and is willing to accept responsibility. As a member of your management staff, I am confident that I can make the same outstanding contribution to your firm that I have made to my present employer and that I can readily capture your share of the high-performance market.

The enclosed resume summarizes my background and experience in the above areas. Should you require additional information, please feel free to contact me at the above address or by phone at (318) 555-5555. I welcome your acknowledgment and look forward to a meeting at your earliest convenience.

Yours sincerely,

Chris Smith

Enc. Resume

▶ Letter illustrates continual career progression.

▶ Beyond matching qualifications with requirements, candidate highlights personal attributes applicable to advertised position.

RESPONSE TO A "BLIND" ADVERTISEMENT
(Manufacturing Test Technician)

178 Green Street
Glendive, MT 59330

June 5, 20--

Human Resources Director
P.O. Box 7777
Billings, MT 59107

RE: Manufacturing Test Technician

Dear Human Resources Director:

I am writing this letter with the expressed intent of applying for your position advertised in the June 3 edition of the *Billings Gazette*. It is my interest to join your engineering staff in an area that allows me to utilize my academic as well as practical experience on new product applications and engineering development.

I offer six years of experience, with three as a Test Technician on top-quality, electronic audio systems and as a member of a technical academic team working on a 3,000-line computer program designed to debug software. I also have supervisory and sales responsibility in a retail setting.

Through study and work, I have directed my career toward the full-time profession of engineering and I feel that my education and diversity of environments and responsibility enable me to make a positive and immediate contribution to your organization.

I would like to arrange a personal interview to further expand upon your requirements and my ability to meet them. I can be reached at the above address or between the hours of 9:00 A.M. and 4 P.M. at (406) 555-5555.

I look forward to meeting you.

Sincerely,

Chris Smith

Enc. Resume

▶ Introduction immediately refers to publication where advertisement appeared.

▶ Candidate invites addressee to respond to inquiry since specific employer is unknown.

RESPONSE TO A "BLIND" ADVERTISEMENT
(Marketing Analyst)

178 Green Street
Beachwood, OH 44122

January 2, 20--

Department of Human Resources
P.O. Box 7777
Dayton, OH 45402

RE: Marketing Analyst

Dear Sir or Madam:

I am writing to request your consideration of my application for the Marketing Analyst position advertised in today's *Dayton Daily News*.

Please note that in addition to a Bachelor of Science degree in Marketing, I have three years of responsible experience ranging from Merchandise Analyst to Senior Analyst with a rapid-growth, nationwide apparel retailer. I am responsible for recruiting, screening, and providing job overview and subsequent personnel training in retailing/distribution. Working with reports generated by a national computer network, I perform in-depth analyses of sales results and inventory levels with a view toward providing the ideal merchandise mix and qualities to targeted markets.

In addition, I have experience working in private clubs, membership operations, banking, and television. I have excellent communication and interpersonal skills, work well under pressure as either an individual contributor or as a team player, and relate easily to all management levels in the performance of responsibilities.

It would be my pleasure to outline my potential for making a significant contribution to your corporation in an interview. I can be reached at the above address or by phone at (216) 555-5555.

I hope to hear from you soon.

Sincerely,

Chris Smith

Enc. Resume

▶ Response letter immediately states candidate's purpose for writing.

▶ Letter avoids abbreviations and slang.

RESPONSE TO A "BLIND" ADVERTISEMENT
(Medical Assistant)

178 Green Street
Lawton, OK 73505

February 10, 20--

P.O. Box 7777
Platteville, WI 53818

RE: Medical Assistant

Dear Sir or Madam:

My interest in the position of Medical Assistant that you advertised in *Health Support Monthly* has prompted me to forward my resume for your review and consideration.

In addition to ten years of experience as a Home Health Aide, In-patient Claims Representative, and, since 20--, Medical Assistant with Smith Rehabilitation Hospital, I have good knowledge of medical terminology, procedure codes, and medical office systems including related computerized applications. I have an Associate degree in Sociology, was graduated as a medical assistant, and am currently a candidate for an Associate degree in Nursing.

My career objective is to develop further my medical and support skills in areas that will give me the opportunity to participate in the administration of quality health care. I would welcome the opportunity to discuss whether my abilities and goals suit your requirements and expectations. Please contact me at the above address or at (405) 555-5555 during the daytime to schedule an interview.

Thank you.

Yours sincerely,

Chris Smith

Enc. Resume

▶ Candidate immediately refers to advertised position.   ▶ Discussion of experience is very specific.

RESPONSE TO A "BLIND" ADVERTISEMENT
(Nurse's Aide)

178 Green Street
Cleveland, OH 44143

November 26, 20--

Hiring Coordinator
P.O. Box 7777
Dayton, OH 45463

RE: Nurse's Aide Position

Dear Hiring Coordinator:

In response to the advertisement in the November 12 edition of the *Dayton Daily News* for a Nurse's Aide, please accept the enclosed resume as my initial application.

I am CPR-certified and possess a strong clinical background. The classes I attend as part of Ohio State University's nursing program have given me the formal training necessary for this position. With my experience and education, I am confident that I would be a valuable asset to the nursing staff.

I would appreciate the opportunity to meet with you to further discuss the position offered. I can be reached at the above address or at (216) 555-5555.

I look forward to your reply.

Sincerely,

Chris Smith

Enc. Resume

▶ Professional certification and strong educational background add strength to cover letter.

▶ Letter uses short sentences and common words.

RESPONSE TO A "BLIND" ADVERTISEMENT
(Operations Manager)

178 Green Street
Siloam Springs, AR 72761

April 2, 20--

Personnel Director
P.O. Box 7777
Little Rock, AR 77203

RE: Operations Manager

Dear Personnel Director:

In response to last Friday's advertisement in the *Arkansas Democrat-Gazette* for an Operations Manager, I am enclosing my resume for your consideration.

During the past seven years, I have gained progressively responsible experience in areas of sales/marketing, technical, and product management, as well as new product introduction/market development, warehousing, and distribution.

My positions have ranged from Sales/Marketing Representative to Product Manager. I have been fully responsible for start-up, marketing, and promotion of new technology for a manufacturer of architectural and industrial coatings and finishes, sold worldwide. Also, I hold a Bachelor of Arts degree in Economics and I have completed advanced professional and technical study in architecture, protective architectural/industrial coating, and finishes.

Although my positions have been challenging and fast-paced, at this point in my career I am seeking a new, long-term association where my expertise, creativity, and motivation can be more fully utilized. I have a proven track record and I feel that a personal meeting would give us an opportunity to expand on our mutual objectives.

I can be reached at the above address or by phone at (501) 555-5555. Thank you for your consideration and response. I look forward to hearing from you.

Sincerely,

Chris Smith

Enc. Resume

▶ Candidate uses closing to suggest possibility of interview.

▶ One page is standard length for cover letters.

RESPONSE TO A "BLIND" ADVERTISEMENT
(Optical Manufacturer)

178 Green Street
Baltimore, MD 21201

July 23, 20--

Senior Manufacturing Manager
P.O. Box 7777
Bethesda, MD 21211

Dear Senior Manufacturing Manager:

My interest in the Optical Manufacturer position advertised in the July 20 edition of the *Baltimore Sun* has prompted me to submit the enclosed resume for your review. During the past fifteen years, my experience has ranged from Lamination Technician to Production and Manufacturing Manager in the optical industry. I offer excellent skills in technical sales and marketing support, production and product management, manufacturing management, communications and presentations, and trade show coordination.

Although my positions have been diverse and challenging, I am currently seeking a new position that will afford me the opportunity to contribute to the growth and profitability of a company with a diverse product line in industrial, commercial, and/or military markets.

I will be glad to furnish you with additional information pertaining to my qualifications. Please feel free to contact me at the above address or by calling (301) 555-5555.

Sincerely,

Chris Smith

Enc. Resume

▶ Introduction demonstrates candidate's suitability for advertised position.

▶ Closing is straightforward and concise.

RESPONSE TO A "BLIND" ADVERTISEMENT
(Payroll Supervisor)

178 Green Street
Big Stone Gap, VA 24219
(703) 555-5555

June 6, 20--

Human Resources Associate
P.O. Box 7777
Richmond, VA 23219

RE: Payroll Supervisor

Good morning!

As an experienced Payroll Administrator, I am confident that I am the qualified Payroll Supervisor candidate you are searching for as listed in the June 5 edition of the *Richmond Times-Dispatch*.

Please note that in addition to a Bachelor of Arts degree in Economics, my background encompasses ten years of progressively responsible and sophisticated hands-on experience ranging from Marketing Research Assistant, Union Benefits Coordinator, and Human Resources Administrator to my present position as Payroll Administrator. In this capacity, I focus on the day-to-day details of financial operations and training in critical organizational and operational sectors of my employer'general business operation.

I am well organized, detail-oriented, and committed to serving your corporation in an efficient and productive way. I am very eager to learn more about the responsibilities of the position and how I can begin to make a contribution to your overall success.

Sincerely,

Chris Smith

Enc. Resume

▶ Letter focuses on filling employer's needs, not the job candidate's.

▶ Powerful adjectives, when used sparingly, ensure maximum impact.

RESPONSE TO A "BLIND" ADVERTISEMENT
(Pharmaceutical Administrator)

178 Green Street
Rock Springs, WY 82902

September 6, 20--

Human Resources Representative
P.O. Box 7777
Casper, WY 82604

RE: Pharmaceutical Administrator

Dear Human Resources Representative:

I recently spotted your advertisement in the September 4 edition of the *Casper Star Tribune*. I am very interested in becoming associated with an established organization as a Pharmaceutical Administrator and have enclosed my resume for your consideration.

I hold a Master's degree in Hospital Pharmacy Administration and two related Bachelor's degrees. In addition, for the past fifteen years I have had progressively responsible experience ranging from Staff Pharmacist to Pharmacy Supervisor at a 300-bed community hospital. I am well versed in medical terminology; have excellent communications and presentation skills; and work effectively with physicians, clinical staffs, and hospital administration.

Based on my extensive experience in pharmaceuticals, combined with my energy and enthusiasm for a career in the health care field, I believe I am well qualified for this position.

Please contact me at the above address, or call (307) 555-5555 to arrange a mutually convenient time for a meeting, during which we may further discuss your current or anticipated needs and my ability to fill the position.

Thank you for your time.

Yours sincerely,

Chris Smith

Enc. Resume

▶ Candidate's highest educational achievement is shown before other less significant degrees.

▶ Response letter emphasizes candidate's supervisory skills.

RESPONSE TO A "BLIND" ADVERTISEMENT
(Production/Materials Control Manager)

178 Green Street
Fairfield, CT 06420

July 21, 20--

P.O. Box 7777
Willimantic, CT 06626

RE: Production/Materials Control Manager

Dear Sir or Madam:

    Production/materials control management is my forte, and I am looking for a new opportunity where I can put these skills to work for a company interested, as I am, in profitable growth and mutual gain for the long term. Please accept the enclosed resume as my expressed interest in applying for the Production/Materials Control Manager position you advertised in the July 19 edition of the *North Jersey Herald and News*.

    I am considered by my associates to be a dynamic, persistent achiever with a composite background of technical, sales, management, and training experience. During the past twenty years my positions have ranged from Production Control Manager to Vice-President of Operations and President with world-leading manufacturers of cutting tools, industrial process controls, and electronics. My expertise encompasses selection, training, and development of competent team leaders and support personnel, with hands-on experience in the design and installation of materials.

    I would be happy to meet with you to discuss, in detail, your requirements and my ability to handle the responsibilities of the position offered. I am very interested in learning more about your company and I am confident I can provide you with effective and profitable management.

    Should you require additional information prior to our meeting, please contact me at the above address or by phone at (203) 555-5555.

Yours sincerely,

Chris Smith

Enc. Resume

▶ Introductory sentence draws attention.

▶ Closing emphasizes candidate's enthusiasm for desired position.

RESPONSE TO A "BLIND" ADVERTISEMENT
(Sales Manager)

---

178 Green Street
Girdletree, MD 21829
(301) 555-5555

October 13, 20--

P.O. Box 7777
Chicago, IL 60605

RE: Sales Manager position

Dear Sir or Madam:

The position of Sales Manager advertised in the *Chicago Tribune* on October 12 intrigues me. I believe you will find me well qualified.

I am an innovative achiever who feels that in a growth industry like cable television, there is the need for a representative who can meet and beat the competition. I believe that I have all the necessary ingredients to contribute to the success of your operation and, if necessary, I am willing to take a step backward as long as I see there is potential for forward momentum. All I need is a starting point.

The enclosed confidential resume summarizes my proven track record as the Vice-President of Sales for a $2 million operation. I have strong communications skills and the ability to prepare and make presentations to decision-makers on all levels.

I feel that a personal meeting would give us the opportunity to discuss your short- and long-term objectives and my ability to direct your organization toward successfully achieving those goals.

Thank you for your attention to this matter. I look forward to speaking with you.

Sincerely yours,

Chris Smith

Enc. Resume

▶ Letter suggests discretion.

▶ Setting desired position apart from body of letter may be advantageous when responding to a "blind" advertisement.

RESPONSE TO A "BLIND" ADVERTISEMENT
(Staff Photographer)

178 Green Street
Tyler, TX 75799

July 20, 20--

Department of Human Resources
P.O. Box 7777
San Antonio, TX 78297

RE: Staff Photographer

To whom it may concern:

I am responding to your July 18 advertisement in the *San Antonio Express* for a staff photographer.

As you will be able to see from my resume, I hold a Bachelor of Fine Arts degree in Photography from the University of Texas. My extensive photography experience includes several years of printing and processing with a variety of black-and-white materials, and custom and production printing of color negatives. In addition, I am familiar with traditional 35 mm, 2-¼, and 4 × 5 equipment, as well as digital formats. I also have experience teaching photography in a bachelor's degree program.

I would very much like to arrange an opportunity to meet with you and review my portfolio. I am confident that I can convince you of my skills as a photographer, as well as my dedication to producing a product of the highest quality.

I can be reached at the above address or by phone during the evening at (903) 555-5555. Thank you for your consideration of my application.

Sincerely,

Chris Smith

Enc. Resume

▶ Stating that a portfolio is available on request is beneficial for certain positions.

▶ Candidate invites addressee to respond to inquiry since specific employer is unknown.

RESPONSE TO A "BLIND" ADVERTISEMENT
(Teacher)

178 Green Street
Newport, RI 02840

May 14, 20--

Search Committee
P.O. Box 7777
Providence, RI 02908

RE: Sixth Grade Teaching Position

Dear Search Committee:

I have enclosed my resume in response to your advertisement in the May edition of *Education in New England.*

During the past several years, I have been preparing myself for a full-time position as a teacher in an established school system, where I can apply my teaching, training, and administrative experience to manage and motivate a classroom of students toward higher education.

As a Student Teacher with the Easton Public School System, I successfully taught literature, public speaking, and creative writing at the secondary level. I received my Bachelor's degree and certification in Elementary Education in 20-- from Stonehill College in Easton, Massachusetts. Also, I have served as a Substitute Teacher in several school districts over a four-year period and have designed, organized, and taught my own summer course for gifted children in the town of Newport for the past two years.

Currently, I am seeking an opportunity with a system that offers continued professional development and the opportunity for advancement in the field of education. I would welcome a personal interview to discuss in detail my ability to handle the teaching position and my compatibility with the rest of your staff.

In the interim, should you require additional information, please contact me at the above address or by phone at (401) 555-5555.

Yours sincerely,

Chris Smith

Enc. Resume

▶ Temporary experience is relevant to full-time employment.

▶ Candidate immediately refers to advertised position.

RESPONSE TO A "BLIND" ADVERTISEMENT
(Technical Sales Associate)

178 Green Street
Valdosta, GA 31698
(912) 555-5555

January 24, 20--

Sales Director
P.O. Box 7777
Macon, GA 31201

RE: Technical Sales Associate position

Dear Sales Director:

I have more than sixteen years of diverse product development, sales and marketing, and technical support experience for a leading internationally recognized computer company. You will note from my enclosed resume that my background runs parallel to the requirements for the Technical Sales Associate position that was advertised in the January 23 edition of the *Macon Telegraph*.

Accustomed to multimillion-dollar marketing and product development responsibilities, I am now prepared to take on the challenges of a new position in technical sales offering me broader opportunities. I can bring dynamic leadership, technical support acumen, and decisive marketing skills to your firm. To illustrate, I have been responsible for conceptualizing and developing software/hardware and marketing techniques, possess solid problem-solving skills, and am known for my proven ability to motivate others.

As you can see, my qualifications closely match your requirements. I am looking forward to a personal meeting with you to discuss this opportunity. Please call to arrange a time for us to meet at your convenience. Salary requirements are open to discussion.

I look forward to your reply.

Sincerely,

Chris Smith

Enc. Resume

▶ Separating major accomplishments from body provides emphasis.

▶ Candidate focuses on applying skills and experiences to advertised position.

RESPONSE TO A "BLIND" ADVERTISEMENT
(Typist)

178 Green Street
Toledo, OH 43660

April 11, 20--

P.O. Box 7777
Toledo, OH 43660

Dear Personnel Manager:

I am interested in the part-time position of At-Home Typist for which you advertised in the February 13 edition of the *Toledo Blade*.

My typing speed is 80 wpm. At present, I am a part-time student at Ohio State University and I am confident your company can utilize my available time and impressive qualifications to fulfill your typing needs.

Please consider the enclosed resume as an application.

I have a desktop PC with an Intel Pentium 4 processor, as well as an HP LaserJet printer, and I am proficient in both Microsoft Word and WordPerfect word processing software. I am anxious to put this equipment and my typing skills to work for your organization.

When would it be a convenient time for an interview? Please call me at (419) 555-5555.

Sincerely,

Chris Smith

Enc. Resume

▶ Mentioning typing speed and proficiency with specific word processing programs can be advantageous for administrative and office support positions.
▶ Response letter immediately introduces candidate's qualifications.

RESPONSE TO A "BLIND" ADVERTISEMENT
(Underwriter)

178 Green Street
Klamath Falls, OR 97601

July 9, 20--

P.O. Box 7777
Anchorage, AK 99514

RE: Underwriter position

Dear Sir or Madam:

I am writing with an expressed interest in applying for your advertised position of Underwriter that appeared in Sunday's edition of the *Anchorage Daily News*. I am an experienced professional underwriter with a successful track record in the development of new business, the management of highly productive and diversified underwriting activities, and the support of sales and marketing operations.

I have a record of outstanding success as a Security Underwriter in establishing and maintaining profitable relationships with accounts and agents throughout the Pacific Northwest. In my current position, I have grown marketing and client contacts from a start-up base to $1.7 million in gross premiums.

I am eager to continue my successful track record with a new company that is in need of an aggressive, dedicated professional. I would like to learn more about your corporation and how I can begin to make a substantial and long-term contribution to your success. I would be glad to travel to Anchorage for a personal interview at your convenience.

Please contact me at the above address or at (503) 555-5555 if I can be of further assistance. I hope to hear from you soon.

Yours sincerely,

Chris Smith

Enc. Resume

▶ Background summary accentuates candidate's acquired professional skills and impressive track record.

▶ Willingness to travel can be advantageous.

RESPONSE TO A "BLIND" ADVERTISEMENT
(Writer/Researcher)

178 Green Street
Pompano Beach, FL 33063
(305) 555-5555

December 27, 20--

Personnel Manager
P.O. Box 7777
Tampa, FL 32714

Dear Personnel Manager:

I feel I have the experience and ability to fill the Writer/Researcher position advertised on December 26 in the *Tampa Tribune*.

Writing Experience: I have written or co-written five books on business management and communications. In addition, I have been a reporter for magazines and newspapers for many years and have written more than 3,000 articles for publication, on topics ranging from crime to sports to medicine to humor. I know how to generate ideas and research topics, and I am comfortable writing on almost any subject and in a range of styles. I would have no trouble matching the established style of your book series.

Editing Experience: I have edited a number of books on business topics and worked as an editor on several newspapers. I am capable of both minor polishing and major rewriting, but more importantly, I am able to tell which level of editing is needed. In addition, I taught English Composition and Communications at the college level for three years. My grammar and editing skills are, I believe, exceptional.

Publications Management Experience: Before moving to Florida, I was the Publications Coordinator for an international business consulting firm and had ultimate responsibility for the production of more than twenty books a year. I have also had responsibility for the production of several daily newspapers and magazines. In each of these positions, I supervised writers, managed the copyediting operation, and oversaw all production activities. I am very comfortable working with tight deadlines—in more than fifteen years, I rarely failed to meet one.

Based on my background, I feel I am the ideal candidate for your position. I have enclosed a resume as well as a brief sample of my writing. I look forward to meeting with you to further discuss how I could work with your organization.

Sincerely,

Chris Smith

Enc. Resume, Writing sample

▶ Categorizing qualifications adds strength to cover letter.

▶ Summary of experience highlights candidate's achievements.

CHAPTER 13

"COLD" LETTER TO A POTENTIAL EMPLOYER

A "cold" cover letter lets you directly contact potential employers without a referral or previous correspondence. Job seekers most commonly use this type of letter to advertise their availability to hiring managers or human resources departments. Presumably, after researching your field, you will have created a list of the top employers for whom you would like to work, and gathered basic company information for each. A cold letter should incorporate your knowledge of the company along with a discussion of your relevant qualifications. When writing a cold letter, keep in mind you are not applying for a specific position. State your skills and accomplishments, but let the employer decide how you may best suit his or her needs.

"COLD" LETTER TO A POTENTIAL EMPLOYER
(Accountant)

178 Green Street
Chester, PA 19013
(215) 555-5555

November 19, 20--

Pat Cummings
Hiring Manager
Any Corporation
1140 Main Street
Philadelphia, PA 19130

Dear Ms. Cummings:

During the past seven years, my experience has ranged from Fixed Asset Accountant/Financial Management Trainee to Senior Cost Accountant of a $250 million processing operation.

Currently, I am seeking a long-term career opportunity with a well-seasoned manufacturer or high-tech firm that has a need for an accountant with a good knowledge of, and experience in, cost accounting, general accounting, and finance.

The enclosed resume outlines my background in the above areas. Throughout my experience, I have been aware of, and continually impressed by, the diverse services offered by Any Corporation. Needless to say, I am eager to join a team such as yours.

I look forward to the opportunity to meet in a personal interview. I will call you November 29 to arrange a convenient time.

Yours sincerely,

Chris Smith

Enc. Resume

▶ Closing specifies that candidate will follow up inquiry.

▶ Career objective gives focus without limiting candidate's opportunities.

"COLD" LETTER TO A POTENTIAL EMPLOYER
(Accounts Receivable Clerk)

178 Green Street
Philadelphia, PA 19134

December 2, 20--

Pat Cummings
Manager, Accounts Receivable
Any Corporation
1140 Main Street
Macungie, PA 18062

Dear Mr. Cummings:

I would like to express my interest in applying my relevant experience and background to a position in the accounts receivable department at Any Corporation.

In addition to an Associate degree in Administration, I possess four years of bookkeeping and general office experience. While at Independence Bank, I performed word processing and data entry involving trust fund information, daily sales records, payroll expenses, and invoices. As an Academic Records Assistant at Drexel University, I was responsible for the maintenance and input of thousands of alumni records. I can type 65 wpm, and am proficient in most major computer word processing programs and spreadsheet applications. Of additional interest, I have a fluent command of the Spanish language, both oral and written, and have a reading knowledge of Italian.

The record-keeping nature of my past experience has given me a facility for detail, patience, and the ability to keep accurate records, all of which I am confident can be successfully applied to an Accounts Receivable position with Any Corporation.

My resume is enclosed for your consideration. Should you have any questions or wish to schedule an interview, please do not hesitate to call me at (215) 555-5555. I look forward to hearing from you soon.

Sincerely,

Chris Smith

Enc. Resume

▶ Unrelated work experience is omitted.

▶ Mentioning speed and word processing skills can be advantageous for administrative and office support positions.

"COLD" LETTER TO A POTENTIAL EMPLOYER
(Administrative Assistant)

178 Green Street
Delaware City, DE 19706
(302) 555-5555

January 18, 20--

Pat Cummings
Director, Human Resources
Any Corporation
1140 Main Street
New Castle, DE 19720

Dear Ms. Cummings:

    I am interested in applying for an Administrative Assistant position with Any Corporation. I graduated in May 20-- with an Associate degree in Computer Information Systems from the University of Delaware.

    I have worked in the university's main computer room for two years, and I have developed advanced skills in a large number of software packages on both PC and Macintosh systems, including WordPerfect and Word for Windows. More recently, I worked as a receptionist for four months with Cammarata Designs, Inc., where I gained exposure to all facets of administrative work: typing 70 wpm, phone contact, and customer relations. With my educational background, proven academic success, and desire to learn and excel, I am confident I can make a significant contribution to your staff.

    My enclosed resume provides additional information about my education and experience. I will be glad to make myself available for an interview at your earliest convenience to discuss how my qualifications would be consistent with your needs. Thank you for your time and consideration.

Sincerely,

Chris Smith

Enc. Resume

▶ Letter immediately states candidate's purpose.

▶ Valuable computer skills are highlighted.

"COLD" LETTER TO A POTENTIAL EMPLOYER
(Administrative Director)

178 Green Street
Sarasota, FL 34236

August 20, 20--

Pat Cummings
Controller
Any Corporation
1140 Main Street
Bangor, ME 04401

Dear Mr. Cummings:

My desire to secure a challenging growth opportunity in a fast-paced business environment has prompted me to forward the attached resume for your evaluation.

Please note that in addition to my formal education, I have eight years of hands-on management experience working in large-scale distribution, shipping and receiving, warehouse, and department store environments, involving up to 50,000 line items.

My primary focus is in areas of distribution, warehousing, and general operations management. My experience, however, also encompasses all aspects of personnel management as well as purchasing, inventory control, security and safety, merchandising, MIS, and quality management.

Please contact me at the above address or call (813) 555-5555, so that we may arrange a mutually convenient time for an interview.

Thank you for your consideration.

Sincerely,

Chris Smith

Enc. Resume

▶ Candidate's practical experience outweighs his/her education.

▶ Closing is brief and to the point.

"COLD" LETTER TO A POTENTIAL EMPLOYER
(Advertising Executive)

178 Green Street
Minster, OH 45865

June 3, 20--

Pat Cummings
Senior Art Director
Any Advertising Agency
1140 Main Street
Dayton, OH 45401

Dear Ms. Cummings:

I am no stranger to hard work, long hours, or tight schedules. To achieve mutual objectives, I am open to training, travel, and new assignments, and will apply dedication and quality performance to whatever tasks I am assigned.

During the past seven years, my experience has been concentrated in directing and coordinating the design, illustration, and concept development of promotional and direct mail marketing pieces for an established advertising agency. I have completed advanced coursework in commercial art and specialized technology.

Although my position is diversified and provides me with challenge and decision-making responsibilities in a creative and highly competitive industry, I feel it is time for a change. I am interested in joining a company, such as Any Advertising Agency, where I can apply my education and experience to develop new skills that will lead to my advancement within your art department.

I have enclosed a resume and project sample. I would welcome the opportunity to present a portfolio of my work and discuss my qualifications in greater detail.

To arrange an interview, please contact me at the above address or by phone at (419) 555-5555 days or (419) 555-4444 evenings.

I look forward to your return response.

Sincerely,

Chris Smith

Enc. Resume, Sample

▶ Introductory sentence draws attention.

▶ Enclosure lines refer to all attached materials.

"COLD" LETTER TO A POTENTIAL EMPLOYER
(Advertising Sales Associate)

178 Green Street
Decatur, GA 30032
(404) 555-5555

August 26, 20--

Pat Cummings
Personnel Director
Any Corporation
1140 Main Street
Augusta, GA 30901

Dear Mr. Cummings:

Given both my sales experience and my objective of pursuing a career in the fast-paced advertising industry, I would like to explore options within the Sales Department at Any Corporation.

I have been involved in sales/customer service with a major U.S. air carrier for four years, in which time I gained the exposure and valuable work experience necessary for success. I have learned the art, as well as the importance of, creating a strong rapport with clients while demonstrating outstanding customer service for successful sales. I have also learned unique approaches to problem-solving and how to handle rejection with renewed optimism and good humor. In addition, I possess exceptional communication and organizational skills. I am proficient in Microsoft Word for Windows and can type effectively at 65 wpm.

I look forward to expanding my career in sales and advertising with Any Corporation. I would certainly appreciate the opportunity to discuss how I might apply my skills and knowledge to benefit your company. I would like to schedule an interview at your convenience, and will call you next week to do so. Thank you.

Sincerely,

Chris Smith

Enc. Resume

▶ Letter focuses on acquired skills relevant to field of interest.

▶ Closing suggests a meeting to follow letter.

"COLD" LETTER TO A POTENTIAL EMPLOYER
(Alumni Relations Coordinator)

178 Green Street
Kirkwood, MO 63122
(314) 555-5555

August 18, 20--
Pat Cummings
Director, Alumni Relations
Any University
1140 Main Street
St. Louis, MO 63141

Dear Ms. Cummings:

In my experience with alumni relations, I have been continually impressed by Any University's outstanding record of annual alumni contributions. Should you be in need of an addition to your staff, I would appreciate your consideration of my qualifications.

Please note that during the past ten years I have held diverse and progressively responsible positions in alumni relations at both the university and private secondary school levels. During this period, I have been heavily involved in strategies, annual fundraising campaigns, marketing/mailing programs, and media/public relations. Although these positions have been challenging and broad in scope, I feel that my expertise would be especially suited to your organization. I have been, and am confident I will continue to be, successful in achieving both short- and long-range objectives.

The enclosed, up-to-date resume details my background in these areas. Would it be possible to schedule a personal interview? I would be happy to make myself available at your convenience.

I look forward to your response.

Sincerely,

Chris Smith

Enc. Resume

▶ Phrasing request in question form is a strong closing.

▶ One page is standard length for cover letters.

"COLD" LETTER TO A POTENTIAL EMPLOYER
(Architectural Engineer)

178 Green Street
Little Rock, AR 77203

March 9, 20--

Pat Cummings
Chief Engineer
Any Corporation
1140 Main Street
Tucson, AZ 85714

Dear Mr. Cummings:

Please accept this letter as an application for a position within your company. I have enclosed a resume for your consideration and review, but would like to draw your attention to several points.

I hold a Bachelor's degree in Architectural Engineering and possess six years of professional experience in increasingly responsible positions in the engineering, architectural, and construction fields. In my most recent position as Project Manager, I have been able to utilize my background in coordinating the structural, mechanical, electrical, and civil disciplines on several different projects.

My specific achievements include conceiving and supervising the construction of a fifty-acre industrial park and helping to reorganize Jiffy Contractors. In addition, the Army Corps of Engineers regularly relies on my expertise for private consultations.

I believe that my qualifications would make me a valuable asset to your firm and I look forward to a personal interview at your earliest convenience. Please contact me at the above address or by phone at (501) 555-5555.

Thank you very much for your time and consideration.

Sincerely yours,

Chris Smith

Enc. Resume

▶ Discussion of experience clearly spells out candidate's area of expertise.

▶ Telephone number included in closing is omitted in return address.

"COLD" LETTER TO A POTENTIAL EMPLOYER
(Art Director)

---

178 Green Street
Schaumburg, IL 60191
(708) 555-5555

March 3, 20--

Pat Cummings
Executive Director
Any Performing Arts Foundation
1140 Main Street
Chicago, IL 60632

Dear Ms. Cummings:

As a studio owner, manager, choreographer, performer, and producer, I feel I have much to offer in support of performing arts.

In addition to my successful experience, I have been actively involved in public relations and promotional activities. Such work requires the ability to communicate and interface effectively with talented professionals as well as patrons of the arts. I am most effective in the capacity of planner, coordinator, manager, and representative in a creative environment and feel confident that I can contribute to the efforts of a performing arts foundation.

I have enclosed a professional profile for your consideration regarding any suitable openings. Perhaps we could meet for a personal interview? I would love to share with you my experiences and dedication to the performing arts.

Sincerely,

Chris Smith

Enc. Professional profile

▶ Experience reinforces candidate's professional objective.

▶ Candidate immediately introduces qualifications.

"COLD" LETTER TO A POTENTIAL EMPLOYER
(Arts Administrator)

178 Green Street
Arlington, VA 22203
(703) 555-5555

June 26, 20--

Pat Cummings
Director
Any Gallery
1140 Main Street
Vienna, VA 22108

Dear Mr. Cummings:

Last weekend I attended the opening of your newest exhibition, "Forming Meaning," and I especially appreciated your commitment to the local art scene. I am currently searching for an opportunity with a reputable gallery, and would be very interested in contributing my skills to your staff.

Please note that in addition to my broad formal education in areas related specifically to art and art education, I hold a Master of Education degree in Administration. I also possess valuable experience in diverse aspects of museum operations, including exhibition and display, media presentation, proposal writing, and associated details of estimation and cost accounting.

I would like to arrange a mutually convenient time for an interview during which we could further discuss your current or anticipated needs.

Thank you for your consideration.

Sincerely,

Chris Smith

Enc. Resume

▶ Letter highlights candidate's acquired professional and educational training.

▶ Closing thanks addressee in advance for attention.

"COLD" LETTER TO A POTENTIAL EMPLOYER
(Associate Editor)

178 Green Street
Needham, MA 02192
(617) 555-5555

June 18, 20--

Pat Cummings
Human Resources Director
Any Publishing Company
1140 Main Street
New York, NY 10128

Dear Ms. Cummings:

I have four years of publishing experience, including two years of scholarly journal experience in social science, physical science, and engineering which I would like to put to work at Any Publishing Company.

Specifically, I am seeking a position as an Associate Editor, Project Editor, or the equivalent in new book or journal development and administration. Originally from Long Island, I am planning to relocate to the New York area later this summer. Please consider the following highlights from my career:

- Developed a new book series in sociology through all phases of publication: from author contract negotiation to the creation of a series marketing plan.
- Acquired *Earth Day Every Day*, which was nominated for the Fortmiller Foundation's Prize and is already an "academic bestseller."
- Participated in a dynamic engineering program which included the launch of three new journals: *Physical Science*, *Micro Journal*, and the *Journal of Alternative Energy*.

In addition to a strong background in English literature and the social sciences at the University of Notre Dame, my training has included courses relevant to a position in medical publishing: Anatomy, Physiology, Medical Terminology, Nursing Procedures, Biology, and Radiographic Physics.

I will be in New York from July 20 to 30, during which time I would appreciate the opportunity to meet with you. Thank you for your consideration, and I look forward to speaking with you soon.

Sincerely,

Chris Smith

Enc. Resume

▶ Courses listed are related to candidate's field of interest.

▶ Closing provides specific time frame to allow for meeting.

"COLD" LETTER TO A POTENTIAL EMPLOYER
(Audio-Visual Specialist)

178 Green Street
Proctorville, VT 05153
(802) 555-5555

July 7, 20--

Pat Cummings
Personnel Manager
Any Corporation
1140 Main Street
Chicago, IL 60605

Dear Mr. Cummings:

In the interest of investigating career opportunities with your company, I am enclosing my resume for your consideration and review.

As you will note, I have fifteen years of educational and media experience. I am proficient in the operation of a wide variety of photographic, video, and audio equipment. In my current position, I am regularly responsible for processing and duplicating slides, as well as designing and setting up slide presentations, from simple slide-only programs to full-blown synchronized slide and audio productions.

I believe that my qualifications would make me an outstanding asset to your organization. I would very much appreciate the opportunity to personally meet with you at your convenience to further discuss my abilities and the needs of Any Corporation.

I look forward to hearing from you soon.

Sincerely,

Chris Smith

Enc. Resume

▶ Letter is easy and quick to read, and only relevant details are included.

▶ Candidate expresses willingness to meet at addressee's convenience in closing.

"COLD" LETTER TO A POTENTIAL EMPLOYER
(Automated Systems Specialist)

178 Green Street
Toledo, OH 43660
(419) 555-5555

January 8, 20--

Pat Cummings
Vice-President
Any Corporation
1140 Main Street
Beachwood, OH 44122

Dear Ms. Cummings:

During the past thirteen years, I have had comprehensive experience in the design, development, sale, and operation of automated equipment designed for the food-processing industry.

Currently, I am seeking a new association with a firm that can benefit from my experience in the areas cited above. I possess a unique combination of skills: technical sales, application engineering, and technical liaison between engineering and production to test, debug, and refine automated food-processing systems. In addition, I have experience as a Production Foreman and Supervisor responsible for postproduction with a manufacturer of a wide variety of power tools distributed through the Midwest.

I am very interested in speaking with you about current opportunities with Any Corporation. I will call your office on Monday, January 16 to schedule a convenient interview time.

Thank you for your consideration.

Sincerely,

Chris Smith

Enc. Resume

▶ Letter cites specific date phone contact will be made.

▶ Candidate does not limit available opportunities by stating specific position desired.

"COLD" LETTER TO A POTENTIAL EMPLOYER
(Aviation Specialist)

178 Green Street
Hunt Valley, MD 21031
(712) 555-5555

January 20, 20--

Pat Cummings
Senior Operations Manager
Any Airline
1140 Main Street
Baltimore, MD 21226

Dear Mr. Cummings:

I am very interested in securing a challenging position in an aviation-related operation, and have admired the fast-growing quality reputation Any Airline has built in the national arena.

I possess nine years of diverse full-time and part-time experience within the airline industry, ranging from Ground Crew and Operations Agent to my current position as Senior Operations Dispatcher for a highly personalized, worldwide courier service. This experience is supplemented by a Bachelor of Science degree in Aviation Science/Aviation Management, and comprehensive advanced training courses in these areas.

My enclosed resume provides a summary of the experience and training I feel can be put to effective use for your company. After you have had an opportunity to review my credentials, I would like to arrange a personal meeting so that I can more fully expand on my immediate and long-term potential. I am happy to make myself available at your convenience.

I look forward to hearing from you.

Sincerely,

Chris Smith

Enc. Resume

▶ Introduction states candidate's desire to join specific organization.

▶ Only relevant educational training is included.

"COLD" LETTER TO A POTENTIAL EMPLOYER
(Banking/Finance Professional)

178 Green Street
Barry Creek, CA 95916

July 7, 20--

Pat Cummings
Chief Hiring Officer
Any Corporation
1140 Main Street
Bakersfield, CA 93301

Dear Ms. Cummings:

I am writing to bring to your attention my years of experience in banking and finance, which include successful performance in such areas as fiduciary trust and real estate administration, investment management, and personal financial planning.

The enclosed resume summarizes my background. Please note that in addition to formal education in business administration and graduate study in banking, I have more than twenty years of progressively responsible experience in positions ranging from Senior Trust Officer and Controller to my most recent involvement as Registered Investment Consultant.

Currently, I am seeking a challenging opportunity in which to apply my background and experience, in a permanent, part-time situation.

I am currently available for an interview and will be glad to meet with you to further discuss additional details of my background and the mutual advantages of my joining your organization. In the interim, should your require additional information, please feel free to contact me by phone at (213) 555-5555 or (213) 444-4444, or at the above address.

Thank you for your consideration. I look forward to speaking with you.

Sincerely,

Chris Smith

Enc. Resume

▶ Letter illustrates continual career progression.

▶ Candidate indicates type of employment desired.

"COLD" LETTER TO A POTENTIAL EMPLOYER
(Business Consultant)

178 Green Street
Medford, WI 54451
(715) 555-5555 (days)
(715) 444-4444 (evenings)

September 12, 20--

Pat Cummings
Chairperson of the Board
Any Corporation
1140 Main Street
Schofield, WI 54476

Dear Mr. Cummings:

In the past several months, I have been studying operations at Any Corporation. By reading your annual report, company profile, and write-ups in several trade publications, I have been able to keep a close eye on both your costs and profits. If you agree that Any Corporation could benefit from an efficient, time-saving plan to cut production dollars, I would like to present my qualifications to you.

I am a skilled business consultant with more than seventeen years of experience concentrated in the advertising field. I believe I can be of assistance to your organization. For your evaluation, I have prepared the attached business proposal that contains a detailed summary of a series of events and observations concerning trends in Any Corporation's operations that could be easily reversed.

I may be reached at either one of the above-listed numbers for a telephone conference, or to establish a mutually convenient time for a personal meeting. At such time, I would been pleased to demonstrate how I might be able to assist in correcting and/or eliminating many of the challenges touched upon in the attached proposal.

Thank you for your consideration.

Sincerely,

Chris Smith

Enc. Business proposal

▶ Introduction expresses candidate's knowledge of firm.

▶ Discussion details how candidate's qualifications will benefit potential employer.

"COLD" LETTER TO A POTENTIAL EMPLOYER
(Buyer)

178 Green Street
El Cajon, CA 92020
(619) 555-5555

May 12, 20--

Pat Cummings
Personnel Coordinator
Any Corporation
1140 Main Street
Santa Ana, CA 97201

Dear Ms. Cummings:

If you are in need of a creative, innovative, professional buyer to add excitement to your inventories while generating bottom-line profits, then we have good reason to meet for further discussion.

During the past sixteen years I have had the opportunity to work in positions ranging from Merchandise Planner to Head Buyer on the headquarters level at two major off-price retail chains. I have enjoyed rapid advancement and experienced the challenge of coordinating new concepts, introducing change associated with upscale fashion, and generating substantial increases in sales and profits.

Currently, I am looking for a new association with a growing chain that will benefit from my experience in identifying fashion trends, developing resources, and negotiating big buys for off-price retail operations. I am interested in a professional opportunity that will utilize my market and product knowledge, and am anxious to achieve the same results for your chain as I have achieved for my current employer.

Since my present employer is unaware of my search, your confidence is appreciated. I look forward to your response.

Sincerely,

Chris Smith

Enc. Employment profile

▶ Experiences are tailored to employer's needs.

▶ Closing informs addressee of need for confidentiality.

"COLD" LETTER TO A POTENTIAL EMPLOYER
(Campaign Manager)

---

178 Green Street
Omaha, NE 68102
(402) 555-5555

December 23, 20--

Pat Cummings
Lieutenant Governor
State of Nebraska
1140 Main Street
Lincoln, NE 68502

Dear Lieutenant Governor Cummings:

Over the past fourteen years, I have had diverse and progressively responsible experience in development for nonprofit service organizations, universities, and educational institutions. These responsibilities have ranged from Secretary to the Director of Development.

During this period, I have been heavily involved in development strategies, annual fund-raising campaigns, marketing and mailing programs, and media and public relations. Although these positions have been both challenging and exciting, I now feel that my expertise would be put to better use in a new environment, namely, the State of Nebraska.

I would appreciate the opportunity to discuss with you the contribution I can make to the state administration. I will call your office the week of January 9 to schedule a mutually convenient time to meet.

Thank you for your consideration.

Sincerely,

Chris Smith

Enc. Resume

▶ Closing indicates specific date when candidate will follow up inquiry.

▶ Language is straightforward and understandable.

"COLD" LETTER TO A POTENTIAL EMPLOYER
(Chef)

178 Green Street
Clarksville, TN 37044
(615) 555-5555

April 15, 20--

Pat Cummings
Manager
Any Hotel
1140 Main Street
Lexington, KY 40508

Dear Ms. Cummings:

During the past six years, my positions have ranged from Sous Chef to Executive Chef of a restaurant continually rated in the top one hundred restaurants and food service institutions nationwide. My experience includes associations with country clubs, hotels, resorts, and four-star restaurants where I held a variety of positions including, Waiter, Line Cook, and Saute Chef.

Because of my ability to organize, train, and work effectively with personnel in quality, high-volume restaurants, I have been able to always maintain a conscientious, highly productive work force. I have expertise in coordinating activities and directing the indoctrination and training of chefs and other kitchen staff to ensure an efficient and profitable food service.

In addition to being an honors graduate of the Culinary Institute of America, I have received several national and regional awards for my creative culinary skills.

The enclosed resume is a brief summary of my qualifications. I would welcome the chance to discuss the culinary opportunities available at Any Hotel, and will call during the week of May 1 to schedule a meeting.

Thank you for your consideration.

Yours sincerely,

Chris Smith

Enc. Resume

▶ Impressive credentials and awards further enhance candidate's qualifications.

▶ Candidate's most relevant work experience is prioritized.

"COLD" LETTER TO A POTENTIAL EMPLOYER
(Civil Engineer)

178 Green Street
Providence, RI 02903

October 10, 20--

Pat Cummings
Hiring Director
Any Firm
1140 Main Street
New Britain, CT 06050

Dear Mr. Cummings:

I am interested in joining Any Firm's team, specifically the civil engineering division. I have ten years of progressively responsible experience acquired during roadway, civil, site, hazardous waste, and waterfront projects. This is supported by a Bachelor of Science degree in Forest Resource Management, Certification in Surveying Technology, completion of the Fundamentals in Surveying Examination, and hazardous site activities study.

Presently, I am investigating new, broader opportunities where my technical and supervisory skills can be effectively utilized.

If relocation is necessary, then I am ready to make that commitment. I am confident of my ability to make a positive and immediate contribution to your firm and would welcome the opportunity to personally discuss your current or anticipated staffing requirements during a face-to-face or phone interview.

I can be reached at the above address or by phone at (401) 555-5555. I look forward to hearing from you.

Sincerely,

Chris Smith

Enc. Resume

▶ Professional certification and strong educational background add strength to cover letter.

▶ Willingness to relocate can be advantageous.

"COLD" LETTER TO A POTENTIAL EMPLOYER
(Clinical Psychologist)

178 Green Street
Athens, GA 30607
March 14, 20--

Pat Cummings
Chair, Board of Directors
Any Hospital
1140 Main Street
Atlanta, GA 30354

Dear Ms. Cummings:

I am interested in joining the progressive health care team at Any Hospital. The enclosed professional profile is a summary of my academic and clinical experience in private practice, mental health clinics, and HMOs.

My experience as a Clinical Psychologist, Clinical Social Worker, and Research Psychologist spans more than twenty-five years working in clinical, academic, industrial, and community settings, where I have treated individuals, couples, groups, and families. I have the professional qualifications and clinical skills to provide the quality psychotherapeutic and counseling services you require of all your health care providers. I am a board-certified Diplomat in Social Work, full member of AGPA and NEGP, and listed in the National Register for Health Service Providers in Psychology.

If you require additional information, please feel free to contact me at (404) 555-5555. I hope to hear from you shortly.

Sincerely,

Chris Smith

Enc. Professional profile

▶ Job-related affiliations demonstrate candidate's active participation in his/her field.

▶ Closing invites addressee to inquire about additional information.

"COLD" LETTER TO A POTENTIAL EMPLOYER
(Clinical Researcher)

178 Green Street
Pueblo, CO 81001

November 7, 20--

Pat Cummings
Product Development Supervisor
Any Corporation
1140 Main Street
Gunnison, CO 81231

Dear Mr. Cummings:

I am interested in a challenging position requiring product management, product development, and clinical research/nursing skills. Any Corporation's research facility has earned a reputation as the most technologically advanced in the field and, for this reason, I am eager to join your staff.

My expertise includes the management of product development from clinical research for FDA approval to commercial marketability. I offer thirteen years of professional clinical experience with major teaching and trauma hospitals as a Staff R.N. and Therapeutic Apheresis Nurse Specialist. My most recent three years have been spent as Project Manager of Clinical Services and Product Manager with a firm specializing in clinical research and product development, concentrating in applications for autolymphocyte therapy (ALT).

I have excellent communication, computer, and writing skills and am well qualified to assume responsibility for clinical, regulatory, and related functions.

I am anxious to discuss how I might contribute to your organization. Please contact me at the above address, or call (719) 555-5555 to arrange a mutually convenient time for a meeting. Thank you for your consideration.

Sincerely,

Chris Smith, R.N.

Enc. Resume

▶ Specific company information illustrates candidate's commitment to his/her field.

▶ Relevant work experience is emphasized while other positions are omitted.

"COLD" LETTER TO A POTENTIAL EMPLOYER
(Clinical Service Administrator)

178 Green Street
Orono, ME 04473
(207) 555-5555

February 21, 20--

Pat Cummings
Senior Administrator
Any Corporation
1140 Main Street
Portland, ME 04101

Dear Ms. Cummings:

If you are in need of a take-charge professional skilled in clinical service administration as well as quality assurance, utilization review, and risk management, then we have good reason to meet for further discussion.

In addition to a Master of Science degree in Business Administration, I offer thirteen years of progressively responsible, comprehensive experience, including five years in my current position as Director of Service Administration at the medical teaching facility of the University of Maine. In this capacity, I have developed a competent quality assurance support staff, and have provided overall leadership and management for a department that supports and generates input to clinical chiefs in highly technical areas.

The enclosed resume summarizes my qualifications. I would appreciate the opportunity to meet with you in order to discuss in greater detail the mutual benefits of my joining your management team. I will call you on February 28 to schedule a convenient time.

Yours sincerely,

Chris Smith

Enc. Resume

▶ Closing suggests a meeting to follow letter.   ▶ Enclosure line suggests candidate is a meticulous, detail-oriented professional.

"COLD" LETTER TO A POTENTIAL EMPLOYER
(Communications Consultant)

178 Green Street
Wayne, NE 68787

November 11, 20--

Pat Cummings
Program Director
Any Corporation
1140 Main Street
Schenectady, NY 12308

Dear Mr. Cummings:

My interest in a consulting position with a communications company offering potential for advancement has prompted me to forward my resume for your review and evaluation.

In addition to a Bachelor of Arts degree in Political Science/Communications, I have three years of concentrated experience in customer contact and service. My positions have ranged from Data Processing Analyst and Brokerage Service Representative to my most current position as New Business Representative. I have exceptional organizational, communication, and interpersonal skills that I am confident could be effectively utilized in a firm such as yours.

If you have room for a highly motivated achiever in your firm, then we have good reason to meet. I feel strongly that my qualifications can be more fully demonstrated during a personal interview. I am able to travel to Schenectady at your convenience for a discussion. I can be reached at the above address or by phone at (402) 555-5555.

Thank you for your consideration and response.

Sincerely,

Chris Smith

Enc. Resume

▶ Letter avoids abbreviations and slang.　　▶ Letter tailors experience and skills to position applied for.

"COLD" LETTER TO A POTENTIAL EMPLOYER
(Computer Applications Programmer)

178 Green Street
Phoenix, AZ 85004
(602) 555-5555

April 15, 20--

Pat Cummings
Vice-President, Human Resources
Any Corporation
1140 Main Street
Anchorage, AK 99514

Dear Ms. Cummings:

I am seeking a position that requires not only technical expertise, but also decision-making skills to provide support and direction to a growing organization. Any Corporation's innovative MoneyManager software has placed your firm at the forefront of financial application developers. I am anxious to join your programming team. Based on my qualifications, I am confident of my ability to provide you with the technical/business planning and follow-through necessary to develop little more than a concept into a marketable, profitable, and competitive product.

During the past fifteen years, my technical and management experience has ranged from Programmer specializing in communications software to Senior Manager of Data Base Management Products and Systems Performance. In all areas, I have played a key role in the development of products in the volatile environment of changing technology, and, as a result, was the recipient of *Financial Quarterly*'s "Product Manager of the Year" Award in 20--.

The enclosed resume summarizes my background and experience in the areas cited above. Please review my qualifications and contact me so that we can discuss your requirements and mutual objectives. Thank you for your consideration.

Sincerely,

Chris Smith

Enc. Resume

▶ Awards draw attention to candidate's significant accomplishments.

▶ Candidate clearly expresses eagerness to work for specific employer.

"COLD" LETTER TO A POTENTIAL EMPLOYER
(Computer Programmer)

178 Green Street
Bunkie, LA 71322
(318) 555-5555

December 5, 20--

Pat Cummings
Hiring Director
Any Corporation
1140 Main Street
Chicago, IL 60605

Dear Mr. Cummings:

 I am an experienced Computer Programmer and I am ready, willing, and able to join Any Corporation.

 I offer extensive knowledge of five computer languages and strong management, sales, and sales support experience. As a Computer Specialist, I was responsible for the management of a center handling the complete line of Honeywell computers and peripherals for home and commercial use. In addition to a Bachelor of Science degree in Business Administration, I will receive a certificate in Programming in May 20--.

 I feel confident that, given the opportunity, I can make an immediate contribution to Any Corporation. I would appreciate the opportunity to meet with you to discuss your requirements. I will call your office on Tuesday, December 12, to schedule an appointment. Thank you for your consideration.

Sincerely,

Chris Smith

Enc. Resume

▶ First paragraph is short and hard-hitting.

▶ Including telephone number is necessary in a cover letter.

"COLD" LETTER TO A POTENTIAL EMPLOYER
(Computer Software Designer)

178 Green Street
Decorah, IA 52101
(319) 555-5555

February 12, 20--

Pat Cummings
Personnel Director
Any Corporation
1140 Main Street
Cedar Rapids, IA 52402

Dear Ms. Cummings:

As a graduate student who will complete a Master of Science degree in Computer Science in March of this year, a challenging application software or system-oriented position interests me very much.

I believe that my two years of experience as a Data Base Designer, as well as my six months as an Intern at Puttnee Bowles, gives me the necessary capabilities to successfully handle the responsibilities of a Computer Software Designer. I have considerable experience with DBMS packages such as Oracle, Ingres, DB2, Foxpro, and OS/2 Data Manager.

My academic training has provided valuable experience with many languages in the Unix/Windows environment. My education has exposed me to extensive programming assignments, preparing me to work individually and as part of a team. With competency in Fortran, C, SAS, Pascal, and a variety of other programming languages, I am comfortable in SUNOS, DOS, Unix, and VAX operating environments. I have effectively used a variety of graphics, spreadsheet, database, desktop publishing, word processing, and telecommunication applications.

I have a high degree of initiative, as well as the ability to communicate effectively and grasp new concepts quickly. Further, I believe that my analytical skills and experience would positively contribute to the design department of your organization.

I would appreciate the opportunity to discuss my qualifications in a personal interview. I will call your office next Monday to follow up on my inquiry. I look forward to learning more about the software design projects at Any Corporation.

Sincerely,

Chris Smith

Enc. Resume

▶ Technical language is acceptable when it relates to candidate's field.

▶ Internship experience is valuable for candidates with little job experience, particularly if it corresponds to the position sought.

"COLD" LETTER TO A POTENTIAL EMPLOYER
(Consulting/Management Specialist)

178 Green Street
Franklin Park, IL 60131

June 28, 20--

Pat Cummings
Operations Manager
Any Company
1140 Main Street
Skokie, IL 60076

Dear Mr. Cummings:

Is Any Company currently in need of a hardworking and intelligent Consultant/Management Specialist with more than ten years of experience? If so, then please consider the following qualifications.

During the past eight years, I have been actively involved in the development and administration of health and welfare funds and defined contribution plans, and have developed, designed, and implemented medical practice systems. This proficiency has been applied to both union and company requirements. My professional background is supported by a Master of Business Administration, Employee Benefits Specialist Certification, and current candidacy for a Master of Science in Computer Information Systems.

If I possess what you are looking for, please call me at (708) 555-5555. I eagerly await your reply.

Sincerely,

Chris Smith

Enc. Resume

► Opening a letter with a question draws attention to candidate.

► Educational credentials strengthen cover letter.

"COLD" LETTER TO A POTENTIAL EMPLOYER
(Controller)

178 Green Street
Sioux Falls, SD 57102

July 22, 20--

Pat Cummings
Hiring Officer
Any Corporation
1140 Main Street
Richmond, VA 23219

Dear Ms. Cummings:

During the past eight years I have held numerous progressively responsible positions in the areas of general accounting, business, office management, and project management.

Currently I am seeking a new association with a company where I can apply my experience and skills toward both company and personal goals.

I consider myself to be well-organized, self-motivated, and productive. I am open to additional training and am looking for a position that offers advancement based on ability to perform.

The enclosed resume summarizes my background and experience. I am available at your earliest convenience to discuss my qualifications with you during a personal interview. I can be reached at the above address or by phone at (605) 555-5555.

Thank you in advance for your response.

Sincerely,

Chris Smith

Enc. Resume

▶ Discussion of experience indicates a series of promotions.

▶ Discussion of personal qualities reiterates candidate's ability to contribute to potential employer.

"COLD" LETTER TO A POTENTIAL EMPLOYER
(Country Club Manager)

178 Green Street
West Palm Beach, FL 33405
(407) 555-5555

April 13, 20--

Pat Cummings
Owner
Any Country Club
1140 Main Street
Sarasota, FL 34236

Dear Mr. Cummings:

I am writing to inquire about available management positions at Any Country Club. I have been an active member since 20--, and my familiarity with the club and its members would make me an excellent candidate for your consideration.

I am presently employed in a position that has presented challenges and personal satisfaction for a job well done. However, I feel that my education, training, and experience have prepared me for a broader scope of responsibility, and for this reason I am seeking a change.

I would like to associate with a quality facility in the hospitality industry that maintains high standards for services offered to guests or members. Based on my education and employment history, I believe I can play a key role in achieving our mutual goals for success and profit by providing cost-effective management.

The enclosed resume summarizes my qualifications. I would welcome the opportunity to discuss my ability to meet your expectations for club management positions. Please contact me to schedule a mutually convenient time for an interview.

Thank you. I look forward to talking with you.

Sincerely,

Chris Smith

Enc. Resume

▶ Letter focuses on the needs of the employer, not the job candidate.

▶ Type of position desired is clearly stated.

"COLD" LETTER TO A POTENTIAL EMPLOYER
(Editorial Assistant)

178 Green Street
New York, NY 10020
(212) 555-5555

March 13, 20--

Pat Cummings
Personnel Director
Any Corporation
1140 Main Street
Chicago, IL 60605

Dear Ms. Cummings:

I would like to inquire about upcoming entry-level editorial openings with Any Corporation.

I am presently a senior in good standing at New York University, due to graduate in May of this year. I am pursuing a Bachelor of Arts degree with a major in Journalism and minors in both Economics and English Literature. I am proficient in both WordPerfect and Microsoft Word, and am familiar with the operation of both PCs and Macintosh machines. I am presently working as a Research Intern for the economics division of Tradewinds Publishing in Newark.

Enclosed you will find a copy of my resume. Letters of recommendation from employers and professors, as well as writing samples, will gladly be provided at your request. I will contact you next week about the possibility of arranging a meeting at your convenience.

I look forward to speaking with you.

Sincerely,

Chris Smith

Enc. Resume

▶ Relevant internship bolsters otherwise limited work experience.

▶ Computer skills listed are related to candidate's field of interest.

"COLD" LETTER TO A POTENTIAL EMPLOYER
(Electrician)

178 Green Street
Lawrence, KS 66409

September 14, 20--

Pat Cummings
Staff Coordinator
Any Corporation
1140 Main Street
Topeka, KS 66607

Dear Mr. Cummings:

I am currently investigating availabilities in electrical operations, and would like to submit my qualifications for your review.

Although I am a newly licensed Journeyman Electrician, I have nine years of experience in the field, five as an Apprentice and four as a Journeyman, handling a variety of electrical installations while working with electrical contractors and as a subcontractor. I am capable of working independently or as a member of a team and feel confident in my ability to handle multiple responsibilities and provide quality performance on any assignment I undertake.

The enclosed resume is a brief summary of my experience. I would appreciate the opportunity to further discuss my qualifications, and with that in mind, I will contact your division next Wednesday to schedule a meeting. Should you require additional information, please contact me at the above address or by phone at (913) 555-5555.

I am very interested in joining Any Corporation and look forward to your return reply.

Yours sincerely,

Chris Smith

Enc. Resume

▶ Candidate includes licensure relevant to his/her field.

▶ Closing informs addressee that resume is enclosed.

"COLD" LETTER TO A POTENTIAL EMPLOYER
(Electromechanical Drafter)

178 Green Street
New Castle, DE 19720
(302) 555-5555

November 20, 20--

Pat Cummings
Chief Engineer
Any Corporation
1140 Main Street
Easton, PA 18044

Dear Ms. Cummings:

As a recent graduate with an Associate degree in Electromechanical Drafting, with concentration in Electromechanical Technology, my goal is to join a firm where I can apply my skills in a drafting environment.

Since 20--, I have held responsible part-time positions as a Marine Technician and a Mason Tender while earning my degree. Able to handle assignments individually or as a team member, I am computer literate, and people-oriented, have good communication skills, and relate well to all levels of authority. Now I am seeking an opportunity for personal development and advancement based on the quality of my technical performance.

My resume provides a summary of my education, background, and experience, but I strongly feel that during the course of a personal interview my potential for making a significant contribution to your firm can be more fully demonstrated. I am hopeful that we can set up a mutually convenient appointment in the near future.

Should you require additional information, please contact me at the above address or phone number. I look forward to your return response.

Yours sincerely,

Chris Smith

Enc. Resume

▶ Part-time work experience during school indicates candidate's strong work ethic.

▶ Closing refers addressee to telephone number in return address.

"COLD" LETTER TO A POTENTIAL EMPLOYER
(Elementary School Teacher)

178 Green Street
Lubbock, TX 79408
(806) 555-5555

July 7, 20--

Pat Cummings, Ph.D.
Superintendent
Any Public School
1140 Main Street
Chickasha, OK 73023

Dear Dr. Cummings:

My interest in contributing to the enhancement of elementary education within the Any Public School System has prompted to forward the enclosed resume for your review and consideration.

Currently, as an Elementary School Teacher responsible for thirty second-grade students, I am actively involved in the development and implementation of reading, writing, and math programs that effectively motivate accomplishment through both individual and group projects. My professional training and experience began with the Rockford Public School System as a Student Teacher at Roosevelt Elementary School and as a Substitute Teacher at various locations within the system. I completed a Bachelor of Arts degree in Elementary Education in May 20--.

Additionally, I have been instrumental in instituting and selecting educational software for a Windows-based PC, system as well as instructing the teaching staff on its use. Presently, I am formulating a proposal to initiate the establishment of a high-ability learning program.

I am confident of my ability to stimulate and motivate children toward personal growth and achievement. I would welcome the opportunity to meet with you to discuss your current staffing requirements. In the interim, if any additional information is required, please contact me at the above address or phone number.

Sincerely,

Chris Smith

Enc. Resume

▶ Computer skills listed are related to candidate's field of interest.

▶ Candidate tailors letter to his/her field of interest.

"COLD" LETTER TO A POTENTIAL EMPLOYER
(Engineer)

178 Green Street
Sacramento, CA 95852

July 20, 20--

Pat Cummings
Project Manager
Any Corporation
1140 Main Street
Modesto, CA 95354

Dear Mr. Cummings:

Are you in need of a highly qualified Engineer to successfully complete diverse construction projects? If so, I would like to offer my resume for your consideration.

In addition to a Bachelor of Science degree with a concentration in Civil Engineering, I hold two Associates degrees in related subjects. My professional experience spans ten years during which I have held progressively responsible part-time and full-time positions in construction. My expertise includes construction of schools, parking areas, museums, medical facilities, office buildings, and other structures. I am experienced in supervision, engineering layout, construction coordination, purchasing, and many aspects related to the organization and business of construction.

After reviewing my resume, if you have a place in your organization for an experienced professional who works only to high standards of excellence, I hope you will contact me at the above address, or call (916) 555-5555. I would like to arrange a personal interview, during which we can further discuss my potential for service at Any Corporation.

Thank you for your consideration.

Sincerely,

Chris Smith

Enc. Resume

▶ Discussion of experience is very specific.　　　▶ Closing encourages reader to respond to letter.

"COLD" LETTER TO A POTENTIAL EMPLOYER
(Engineering Instructor)

178 Green Street
Macon, GA 31201
(912) 555-5555

August 20, 20--

Pat Cummings
Headmaster
Any School
1140 Main Street
Evansville, IN 47713

Dear Ms. Cummings:

If you are in need of an Engineering Instructor to teach accredited classroom courses or conduct in-house seminars and training, then we have good reason to meet for further discussion.

I have extensive experience in teaching courses on proposal writing, pricing, component design, and equipment operation and control. My practical expertise is in electromechanical design and the analysis of mechanical systems. In addition, I offer five years of experience teaching engineering.

My experience as an Engineer, Principal Engineer Manager, Author, and Technical Writer is extensive. I am skilled in preparing and presenting complex technical reports to corporate clients and/or company management in support of contracts or proposed new developments. Currently, I am interested in joining an educational system where I can impart my engineering knowledge, experience, and writing skills to students in an academic or vocational environment, preferably on a per diem or course assignment basis. I have an excellent grasp of highly sophisticated systems and instrumentation, and I can provide your students with essential technical knowledge and support.

I would appreciate the opportunity to discuss my qualifications. I will call the school next week to schedule an interview. In the meantime, I have enclosed my professional profile for your review. Thank you for your time.

Sincerely,

Chris Smith

Enc. Professional profile

▶ Four short paragraphs is the ideal length for a cover letter.

▶ Letter focuses on acquired skills relevant to field of interest.

"COLD" LETTER TO A POTENTIAL EMPLOYER
(Esthetician)

178 Green Street
Hartford, CT 06115

April 2, 20--

Pat Cummings
Vice-President, Personnel
Any Corporation
1140 Main Street
New Haven, CT 06511

Dear Mr. Cummings:

Currently I am seeking a position with the international sales/marketing division of Any Corporation. I offer professional expertise in opening new markets, launching new salons/spas, introducing beauty products and services, and training personnel.

I am a Licensed Esthetician who, during the past ten years, has held positions in France as Director of Education for a manufacturer of beauty products sold to select European spas and in the United States as Skin Care Director for an exclusive beauty spa.

I am a multilingualist fluent in French (native speaker) and German, and I feel confident that I could make a valuable contribution toward increasing your product name visibility and market share in today's increasingly global economy.

I would appreciate the opportunity to discuss your requirements for penetrating international markets. Should you require additional information, please contact me at the above address or by phone at (203) 555-5555.

I look forward to your return response.

Sincerely,

Chris Smith

Enc. Resume

▶ International work experience and foreign language fluency add weight to candidate's qualifications.

▶ Candidate immediately expresses suitability for desired position.

"COLD" LETTER TO A POTENTIAL EMPLOYER
(Executive Secretary)

178 Green Street
Allentown, PA 18105

August 5, 20--

Pat Cummings
Human Resources Manager
Any Corporation
1140 Main Street
Philadelphia, PA 19130

Dear Ms. Cummings:

If you are in need of an Executive Secretary who can double as an Administrative Assistant and handle the day-to-day details necessary to keep an operation running smoothly, then we have good reason to meet.

During the past seven years, I have provided administrative support to senior-level officers and account executives in a domestic and international sales and marketing environment. Although this position has been interesting, I am presently considering a position change with a company offering greater responsibility and growth potential than is possible with my present employer.

So that I can be considered for a position with your firm, I am enclosing a copy of my professional profile for your review. I would appreciate the opportunity to discuss my past achievements, along with ways in which I might excel in a future position with Any Corporation.

Thank you for reviewing my credentials. I can be reached at the above address or by phone between 9 A.M. and 1 P.M. at (215) 555-5555.

Sincerely,

Chris Smith

Enc. Professional profile

▶ Candidate expresses best time of day to be reached in closing.

▶ Letter is short and to the point.

"COLD" LETTER TO A POTENTIAL EMPLOYER
(Facilities Specialist)

178 Green Street
Riverside, CA 92502
(714) 555-5555

December 28, 20--

Pat Cummings
Human Resources Manager
Any Corporation
1140 Main Street
Fresno, CA 93786

Dear Mr. Cummings:

I am interested in exploring the possibility of joining your company as a Facilities Specialist, or in a related role. The enclosed resume provides you with information concerning my background and abilities.

For more than seven years, I have been employed in the commercial interior design field. During this time, I have progressed from Draftsperson to Project Manager. I have successfully designed and implemented a variety of new systems and procedures during my tenure, and have been recognized for having effected considerable increased revenues and measurable cost savings.

I admire Any Corporation's position on the cutting edge of design and I am anxious to join your firm. I would appreciate the opportunity for a personal interview at your convenience to discuss how my skills and abilities would be assets to your organization. If you desire further information at this time, I will be happy to supply whatever you need.

Thank you again for your time. I will call the week of January 16 to schedule a mutually convenient meeting time.

Sincerely,

Chris Smith

Enc. Resume

▶ In closing, candidate specifically requests interview.

▶ Letter incorporates company knowledge into discussion of qualifications.

"COLD" LETTER TO A POTENTIAL EMPLOYER
(Field Coordinator)

178 Green Street
Greenville, SC 29601
(803) 555-5555

July 10, 20--

Pat Cummings
Chief Executive Director
Any Campaign
1140 Main Street
Clinton, SC 29325

Dear Ms. Cummings:

Are you searching for a dynamic Field Coordinator or Campaign Manager for your upcoming campaign?

During the past two years, both my graduate education at the University of Southern Carolina and my professional experience have been focused on government issues and political campaigns. I have worked as a Campaign Manager, Field Coordinator, Volunteer Organizer, and Fund Raiser.

My motivation has always been toward a "behind-the-scenes" career in politics that would allow me to play a key role in electing qualified candidates, the kind who can make a significant difference for the constituents they represent. As the enclosed resume reflects, I have had experience with numerous campaigns on the local, state, and federal levels. I feel confident that I have the skills necessary to make voters aware of the importance of electing your candidate into office.

I will call your office on Wednesday, July 19, to assure receipt of my letter and to schedule an interview. Thank you for your consideration. I am eager to join your team!

Sincerely,

Chris Smith

Enc. Resume

▶ Letter clarifies candidate's career goals.　　　▶ Closing reiterates candidate's interest in position.

"COLD" LETTER TO A POTENTIAL EMPLOYER
(Financial Associate)

178 Green Street
Eugene, OR 97401
(503) 555-5555

October 17, 20--

Pat Cummings
Human Resources Director
Any Corporation
1140 Main Street
Portland, OR 97201

Dear Mr. Cummings:

I am a new graduate with a Bachelor of Arts degree in Political Science who can offer your firm dedication, skill, and a willingness to learn your industry while aspiring to performance-based advancement.

My interests are in business, investments, and finance. In keeping with these, I have developed a strong work ethic, which is evidenced by the fact that I have maintained a part-time job throughout my four years of college. My work has included operating my own successful small business, as well as employment with outside firms and internships related to my career interests. I function equally well working independently or as a member of a team, and feel confident that given the opportunity, I can make a positive difference as a member of your organization.

The enclosed resume summarizes my experience. I am eager to meet for an interview during which I can fully express my capacity and desire to contribute to Any Corporation. I will call your office the week of October 23 to schedule an appointment.

Thank you for your time and consideration. I look forward to speaking with you in the near future.

Sincerely,

Chris Smith

Enc. Resume

▶ Part-time work experience during school indicates candidate's strong work ethic.

▶ Letter expresses commitment to field of interest.

"COLD" LETTER TO A POTENTIAL EMPLOYER
(Financial Consultant)

178 Green Street
Clinton, MS 39058

May 8, 20--

Pat Cummings
Manager, Accounts Receivable
Any Corporation
1140 Main Street
Florence, MS 39073

Dear Ms. Cummings:

As a Credit and Collections Consultant, I have been instrumental in substantially improving accounts receivable management and cash flow control, while reducing bad debt risk, for a rapidly growing, high-tech company.

Because of my performance during the past twelve years as Staff Accountant, Credit Analyst, Credit and Collections Manager, and Consultant, I have been consistently retained by new management during several acquisitions, mergers, and consolidations. I have held positions that have provided me with increasingly responsible experiences and challenges. However, due to the planned move of my function to Canadian headquarters, I am currently investigating new consulting opportunities with companies that can benefit from my expertise as a Credit and Collections Specialist dedicated to improving their cash position.

Despite current economic conditions, I am confident of my ability to establish and manage credit and collection systems, procedures and controls, and employee training programs that will generate the same positive results as experienced by my current employer.

The enclosed profile is a summary of my experience. I would appreciate the chance to discuss your credit/collection problems and my ability to arrive at solutions that will achieve positive financial results without alienating your customer base. I will call your office on May 15 to arrange a mutually convenient time for an interview.

Should you require additional information prior to my call, please contact me at the above address or by phone at (601) 555-5555. I look forward to your return response.

Sincerely,

Chris Smith

Enc. Professional profile

▶ Job descriptions emphasize candidate's accomplishments.

▶ Candidate discusses how past business experience can benefit potential employer.

"COLD" LETTER TO A POTENTIAL EMPLOYER
(Financial Planner)

178 Green Street
Gardenia, ND 58739

April 15, 20--

Pat Cummings
Personnel Manager
Any Corporation
1140 Main Street
Chicago, IL 60605

Dear Mr. Cummings:

Having had the opportunity to meet with Deborah Sturgis and the rest of the staff at the Fargo office, I am very much interested in starting my career in finance at Any Corporation.

I am planning a permanent relocation to the Chicago area in the late summer. Therefore, I am submitting my resume for consideration for admittance into your Financial Planner Training Program.

Please note that I am currently completing my senior year at North Dakota University and will receive my Bachelor of Science degree with a major in Accounting and a concentration in Computer Programming this May. Throughout four years of college, and during full-time and part-time employment, I have continued to strengthen my focus in these areas. In addition, I have excellent problem-solving skills and feel that, given the opportunity, I would be both an immediate and long-term asset to your firm.

While my resume is a good summary of my qualification, I feel strongly that my potential to be of service to your organization could be more fully demonstrated during a personal interview. I plan to be in the Chicago area the week of May 1 and would welcome the opportunity to meet with you. I will follow up with a phone call on April 25 to arrange such a meeting. In the interim I can be reached at the above address or by telephone at (701) 555-5555.

Thank you for your time and consideration.

Sincerely,

Chris Smith

Enc. Resume

► Candidate immediately introduces purpose for writing.

► Candidate indicates time frame for follow-up contact.

"COLD" LETTER TO A POTENTIAL EMPLOYER
(Flight Attendant)

178 Green Street
Helena, MT 59601
(406) 555-5555

January 3, 20--

Pat Cummings
Attendant Supervisor
Any Airline
1140 Main Street
Phoenix, AZ 85023

Dear Ms. Cummings:

I am an ambitious, career-oriented, energetic individual with a keen interest in becoming a Flight Attendant for Any Airline.

I possess six years of diverse business experience in both the retail and hospitality industries. I understand the importance of excellent customer/public relations and support, along with strong communication skills, for maintaining efficient airline operations and a strong, positive public image.

I feel confident that, given the opportunity, I can make an immediate contribution to the flight system at Any Airline. I would appreciate the chance to personally sit down with you to discuss your requirements and my ability to meet them.

I look forward to meeting with you.

Yours sincerely,

Chris Smith

Enc. Resume

▶ Discussion of personal qualities reiterates candidate's ability to contribute to potential employer.

▶ Closing reiterates candidate's interest in specific corporation.

"COLD" LETTER TO A POTENTIAL EMPLOYER
(Foreperson/Ironworker)

178 Green Street
Spartanburg, SC 29304

August 4, 20--

Pat Cummings
Personnel Manager
Any Corporation
1140 Main Street
Sioux City, IA 51102

Dear Mr. Cummings:

Please accept the enclosed resume as indication of my interest in securing a position with Any Corporation. During the past ten years, my career has grown steadily. I began as Journeyman Ironworker/Foreman Ironworker with Local #10, and have progressed to Senior Project Manager, with responsibility for constructing commercial and industrial steel buildings in the United States and Canada.

I am an effective negotiator skilled in dealing with subcontractors, vendors, and suppliers, and in the coordination and scheduling of manpower, equipment, and materials to meet deliveries, time schedules, and budgets. I am well qualified to assume responsibilities for projects from pre-job site inspections to final completion.

I would welcome the chance to personally discuss my capabilities and your anticipated requirements. Please contact me at the above address or by phone at (803) 555-5555 to arrange for a mutually convenient time for such a meeting.

Thank you for your consideration and early response.

Sincerely,

Chris Smith

Enc. Resume

▶ Letter focuses on candidate's past job experience while incorporating functional qualifications.

▶ Candidate expresses knowledge in his/her field of interest.

"COLD" LETTER TO A POTENTIAL EMPLOYER
(Fund Raiser)

178 Green Street
Rollins College, FL 32789
(407) 555-5555

June 1, 20--

Pat Cummings
Staff Coordinator
Any Organization
1140 Main Street
Orlando, FL 32809

Dear Ms. Cummings:

As a committed, creative, and industrious professional eager to use my skills in a challenging fundraising position, I am very interested in learning more about the opportunities available at Any Organization.

My experience in nonprofit development, public relations, and especially fundraising, would be a strong asset to your organization. I have spent more than three years as the Development and Public Relations Assistant at the Women's Educational Society, where my experience has encompassed preparing grant proposals, compiling program books for fund-raising events, writing correspondences for the executive director, contributing to the quarterly newsletter, and generating donation acknowledgments. I am involved with the implementation of two yearly appeals, and publish the employee newsletter. In addition, as a member of the Executive Committee for my alumni class at Rollins College, I produce a quarterly newsletter, compiling news from more than 1,500 classmates.

I am Macintosh and PC literate, and I am familiar with many of the most popular word processing programs. I am not afraid to tackle new challenges, as evidenced by the fact that I taught myself desktop publishing on a Macintosh in order to produce my alumni newsletter. In addition, I am solely responsible for the fundraising database program in my office, which involves updating and maintaining donor records, generating daily income reports and financial analyses, and training staff and volunteers in data entry procedures.

I have enclosed a resume, as well as copy of my employee newsletter and a program book to serve as writing samples. Please contact me if you need further information. Thank you.

Sincerely,

Chris Smith

Enc. Resume, Writing samples

▶ Candidate's most recent position is outlined in detail.

▶ Letter emphasizes achievements, and does not simply list job responsibilities.

"COLD" LETTER TO A POTENTIAL EMPLOYER
(Graphic Artist)

178 Green Street
Bridgeville, PA 15017
(412) 555-5555

September 20, 20--

Pat Cummings
Director of Human Resources
Any Corporation
1140 Main Street
New York, NY 10108

Dear Mr. Cummings:

I am extremely interested in putting my graphics expertise to work for Any Corporation. Your great successes in the past year, including your six-figure accounts with Kitters Cola and the Mooburger Company, impressed all of us in the advertising business. Now I want to get in on the fun and excitement! Enclosed is a copy of my resume.

I operate from my own computerized studio where I design using the latest graphic-related hardware and software. I offer extensive experience in:

- Designing marketing literature with QuarkXpress, Aldus Freehand, and Photoshop.
- Preparing complicated files on the Macintosh as final mechanicals, for direct export to the printing company.
- Communicating and working directly with clients, supervisors, and department heads.
- Estimating jobs firsthand and working directly with vendors.
- Directing graphic art departments and supervising projects.

Do my credentials sound suitable for a position at Any Corporation? I would be more than happy to meet with you and show you a portfolio of my work at your convenience. I will call your office next week to schedule an interview. Thank you for your consideration.

Sincerely,

Chris Smith

Enc. Resume

▶ Bulleted statements highlight candidate's on-the-job achievements.

▶ Letter reveals candidate's continued research in his/her field of interest.

"COLD" LETTER TO A POTENTIAL EMPLOYER
(Head Nurse)

178 Green Street
Woodland Hills, CA 91367
(818) 555-5555

May 29, 20--

Pat Cummings, R.N.
Director of Nursing
Any Facility
1140 Main Street
Long Beach, CA 90844

Dear Ms. Cummings:

Last week, I read an article in the *Press Telegram* praising Any Facility's excellent staff and patient services among area health care centers. I am looking for a nursing opportunity in the Long Beach area, and this piece confirmed my desire to join your esteemed organization.

I offer more than twelve years of experience ranging from Nursing Assistant and Charge Nurse to Nursing Supervisor for a 120-bed, multilevel nursing facility catering to patients afflicted with Alzheimer's, renal disease, and other chronic geriatric conditions. My experience encompasses diverse areas of health care supervision, including patient assessment and staff development, as well as the coordination of such resident care services as physical therapy, dietary, housekeeping, pharmacy, and social services.

I am interested in joining the staff at Any Facility. I would welcome the opportunity to arrange a mutually convenient time in which we could further discuss your current or anticipated needs in terms of my qualifications.

Thank you for your consideration.

Sincerely,

Chris Smith, R.N.

Enc. Resume

▶ Letter outlines series of promotions.

▶ Letter emphasizes candidate's strong work history.

"COLD" LETTER TO A POTENTIAL EMPLOYER
(Health Services Coordinator)

178 Green Street
Providence, RI 02903

January 8, 20--

Pat Cummings
Controller
Any Corporation
1140 Main Street
Providence, RI 02903

Dear Mr. Cummings:

Over the past fifteen years, I have been involved in many aspects of health care administration and management. Currently I am seeking a senior-level position in home/health care services in a public health hospital or hospital-based home care agency, where I can apply my expertise in the planning and administration of service delivery systems.

In addition to a Master of Science degree in Community Health Nursing, I have extensive experience in home care program planning, as well as all areas of proposal writing and funding requests, budget administration, and third-party payments.

The enclosed resume summarizes my background and experience in the areas I have cited above. I would appreciate the opportunity to meet with you to discuss your professional requirements and my ability to direct an organization, such as yours, that is dedicated to quality health care systems and services.

I feel confident, based on my strong academic and professional credentials, that I can create an effective professional environment. If you require additional information, please feel free to contact me at the above address, or by phone at (401) 555-5555.

Thank you for your consideration.

Yours sincerely,

Chris Smith

Enc. Resume

▶ Closing reiterates candidate's qualifications for position.　　▶ Unrelated work experience is omitted.

"COLD" LETTER TO A POTENTIAL EMPLOYER
(Human Resources Professional)

178 Green Street
Grenvil, NE 68941
(402) 555-5555

October 19, 20--

Pat Cummings
Staff Coordinator
Any Corporation
1140 Main Street
St. Louis, MI 63130

Dear Ms. Cummings:

I am writing regarding opportunities your firm may have for experienced human resources professionals.

I have a solid track record as a Human Resources Generalist working in a fast-paced environment with a reputable professional services firm in the Omaha area. I have successfully provided staff planning, recruiting, and employee relations support for several of the firm's key high-technology practices, which provide systems engineering and management consulting services. In addition, I have more than six years of solid accomplishment as a Management Analyst, Systems Analyst, and Environmental Management Consultant providing technical and management services to both government and commercial clients.

I am now seeking new and challenging responsibilities in an organization that would benefit from my background and specific mix of skills. I am willing to relocate and/or travel for the right opportunity.

Perhaps we could meet soon to discuss available openings at Any Corporation? Thank you for your time and consideration.

Sincerely,

Chris Smith

Enc. Resume

▶ Letter stresses candidate's extensive experience and significant accomplishments.

▶ Candidate uses closing to suggest possibility of interview.

"COLD" LETTER TO A POTENTIAL EMPLOYER
(Human Services Coordinator)

178 Green Street
Washington, DC 20024

November 6, 20--

Pat Cummings
Director
Any Agency
1140 Main Street
Washington DC 20005

Dear Mr. Cummings:

During the past ten years, my experience has been concentrated as an Area Office Manager and Child Advocate Coordinator in the coordination and management of human services information and resources for multicultural, multilingual populations in the Washington, D.C. area.

Currently, I am seeking a new association with an agency, in the public or private sector, which has a need for a qualified professional. I can offer broad experience working with and coordinating the efforts of, public, private, and charitable resources, educational systems, and providers of human services to community residents or company employees.

I am especially interested in the field of human services as I am dedicated to improving the quality of life and learning for the less fortunate. I possess strong organizational, communication, and teaching skills, as well as the ability to work well under stressful or crisis situations.

I would be glad to make myself available for an interview at your convenience to discuss how I might put my knowledge and experience to work for Any Agency. Should you require additional information prior to our meeting, please contact me at the above address or by phone at (202) 555-5555. I plan to make a follow-up call within a few days.

I look forward to speaking with you.

Yours sincerely,

Chris Smith

Enc. Resume

▶ Dedication to candidate's field of interest is emphasized.

▶ Related work experience is accentuated.

"COLD" LETTER TO A POTENTIAL EMPLOYER
(Insurance Salesperson)

178 Green Street
Lubbock, TX 79408
(806) 555-5555

July 16, 20--

Pat Cummings
Sales Director
Any Insurance Company
1140 Main Street
Houston, TX 77027

Dear Ms. Cummings:

Currently, I am seeking a new association within the insurance industry where I can apply my combined knowledge experience to the sale of insurance products and services. I am interested in a home office staff or sales position where there is opportunity for increased responsibility and compensation based on personal performance.

During the past thirteen years, I have built a successful career in the insurance industry, first as a Sales Representative with Unlimited Trust Insurance and then for ten years with Lubbock Mutual Life Insurance. In both positions I established myself as a consistent top producer selling a broad scope of insurance and investment products to businesses and individuals.

I have enclosed a resume for your consideration. I am anxious to discuss in greater detail my credentials for contributing to the profitability and increased customer satisfaction of your firm. Please contact me so that we may explore the possibility of a mutually beneficial association. Thank you.

Sincerely,

Chris Smith

Enc. Resume

▶ Job descriptions indicate how candidate contributed to his/her previous employers.

▶ Letter immediately states candidate's purpose.

"COLD" LETTER TO A POTENTIAL EMPLOYER
(Interior Designer)

178 Green Street
Lindsay, NE 68644
(402) 555-5555

May 18, 20--

Pat Cummings
Senior Interior Designer
Any Design Company
1140 Main Street
Lincoln, NE 68521

Dear Mr. Cummings:

I am an energetic, creative, career-oriented individual with a genuine interest in pursuing a professional career in the area of interior design. For this reason, I am forwarding my resume for your consideration.

Please note that in addition to a Bachelor of Arts degree in Interior Design/Visual Arts, I have more than seven years of part-time and full-time experience encompassing the sale and follow-through of complete design concepts for both commercial and residential clientele.

Throughout my career, I have kept myself updated on trends and major players in the industry. I am familiar with your work at Any Design Company and would be honored to join your talented team. Could we meet for further discussion? I would love to show you my portfolio and convince you of my abilities.

I look forward to hearing from you.

Sincerely,

Chris Smith

Enc. Resume

▶ Stating that a portfolio is available on request is beneficial for certain positions.

▶ Closing reiterates candidate's knowledge of organization.

"COLD" LETTER TO A POTENTIAL EMPLOYER
(International Sales Associate)

178 Green Street
Los Angeles, CA 90066
(213) 555-5555

April 1, 20--

Pat Cummings
Controller
Any Corporation
1140 Main Street
Boston, MA 02215

Dear Ms. Cummings:

During the past fifteen years I have played a key role in the development of international markets for the sale of capital and laboratory equipment, systems, and services. Currently, I am seeking a new position with a firm that can benefit from my expertise in the development of profitable overseas markets. Any Corporation's commitment to developing overseas accounts makes me eager to join your international team.

Throughout my career in foreign service and international sales, I have developed and currently maintain excellent personal, business, and government contacts with key product movers in pharmaceuticals, cosmetics, and chemical manufacturing; food processors; scientific laboratories; and health institutions worldwide.

My peers and associates consider me to be a goal setter and achiever, and I am confident I can produce the same beneficial results in the development of international markets for your products that I have for my present employer. If you can use an executive who is thoroughly familiar with international market development and sales, I would like to discuss my qualifications with you during a personal interview. At that time, I will be glad to expand on my experience and answer any questions you might have. I will call your office next week to schedule a mutually convenient meeting time.

Sincerely,

Chris Smith

Enc. Resume

▶ International work experience adds weight to candidate's qualifications.

▶ Letter clarifies candidate's career goals.

"COLD" LETTER TO A POTENTIAL EMPLOYER
(Jewelry Designer)

178 Green Street
Fresno, CA 93786
(209) 555-5555

August 15, 20--

Pat Cummings
Creative Director
Any Corporation
1140 Main Street
Los Angeles, CA 90053

Dear Mr. Cummings:

Of all the fine jewelry designs being produced today, in my estimation yours is singularly the best. I would like to put my talent as a Jewelry Designer to work for Any Corporation.

I have devoted the past seven years to developing and refining my design skills while maximizing my technical knowledge. In addition to producing my own designs, I currently work as a model maker for Gemmz, Inc., a Fresno-based jewelry maker. Over the course of my career, I have continued to make several significant contributions to the field of jewelry design:

- Three of my designs were featured as part of Gemmz's flagship line at the 20-- International Jewelry Bazaar.
- Developed a buffing method in our Fresno production facility that is being implemented nationwide.
- Earned a fine arts degree in jewelry design.
- Won several design awards.

I would like to discuss some of the options available at Any Corporation and the possibility of my designing jewelry for you. I will call on September 1 to arrange an interview.

Thank you for your consideration.

Sincerely,

Chris Smith

Enc. Resume

▶ Bullets provide a clear and crisp presentation.

▶ Career objective is supported by awards and accomplishments.

"COLD" LETTER TO A POTENTIAL EMPLOYER
(Jewelry Sales/Buyer)

178 Green Street
Neptune, NJ 07754
(415) 555-5555

July 18, 20--

Pat Cummings
General Manager
Any Store
1140 Main Street
Cherry Hill, NJ 08002

Dear Ms. Cummings:

I am a recent graduate of the Gemological Institute of America with a year of successful experience in the purchase and sale of precious metals, gems, and antique jewelry.

Currently, I am looking for a new position with a major jewelry store where I can apply my sales and customer relations skills to continue my proven track record of increasing profit and market share. During my year at Monahan Jewelers, I was responsible for increasing company sales by 10 percent while creating a substantially larger customer base.

The enclosed resume summarizes my experience. I am very much interested in Any Store because of your top-notch reputation in the field. I am confident of my ability to represent you in an ethical and professional manner, and look forward to hearing from you soon.

Yours sincerely,

Chris Smith

Enc. Resume

▶ Closing reiterates candidate's interest in specific corporation.

▶ Letter focuses attention on candidate's major skills and accomplishments.

"COLD" LETTER TO A POTENTIAL EMPLOYER
(Landscape Designer)

178 Green Street
Puyallip, WA 98374
(206) 555-5555

July 6, 20--

Pat Cummings
Manager
Any Corporation
1140 Main Street
Seattle, WA 98109

Dear Mr. Cummings:

During the past twenty-five years, my education, training, and experience have been concentrated as an Arborist and Landscape Designer; for nineteen of those years I have been with the same tree and landscape company. Although my projects were diverse and have afforded me the opportunity to work with clients on creative project design and maintenance, I am ready for a change.

I am interested in bringing my experience and education to a distinguished corporate entity such as Any Corporation. As a seasoned, dependable professional skilled in creative planning and maintenance, I believe I have much to offer your firm. In addition to my hands-on experience, I am a certified Arborist and hold a Bachelor of Science in Environmental Design from the University of Washington in Seattle.

The enclosed resume is a summary of my qualifications. I look forward to the opportunity to discuss, in detail, your requirements and my ability to perform the responsibilities the position of Landscape Designer would demand at Any Corporation.

Should you require any additional information, please contact me at the above address or by phone. I look forward to your return response.

Yours sincerely,

Chris Smith

Enc. Resume

▶ Candidate refers to attached resume in closing.

▶ Qualifications are geared to candidate's field of interest.

"COLD" LETTER TO A POTENTIAL EMPLOYER
(Lawyer)

178 Green Street
Glendale Heights, IL 60139
(708) 555-5555

February 26, 20--

Pat Cummings
Hiring Coordinator
Any Law Firm
1140 Main Street
Chicago, IL 60606

Dear Ms. Cummings:

    I am a 20-- graduate of Chicago-Kent College of Law interested in a position as an Associate with Any Law Firm. I am particularly interested in the firm's real estate, corporate, finance, and litigation departments.

    As my enclosed resume indicates, upon graduation I accepted a job with the Chicago-based law firm Glavin and Joyce. As a first-year associate, I worked in the firm's litigation, real estate, finance, and corporate departments. In May of 20--, I accepted a position with the Brussels-based international consulting firm Brunkhorst and Associates. On their behalf, I act as a consultant and advisor on American law as it relates to the offshore funding of U.S. commercial real estate.

    Although I enjoy my present position, I would very much like to become associated with an up-and-coming firm such as yours so that I can continue my development as a lawyer. My association with a well-established, full-service law firm would also enable me to better service Brunkhorst and Associates and its clients.

    If my qualifications are of interest to you, I would like to visit your offices for an interview. I will contact you Monday, March 4, to discuss available opportunities. Thank you for your attention and I look forward to speaking with you.

Sincerely,

Chris Smith

Enc. Resume

▶ Candidate tailors letter to his/her field of interest.

▶ Including a telephone number is essential in a cover letter.

"COLD" LETTER TO A POTENTIAL EMPLOYER
(Legal Assistant)

178 Green Street
Kankakee, IL 60901
(815) 555-5555

April 16, 20--

Pat Cummings
Director of Human Resources
Any Law Firm
1140 Main Street
Chicago, IL 60611

Dear Mr. Cummings:

During the course of my research into area law firms, I learned that Any Law Firm was consistently ranked as one of the leading organizations in the greater Chicago area. For this reason, I would like to submit my resume for your consideration.

In addition to a Comprehensive Certificate in Paralegal Studies and a Bachelor of Science degree in Business Administration, I offer your firm more than five years of experience as a Consumer Mediator with the Attorney General's office. In addition, I possess more than seven years of comprehensive business experience working and negotiating with senior-level management and decision-makers associated with *Fortune* 500 consumer products manufacturers and key account retailers. I am fully trained in all aspects of office management and have proficiency in Microsoft Word and WordPerfect word processing programs. I maintain a typing speed of 75 wpm.

My positions to date have both challenged and provided me with continual growth and success, but I recently made the decision to change my career direction. Instead of accepting a position at our company headquarters, I opted to complete a program in paralegal studies and to work toward making a meaningful contribution through legal avenues.

My first interest is in applying my legal studies to further my development and advancement in the profession. I am flexible, adaptable, a good writer and a fast study. I feel confident that with minimal supervision, I will be able to provide paralegal support service to your staff in any area of the law.

I am eager to continue my career in legal assistance with Any Law Firm, and would like to arrange for a meeting at your convenience. I will phone your office on April 26 to discuss this matter further.

I look forward to speaking with you.

Yours sincerely,

Chris Smith

Enc. Resume

▶ Closing expresses enthusiasm for follow-up phone contact.

▶ Interest in new field is emphasized.

"COLD" LETTER TO A POTENTIAL EMPLOYER
(Legal Associate)

178 Green Street
New York, NY 10128

July 10, 20--

Pat Cummings
Hiring Officer
Any Law Firm
1140 Main Street
Syracuse, NY 13221

Dear Ms. Cummings:

I am enclosing a copy of my resume for your review. Please consider me for an associate position with Any Law Firm.

During the past three years, I have been employed in several law-related positions while completing my requirements for a Juris Doctor degree at Yale Law School. These positions have given me the opportunity to gain firsthand experience in legal drafting and research in those areas of the legal profession having to do with real estate, corporate finance, and litigation. As a result of my studies, I was admitted to the Connecticut Bar in December 20--.

I would like the opportunity to meet with you for further discussion. I am very interested in joining your firm and would look forward to an interview at your earliest convenience. I can be reached at the above address or by phone between 6 P.M. and 10 P.M. at (212) 555-5555.

Sincerely,

Chris Smith

Enc. Resume

▶ Impressive educational background strengthens cover letter.

▶ Closing cites specific times candidate may be reached.

"COLD" LETTER TO A POTENTIAL EMPLOYER
(Librarian)

178 Green Street
Boston, MA 02215

December 28, 20--

Pat Cummings
Director, Personnel
Any Library
1140 Main Street
Cambridge, MA 02138

Dear Mr. Cummings:

   I am an experienced researcher who has worked extensively with archival records and secondary sources. Currently, I am seeking an opportunity to apply my acquired research skills to a full-time position as a Librarian.

   My training has emphasized the importance of precise organization and the thoughtful use of evidence to make clear historical arguments, and my work at the Library of Congress, the Boston Public Library, and the Hauptstaatarchiv Stuttgart has shown me the usefulness of these skills in an actual research environment. As a Librarian and as a Consultant at Boston University, I have gained valuable experience supervising staff members, working directly with students and professors, and choosing and instructing departments on new reference procedures. I have also achieved expertise in the following areas: Microsoft Word and WordPerfect software, automated library reference networks, copying, and filing.

   I would welcome the opportunity to work at Any Library. While I have enjoyed my time at Boston University, I am eager to put my skills to work in a nonacademic environment.

   Enclosed please find a copy of my resume, which summarizes my qualifications. I will be glad to furnish any additional information that you desire, and you may reach me at (617) 555-5555 to discuss opportunities. I look forward to speaking with you.

   Thank you very much for your consideration.

Sincerely,

Chris Smith

Enc. Resume

▶ Letter tailors experience and skills to position applied for.

▶ Type of position desired is clearly stated.

"COLD" LETTER TO A POTENTIAL EMPLOYER
(Manufacturer)

178 Green Street
Little Compton, RI 02837
(401) 555-5555

August 27, 20--

Pat Cummings
Personnel Manager
Any Corporation
1140 Main Street
Chicago, IL 60605

Dear Ms. Cummings:

During the past fourteen years, my experience has been in all phases of custom casework and millwork manufacturing. Currently, I am investigating new opportunities in the Chicago area where my family and I are planning permanent relocation.

The enclosed resume summarizes my background and experience in the areas cited above. I am highly motivated, profit-oriented, and recognized for my ability to direct a manufacturing function and produce quality goods within cost-budget and time schedules.

I am very much interested in joining your organization, and am currently available for interviews. I will call you on Wednesday, September 6, to confirm that you received my resume and to answer any questions you might have.

Sincerely,

Chris Smith

Enc. Resume

▶ Letter is short and to the point.

▶ Closing indicates specific date when candidate will follow up inquiry.

"COLD" LETTER TO A POTENTIAL EMPLOYER
(Marketing Director)

---

178 Green Street
Ada, OK 74820
(405) 555-5555

January 2, 20--

Pat Cummings
Director of Recruiting
Any Corporation
1140 Main Street
Sandy Springs, SC 29677

Dear Mr. Cummings:

It takes a seasoned professional to provide the leadership, motivation, and strategies to introduce new products, develop lucrative territories, and direct the marketing activities of a productive and profitable organization. Because I have the experience and skills to build a sound customer base for your firm, I feel we have good reason to meet.

I offer extensive marketing experience, including twenty years as Director of Marketing for a multimillion-dollar sportswear manufacturer. This position required the successful establishment of new markets and major contacts at both regional and national levels. During my tenure in this position, I was able to secure thirteen long-term contracts with national retail chains.

Currently, I am seeking a new, more challenging position with a company that can benefit from my expertise. I would welcome the opportunity for a personal interview that would allow me to further expand on my background and help us determine the mutual benefits my joining your firm would imply.

I will call you the week of January 23 to arrange a mutually convenient meeting time. Thank you for your consideration.

Yours sincerely,

Chris Smith

Enc. Resume

▶ Candidate immediately expresses suitability for desired position.

▶ Summary of experience highlights candidate's achievements.

"COLD" LETTER TO A POTENTIAL EMPLOYER
(Marketing/Development Executive)

---

178 Green Street
Troy, MI 48098
(313) 555-5555

June 14, 20--

Pat Cummings
Staff Manager
Any Corporation
1140 Main Street
Grand Rapids, MI 49503

Dear Ms. Cummings:

During twenty years of employment with major corporations such as Peters and Miller, B.K. Murphy Company, and Bennett Trade Company, I played a key role in both marketing and the development/introduction of new product lines at national and regional levels.

Currently, I am seeking a new position in which I can utilize my marketing expertise to provide planning and support to a chief executive officer or general manager with marketing responsibility.

The enclosed business profile summarizes my experience in the development, marketing, and sale of food and nonfood products for domestic, overseas, and military markets. I am very much interested in your company and its products and would welcome the opportunity to meet with you at your convenience. In the interim, should you require additional information, please do not hesitate to contact me.

Sincerely,

Chris Smith

Enc. Business profile

▶ Letter indicates how candidate contributed to his/her previous employers.

▶ Letter relies on action rather than passive verbs for emphasis.

"COLD" LETTER TO A POTENTIAL EMPLOYER
(Marketing Intern)

---

178 Green Street
Augusta, GA 30901
(706) 555-5555

July 21, 20--

Pat Cummings
Personnel Director
Any Corporation
1140 Main Street
Detroit, MI 48226

Dear Mr. Cummings:

My interest in a marketing internship with your reputable firm has prompted me to forward my resume for your review.

As a fourth-year student and candidate for a Bachelor of Arts degree in Marketing, I am looking for an opportunity to develop my skills in marketing and product management. In return, I offer academic marketing experience, superb written and verbal communication skills, and a keen desire to learn the ins and outs of the marketing business.

I will call your office the week of July 24 to schedule an interview. Thank you for your consideration, and I look forward to speaking with you.

Yours sincerely,

Chris Smith

Enc. Resume

▶ Letter emphasizes valuable skills.

▶ Powerful adjectives, when used sparingly, ensure maximum impact.

"COLD" LETTER TO A POTENTIAL EMPLOYER
(Massage Therapist)

178 Green Street
Houston, TX 77091
(713) 555-5555

July 5, 20--

Pat Cummings
Massage Therapist
Any Clinic
1140 Main Street
Dallas, TX 75738

Dear Ms. Cummings:

I am a graduate of the Morgan School of Massage Therapy and a Licensed Massage Therapist with experience in several innovative methods of massage therapy. I am confident that, as the first organization in Dallas to believe in and promote the therapeutic advantages of massage therapy, Any Clinic continues to play a leading role in this growing segment of the health care industry. For this reason, I would like to submit my credentials for consideration in reference to any openings you might have now or in the future for a Massage Therapist.

With twelve years of experience, I have the specialized professional training and practical skills necessary to evaluate clients and to provide them with the treatment modalities that will best address problems relating to their rehabilitation and overall health maintenance. I am dedicated to applying my acquired skills and I feel confident that I can provide Any Clinic with the ethical, professional services you would expect from a Licensed Massage Therapist.

The enclosed resume briefly summarizes my experiences. I would be glad to meet with you at your convenience. I look forward to hearing from you.

Sincerely,

Chris Smith

Enc. Resume

▶ Including professional accreditation and licensure may be advantageous for certain kinds of work.

▶ Specific company information illustrates candidate's commitment to his/her field.

"COLD" LETTER TO A POTENTIAL EMPLOYER
(Mechanical Engineer)

178 Green Street
Laconia, NH 03102
(603) 555-5555

January 6, 20--

Pat Cummings
Recruitment Officer
Any Corporation
1140 Main Street
Newark, NJ 07101

Dear Mr. Cummings:

For more than twenty years, I have been actively involved in precision machining work encompassing the development of working prototypes, specialty machine building/design, and precision tool/die production for high-speed equipment.

My work is diverse and challenging, requiring talent and technical skill to evaluate needs and solve complex problems. While I have been challenged by my previous experiences, I would like now to join a professional group where I can concentrate my skills on the design and development of prototypes and models for projects on the leading edge of discovery.

I have hands-on experience with the use, maintenance, and programming of all types of mechanical and hydraulic equipment used in precision machining, and can provide you with the quality work necessary for your purposes. The enclosed resume summarizes the details of my education and experience. Should you have any questions, please contact me at the above address or phone. I plan to make a follow-up call on January 16. Perhaps we can set up an appointment for an interview at that time?

I look forward to your return response.

Yours sincerely,

Chris Smith

Enc. Resume

▶ Discussion of experience clearly spells out candidate's area of expertise.

▶ Qualifications highlight candidate's problem-solving ability.

"COLD" LETTER TO A POTENTIAL EMPLOYER
(Multimedia Manager)

178 Green Street
Cinnaminson, NJ 08077
(609) 555-5555

November 1, 20--

Pat Cummings
Hiring Director
Any Corporation
1140 Main Street
Chicago, IL 60605

Dear Ms. Cummings:

As a member of the Newark Computer Society, I have followed with interest Any Corporation's growth and innovation in the field of multimedia technology. I am currently conducting a job search in the Chicago area, and would like to apply for a position within your management structure.

During the past fourteen years, my experience has ranged from Senior Auditor with Keane & Co. Peripherals to my current position as Vice-President/Controller of a $90 million, multiplant CD-ROM manufacturing operation. I believe that my expertise and entrepreneurial insight can be utilized to the advantage of a growing enterprise with a need for effective and efficient financial management and cost control.

If your company can use a profit-oriented and financially astute executive, I would like to discuss my qualifications with you during a personal interview. Thank you for your time and consideration.

Sincerely,

Chris Smith

Enc. Resume

▶ Discussion details how candidate's qualifications will benefit potential employer.

▶ Candidate clearly expresses eagerness to work for specific employer.

"COLD" LETTER TO A POTENTIAL EMPLOYER
(Mutual Funds Broker)

178 Green Street
Honolulu, HI 96813
(808) 555-5555

April 14, 20--

Pat Cummings
Controller
Any Corporation
1140 Main Street
Chicago, IL 60611

Dear Mr. Cummings:

I am writing to inquire about employment opportunities within your organization, which, according to *Money Managers' Report*, is the fastest-growing mutual funds broker in the country.

I have been involved in the brokerage business for the better part of the last twenty years. On "Black Monday" I solidified a $1 million lease in the largest mall in the West, and then consummated the agreement during one of the worst economic scares since the Great Depression of the 1930s. I am the only private broker to raise construction money from Warga Property Investors, the top-grossing real estate trust in the world.

I am a highly motivated and principled professional who knows that her energy level, expertise, and commitment to success will produce results. I would be interested in meeting with you to discuss your current or anticipated needs in terms of my qualifications and career objectives. I will contact your office in the coming weeks to schedule an interview.

Thank you for your consideration.

Sincerely,

Chris Smith

Enc. Resume

▶ Introduction expresses candidate's knowledge of firm.

▶ Use of concrete examples highlights candidate's achievements.

"COLD" LETTER TO A POTENTIAL EMPLOYER
(Nurse)

178 Green Street
New York, NY 10128

September 9, 20--

Pat Cummings, R.N.
Nursing Director
Any Hospital
1140 Main Street
Pittsburgh, PA 15217

Dear Ms. Cummings:

I am eager to continue my professional nursing career in a midsize metropolitan hospital, and am especially interested in your organization's widely respected Disease Task Force Unit. Please consider the enclosed resume as application for suitable positions at Any Hospital.

Please note that in addition to fourteen years of experience ranging from Staff Nurse (ER) to Head Nurse/Supervisor (orthopedics/OR), I have had extensive, ongoing responsibilities in the areas of staff selection and training, purchasing/vendor negotiations, budget responsibilities, and committee and task force implementation and involvement.

I am presently planning to relocate permanently to Pennsylvania, and I am seeking appointments for serious interviews in the near future. I would welcome the opportunity to put my experience to work for Any Hospital, and I feel confident that I can make an immediate and valuable contribution to your facility.

Please feel free to contact me at the above address or by phone at (212) 555-5555. I look forward to hearing from you soon.

Sincerely,

Chris Smith

Enc. Resume

▶ Experience reinforces candidate's professional objective.

▶ Career objective gives focus without limiting candidate's opportunities.

"COLD" LETTER TO A POTENTIAL EMPLOYER
(Nurse: Anesthesia)

178 Green Street
Trenton, NJ 08618
(609) 555-5555

April 3, 20--

Pat Cummings
Human Resources Coordinator
Any Hospital
1140 Main Street
Trenton, NJ 08618

Dear Mr. Cummings:

As a recent graduate of the New Jersey Medical Center School of Nurse Anesthesia, I am anxious to explore the possibility of a position within your anesthesia department. My resume is enclosed for your review.

In addition to technical academic coursework and extensive exposure to the administration of anesthetics during all surgical specialties, I have six years of professional experience in med/surg and SICU nursing. Early on, I established, and continue to maintain, an excellent record for dedication, quality of direct patient care, and clinical interface with multidisciplinary health care systems.

I offer a strong work ethic combining flexibility, reliability, and stamina. I consider myself a professional dedicated to providing patients with the highest quality of health care throughout the treatment and recovery processes.

I will call you within the week to schedule a mutually convenient time to meet. Thank you for your consideration.

Sincerely,

Chris Smith

Enc. Resume

▶ Only relevant educational training is included.

▶ Closing specifies that candidate will follow up inquiry.

"COLD" LETTER TO A POTENTIAL EMPLOYER
(Office Manager)

178 Green Street
Kingsport, TN 37660

January 11, 20--

Pat Cummings
Director of Human Resources
Any Corporation
1140 Main Street
Yukon, MO 65589

Dear Mr. Cummings:

My interest in associating with an established firm such as Any Corporation has prompted me to forward my resume, which briefly summarizes my experience in office and departmental management.

As Office/Department Manager at Kimco, I was responsible for directing and coordinating the activities of accounting and support personnel in a $10 million manufacturing operation. I concurrently managed the cutting room and handled the purchasing of approximately $5 million in raw materials, supplies, and capital equipment used in manufacturing, sales, and distribution of branded and private label products through mass merchandisers.

This position required entrepreneurial skills and the capability to "wear many hats" in a small, active manufacturing operation. During my six years at Kimco, the company nearly doubled its profits and was able to expand its staff by 15 percent.

I would appreciate the opportunity to discuss, on a one-on-one basis, openings within your company. I can be reached at the above address or by phone at (615) 555-5555. If I do not receive a response, I will call within a few days to arrange a mutually convenient meeting time.

Sincerely,

Chris Smith

Enc. Resume

▶ Candidate's most recent position is outlined in detail.

▶ Dollar amounts quantify candidate's accomplishments.

"COLD" LETTER TO A POTENTIAL EMPLOYER
(Operations Executive)

178 Green Street
Alexandria, LA 71301
(703) 555-5555

March 17, 20--

Pat Cummings
Hiring Manager
Any Corporation
1140 Main Street
Birmingham, AL 35229

Dear Ms. Cummings:

If you are in need of an aggressive, highly motivated Operations Executive, then we have good reason to meet.

During the past twelve years, I have held progressively responsible positions ranging from Field Representative to General Manager of a $10 million multi-branch operation. Currently, I am seeking an opportunity to apply this experience to foster the growth and profits of your company through greater market penetration and increased sales volume.

The enclosed resume summarizes my background and experience. I am very interested in joining the operations team at Any Corporation and feel that I can produce the same beneficial results for your firm as I have for my current and prior employers. I would consider a personal discussion to be mutually advantageous. I am open to relocation and/or travel, and the compensation package is negotiable.

I will call your office on March 27 to follow up on my inquiry. Thank you for your time and consideration.

Sincerely,

Chris Smith

Enc. Resume

▶ Closing thanks addressee in advance for attention.

▶ Introductory sentence draws attention.

"COLD" LETTER TO A POTENTIAL EMPLOYER
(Operations Manager)

---

178 Green Street
Santa Ana, CA 97201
(714) 555-5555

April 10, 20--

Pat Cummings
Staff Director
Any Corporation
1140 Main Street
St. Petersburg, FL 35701

Dear Mr. Cummings:

I am presently searching for a position at the decision-making level in areas of customer service/sales support. I read about Any Corporation's recent expansion in this month's *Investing Now,* and am interested in exploring employment opportunities at your firm.

Please note that my fifteen years of broad-based management experience encompasses a full range of customer service functions. Most recently my talents were put to use as Customer Service Manager for a well-established and growing computer service company providing computer systems, time-sharing business application programs, software packages, and associated support services on an international level. My intensive experience in sophisticated aspects of customer support management includes on-site training of front-line staff and management in diverse computer business and manufacturing applications, and associated sales support activities. I am willing to relocate for the right opportunity.

I would like to arrange a mutually convenient time for a meeting, during which we may further discuss your current or anticipated needs. I will call your office next week to schedule an interview.

Thank you for your consideration.

Sincerely,

Chris Smith

Enc. Resume

▶ Letter emphasizes candidate's strong work history.

▶ Only relevant work experience is emphasized.

"COLD" LETTER TO A POTENTIAL EMPLOYER
(Pharmacy Director)

178 Green Street
Santa Clara, CA 95053

June 22, 20--

Pat Cummings
Director, Health Care Services
Any Corporation
1140 Main Street
Colorado Springs, CO 80903

Dear Ms. Cummings:

As Assistant Director of Pharmacy with a high-volume, forty-store chain, I have the management and sales expertise necessary to deal with multidisciplinary health care professionals as a member of your management team.

In addition to holding a Bachelor of Science degree in Pharmacy, I am a Registered Pharmacist with eight years of progressively responsible experience encompassing general management and in-house and field sales experience in a rapid growth environment.

I am well versed in regulations controlling therapeutic drug treatment, have sound knowledge of medical terminology, work well in either an independent setting or team effort, and enjoy both the clinical and nonclinical aspects of working with health care products and/or services. Based on my experience and professional credentials, I consider myself well qualified to handle the responsibilities of a management position at your company.

I hope to hear from you to schedule a personal interview at your convenience. I can be reached at the above address or at (408) 555-5555 from 9 A.M. to 5 P.M. weekdays or at (408) 555-4444 on weekends. I am willing to relocate for the right professional challenge and compensation package.

Sincerely,

Chris Smith

Enc. Resume

▶ Candidate immediately introduces his/her qualifications.　　　▶ Experiences are tailored to employer's needs.

"COLD" LETTER TO A POTENTIAL EMPLOYER
(Plant Manager)

178 Green Street
Little Rock, AR 72204
(501) 555-5555

July 7, 20--

Pat Cummings
Personnel Manager
Any Corporation
1140 Main Street
Chicago, IL 60605

Dear Mr. Cummings:

Are you looking for a competent plant manager who will effectively handle all aspects involved in the smooth operation of your organization? If so, I would like to present my confidential resume for your consideration.

Please note that, in addition to more than five years of vocational training and hands-on experience with automated, semiautomated, and mechanical plant equipment and systems, I have been involved in purchasing and negotiations. Although presently employed in a responsible position, I feel that an association with your firm may offer better growth potential than I can foresee with my present employer.

Thank you for your consideration. I look forward to hearing from you.

Sincerely,

Chris Smith

Enc. Resume

▶ Letter is easy and quick to read, and only relevant details are included.

▶ Letter suggests discretion.

"COLD" LETTER TO A POTENTIAL EMPLOYER
(Printer)

178 Green Street
Athens, GA 30601
(404) 555-5555

May 29, 20--

Pat Cummings
Manager, Production Department
Any Corporation
1140 Main Street
Atlanta, GA 30340

Dear Ms. Cummings:

My interest in a position in printing or related areas of graphic arts prompts me to forward my resume for your review.

During the past six years, I have been employed with a major insurance company where I rapidly advanced from an entry-level position to Operator of a Xerox 9900 printing system. This experience, combined with my formal education in graphic arts, college-level courses in business administration, and experience in various areas of retail business operations, has equipped me with a sound and varied background. I am confident of my ability to make a creative and productive contribution as a member of your publications and training department.

I will be spending the week of July 29 to August 4 in your area prior to permanent relocation. I hope to meet with you during my visit, and would like to hear from you to set a convenient time and date for an interview. At that time, we will have the opportunity to discuss your requirements and my ability to handle the responsibilities of a position at Any Corporation.

I look forward to your return response.

Sincerely,

Chris Smith

Enc. Resume

▶ Closing provides specific time frame to allow for meeting.

▶ Candidate expresses knowledge in his/her field of interest.

"COLD" LETTER TO A POTENTIAL EMPLOYER
(Production Manager)

178 Green Street
Tampa, FL 33620
(813) 555-5555

January 13, 20--

Pat Cummings
Vice-President, Operations
Any Corporation
1140 Main Street
Babson Park, FL 33827

Dear Mr. Cummings:

If you are in need of an experienced manager skilled in production planning, scheduling, and control for a quality production operation, then we have good reason to meet.

During the past seven years, I have held progressively responsible positions, leading to Senior Production Control/Personal Computer Planner in a multiple product line operation. This association has afforded me the opportunity for personal development, while allowing me to make a significant contribution to the company's rapid growth.

My complex and diverse assignments require that I troubleshoot, investigate, and resolve problems by developing solutions that save money, increase productivity, and improve quality during high-volume production.

Although my job is secure, I feel the time has come to secure a position that offers greater responsibility, as well as the authority to make decisions that are in the best interest of the company.

My achievements in the past, which I have detailed on the enclosed employment profile, attest to my ability to contribute to a winning team. I am anxious to discuss how I may continue to uphold my personal standards of excellence as a member of the Any Corporation team. For this reason, I will call to schedule a mutually convenient interview time.

I look forward to speaking with you.

Yours sincerely,

Chris Smith

Enc. Employment profile

▶ One page is standard length for cover letters.   ▶ Unrelated work experience is omitted.

"COLD" LETTER TO A POTENTIAL EMPLOYER
(Project Manager)

178 Green Street
Deer Park, NY 11729

March 19, 20--

Pat Cummings
Recruitment Manager
Any Corporation
1140 Main Street
New York, NY 10022

Dear Ms. Cummings:

During the past eight years, I have been actively involved as a Mechanical Engineer and Project Manager with companies specializing in commercial building and highway bridge reconstruction as well as full turnkey nuclear and fossil fuel plant construction.

Presently, I am phasing out of a general management position, and looking to make a new start with a firm that will allow me to apply my combined technical, management, and administrative skills to achieve cost-effective and profitable completion of heavy construction and/or engineering projects.

The enclosed resume summarizes my background and experience in the areas I have cited above. I am available for an interview at any time and would like to arrange an appointment at your earliest convenience.

I can be reached at the above address or by phone at (516) 555-5555. I am sincerely interested in career possibilities at your firm, and plan to make a follow-up call within a few days.

Sincerely,

Chris Smith

Enc. Resume

▶ Candidate does not limit available opportunities by stating specific position desired.

▶ Letter avoids abbreviations and slang.

"COLD" LETTER TO A POTENTIAL EMPLOYER
(Property Manager)

178 Green Street
Mill Valley, CA 94941
(415) 555-5555

May 19, 20--

Pat Cummings
Personnel Director
Any Corporation
1140 Main Street
Fresno, CA 93786

Dear Mr. Cummings:

    I am writing to investigate opportunities in which I could apply my skills in property management and real estate investments with your company's holdings.

    As you will note from the enclosed resume, I have more than fifteen years of experience in general property management, including both residential and commercial properties. During the past five years, I have headed an absentee-owner property management company that has grown from 400 to 750 units while maintaining a vacancy rate below 5 percent. I offer a thorough knowledge of all aspects of property management, from locating, negotiating, and acquiring property through leasing, maintenance, and financial management.

    I strongly believe my qualifications would prove to be an asset to Any Corporation. I would greatly appreciate the opportunity to present my skills in a personal interview.

    Thank you for your time and consideration.

Sincerely,

Chris Smith

Enc. Resume

▶ Letter focuses attention on candidate's major skills and accomplishments.

▶ Enclosure line suggests candidate is a meticulous, detail-orientated professional.

"COLD" LETTER TO A POTENTIAL EMPLOYER
(Public Relations Assistant)

178 Green Street
Wheatland, ND 58079
(701) 555-5555

September 10, 20--

Pat Cummings
Vice-President, Human Resources
Any Public Relations
1140 Main Street
Los Angeles, CA 90053

Dear Ms. Cummings:

Please accept the enclosed copy of my resume as a preliminary application for a position with Any Public Relations.

In addition to my degree in Journalism and Public Relations, I have four years of experience working with a modeling/talent agency and modeling school. In both the teaching and model recruitment/placement environments, I have worked with key accounts in areas where image building and high visibility for client services and/or products were the ultimate objectives. Through activities which included the selection and placement of models for union and nonunion television commercials, I honed my abilities to coordinate creative programs and innovative functions involving clients and the general public. As a result, I feel confident that I could successfully apply my experience to a position in your firm.

I will be in the Los Angeles area at the end of the month and will call your office during the week of September 25. I look forward to talking with you.

Sincerely,

Chris Smith

Enc. Resume

▶ Discussion of experience is very specific.　　▶ Letter emphasizes valuable skills.

"COLD" LETTER TO A POTENTIAL EMPLOYER
(Quality Control Specialist)

178 Green Street
San Bernardino, CA 92403

May 27, 20--

Pat Cummings
Director, Personnel
Any Corporation
1140 Main Street
Burbank, CA 91510

Dear Mr. Cummings:

During the past twelve years, my experience has been concentrated in quality assurance and quality control in the coated paper and plastics industry.

I have remained with the company through several acquisitions and staff reductions and in each case, have advanced to positions of broader responsibility. However, I feel it is time for a change. I would like to join a firm that has a need for someone like myself, skilled in the development of preventive maintenance programs that improve productivity, material handling procedures, and inventory availability.

I am thoroughly experienced with quality control methods and environmental regulations involving material waste processing and disposal, and I am fully qualified to supervise and coordinate a full range of quality control/assurance activities in a high-volume, custom product manufacturing or processing operation.

The enclosed resume is a summary of my background and experience. If you are in need of additional information, please contact me at the above address or by phone at (714) 555-5555.

I am very interested in opportunities with Any Corporation and look forward to hearing from you.

Sincerely,

Chris Smith

Enc. Resume

▶ Telephone number included in closing is omitted in return address.

▶ Letter focuses on candidate's past job experience while incorporating functional qualifications.

"COLD" LETTER TO A POTENTIAL EMPLOYER
(Real Estate Banker)

178 Green Street
Sunnyvale, CA 94088
(408) 555-5555

August 3, 20--

Pat Cummings
Associate Director
Any Bank
1140 Main Street
Newtown Square, PA 19093

Dear Ms. Cummings:

I am interested in exploring opportunities within the real estate investment/ mortgage lending department of Any Bank. Should you be in need of someone with my qualifications, I would be eager to lend assistance to your organization.

In addition to a Bachelor of Science degree in Management with a major in Finance and a real estate sales license, I have diverse experience in positions that have required strong communication and interpersonal skills in dealing with associates, customers, and personnel. My current position as Portfolio Administrator/Fund Accountant is diverse and detailed; however, I am interested in applying my financial background to areas involving new business development and account administration.

I am confident that my skills and abilities could benefit Any Bank. I would appreciate the opportunity to talk with you regarding suitable opportunities within your organization.

Sincerely,

Chris Smith

Enc. Resume

▶ Including professional accreditation and licensure may be advantageous for certain kinds of work.

▶ Letter immediately refers addressee to attached resume.

"COLD" LETTER TO A POTENTIAL EMPLOYER
(Repair Technician)

178 Green Street
Sioux Falls, SD 57105
(605) 555-5555

January 29, 20--

Pat Cummings
Repair Maintenance Operator
Any Corporation
1140 Main Street
Salt Lake City, UT 84111

Dear Mr. Cummings:

Please accept the enclosed resume as an expressed interest in exploring employment opportunities available in the repair and maintenance division of Any Corporation.

I have acquired training and extensive experience in the installation and repair of various heating, electrical, and power systems for commercial, industrial, and residential properties. My employment has required that I develop proficiency in the fabrication of plumbing systems and in the coordination of repair service for equipment malfunctions. In various management capabilities, I have facilitated all administrative and fiscal operations for service companies, in addition to managing personnel. I possess exceptional communication, leadership, and troubleshooting skills. In response to an increasingly multicultural industry, I have acquired fluency in Portuguese and conversational abilities in Spanish and French. I feel that my accomplishments have prepared me to assume the responsibilities demanded at Any Corporation.

I would welcome the opportunity to meet with you and discuss ways in which my capabilities could be guided to suit your needs. Please consider the enclosed resume and direct your response to the above address or telephone number. I will follow up this correspondence with a phone call early next week.

I look forward to speaking with you in the near future. Thank you for your time.

With best regards,

Chris Smith

Enc. Resume

▶ Foreign language skills strengthen candidate's qualifications.

▶ Closing refers addressee to telephone number in return address.

"COLD" LETTER TO A POTENTIAL EMPLOYER
(Research Assistant)

178 Green Street
Manchester, NH 03104
(603) 555-5555

July 31, 20--

Pat Cummings
Human Resources Director
Any Bank
1140 Main Street
Chicago, IL 60605

Dear Ms. Cummings:

Having majored in Mathematics at Rice University, where I also worked as a Research Assistant, I am confident that I would make a successful addition to your economics research department.

In addition to my strong background in mathematics, I offer significant business experience, having worked in a data processing firm, a bookstore, and a restaurant. I am sure that my courses in statistics and computer programming will prove particularly useful in an entry-level position.

I am attracted to Any Bank by your recent rapid growth and the superior reputation of your economic research department. After studying different commercial banks, I have concluded that Any Bank will be in a strong competitive position to benefit from upcoming changes in the industry.

I would like to interview with you at your earliest convenience.

Sincerely,

Chris Smith

Enc. Resume

▶ Closing reiterates candidate's company knowledge.

▶ Letter includes course work that corresponds to position desired.

"COLD" LETTER TO A POTENTIAL EMPLOYER
(Retail Sales Manager)

178 Green Street
Fairfax, VA 22030

April 11, 20--

Pat Cummings
Retail Sales Director
Any Corporation
1140 Main Street
Charleston, WV 25301

Dear Mr. Cummings:

During the past twenty years, I have played a key role in the development of new markets and increased profitability for the sales of women's and junior apparel to large department stores and mass merchandisers.

Currently, I am seeking a position with a company that can benefit from my expertise as a highly productive, dynamic, profit-oriented manager with a proven record of achievement in sales and sales management. I have a consistent record for achieving sales goals, expanding market share, reducing costs, and increasing profits.

The enclosed resume summarizes my background and experience. If Any Corporation can use an executive who is qualified to assume responsibility for the profitable direction of expanding or diversifying market strategy, I would like to discuss my qualifications with you during a personal interview.

I look forward to an opportunity to produce the same beneficial results for your corporation as I have for previous employers. I can be reached at the above address or by phone at (703) 555-5555.

Thank you for your consideration.

Yours sincerely,

Chris Smith

Enc. Resume

▶ Dynamic action verbs give letter impact.

▶ Background summary accentuates candidate's acquired professional skills and impressive track record.

"COLD" LETTER TO A POTENTIAL EMPLOYER
(Retail Salesperson)

178 Green Street
Cherry Fork, OH 95618
(513) 555-5555

July 21, 20--

Pat Cummings
Hiring Manager
Any Corporation
1140 Main Street
Cincinnati, OH 45202

Dear Ms. Cummings:

During the past three years as a Sales Representative with Fits Like a Glove, Inc., I have successfully sold to and serviced retail accounts throughout the Midwest. In this capacity, I established a record for the development of new business and solid client relationships which have generated additional customers and referrals. In addition, as principal owner of a retail establishment, I managed all areas of independent department store operations specializing in family ready-to-wear accessories, athletic wear, and athletic footwear and equipment.

Currently I am looking for a new opportunity where I can utilize my sales, merchandising, management, and communications skills to contribute to the efficiency and bottom-line results of a firm providing quality products and service to a diverse consumer population or dealer network.

Among retailers, Any Corporation's name emerges as the industry leader with respect to aggressive sales techniques. I feel that I can play a valuable role in such an environment.

My resume is enclosed for your review. In the near future, I will call your office to schedule an interview. Thank you for your consideration and I look forward to speaking with you.

Sincerely,

Chris Smith

Enc. Resume

▶ Summary of experience highlights candidate's achievements.

▶ Closing reiterates candidate's knowledge of organization.

"COLD" LETTER TO A POTENTIAL EMPLOYER
(Sales Executive)

178 Green Street
Beetown, WI 53802

June 6, 20--

Pat Cummings
Staff Coordinator
Any Corporation
1140 Main Street
Milwaukee, WI 53201

Dear Mr. Cummings:

Your firm has been brought to my attention as one that can provide the challenge, diversification, and stability I am looking for in a company.

For more than fifteen years, I have held progressively more responsible jobs selling industrial and agricultural chemicals, pharmaceuticals, and related products with a multinational manufacturer and distributor. I am an effective time-and-territory manager, have sound knowledge of sales techniques and strategies, and have been successful in new business and marketing development in every position I have held to date.

The enclosed resume summarizes my background and experience. While I am interested in permanent relocation to your area, I am also willing to travel.

I am highly productive, profit oriented, and cost conscious, and can contribute much to increasing your share of the market. I feel that a meeting, at your convenience, could be mutually beneficial. I can be reached at the above address or by phone at (414) 555-5555.

Yours sincerely,

Chris Smith

Enc. Resume

▶ Willingness to travel can be advantageous.   ▶ Candidate details applicable work experience.

"COLD" LETTER TO A POTENTIAL EMPLOYER
(School Administrator: Secondary Level)

178 Green Street
Hartford, CT 06120
(203) 555-5555

July 14, 20--

Pat Cummings
Superintendent
Any Public School System
1140 Main Street
Bridgeport, CT 06604

Dear Dr. Cummings:

During the past twelve years as Principal of Murray Central High School, I have had the opportunity to provide leadership in a multiracial, multilingual urban high school during a complex, volatile era. Please accept the enclosed resume as an application for an administrative position with the Any Public School System.

My positions with the Murray School System have been challenging and have provided a setting in which I have been able to develop a variety of new programs as well as implement existing programs to create a winning tradition of academic excellence. My primary purpose has always been to motivate students toward educational excellence, higher education, improved self-image, and job preparedness.

In my years with Murray Central High, I have achieved the goals I projected for the school, students, parents, and business and residential communities. Now, I am ready for a change to a school system where I can once again provide the leadership needed to uphold and strengthen educational standards while achieving desired objectives. With my background, experience, proven leadership skills, and dedication to quality education, I am well qualified and prepared to make the same commitment to the Any Public School System.

The enclosed professional profile is a summary of my experience. I look forward to the opportunity to discuss, in further detail, my educational philosophy, my ability to fill your requirements, and why I am qualified for an administrative position with the Any Public School System. I anxiously await your response.

Yours sincerely,

Chris Smith

Enc. Professional profile

▶ Qualifications are geared to candidate's field of interest.

▶ Letter indicates how candidate contributed to his/her previous employers.

"COLD" LETTER TO A POTENTIAL EMPLOYER
(Security Specialist)

178 Green Street
Ranier, OR 97048
(503) 555-5555

May 31, 20--

Pat Cummings
Personnel Manager
Any Corporation
1140 Main Street
Chicago, IL 60605

Dear Mr. Cummings:

Are you currently seeking a Security Specialist to maintain or upgrade the security of your organization? If so, I would like to apply for the position.

During the past twenty years, I have gained experience and education encompassing all aspects of law enforcement, and security procedures and implementation.

I feel confident that I can make an immediate contribution to Any Corporation, and I believe that a personal conversation would be to our mutual advantage. I will call your office on Tuesday, June 13, to schedule an appointment at your convenience.

Thank you for your attention. I look forward to speaking with you.

Sincerely,

Chris Smith

Enc. Resume

▶ Introducing letter with a question draws attention to candidate.

▶ Closing is brief and to the point.

"COLD" LETTER TO A POTENTIAL EMPLOYER
(Social Worker: Counseling)

178 Green Street
Fort Worth, TX 76114
(817) 555-5555

March 17, 20--

Pat Cummings
Director, Mental Health Services
Any Center
1140 Main Street
Dallas, TX 75206

Dear Ms. Cummings:

    My involvement with a number of local counseling centers has given me the opportunity to become familiar with Any Center's work. My observation of your facility and its staff has confirmed my desire to join your organization in a counseling or group leadership capacity.

    For the past fifteen years, my experience has ranged from Mental Health Aide to Peer Counselor and Group Leader working with alcoholics, drug abusers, and mentally/emotionally disabled adults. I am a candidate for a Master's degree in Counseling/Psychology, and am well trained in alcohol/substance abuse counseling and the provision of related health care services to individuals and/or groups at all age levels.

    I am very interested in joining your staff. I will call your office next week to schedule an interview at your convenience.

Yours sincerely,

Chris Smith

Enc. Resume

▶ Letter highlights candidate's acquired professional and educational training.

▶ Only related work experience is included.

"COLD" LETTER TO A POTENTIAL EMPLOYER
(Social Worker: Geriatrics)

178 Green Street
Great Falls, MT 59403
(406) 555-5555

July 3, 20--

Pat Cummings
Director, Human Services
Any Corporation
1140 Main Street
Billings, MT 59107

Dear Mr. Cummings:

My interest in continuing my professional career as a clinical social worker in the geriatric area of human services has prompted me to forward my resume for your consideration.

In addition to graduate work, licenses, and registration in the field of social work, I have nine years of professional experience ranging from Psychiatric Caseworker to Clinical/Research Social Worker at Worthy Hospital. Recently, I conducted research and coauthored a publication on geriatrics, an undertaking that has focused my interest on the problems of aging and the older adult population.

I would appreciate meeting with you for further discussion after you review my qualifications. In the interim, please feel free to contact me if you have any questions.

I look forward to learning more about Any Corporation.

Sincerely yours,

Chris Smith

Enc. Resume

▶ Publication is impressive and adds weight to cover letter.

▶ Closing invites addressee to inquire about additional information.

"COLD" LETTER TO A POTENTIAL EMPLOYER
(Social Worker: Medical)

178 Green Street
Geneseo, NY 14454
(716) 555-5555

April 2, 20--

Pat Cummings
Outreach Director
Any Hospital
1140 Main Street
Oneonta, NY 13820

Dear Ms. Cummings:

I am a newly Licensed Medical Social Worker investigating new opportunities in which to apply my education and experience. I am capable of working independently or as a member of a team, and I feel confident in my ability to handle the responsibilities of the position and to provide quality performance in any assignment I undertake.

In addition, I offer excellent administrative and clinical experience and am anxious to put my skills to work for Any Hospital. With that in mind, I enclose my resume for your consideration.

I look forward to your immediate reply.

Sincerely,

Chris Smith

Enc. Resume

▶ Candidate includes licensure relevant to his/her field.

▶ Language is straightforward and understandable.

"COLD" LETTER TO A POTENTIAL EMPLOYER
(Telemarketer)

178 Green Street
Juneau, AK 99801
(907) 555-5555

February 23, 20--

Pat Cummings
Director, Marketing
Any Corporation
1140 Main Street
Anchorage, AK 99514

Dear Mr. Cummings:

I am a highly motivated individual with a proven sales record who is interested in securing a challenging telemarketing position. I have enclosed my resume for your consideration.

During the past ten years, I have been employed as a Telemarketer selling sophisticated products and services to hospitals, clinics, and medical professionals, as well as filtration systems to end-users. During this time, I have successfully increased company sales by 40 percent and have established an impressive customer base. I possess extensive telephone and interpersonal skills, and am proficient with all aspects of office operations, including dBase and Lotus 1-2-3 computer applications.

I feel confident that my experience can be successfully applied to a telemarketing position at Any Corporation. I will call your office next week to discuss this matter further.

Yours sincerely,

Chris Smith

Enc. Resume

▶ Letter emphasizes achievements, and does not simply list job responsibilities.

▶ Letter immediately refers addressee to attached resume.

"COLD" LETTER TO A POTENTIAL EMPLOYER
(Television Production Assistant)

178 Green Street
Hito, HI 96720
(606) 555-5555

June 24, 20--

Pat Cummings
Production Director
Any Television Station
1140 Main Street
Honolulu, HI 96822

Dear Ms. Cummings:

I am very interested in launching a career in the broadcast communications industry, and have enclosed my resume for consideration with regard to any entry-level, production positions you might have available at Any Television Station.

I was graduated in May from the University of Hawaii-Hilo with a Bachelor of Arts degree in Communications. Throughout my college career, I enrolled in relevant broadcast communication courses dealing with production, writing, and research. Also, I was actively involved in the university newspaper, where my duties entailed researching events and local talent, conducting interviews, and writing articles for the entertainment section.

While working as an intern last summer for WBZT-TV's "Island Beat," I was given the opportunity to coproduce a local talk show, an assignment that required exceptional organizational and interpersonal skills. I pre-interviewed and scheduled guests for the show, handled financial and transportation details, and researched show topics. I also networked with resource organizations to locate potential guests and panel members. I believe that with my working knowledge of the broadcast and television industries, combined with my ability to adapt quickly to new situations and activities, I would be able to make a valuable contribution to your station.

I would like to meet with you to further discuss possible job openings at Any Television Station and to present my qualifications in greater detail. I will be in the Honolulu area the week of July 3, and would appreciate an interview at your convenience.

I look forward to hearing from you.

Sincerely,

Chris Smith

Enc. Resume

▶ Personal interests and activities are relevant to candidate's field of interest.

▶ Internships strengthen candidate's short work history.

"COLD" LETTER TO A POTENTIAL EMPLOYER
(Textile Specialist)

178 Green Street
Bloomington, IN 47405
(812) 555-5555

April 18, 20--

Pat Cummings
Vice-President, Human Resources
Any Corporation
1140 Main Street
Chicago, IL 60601

Dear Mr. Cummings:

During my successful career in textiles, I have advanced to such positions as Director of Wool Procurement for an international corporation and Senior Vice-President of a national profit trading center. These responsible positions have provided me with the administrative and management expertise to contribute to the efficiency, growth, and profitability of Any Corporation.

I possess extensive experience in trading, sourcing, and purchasing, as well as new market and business development, import/export coordination, and profit center management. Although my current position has been challenging and rewarding, my decision to relocate permanently to Chicago makes it necessary for me to seek new opportunities with a company, such as yours, that can utilize the full scope of my experience in order to achieve mutual objectives.

I have enclosed a resume for your consideration. As of May 1, I will be residing in Chicago and will be available for an interview at your convenience. I will make a follow-up phone call next Monday (April 24) to schedule a meeting time.

Sincerely,

Chris Smith

Enc. Resume

▶ Candidate emphasizes how past business experience can benefit potential employer.

▶ Letter cites specific date phone contact will be made.

"COLD" LETTER TO A POTENTIAL EMPLOYER
(Underwriter)

178 Green Street
Syracuse, NY 13221

April 10, 20--

Pat Cummings
Senior Claims Adjuster
Any Corporation
1140 Main Street
New York, NY 10010

Dear Ms. Cummings:

Currently, I am seeking new opportunities with an underwriter or corporate liability insurance department in which there is a need for expertise in claims settlement.

During the past ten years, my experience in the liability insurance field has ranged from Transcriber to Senior Field Claims Representative. My skills include fact-finding analysis, and negotiating settlements, both of which demand strong training and management skills.

The enclosed resume summarizes my background in the areas I have cited above. I am very much interested in Any Corporation and would be glad to furnish you with additional information during a personal interview. I can be reached at the above address or by phone at (315) 555-5555.

Thank you for your consideration.

Sincerely yours,

Chris Smith

Enc. Resume

▶ First paragraph is short and hard-hitting.

▶ Including telephone number is necessary in a cover letter.

"COLD" LETTER TO A POTENTIAL EMPLOYER
(Upper-Level Manager: Accounting)

178 Green Street
Giants Pass, OR 97526
(503) 555-5555

October 21, 20--

Pat Cummings
Controller
Any Corporation
1140 Main Street
Boston, MA 02101

Dear Mr. Cummings:

In the interest of investigating career opportunities with Any Corporation, I am enclosing my resume for your review.

As you can see, my proven record of achievement has led to rapid promotions. During the past fourteen years, my experience has ranged from Senior Auditor with Hans Anderson and Company, Public Accountant, to Controller and, subsequently, Vice-President of a $50 million multiplant manufacturing operation.

These positions have been fast-paced, challenging, and broad in scope, requiring strong financial and strategic planning capabilities. I am a CPA with the ability to recognize, troubleshoot, and resolve financial and administrative problems. I feel that my experience and entrepreneurial insight can be utilized to the advantage of a growing enterprise with a need for effective and efficient financial management and cost control.

If your company can use a profit-oriented and financially astute executive, I would like to discuss my qualifications with you during a personal interview. I can be reached at (503) 555-5555, at which time I will be glad to provide you with additional information.

Thank you for your time and consideration.

Sincerely,

Chris Smith

Enc. Resume

▶ Discussion of experience indicates a series of promotions.

▶ Background summary accentuates candidate's acquired professional skills and impressive track record.

"COLD" LETTER TO A POTENTIAL EMPLOYER
(Veterinarian)

178 Green Street
Nanticoke, PA 18634
(717) 555-5555

September 17, 20--

Pat Cummings, D.V.M.
Head Veterinarian
Any Animal Hospital
1140 Main Street
Easton, PA 18042

Dear Dr. Cummings:

I am a graduate of the Wiley College School of Veterinary Medicine where I received my D.V.M. degree in 20--. I am interested in pursuing a career in which I can apply my academic and practical skills.

In addition to a graduate and two undergraduate degrees, I offer research and clinical experience obtained through three separate externships that involved studying dairy herds in Switzerland, orangutans in Borneo, and domestic work elephants in India.

As a Medical Engineer for Lorri Electric and a Medical Assistant for a general practitioner, I was exposed to clinical procedures and gained hands-on experience in the installation and servicing of computerized diagnostic equipment. As a Behavioral Specialist, I worked with clients and families in a psychiatric setting. Based on these experiences and my dedication to the veterinary profession, I believe that I am well suited for a position with your animal hospital.

I am eager to offer my skills and experience to Any Animal Hospital. I will contact your office to arrange a time when we may discuss mutually beneficial opportunities.

Sincerely,

Chris Smith, D.V.M.

Enc. Resume

▶ Educational credentials strengthen cover letter.

▶ Externships strengthen candidate's short work history.

"COLD" LETTER TO A POTENTIAL EMPLOYER
(Visual Media Production Assistant)

178 Green Street
San Francisco, CA 94111
(415) 555-5555

October 16, 20--

Pat Cummings
Media Coordinator
Any Corporation
1140 Main Street
Santa Ana, CA 92701

Dear Mr. Cummings:

I am a recent graduate of the University of Southern California seeking opportunities in the photographic and visual media fields. I feel my experience could provide a significant contribution to your corporation. Some of my accomplishments include:

- Direction and supervision of computer-aided graphic design and manual pasteup procedures for the *College Companion*, the largest college newspaper in California.
- Proficiency in page layout, both manual and electronic; photographic imaging; and computerized scanning procedures.
- Conception and production of cover layouts for *The Week Gone By*.
- Hands-on training in electronic still photography, computer graphics, lithography, and illustration.

I am confident that the skills I have acquired both in the classroom and through hands-on experience make me an ideal candidate for a position in visual media production. I would like to meet with you to discuss my qualifications further and will call next week to schedule an interview. In the meantime, I have enclosed a copy of my resume for your review.
Thank you for your time and consideration.

Yours sincerely,

Chris Smith

Enc. Resume

▶ Bulleting draws attention to major accomplishments.

▶ College activities are related to candidate's field of study and career objective.

CHAPTER 14

LETTER TO AN EMPLOYMENT AGENCY

When searching for a job, many candidates rely on the help of employment agencies. These agencies offer services to a wide range of job seekers, primarily for clerical or support staff positions. Letters addressed to employment agencies should focus on who you are, what type of position you are looking for and in what specific industry, and some of your strongest skills related to that field. In order for the agency to place you in an appropriate position, you should mention personal preferences, including geographic and salary requirements. Conclude your letter with a statement specifically indicating how you can be reached, or when you will follow up on your letter.

LETTER TO AN EMPLOYMENT AGENCY
(Accounting Manager)

178 Green Street
Hazelwood, MO 63042
(606) 555-5555

July 18, 20--

Pat Cummings
Director
Any Employment Agency
1140 Main Street
Bridgeton, MO 63042

Dear Ms. Cummings:

The enclosed resume outlines my diverse experience in accounting and finance management. I am in search of an appropriate opportunity in the greater St. Louis area.

The following are some of the strengths and capabilities that I can bring to a position:

- Solid understanding of financial statement preparation and review.
- Proficiency at budget preparation and various written analysis.
- Proven ability to organize department goals to meet overall corporate goals.
- Competency in terms of resource management, including people and systems.
- Strong leadership qualities including upgrading and motivating staff resources.

I would welcome the opportunity to meet with you to discuss my background and credentials. Thank you for your time and consideration.

Sincerely,

Chris Smith

Enc. Resume

▶ Bullets inform agency contact of candidate's qualifications.

▶ Candidate informs agency of geographical preference.

LETTER TO AN EMPLOYMENT AGENCY
(Administrative Assistant)

178 Green Street
Madison, WI 53706

July 17, 20--

Pat Cummings
Representative
Any Employment Agency
1140 Main Street
Milwaukee, WI 53201

Dear Mr. Cummings:

I am searching for an administrative position in the real estate, international finance, or import/export industry. Such a position seems a good match for my education and achievements, as well as my career interests.

As a B.A. graduate of the University of Wisconsin's School of Business, I have been thoroughly educated in all aspects of the business environment. In addition, I consider myself a highly motivated and ambitious person. While pursuing my academic studies, I was accepted into and participated in the University Study Abroad Program in Tokyo, Japan.

I am interested in pursuing a full-time, entry-level position that would allow me to utilize my computer, administrative, and finance skills, as well as my interests in real estate and travel. I would be willing to relocate, given a salary range of $22,000 to $28,000.

I would appreciate consideration for any suitable opportunities. You can contact me between 8 A.M. and 6 P.M. weekdays at (608) 555-5555.

Thank you for your consideration.

Sincerely,

Chris Smith

Enc. Resume

▶ Foreign language skills and international exposure, in exchange programs and/or internships, are valuable assets in today's global market.
▶ When writing to an employment agency, including compensation requirements is optional.

LETTER TO AN EMPLOYMENT AGENCY
(Advertising/Graphic Design Assistant)

178 Green Street
Topeka, KS 66612

April 18, 20--

Pat Cummings
Director
Any Employment Agency
1140 Main Street
St. Paul, MN 55401

Dear Ms. Cummings:

I am writing with the hope that one of your clients in the field of Advertising/ Graphic Design is in need of an entry-level assistant.

I possess strong verbal and written communication skills and pay close attention to detail, while maintaining a flair for creativity. I feel that I am a well-disciplined, highly motivated person with a strong desire to succeed in Advertising/Graphic Design. To support my enthusiasm, I possess excellent PC and Macintosh computer skills and a typing speed of 55 wpm.

Thank you in advance for reviewing the enclosed resume. I would be happy to further discuss my experience and qualifications with you in person. Please feel free to contact me at (913) 555-5555 if I can be of further assistance. Once again, thank you for your consideration.

Sincerely,

Chris Smith

Enc. Resume

▶ Including computer skills may be advantageous for certain fields of work.

▶ Candidate informs agency contact only of experiences and skills related to his/her field of interest.

LETTER TO AN EMPLOYMENT AGENCY
(Bookkeeper)

178 Green Street
Kunia, HI 96759

July 17, 20--

Pat Cummings
Partner
Any Employment Agency
1140 Main Street
Honolulu, HI 96813

Dear Mr. Cummings:

If one of your clients is in need of a highly motivated Bookkeeper who can handle the day-to-day details necessary to continue a smooth operation, I would appreciate your consideration of my enclosed resume.

During the past nine years, I have gained diverse experience in accounting, bookkeeping, administration, office maintenance, and customer service within the manufacturing, distribution, property management, retail, and automotive services industries. I have sound knowledge of credit policies and collection procedures to control accounts receivable and loss reduction while retaining good customer relations and building a profitable business.

Although my preference is to stay on the Pacific Coast, I would consider relocation based upon salary, benefits, and future opportunity for growth. My present salary is $28,000.

I am most interested in the opportunities available with your client base and hope to hear from you to arrange a meeting. I can be reached at the above address or by phone at (808) 555-5555.

Sincerely,

Chris Smith

Enc. Resume

▶ Candidate includes all relocation information.   ▶ Candidate includes only applicable skills.

LETTER TO AN EMPLOYMENT AGENCY
(Chemist)

178 Green Street
Tacoma, WA 98405
(206) 555-5555

April 16, 20--

Pat Cummings
Chief Researcher
Any Corporation
1140 Main Street
Wichita, KS 67202

Dear Ms. Cummings:

Thank you for the time you extended to me during our recent conversation. I have enclosed a current resume for your review with reference to one of your client firms.

For the past eight years, my experience has been as a Teacher of Secondary and College-level Chemistry. During the past year, I was one of two educators chosen for the first Henderson Fellowship, where I had the opportunity to apply my education, training, and experience in chemistry and physical science to industry.

It was such an exciting and challenging experience that I am presently investigating new opportunities that will allow me to transfer my technical and teaching skills to a permanent assignment in the corporate arena.

Again, allow me to reiterate my willingness to relocate should an attractive opportunity present itself. I look forward to speaking with you.

Sincerely,

Chris Smith

Enc. Resume

▶ Candidate thanks addressee for time extended.

▶ Awards draw attention to candidate's significant accomplishments.

LETTER TO AN EMPLOYMENT AGENCY
(Claims Processor)

178 Green Street
Tarrytown, NY 10591

December 4, 20--
Pat Cummings
Employment Specialist
Any Employment Agency
1140 Main Street
Bronx, NY 10474

Dear Mr. Cummings:

My interest in securing a position of Claims Processor with one of your client companies has prompted me to forward my resume for your review.

In addition to six years of experience as Home Health Aide, In-patient Claims Representative, and, since 20--, Medical Assistant with Marifield Rehabilitation Hospital, I have sound knowledge of medical terminology, procedure codes, and medical office systems, including related computerized applications. I possess an Associate degree in Sociology, have trained as a Medical Assistant, and am currently a candidate for an Associate degree in Nursing.

My career objective is to further develop my medical and support skills in areas that will give me the opportunity to contribute to the quality and efficiency of health care. My salary is negotiable, depending on the opportunity.

Should you require additional information, please contact me at the above address or by phone at (914) 555-5555. I can be available for a meeting at your convenience.

Thank you for your consideration.

Sincerely,

Chris Smith

Enc. Resume

▶ Candidate informs agency contact of career goals.

▶ Candidate informs agency contact of relevant educational training.

LETTER TO AN EMPLOYMENT AGENCY
(Computer Operations Supervisor)

178 Green Street
Sinking Spring, PA 19608
(215) 555-5555

July 14, 20--

Pat Cummings
Associate
Any Employment Agency
1140 Main Street
Lancaster, PA 17605

Dear Ms. Cummings:

During the past several years, I have gained broad-based experience in data communications, telecommunications, and personnel supervision with major information resource corporations. Presently, I am looking for a new position that will allow me to combine my computer science and supervisory skills.

Should you be aware of any suitable opportunities, please contact me. I look forward to hearing from you.

Sincerely,

Chris Smith

Enc. Resume

▶ Candidate does not restrict job opportunities.

▶ Candidate invites employment contact to respond to inquiry.

LETTER TO AN EMPLOYMENT AGENCY
(Cook)

178 Green Street
Sioux Falls, SD 57117
(605) 555-5555

April 5, 20--

Pat Cummings
Director
Any Employment Agency
1140 Main Street
Dayton, OH 45402

Dear Mr. Cummings:

I will be moving to the Dayton area next month, and would like to submit my qualifications for any suitable opportunities available through your agency.

I am an accomplished cook with experience in a wide variety of food service institutions, including restaurants, catering services, and banquet functions. My areas of expertise include all aspects of food preparation, from ordering ingredients to presentation.

As you can see from my enclosed resume, I most recently worked as a Rounds Cook at the McGuiness Inn. In addition to cooking to order, I performed several supervisory duties, such as scheduling shifts, overseeing inventory control, and troubleshooting problems.

I will be visiting Dayton to secure housing arrangements during the week of April 17-23. I would be available to meet with you or a client within this time frame. In the interim, I will call your office next week to see if I can provide you with any additional information.

Thank you in advance for your consideration.

Sincerely,

Chris Smith

Enc. Resume

▶ Writing to an employment agency may only be applicable for certain service-oriented and/or support positions.

▶ Closing provides specific time frame to allow for meeting.

LETTER TO AN EMPLOYMENT AGENCY
(Cosmetologist)

178 Green Street
Arlington, TX 76015

March 4, 20--

Pat Cummings
Associate
Any Employment Agency
1140 Main Street
Fort Worth, TX 76110

Dear Ms. Cummings:

Please accept the enclosed resume as my expressed interest in obtaining your job search assistance.

For the past twenty years, I have been employed in the field of cosmetology, in positions ranging from Hairdresser and Instructor to Owner/Operator of my own salon. I possess a valid cosmetology license and have completed several courses in related subjects. I am thoroughly trained in:

- Instruction of all levels of cosmetology theory and practical applications.
- Store promotions and customer relations.
- Hairdressing, permanents, and hair coloring.
- Manicuring, skin care, and facials.

I am currently investigating opportunities that will allow me to apply these skills in either a training school or salon setting. I would greatly appreciate any assistance you could provide in identifying area employers who might be looking for a professional with my qualifications.

My resume is enclosed. Please feel free to contact me at (817) 555-5555. Thank you.

Sincerely,

Chris Smith

Enc. Resume

▶ Bullets make cover letter easy to read.　　　▶ Candidate includes training pertinent to his/her field of interest.

LETTER TO AN EMPLOYMENT AGENCY
(Dental Assistant)

178 Green Street
Lafayette, IN 47902
(317) 555-5555

May 3, 20--

Pat Cummings
Associate
Any Employment Agency
1140 Main Street
Indianapolis, IN 46225

Dear Mr. Cummings:

I am a trained Dental Assistant with several years of both clinical and administrative experience. Currently, I am conducting a job search in this area and have heard about your agency's placement record through several acquaintances. Please allow me to familiarize you with my qualifications in an effort to secure your assistance:

- More than six years of experience as a Dental Assistant, contributing to direct patient care and patient relations.
- Honor graduate as a Dental Assistant from National Education Center.
- Sound knowledge of medical terminology and clinical procedures.
- Certified in first aid, cardiopulmonary resuscitation, and electrocardiography.
- Additional experience as a Receptionist/Secretary with an executive search/management consulting firm, a financial management company, and realty firms.

I would like to find a full-time position in the greater Indianapolis vicinity that would allow me to extensively utilize these skills. My compensation requirement is in the mid- to high twenties.

If your agency could provide me with any assistance in securing such a position, I would appreciate hearing from you. Also, please contact me if you require any additional information.

I look forward to working with you to find gainful employment.

Sincerely,

Chris Smith

Enc. Resume

▶ Introduction indicates candidate's familiarity with specific agency.

▶ Professional certification and strong educational background add strength to cover letter.

LETTER TO AN EMPLOYMENT AGENCY
(Director of Operations)

178 Green Street
Dallas, TX 75240

July 26, 20--

Pat Cummings
Director
Any Employment Agency
1140 Main Street
Houston, TX 77251

Dear Ms. Cummings:

If one of your client companies is in need of a person who can handle the day-to-day details necessary to ensure a smooth operation, then we have good reason to meet.

During the past twelve years my experience has ranged from Credit and Collection Manager with a high-tech company to Service Coordinator with a manufacturer of sophisticated medical systems. In these capacities, I provided detailed administrative support to senior-level managers, field service engineers, and other department personnel.

I am currently contemplating a change and would like to be considered for a position with a progressive management team. I have expertise in complex manual- and computer-generated reports, work well independently or as a member of a team, and have extensive troubleshooting, problem-solving, customer service, interpersonal, and communication skills.

Should my qualifications meet the needs of a client, I would be happy to learn of the opportunity. Please note, I am available for immediate, full-time work. I can be reached at (214) 555-5555.

I hope to hear from you soon.

Sincerely,

Chris Smith

Enc. Resume

▶ Candidate informs agency of his/her date of availability.

▶ First paragraph is short and hard-hitting.

LETTER TO AN EMPLOYMENT AGENCY
(Director of Pharmacy)

178 Green Street
Weston, WV 26452
(304) 555-5555

June 22, 20--

Pat Cummings
Director
Any Employment Agency
1140 Main Street
Clarksburg, WV 26302

Dear Mr. Cummings:

I am a Registered Pharmacist with eight years of progressively responsible experience encompassing general management, in-house, and field sales experience in the pharmaceuticals industry. I would like to request your assistance as a professional employment agency, should one of your clients have a need for a Director of Pharmacy.

I am well versed in regulations controlling therapeutic drug treatment, have sound knowledge of medical terminology, and enjoy the clinical and nonclinical but professional aspects of services involving health care products or services. I am currently seeking a management position supervising either several chain locations or a large in-house staff. I am willing to relocate and/or travel to find the right position. My present salary is $50,000.

I look forward to hearing from you, should my qualifications prove to be a match.

Sincerely,

Chris Smith

Enc. Resume

▶ Candidate immediately informs employment agency of job objective.

▶ Candidate informs agency contact of all relevant information, including travel availability and salary requirements.

LETTER TO AN EMPLOYMENT AGENCY
(Executive Assistant)

178 Green Street
Mobile, AL 36625
(203) 555-5555

July 18, 20--

Pat Cummings
Associate
Any Employment Agency
1140 Main Street
Birmingham, AL 25202

Dear Ms. Cummings:

I am an experienced Executive/Administrative Assistant seeking appropriate career opportunities in the corporate arena.

In addition to five years of staff experience at Bradstreet and Associates, I have worked for three years as an Executive Assistant to the President and Executive Vice-President of a software development company. In that capacity, my responsibilities included a variety of assignments, both individual and team projects, writing and typing executive correspondence, and other administrative activities. My word processing and spreadsheet expertise includes Microsoft Word for Windows, Lotus 1-2-3, and Excel, and my technical background enables me to quickly develop expertise in other similar software programs. I am an organized, detail-oriented individual who enjoys staff projects and produces high-quality work. My resume is enclosed.

Should your client needs and my experience prove to be a good match, I would welcome an opportunity to meet with you.

Sincerely,

Chris Smith

Enc. Resume

▶ Introductory sentence specifies position desired.

▶ Including computer skills may be advantageous for certain fields of work.

LETTER TO AN EMPLOYMENT AGENCY
(Hotel Administrator)

178 Green Street
Murfreesboro, TN 37133

April 2, 20--

Pat Cummings
Manager
Any Employment Agency
1140 Main Street
Nashville, TN 37214

Dear Mr. Cummings:

I would like to request your assistance. I am searching for a way to contribute my highly developed customer relations and administrative skills to a challenging position in a hotel. My qualifications include:

- Well-developed interpersonal skills, having dealt with a diversity of clients, professionals, and staff members.
- Detail- and goal-orientated approach to work.
- Ability to function well in a high-stress atmosphere.
- Knowledge of both EECO and APTEC computer systems.

As my enclosed resume reveals, I have direct experience as a Hotel Clerk in two large capacity properties. Additionally, my work as a Secretary has provided me with knowledge of basic clerical duties and customer relations.

Please contact me at (615) 555-5555 if you feel that my qualifications match the needs of one of your clients. I would be happy to meet with you for further discussion, should you need any additional information.

I appreciate your consideration of my request.

Sincerely,

Chris Smith

Enc. Resume

▶ Candidate suggests informational meeting with agency.

▶ Bullets inform agency contact of candidate's qualifications.

LETTER TO AN EMPLOYMENT AGENCY
(Housekeeper)

178 Green Street
Melrose Park, IL 60160

March 27, 20--

Pat Cummings
Associate
Any Employment Agency
1140 Main Street
Twin Falls, ID 83303

Dear Ms. Cummings:

My interest in securing a position in housekeeping or related support activities has prompted me to forward my resume for your review.

During the past seven years, my experience has been concentrated in housekeeping and related nonclinical services with a quality professional nursing home operation. I enjoy working with people in a professional or resort environment and feel confident that I can make a contribution, as a member of the housekeeping staff, to the quality image an institution would like to uphold.

I will be spending a week, from April 29 to May 5, with family in your area prior to permanent relocation. I would welcome the opportunity to meet with you or one of your clients at that time.

If I can provide you with additional information, please contact me at the above address or by phone at (312) 555-5555.

Thank you for your consideration.

Sincerely,

Chris Smith

Enc. Resume

▶ Candidate describes work environment preferences.

▶ Candidate invites employment contact to respond to inquiry.

LETTER TO AN EMPLOYMENT AGENCY
(Insurance Account Manager)

178 Green Street
Las Cruces, NM 88003

October 7, 20--

Pat Cummings
President
Any Employment Agency
1140 Main Street
Albuquerque, NM 87103

Dear Mr. Cummings:

As per your request during our recent conversation, I am enclosing my business profile for your review and for submission to one of your client firms.

My experience as an Account Manager and Office Manager has provided me with expertise in all facets of insurance agency operation. Once oriented to the policies of a new firm, I have the knowledge and skill to assume responsibility for either of the above positions.

Any assistance you can provide in arranging interviews with prospective employers will be most appreciated. Should you require additional information prior to our meeting, please contact me at the address listed above or call me at (505) 555-5555.

Sincerely,

Chris Smith

Enc. Business profile

▶ Letters to employment agencies are generally brief and to the point.

▶ Candidate requests agency's assistance in scheduling interviews.

LETTER TO AN EMPLOYMENT AGENCY
(Insurance Underwriter)

178 Green Street
Flandreau, SD 57028

March 4, 20--
Pat Cummings
Director
Any Corporation
1140 Main Street
Chicago, IL 60605

Dear Ms. Cummings:

During the past ten years, my experience has been in the liability insurance field in positions ranging from Transcriber to Senior Field Claims Representative. Currently, I am seeking a new association with an underwriter or a corporate liability insurance department in which there is a need for expertise in claims settlement, from fact-finding analysis to negotiation.

I am hoping that among your many clients there may be one or two who are looking for someone who is knowledgeable in the area of corporate liability insurance; if so, I would like to explore the opportunity. I may be reached at (605) 555-5555 during regular business hours or evenings at (605) 555-4444.

I look forward to hearing from you.

Sincerely,

Chris Smith

Enc. Resume

▶ Including a business number is optional in a cover letter.

▶ Letters to employment agencies are generally brief and to the point.

LETTER TO AN EMPLOYMENT AGENCY
(Legal Administrator)

178 Green Street
Jacksonville, FL 32203

August 7, 20--

Pat Cummings
Partner
Any Employment Agency
1140 Main Street
Tallahassee, FL 32302

Dear Mr. Cummings:

I would like to be considered for a court- or legal-related administrative position with any appropriate clients you may serve. I have recently relocated to the Florida from the Washington, D.C. area, and am seeking employment that would utilize my leadership skills, education, and experience.

In Washington, I was the Office Manager for a respected court-reporting firm. All of my primary job responsibilities required organization, attention to detail, writing, and significant computer skills. I have extensive experience working multitasking and in meeting deadlines in a team-oriented environment. As a result, I have developed strong time management and interpersonal skills.

I have enclosed my resume for your review. Should you need additional information, please do not hesitate to contact me at (904) 555-5555. I look forward to hearing from you. Thank you for your time.

Sincerely,

Chris Smith

Enc. Resume

▶ Candidate immediately informs employment agency of job objective.

▶ Letter focuses on acquired skills rather than detailing past employers.

LETTER TO AN EMPLOYMENT AGENCY
(Medical Assistant)

178 Green Street
Cedar City, UT 84720

July 3, 20--

Pat Cummings
Director
Any Employment Agency
1140 Main Street
Smithfield, UT 84335

Dear Ms. Cummings:

Your agency has been recommended to me for job placement within the health care field. I am a trained Medical Assistant searching for a new association with a firm in the Southwest.

Prior to working with professional service firms and a manufacturing company, I spent four years as a Medical Receptionist. My continued interest in, and dedication to, the health care field recently prompted me to pursue additional study at Salt Lake Community College. I have enclosed my resume, which further outlines my background.

After you have reviewed my qualifications, I would appreciate hearing from you with reference to available Medical Assistant positions where I can, perhaps, also apply my business experience. I am looking for an opportunity in the $25,000 to $30,000 range. If I can be of any further assistance, please contact me at the above address or by phone at (801) 555-5555.

Sincerely,

Chris Smith

Enc. Resume

▶ Introduction indicates candidate's familiarity with specific agency.

▶ Continuing education demonstrates candidate's dedication to his/her field.

LETTER TO AN EMPLOYMENT AGENCY
(Office Manager)

178 Green Street
La France, SC 29656
(803) 555-5555

March 30, 20--

Pat Cummings
Associate
Any Employment Agency
1140 Main Street
Spartanburg, SC 29304

Dear Mr. Cummings:

Finding the right person for the job is often difficult, costly, and at times disappointing. However, if one of your clients is in need of a reliable, competent, and well-organized individual for his or her office management staff, I have the qualifications and dedication for the position.

During the past ten years, I have held progressively responsible positions in office management with manufacturing, distribution, export, and service companies. Recently, I made a permanent relocation to La France, and am interested in joining a company in the greater Spartanburg area that can benefit from my experience.

I have broad experience with manual and automated accounting/administrative systems, customer service, personnel supervision, event/meeting planning, credit and collection, and executive support. I function best in a diverse, busy environment and have established a reputation for being organized and capable of coordinating and handling multiple assignments cost-effectively and to schedule.

The enclosed business profile summarizes my qualifications. Should you know of any suitable opportunities, I would appreciate your consideration.

I look forward to hearing from you.

Sincerely,

Chris Smith

Enc. Business profile

▶ Introduction captures addressee's attention.　　▶ Candidate describes work environment preferences.

LETTER TO AN EMPLOYMENT AGENCY
(Operations Manager)

178 Green Street
Phoenix, AZ 85012
(602) 555-5555

January 15, 20--

Pat Cummings
Director
Any Employment Agency
1140 Main Street
Keyport, WA 98101

Dear Ms. Cummings:

I am relocating to your area next month. Your agency's name comes highly recommended as a superior job placement service and, for this reason, I am enclosing my resume for your review.

I am interested in locating a challenging position in which to consolidate my experience and utilize my chemical, electro-mechanical, and mechanical skills. I would be a good match for a progressive, technically oriented company seeking conscientious, intelligent support in the areas of research, manufacturing, or production.

Please note that in fifteen years I have occupied progressively responsible and sophisticated positions with RHG Corporation, ranging from Automated Manufacturing Machine Operator to Research and Development Assistant and Senior Laboratory Technician. I am highly skilled in all trades and have more than six years of experience in the management and supervision of fleet maintenance operations for cars and trucks. I have additional training in accounting, real estate, supervision, and management and I am considered an expert in automotive and general mechanics.

Do you know of any available or anticipated openings that match my qualifications? If so, I can be reached at the address and telephone number listed above until February 1.

I appreciate your time.

Sincerely,

Chris Smith

Enc. Resume

▶ Qualifications call attention to candidate's relevant supervisory and administrative experience.

▶ Candidate does not restrict job opportunities.

LETTER TO AN EMPLOYMENT AGENCY
(Property Manager)

178 Green Street
Salamanca, NY 14779
(716) 555-5555

May 13, 20--

Pat Cummings
Director
Any Corporation
1140 Main Street
Chicago, IL 60605

Dear Mr. Cummings:

In July of this year I will be permanently relocating to the Chicago area. I am forwarding the attached resume for your evaluation because of my desire to contribute my comprehensive experience in real estate/property management to a locally based company.

I have two years of direct experience involving all aspects in the management of 275 apartments and four commercial units in three buildings. My responsibilities include a range of activities, from advertising and promotion of apartments to competitive analysis of rate structures.

My experience also includes contractor negotiations, liaison with government and service agencies, personnel relations, financial management, and other functions basic to the effective management of complex properties.

If you know of any company with a current need for a bright, outgoing property manager with an orientation to sales, please do not hesitate to contact me.

Thank you for your consideration.

Sincerely,

Chris Smith

Enc. Resume

▶ Candidate includes only applicable skills.   ▶ Closing encourages reader to respond to letter.

LETTER TO AN EMPLOYMENT AGENCY
(Purchasing Agent)

178 Green Street
Walla Walla, WA 99362
(509) 555-5555

December 4, 20--

Pat Cummings
Manager
Any Employment Agency
1140 Main Street
Yakima, WA 98909

Dear Ms. Cummings:

I am an experienced professional interested in pursuing my purchasing career within a progressive and challenging environment. Glen Guapo, an associate of mine, referred me to your agency, noting your excellent placement record for those with similar qualifications.

During the past five years, I have held progressively responsible positions ranging from Purchasing Secretary to Regional Distribution Supervisor and Purchasing Agent in the high-tech manufacturing and retail industry. I have been actively involved in vendor evaluation, vendor lead time, and customer delivery scheduling, sourcing, negotiating, and monitoring, and have followed through on purchases from sampling to accounts payable.

Although these positions have been fast-paced, challenging, and broad in scope, I feel that my expertise in purchasing can be utilized to better advantage by one of your client companies. I am confident that my diverse background has given me the flexibility to undertake varied and expanding responsibilities in these areas, and I am open to travel to secure the right opportunity. I am interested in positions with a salary range from $30,000 to $45,000.

Please do not hesitate to contact me if you need any additional information. I would be happy to come in and speak with you or a potential employer. Thank you for your time.

Sincerely,

Chris Smith

Enc. Resume

▶ Candidate informs agency contact of all relevant information, including travel availability and salary requirements.

▶ Candidate immediately names referral.

LETTER TO AN EMPLOYMENT AGENCY
(Quality Control Specialist)

178 Green Street
South Bend, IN 46619

July 23, 20--

Pat Cummings
Director
Any Employment Agency
1140 Main Street
Memphis, TN 38109

Dear Mr. Cummings:

My interest in locating a position in quality control/quality assurance with a firm in the Memphis area has prompted me to forward this up-to-date resume for your review. I am planning permanent relocation to Tennessee in September and I would appreciate any assistance in finding a suitable employer.

My background includes a Bachelor of Science degree in Biology and Associate degrees in Math and Science. I also have seventeen months of solid, hands-on experience as a Quality Control Analyst with a manufacturer of instrumentation for environmental analysis. My knowledge in these areas includes all current inspection systems, procedures, and equipment used to maintain standards to critical tolerance. I am certain of my ability to make an immediate, long-term contribution to my employer.

Please contact me at the above address or by phone at (219) 555-5555 if you know of any quality control vacancies or related positions. I look forward to hearing from you in the near future.

Sincerely,

Chris Smith

Enc. Resume

▶ Impressive educational experience and qualifications help compensate for candidate's short employment history.

▶ Introductory sentence specifies position desired.

LETTER TO AN EMPLOYMENT AGENCY
(Retail Manager)

178 Green Street
Landover, MD 20785
(410) 555-5555

June 16, 20--

Pat Cummings
Director
Any Employment Agency
1140 Main Street
Detroit, MI 48203

Dear Ms. Cummings:

In a month I plan to permanently relocate to the Detroit area. I am forwarding the attached resume for your consideration due to my desire to contribute my experience in retail management to a nationally recognized grocery chain.

During the past eighteen months I have advanced to Shift Manager with Any Natural Foods Market. Working with natural foods is both a vocation and an avocation for me. I have the ability to work with employees and customers to establish high visibility and a quality image for the market, and also, stress the benefits of natural foods to health and fitness. I am service-oriented and feel confident that I can implement and maintain the quality standards of employee performance expected of a first-rate management team.

After you have had a chance to review my qualifications, I would appreciate a meeting to discuss market manager positions.

Sincerely,

Chris Smith

Enc. Resume

▶ Candidate suggests informational meeting with agency.

▶ Letter expresses commitment to field of interest.

LETTER TO AN EMPLOYMENT AGENCY
(Sales/Customer Service Representative)

178 Green Street
Trenton, NJ 08619
(609) 555-5555

November 4, 20--

Pat Cummings
Employment Representative
Any Employment Agency
1140 Main Street
Linwood, NJ 08221

Dear Mr. Cummings:

I am writing to inquire if your agency might be able to assist me in my search for a position in either sales or customer service.

As you can see from my enclosed resume, I have more than seven years of experience in positions ranging from Sales Assistant to Claims Investigator and Bank Teller. Some of my applicable skills include:

- Acting as liaison between customers, staff, and management.
- Investigating and resolving customer requests and problems.
- Tracking and expediting sales orders; ascertaining order accuracy.
- Processing a wide range of financial transactions; maintaining accuracy and balance.
- PC and Macintosh word processing, Lotus 1-2-3 and Excel.

I would be interested in discussing any employment opportunities you feel would be applicable to my skills. Please note that I am willing to travel, and negotiate a salary in the $28,000 to 35,000 range. Do not hesitate to contact me if you need any additional information.

I will follow up this inquiry with a phone call next week.

Sincerely,

Chris Smith

Enc. Resume

▶ Letter focuses on functional skills applicable to potential employer.

▶ When writing to an employment agency, including compensation requirements is optional.

LETTER TO AN EMPLOYMENT AGENCY
(Secretary)

178 Green Street
Clinton, MS 39060

January 18, 20--

Pat Cummings
Staff Associate
Any Employment Agency
1140 Main Street
St. Louis, MO 63122

Dear Ms. Cummings:

Enclosed please find my resume for your review regarding potential employment with your client community. I would be interested in a secretarial position where I could utilize my administrative and secretarial skills.

I have earned an Associate degree in the Secretarial Program at Macomb Community College. In addition, my current tenure at Gaudet and Growney has afforded me the opportunity to further develop competent organizational and analytical skills. In the everyday operations of the department, the general merchandise manager relies on me to organize meetings and coordinate all communications to our ten-store chain. These responsibilities have enabled me to expand my general office skills.

Although my employment at Gaudet and Growney has been a positive experience, I am seeking a position that will offer more advancement opportunity.

I possess excellent secretarial and administrative skills. I have nine years of administrative experience working both in the merchandising department and in the executive offices of my current employer. I am also knowledgeable in a variety of software programs. My compensation requirements are in the $25,000 to $35,000 range, and I would be willing to relocate.

I would welcome the opportunity to speak with you regarding my qualifications. I can be reached at (601) 555-5555, ext. 226 (days) or (601) 555-4444 (evenings).

Thank you for your consideration.

Sincerely,

Chris Smith

Enc. Resume

▶ Writing to an employment agency may only be applicable for certain service-oriented and/or support positions.

▶ Candidate informs agency contact only of experiences and skills related to his/her field of interest.

LETTER TO AN EMPLOYMENT AGENCY
(Security Guard)

178 Green Street
Minden, NV 89423

May 4, 20--

Pat Cummings
Director
Any Employment Agency
1140 Main Street
Las Vegas, NV 89125

Dear Mr. Cummings:

I understand that your agency provides job placement services in the greater Las Vegas area. Having recently moved here, I would greatly appreciate your assistance in securing a position.

For the past eight years, I have worked in the security industry as a Guard. My interest in this field developed from a position with the Willow Mead Art Museum in Wyoming. As a Security Guard at the museum, my duties included patrol, surveillance, and control of facilities and areas. I also maintained reports, records, and documents as required by administration.

For the past three years as a bank Security Guard, I was responsible for ensuring safety and security of customers, bank employees, and bank assets. My compensation for that position was in the high $20,000 range.

I look forward to finding a similar position through your agency. I can begin working immediately. Please contact me to schedule interviews at (702) 555-5555.

Sincerely,

Chris Smith

Enc. Resume

▶ Candidate requests agency's assistance in scheduling interviews.

▶ Candidate informs agency of his/her date of availability.

LETTER TO AN EMPLOYMENT AGENCY
(Stenographer)

178 Green Street
Troutdale, OR 97060
(503) 555-5555

January 3, 20--

Pat Cummings
Representative
Any Employment Agency
1140 Main Street
Portland, OR 97208

Dear Ms. Cummings:

Recently, a friend of mine, Sean Wilson, recommended your agency to assist me in my job search. I understand you successfully found Sean a clerical position last month. I am searching for a challenging position as a Stenographer, to which I could apply the following qualifications:

- Strong shorthand and speed-writing skills at 120 wpm.
- Expertise in Gregg Simplified and Diamond Jubilee methods; proficiency with the Pitman method.
- Experience in the transcription, editing, and interpreting of stenographic characters into clear, concise, and precise English.
- Typing skills that include word processing at 80 wpm.

My experience is supplemented by an Associate degree in Secretarial Sciences and a certificate of accomplishment from the Executive Secretarial Program at Katherine Gibbs secretarial school.

I would prefer to stay in the greater Portland area, and would ask for a salary starting between $24,000 and $28,000. If you could provide me with any assistance in this regard, I would be most appreciative.

I look forward to hearing from you.

Sincerely,

Chris Smith

Enc. Resume

▶ Candidate informs agency of geographical preference.

▶ Candidate informs agency contact of relevant educational training.

LETTER TO AN EMPLOYMENT AGENCY
(Waitperson)

178 Green Street
Reston, VA 22091
(703) 555-5555

December 19, 20--

Pat Cummings
Representative
Any Employment Agency
1140 Main Street
Vienna, VA 22180

Dear Mr. Cummings:

I am searching for a challenging position in the fast-food industry in which work experience and a commitment to excellence will have valuable application.

Currently, I am working as a Server/Bartender for a 250-seat restaurant in Reston, VA. In addition to my serving duties, I am responsible for register control, assistant shift supervision, and conflict resolution. I work well in both relaxed or fast-paced, high-pressure environments.

I would like to continue my career in food service upon my relocation to your area next month. If you should be aware of any available opportunities, I would appreciate your assistance. Until January 1, I can be reached at (215) 555-5555. After that date, I will be residing at the address and telephone number cited above.

Thank you for your time. I will be in contact soon to confirm that you have received this inquiry and attached resume.

Sincerely,

Chris Smith

Enc. Resume

▶ Candidate includes all relocation information.

▶ Candidate describes work environment preferences.

CHAPTER 15

LETTER TO AN EXECUTIVE SEARCH FIRM

Although executive search firms like to recruit their own candidates for client companies, don't let this discourage you from making the first contact yourself. A well-crafted cover letter can alert an otherwise unknowing recruiter of your availability. Remember, this is your chance to shine. Highlight your most impressive accomplishments and attributes and briefly summarize all relevant experience. If you have certain preferences, such as geographical location, travel, and salary, mention them in your cover letter. As a rule, if executive search firms are interested in learning more, they'll call you, so keep your closing succinct.

LETTER TO AN EXECUTIVE SEARCH FIRM
(Buyer)

178 Green Street
Charleston, WV 25322
(304) 555-5555

March 7, 20--

Pat Cummings
Executive Recruiter
Any Company
1140 Main Street
Huntington, WV 25755

Dear Ms. Cummings:

I am a creative, innovative buyer who can add excitement to your clients' inventories while generating bottom-line profits.

During the past eighteen years, I have had the opportunity to work in positions ranging from Merchandise Planner to Head Buyer at the headquarters level of major off-price retail chains. I have enjoyed rapid advancement and experienced the challenge of coordinating new concepts and introducing change associated with upscale fashion and trends. Recently, my efforts generated a 75 percent increase in sales and profits.

Currently, I am looking for a new association with a growing chain that will benefit from my experience and successes in identifying fashion trends, developing resources, and negotiating big buys for off-price retail operations. The professional opportunity I am looking for will utilize my market and product knowledge and ingenuity to achieve the same results for your clients as I have for my current employer.

I am interested in positions with a salary range from $75,000 to $90,000 and will relocate for the right opportunity.

Since my current employer is unaware of my current search, your confidence is appreciated.

Sincerely,

Chris Smith

Enc. Resume

▶ Compensation requirements are often included in executive search letters.

▶ Candidate informs recruiter of need for confidentiality.

LETTER TO AN EXECUTIVE SEARCH FIRM
(Chief Executive Officer)

178 Green Street
Irmo, SC 29063

October 25, 20--

Pat Cummings
Executive Recruiter
Any Corporation
1140 Main Street
Chicago, IL 60605

Dear Mr. Cummings:

During the past twenty years, I have gained experience ranging from National Sales Manager/Director of Marketing to CEO of a $25-million athletic shoe manufacturer. I have earned the reputation for being a highly skilled senior-level manager in the areas of manufacturing, new business start-up and management, company reorganization and expansion, and design and development, at both regional and national levels.

Although my positions have been challenging and fast-paced, at this point in my career I am seeking new opportunities in an advisory capacity, which may ultimately lead to an equity position. I am looking for an environment where my expertise, creativity, and motivation can be fully utilized toward upgrading and/or expanding new or existing businesses. My salary requirement is $80,000 to $100,000.

If you would like any additional information, please do not hesitate to call me at (803) 555-5555. I am best reached weekdays between 8 A.M. and 1 P.M.

I look forward to your response.

Sincerely,

Chris Smith

Enc. Resume

▶ Executive search letters are especially effective for top-level professionals.

▶ Candidate focuses on responsibilities of most recent position.

LETTER TO AN EXECUTIVE SEARCH FIRM
(Commercial Transportation Specialist)

178 Green Street
New Castle, DE 19720
(302) 555-5555

January 7, 20--

Pat Cummings
Superintendent
Any Shipping Company
1140 Main Street
Wilmington, DE 19850

Dear Ms. Cummings:

My interest in an executive position with a major maritime shipper, such as one of your client companies, has prompted me to forward my resume for your review and consideration.

During the past eight years, I have had concentrated management experience in marine transportation with the United States Military Sealift Command. A major portion of my responsibilities involved navigation in heavily traveled areas, as well as the supervision and training of anywhere from one hundred to two hundred personnel during watch.

Although my present assignments are challenging, I am ready for a change to commercial marine transportation and I feel that I can offer one of your client companies a great deal of relevant experience and commitment.

Please do not hesitate to contact me should you know of a suitable match for my skills. I am willing to travel for the right opportunity.

I look forward to speaking with you.

Sincerely,

Chris Smith

Enc. Professional profile

▶ Specifically sighting number of personnel supervised draws attention to candidate's leadership abilities.

▶ Candidate details how past military experience will benefit potential employer.

LETTER TO AN EXECUTIVE SEARCH FIRM
(Corporate President)

178 Green Street
Redmond, WA 98052
(206) 555-5555

December 24, 20--

Pat Cummings
Executive Recruiter
1140 Main Street
Seattle, WA 98103

Dear Mr. Cummings:

   I have enclosed a business profile and request your consideration for any current or anticipated search assignments.

   During the past twenty years, I have had the opportunity to apply innovative, leadership, and profit-making skills in positions ranging from President of a successful start-up business developed to $7 million in annual sales, to Vice-President, Product Management/Business Development, with a $750 million rapid growth computer resale company.

   My skill in undertaking new challenges, ability to implement change, and expertise in developing compatible, professional teams during the transition phases of acquisitions, mergers, and consolidations enables me to provide stability and profitability to growth situations. Presently, I am looking for a position change to a company where I have the responsibility for making meaningful decisions and the authority to implement plans to achieve corporate objectives.

   My desire is to find an exciting, growth-oriented position. Thus, I would be willing to relocate to secure a salary in the $100,000 range.

   Please contact me should my qualifications be of interest to one of your client firms. Thank you for your consideration.

Sincerely,

Chris Smith

Enc. Business profile

▶ Executive search letters provide detailed information regarding candidate's impressive track record.

▶ Candidate immediately and concisely informs recruiter of his/her qualifications.

LETTER TO AN EXECUTIVE SEARCH FIRM
(Director of Administration)

178 Green Street
York, PA 17405

January 13, 20--

Pat Cummings
Executive Recruiter
1140 Main Street
Philadelphia, PA 19130

Dear Ms. Cummings:

Although my present position as Director of Administration has been a most responsible and rewarding experience, personal and family obligations have influenced my decision to return to the Pennsylvania area. For this reason, I am contacting you, in confidence, for assistance in my job search.

During the past fourteen years, my positions as Operations Manager and Director of Administration, with both large and small firms, have given me the hands-on experience and expertise to do a fine job for one of your client companies.

I have enclosed a business profile that briefly outlines my background and experience. I would be happy to meet with you so that you can evaluate and match my skills with the needs of one of your clients. My prime requirements for a position are job satisfaction, good growth potential, a compatible environment, and compensation within the $75,000 to $90,000 range.

I plan to be in your area from February 6 to 17, and hope to meet with you at that time. In the interim, should you require additional information, please contact me at the above address or by phone at (717) 555-5555.

Sincerely,

Chris Smith

Enc. Business profile

▶ Explaining reason for job search is optional.

▶ Benefits to potential employer are emphasized.

LETTER TO AN EXECUTIVE SEARCH FIRM
(Director of Information Services)

178 Green Street
Idaho Falls, ID 83415
(208) 555-5555

August 15, 20--

Pat Cummings
Executive Recruiter
1140 Main Street
Boise, ID 83706

Dear Mr. Cummings:

During our meeting at the Minority Professional Recruiting Center on July 24, we had a chance to discuss opportunities available with several of your client firms that are of great interest to me.

Although my position with McDavid Associates provides an environment that is both interesting and professional, I feel it is time for a change. I am currently seeking a challenging position with a firm that will allow me to apply my combined technical knowledge, experience, and ability to create and implement innovative concepts for greater information systems efficiency. I can offer:

- Thirteen years of experience with MIS corporate information systems.
- Experience in the operation and supervision of administrative functions of several UNIX systems using UNIX System V operating software.
- Skill in communicating with domestic/international networks/mainframes and network system support.
- Capability to work as a team member, team leader, and/or independent contributor, working off-site via modem and data network, to assist users in sales, finance, manufacturing, and production.
- Ability to generate positive results in a company's information systems and networks by streamlining systems and improving personnel/user training and performance.

I have enclosed a resume and would appreciate meeting with you to discuss my qualifications. Relocation is not a problem and my compensation requirements are in the low $70,000 range.

Thank you for your consideration.

Yours sincerely,

Chris Smith

Enc. Resume

▶ Separating major accomplishments from body draws attention.

▶ Avoid technical jargon unless it is specific to candidate's field.

LETTER TO AN EXECUTIVE SEARCH FIRM
(Engineering Administrator)

178 Green Street
Lansdale, PA 19446

November 4, 20--

Pat Cummings
Executive Recruiter
Any Firm
1140 Main Street
Philadelphia, PA 19114

Dear Ms. Cummings:

I am currently exploring administrative opportunities in the engineering field. Enclosed is my resume for your consideration.

Please note that my seventeen years of practical experience have involved working on major commercial and industrial projects in the Middle East as a Construction Engineer, Construction Manager, and Planning and Systems Engineer. This experience is supported by a multilingual capability, a Bachelor of Science degree in Civil Engineering, a Master of Science degree in Engineering Administration with concentration in Construction Management, and broad experience with computers.

I look forward to discussing with you my potential to contribute to your clients' needs. If you will please contact me at the above address or by phone at (215) 555-5555, I would like to establish a mutually convenient time for a personal interview. My salary has ranged from $75,000 to its most current $95,000, and I am open to opportunities that offer similar compensation.

Thank you for your attention.

Sincerely,

Chris Smith

Enc. Resume

▶ Letters to executive search firms are best utilized by a candidate with extensive experience in his/her field of interest.

▶ Executive search letters generally allow recruiter to respond to candidate's inquiry.

LETTER TO AN EXECUTIVE SEARCH FIRM
(Executive Administrator)

178 Green Street
Columbia, SC 29202

December 15, 20--

Pat Cummings
Director
Any Executive Search Firm
1140 Main Street
Spartanburg, SC 29304

Dear Mr. Cummings:

If one of your client firms is in need of an innovative executive with broad experience in product management, business development, and high-tech product service operations, then we have good reason to meet for further discussion.

I am an aggressive professional who enjoys a challenge and is willing to accept the responsibility for capturing my corporate share of targeted and strategic markets. As a leader or member of a professional national and/or international marketing staff, I am confident that I can make the same outstanding contribution to one of your client firms as I have to my present employer.

During the past seventeen years, I have progressively advanced from positions ranging from Senior Sales Representative, Strategic Account Manager, and Marketing Manager to my most current position as Strategic Alliance Marketing and Business Development Manager with an internationally recognized computer company.

Although these positions have been fast-paced and challenging, I feel that my expertise in selling concepts and working with vendors worldwide on the development and execution of joint marketing ventures can be effectively utilized to provide high visibility and develop new applications for increased sales. Please note, I am willing to relocate for the right opportunity.

The enclosed resume summarizes my background and experience in the areas cited above. Should you require additional information, please feel free to contact me at the above address or by phone at (803) 555-5555. I would welcome your acknowledgment and look forward to a meeting at your earliest convenience.

Sincerely,

Chris Smith

Enc. Resume

▶ Candidate details all relevant experience.

▶ Candidate informs recruiter of willingness to travel and/or relocate.

LETTER TO AN EXECUTIVE SEARCH FIRM
(Financial Administrator)

178 Green Street
Albany, GA 31708

November 15, 20--

Pat Cummings
Senior Consultant
Any Search Firm
1140 Main Street
Jacksonville, FL 32207

Dear Ms. Cummings:

Should one of your clients find themselves in need of a business professional with expertise in strategic planning, domestic and international finance, marketing, and general management, I ask that you consider my enclosed executive profile.

My expertise derives from thirteen years of experience in profit-center management, investment banking, and asset management for Fortune 100 and 500 companies, institutions, and individual investors with diverse holdings in ranges from $1 million to $500 million. I have sound knowledge concerning the implementation of mergers/acquisitions, developmental strategies, and business plans for major corporate and independent investors in the United States and abroad.

My decision to permanently relocate to Florida now makes it necessary for me to look into new opportunities. I am interested in joining the management staff of an established financial corporation. My current annual compensation is $80,000.

I am innovative, well organized, skilled in working with decision-makers, and capable of directing a well-disciplined management organization that can accept the challenge of bringing business plans into functioning profit modes.

Should you be aware of a suitable opportunity, please contact me at the above address or my business phone at (912) 555-5555. I appreciate your consideration.

Yours sincerely,

Chris Smith

Enc. Executive profile

▶ Summary of experience accentuates candidate's acquired professional skills and impressive track record.

▶ Including a business number is optional in a cover letter.

LETTER TO AN EXECUTIVE SEARCH FIRM
(Labor Relations Specialist)

178 Green Street
Kalamazoo, MI 49006

June 15, 20--

Pat Cummings
Executive Recruiter
1140 Main Street
Chicago, IL 60605

Dear Mr. Cummings:

My experience encompasses more than ten years of decision-making responsibility for human resource development, manpower planning, and labor law and relations, affecting hundreds of employees in the public and private sectors. In addition to the training and supervision of sizable staffs, I have been involved in collective bargaining for management, wage and salary administration, employee benefits, safety and training, and making and enforcing labor law considerations.

I am currently interested in a firm that offers stability, growth, and profits. I am willing to relocate if offered a challenging assignment. My salary requirement is $50,000 to $65,000.

I have enclosed my resume for your review. If I may provide you with additional information, please call me at (616) 555-5555. I look forward to discussing my qualifications with you in more detail.

Sincerely,

Chris Smith

Enc. Resume

▶ Candidate highlights areas of expertise.   ▶ Experiences are tailored to employer's needs.

LETTER TO AN EXECUTIVE SEARCH FIRM
(Lawyer: International Law)

178 Green Street
New Hope, MN 55428
(612) 555-5555

March 24, 20--

Pat Cummings
Executive Recruiter
1140 Main Street
Minneapolis, MN 55426

Dear Ms. Cummings:

I feel that as an executive in a search company, you might be effective in matching me with the legal staff of one of your client firms.

In addition to a Juris Doctor degree, I recently received a Master of Laws in Banking Law Studies with a concentration in International Law. My expertise is in the supervision of associate and support legal staff in research, document preparation, and coordination as required for all legal issues. I am well organized, accurate, and conscientious, interface well with individuals and groups, and feel confident that I can be a contributing asset to one of your client firms.

I have enclosed a professional profile of my academic accomplishments and work experience. My last compensation was $90,000, although I feel my value has substantially increased with the attainment of my recent degree. Should you wish to discuss my qualifications further, I can be reached at my office at (612) 555-4444, extension 22.

I look forward to working together.

Sincerely,

Chris Smith

Enc. Professional profile

▶ Advanced degrees add weight to cover letter.

▶ Benefits to potential employer are emphasized.

LETTER TO AN EXECUTIVE SEARCH FIRM
(Management Consultant)

178 Green Street
Gusher, VT 84030
(802) 555-5555

April 1, 20--

Pat Cummings
Executive Recruiter
Any Corporation
1140 Main Street
Chicago, IL 60605

Dear Mr. Cummings:

I have played a key role in designing, implementing, reorganizing, and managing a variety of functions—including operations, manufacturing, materials, engineering, and quality assurance—for nationally and internationally recognized corporations.

Currently, I am seeking a position with a company that can benefit from my twenty years of progressively responsible management experience in the above areas. My expertise is diverse and includes:

- Five years as Director of Operations for a $60 million manufacturer.
- More than six years as Materials Manager with a multiplant, multiwarehouse, $10 million manufacturer of industrial rubber products.
- More than nine years as Manufacturing Coordinator with a toy manufacturer, with responsibilities related to the physical set-up of new or expansion of existing manufacturing and support facilities; manpower planning; industrial union relations; and capital equipment investment and materials purchases.

I have enclosed my resume for your review. Should you be conducting a search for someone with my background at the present time or in the near future, I would greatly appreciate your consideration. I would be happy to discuss my background in greater detail with you, on the phone or in person. Thank you for your time.

Yours sincerely,

Chris Smith

Enc. Resume

▶ Candidate highlights areas of expertise.

▶ Separating major accomplishments from the body of the letter draws attention.

LETTER TO AN EXECUTIVE SEARCH FIRM
(Operations Manager)

178 Green Street
Minnetonka, MN 55343
(612) 555-5555

March 23, 20--

Pat Cummings
President
Any Search Firm
1140 Main Street
Minneapolis, MN 55408

Dear Ms. Cummings:

Based on my diverse background and experience with high-end, mid-range, and low-end hardware, software, and network products designed for many industries, I feel confident that I can make a valuable contribution toward new product planning, market development, and expansion at a firm within your client base.

Over the last seventeen years, I have developed and marketed packaged and customized software for many industries in domestic and international markets, but also provided the support products for end-users at all levels. Because of this diversity, I am easily able to transfer my skills to marketing other products.

In addition to a strong marketing and sales background, I have established a record for setting up, staffing, and managing top-producing, profitable district offices.

The enclosed profile is a brief summary of my qualifications. Should you be aware of an advanced marketing and development position within the $70,000 to $80,000 range, please consider my qualifications.

Thank you in advance for your attention to this matter.

Sincerely,

Chris Smith

Enc. Professional profile

▶ Letters to executive search firms are best utilized by a candidate with extensive experience in his/her field of interest.

▶ Letter focuses on candidate's major skills and accomplishments.

LETTER TO AN EXECUTIVE SEARCH FIRM
(Plant Manager)

178 Green Street
Madison Heights, MI 48071
(313) 555-5555

July 18, 20--

Pat Cummings
President
Any Search Firm
1140 Main Street
Detroit, MI 48239

Dear Mr. Cummings:

During the past ten years, I have held positions ranging from Production Supervisor to Plant/Operations Manager with a $16 million manufacturer and importer of electrical products. Presently, I am seeking a new association with a firm, where I, as a seasoned manager, can contribute to its cost-effective, quality operation and profitability in keeping with management objectives.

In my current position as Plant Manager, I have restructured and developed a stable work force and environment. Under my direction, the company has benefited from the efficient performance of a supervisory staff and support personnel in all phases of plant operations including production, purchasing, inventory control, warehousing, distribution, and maintenance of a 325,000+ square-foot facility.

The enclosed resume summarizes my background and experience in the above areas. Based on my skills in dealing with employees, vendors, and management, I would welcome the opportunity to apply my proven track record to one of your client firms as I have for my present and prior employers. Relocation is not a problem and my compensation requirements are in the $60,000 to $70,000 range.

If you need additional information, I can be reached at the above address or phone.

Thank you for your consideration.

Sincerely,

Chris Smith

Enc. Resume

▶ Candidate immediately highlights substantial accomplishments that would interest industry professional.

▶ Letter indicates how candidate contributed to his/her previous employers.

LETTER TO AN EXECUTIVE SEARCH FIRM
(President/CEO)

---

178 Green Street
Warwick, RI 02886
(401) 555-5555

August 3, 20--

Pat Cummings
Personal Consultant
Any Search Firm
1140 Main Street
Pawtucket, RI 02860

Dear Ms. Cummings:

In the course of your search assignments, you might have a need for an experienced President/CEO with expertise in all phases of real estate development and construction. If so, I would like to be considered.

During the past twenty years as a Developer of large real estate complexes and President of a major real estate development group, I managed large projects, from site acquisition and master planning through approvals. I have successfully marketed award-winning residential and commercial mixed-usage developments representing $185 million in sales. Currently, I am involved in negotiating site acquisitions, and planning, coordinating, and managing large real estate development/construction projects for both foreign and domestic investors with interests throughout the Northeast.

My positions require strong administrative, management, financial, and interpersonal skills, as well as the capability to negotiate effectively and successfully with financial institutions, regulatory agencies, development professionals, and contractors. Presently, I am looking for a new association with a firm where my expertise can be used to achieve mutual objectives for growth and profit.

My preference is to remain in my present regional location, with which I am most familiar. My current salary is in the low six figures. After you have reviewed my qualifications, I can arrange to meet with you at your convenience.

Thank you for your attention to this matter.

Sincerely,

Chris Smith

Enc. Professional profile

▶ Candidate informs recruiter of preference for remaining in present location.

▶ Letter stresses candidate's extensive experience and significant accomplishments.

LETTER TO AN EXECUTIVE SEARCH FIRM
(Senior Accountant)

178 Green Street
Concord, NH 03302
(603) 555-5555

July 20, 20--
Pat Cummings
Executive Recruiter
1140 Main Street
New York, NY 10022

Dear Mr. Cummings:

I believe that the varied accounting, finance, and general management experience I have gained over the course of my career will be of significant interest to you in your current or anticipated client searches.

As a seasoned, certified Accountant, I have successfully managed general ledger, cash accounting, accounts payable, employee disbursements, and fixed asset operations. As a Manufacturing Plant Controller, I managed the accounting activities and the general administrative functions of a $35 million manufacturing plant. I have:

- Prepared, analyzed, and presented P&L, balance sheet, departmental expense, manufacturing variance, and other operating reports.
- Prepared $2 million annual departmental operating budgets, analyzed results, initiated required operational improvements, and prepared forecasts.
- Developed annual strategic and operational improvements that resulted in a 15 percent increase in efficiency.
- Oversaw human resources, purchasing, payroll, and other plant administrative functions.
- Maintained quality accounting operations by implementing internal controls testing programs.

I have also managed the interface between my group and the data center running my applications, directed the MIS professionals that supported my applications and systems, and managed the enhancement projects that steadily improved day-to-day operations. I am also comfortable with the operation of several different spreadsheet and word processing applications on PC and Macintosh systems.

My resume is enclosed. While my prime interest is in securing a position on the East Coast, I am willing to relocate for the right opportunity and compensation ($80,000 to $95,000).

Thank you for your consideration.

Sincerely,
Chris Smith
Enc. Resume

▶ Candidate quantifies accomplishments with dollar figures and percentages.

▶ Candidate focuses on responsibilities of most recent position.

LETTER TO AN EXECUTIVE SEARCH FIRM
(Senior Business Analyst)

178 Green Street
Blacksburg, VA 24061
(703) 555-5555

April 7, 20--

Pat Cummings
Executive Recruiter
1140 Main Street
Manassas, VA 22110

Dear Ms. Cummings:

During the past twenty years, I have played a significant role in financial systems development as well as in accounting, financial planning, and audit management dealing with international and domestic markets.

Although I am presently employed as Senior Business Analyst, with a $150 million division of Medfort Corporation, I feel it is time for a change. I am currently seeking a new position with a company that can benefit from my expertise in:

- Accounting systems design and installation
- Account department organization and management
- Financial planning management (domestic and international marketing)
- Financial project design and management.

I am an effective developer of strategic financial and accounting systems with special skills as a problem-solver and professional group manager. While my preference is to stay within the mid-Atlantic region, I would consider relocation should the right position present itself. My salary requirements are in the $70,000 to $85,000 range.

I look forward to hearing from you should a suitable match for my qualifications become available.

Sincerely yours,

Chris Smith

Enc. Resume

▶ Candidate informs recruiter of acceptable relocation areas.

▶ Candidate immediately and concisely informs recruiter of his/her qualifications.

LETTER TO AN EXECUTIVE SEARCH FIRM
(Vice-President of Banking)

178 Green Street
Atlanta, GA 30303
(404) 555-5555

December 21, 20--

Pat Cummings
President
Any Search Firm
1140 Main Street
Atlanta, GA 30340

Dear Mr. Cummings:

I am an accomplished Vice-President who can significantly contribute to the successful operations of one of your client banking institutions.

I possess extensive experience in multibranch operations, including the following areas:

- Successfully developing and personally marketing new products for small businesses.
- Rewriting and implementing branch system policies and procedures.
- Troubleshooting operations and establishing improved financial controls.
- Budget planning and controls, audits.

My compensation requirement is within the $75,000 to $85,000 range, and I would consider making a long-distance move to a new job location. I have enclosed a professional profile and would be happy to provide additional information if needed.

I look forward to hearing from you regarding placement possibilities.

Sincerely,

Chris Smith

Enc. Professional profile

▶ Executive search letters generally allow recruiter to respond to candidate's inquiry.

▶ Discussion of experience is very specific.

LETTER TO AN EXECUTIVE SEARCH FIRM
(Vice-President of Nursing)

178 Green Street
Woonsocket, RI 02895
(401) 555-5555

April 15, 20--

Pat Cummings
Consultant
Any Search Firm
1140 Main Street
Warwick, RI 02893

Dear Ms. Cummings:

At a recent conference, I was made aware that your firm is in the process of searching for the Vice-President of Nursing at Any Hospital.

During the past sixteen years, my experience has been with referral hospitals—eleven years as Assistant Director of Nursing, with Emory Hospital and five years in my current position as Vice-President, Nursing with Newman General Hospital. My experience working with private practice physicians and my proven ability to establish a collegial and cooperative team effort between doctors and nurses, in both hospitals, has enabled me to successfully achieve the best in cost-effective, quality patient care.

My past and current positions have been challenging and have provided me with the satisfaction of developing programs that made positive contributions to the professional and quality image of both hospitals and research projects. However, at this point in my career, the position of Vice-President of Nursing at Any Hospital particularly interests me. It will offer me a broader scope of responsibility and the opportunity to utilize my administrative experience and clinical background in a larger facility and in a setting with which I am thoroughly familiar.

The enclosed confidential profile summarizes my experience. I could be available at your convenience to discuss your client's requirements and my ability to handle the responsibilities of the position offered.

Thank you for your consideration of my application.

Sincerely,

Chris Smith

Enc. Professional profile

▶ Candidate informs recruiter of need for confidentiality.

▶ Executive search letters provide detailed information regarding candidate's impressive track record.

LETTER TO AN EXECUTIVE SEARCH FIRM
(Vice-President of Sales)

178 Green Street
Houston, TX 77248
(713) 555-5555
(713) 444-4444 (Fax)

August 2, 20--

Pat Cummings
Recruiter
Any Search Firm
1140 Main Street
Hartford, CT 06102

Dear Mr. Cummings:

Currently, I am considering a move to the Northeast and am pursuing executive positions with profitable, aggressive retail corporations. Your firm has been recommended to me as one that services a wide client base in this area. In this regard, I would request your consideration of my qualifications.

As a corporate Vice-President of Sales with an established record for the development of approximately $215 million in sales, my responsibilities have covered the gamut of successful strategies and techniques for growth and profitability. My involvement in sales, marketing, staff development, and production interface has been extensive, and my ability to organize and manage is well documented in goals I have achieved with my present and prior employers. My salary requirements lie in the $200,000 to $250,000 range, plus bonuses.

The enclosed resume highlights my accomplishments. I would welcome the opportunity to discuss my qualifications further should a client wish to consider me for a position.

Thank you for your time.

Sincerely,

Chris Smith

Enc. Resume

▶ Executive search letters are especially effective for top-level professionals.

▶ Candidate immediately highlights substantial accomplishments that would interest industry professional.

CHAPTER 16

NETWORKING LETTER

A networking letter is a letter you send to a third party, usually an industry contact, in order to seek some assistance with your job search. Since you are essentially asking for a favor from the recipient—who is often someone you don't know personally—it is important that your letter carry just the right tone—not too friendly, but not overly formal either. Unless you know your contact well, you should word your networking letter as you would any business letter. In other words, do not use your addressee's first name, or rely on an overly casual writing style. By the same token, if you have been in contact with this person recently, it is certainly appropriate to remind him or her of the occasion: "It was great seeing you at the Chicago Writers' Convention last month," or "It has been several months since we bumped into each other on that flight to London. How are you?"

In all likelihood, many of your networking letters will be written to people you've never met, but who have been referred to you by a mutual acquaintance. In such cases, you should immediately state the name of the person who referred you, as in "Jean Rawlins suggested I contact you." Don't begin your letter by asking for a job outright; that's a little too presumptuous. With unfamiliar contacts, you'll find that it's generally more effective to start out by telling a little about yourself and your qualifications, then move on to request the information you need, be it insights on breaking into a particular industry, suggestions for names of other people you might contact, or consideration for an available position. If your letter is politely persuasive, the chances are good that people will be quick to respond and happy to help you out.

NETWORKING LETTER
(Administrative Assistant)

178 Green Street
Durango, CO 81301

November 16, 20--

Pat Cummings
Attorney at Law
Any Firm
1140 Main Street
Pueblo, CO 81001

Dear Mr. Cummings:

Recently, Luke Gokey suggested I contact you concerning any assistance you might be able to provide with my job search. I am interested in joining an organization in a position that would utilize my legal, administrative, and managerial knowledge and experience. The enclosed resume will provide you with information concerning my background and abilities.

As indicated, my law-related background is extensive and varied. For twelve years, I have supervised records and staff activities within the Any County Registry of Deeds. Unfortunately, I have reached the plateau of responsibility level within the structure of this position, and am now seeking to continue in my career progression.

I am especially interested in a legal administrative position, preferably with a private firm or corporation. I am willing to relocate and/or travel and am open to negotiation in terms of starting salary.

Should you know of any related openings or contacts to whom I should pass my resume, please do not hesitate to call me at (303) 555-5555. Thank you for your time. I look forward to hearing from you in the near future.

Sincerely,

Chris Smith

Enc. Resume

▶ Candidate requests additional referrals from networking contact.

▶ Candidate clearly indicates type of position desired.

NETWORKING LETTER
(Advertising Executive)

178 Green Street
Neptune, NJ 07754
(908) 555-5555

August 14, 20--

Pat Cummings
Communications Director
Any Agency
1140 Main Street
Hackensack, NJ 07601

Dear Ms. Cummings:

Please find attached my resume. I spoke with Jim Shaffer last week and he suggested I send my credentials to you prior to meeting in person.

As we discussed, I have five-plus years of advanced media, governmental, and business experience. My background provides a broad base of skills that allows me to handle a variety of situations and responsibilities.

I look forward to meeting with you at your earliest possible convenience.

Sincerely,

Chris Smith

Enc. Resume

▶ Introduction refers to attached resume.

▶ Letter is easy and quick to read, and only relevant details are included.

NETWORKING LETTER
(Advisor)

178 Green Street
Burbank, CA 91501

January 18, 20--

Pat Cummings
Director
Any Corporation
1140 Main Street
Vernon, CA 90058

Dear Mr. Cummings:

At the suggestion of Walter Durrane, I am enclosing my resume for your consideration pertaining to advising or related assignments with Any Corporation.

I have recently retired from a long and successful general medical practice. However, I am interested now in contributing my expertise as a representative for a public agency such as the Fraud Control Unit at Any Corporation. I have had prior experience as an Evaluator and Advisor for insurance companies and attorneys with regard to industrial and insured claims, and I would like to apply these skills to the continuation of my profession.

I look forward to meeting with you to further discuss my ability to fulfill your requirements. In the interim, I may be reached at the above address or by phone at (818) 555-5555.

Sincerely,

Chris Smith, M.D.

Enc. Resume

▶ Basis for referral is immediately established.

▶ Language is straightforward and understandable.

NETWORKING LETTER
(Architectural Designer)

178 Green Street
Mount Laurel, NJ 08054

November 13, 20--

Pat Cummings
Principal Engineer
Any Corporation
1140 Main Street
Minneapolis, MN 55440

Dear Ms. Cummings:

During a recent discussion with Mackenzie Simon, a member of your firm, I expressed an interest in making a change and he suggested that I contact you with reference to opportunities within your organization.

In conjunction with five years of experience as a Chief Engineer and ten years as an Architectural/Environmental Designer, I hold a Bachelor's degree in Architectural Design. This combination is ideally applicable to projects and programs involving those areas of asbestos abatement, specifications writing, and the monitoring of in-force contracts which I understand are all an integral part of your business. My background in architectural design and construction as well as engineering management, from design to production, would enable me to become a valuable contributor to one or more areas of your firm.

My resume is enclosed. I am especially interested in working in areas to which your firm is dedicated, and I would like to meet with you for further discussion. My preference is to remain in the Northeast area; however, traveling is not a problem. I can be reached at the above address or by phone at (609) 555-5555, extension 234, between 8:30 A.M. and 5:00 P.M. EST.

Yours sincerely,

Chris Smith

Enc. Resume

▶ Candidate informs networking contact of all relevant information, including geographical preference.

▶ Candidate focuses on relevant functional skills.

NETWORKING LETTER
(Assistant Hospital Administrator)

178 Green Street
Rapid City, SD 57007
(605) 555-5555

July 4, 20--

Pat Cummings
Hospital Administrator
Any Hospital
1140 Main Street
Rapid City, SD 57007

Dear Mr. Cummings:

Upon completion of my coursework this month, I will be searching for a full-time position in hospital administration. During the past year as a volunteer at your hospital, I have gained a great deal of personal satisfaction and continued interest in working at a facility caring for older citizens. I would like to call upon your experience in this field to assist me in any way possible as I begin my job search.

Although you may already be aware of my qualifications, I have enclosed my resume for your perusal. In addition to a Bachelor of Science degree in Business Administration, I can offer five years of part-time and full-time experience in office administration, accounting, computer operations, and credit/collections that may be beneficial to Any Hospital. I am willing to work in an entry-level position that would allow me to interface with professionals from whom I can learn and further develop my skills to handle greater responsibilities.

I would like to meet with you briefly when I come in to volunteer for the final time on July 17. Any organization/contact names or industry insight you could provide would greatly enhance my search efforts. I will call your office this Friday to arrange a time on the 17th that would be convenient for you.

Thank you for your time, Mr. Cummings.

Sincerely,

Chris Smith

Enc. Resume

▶ Reminds networking contact of common experience.

▶ Letter clarifies candidate's career goals.

NETWORKING LETTER
(Auto Salesperson)

178 Green Street
Brooklyn, NY 11201
(718) 555-5555

December 5, 20--

Pat Cummings
Regional Manager
Any Corporation
1140 Main Street
Rochester, NY 14623

Dear Ms. Cummings:

During a recent visit to Rochester, my longtime friend Bill Atwood suggested your name as a valuable contact in the field of auto sales. I understand that your corporation has contracted Bill's agency several times to promote your regional dealerships. I would like to take this opportunity to ask for any assistance you might be able to provide with my job search.

Due to recent downsizing, I am seeking a new, long-term association with an aggressive, fast-paced dealership. During the past eight years, my positions have ranged from Salesperson to Sales Manager with a high-volume dealership. My expertise is in developing, training, motivating, and managing a top-producing sales team in a highly competitive market. I am an effective communicator with presentation skills designed to generate results when dealing with management, personnel, and the general public. I established and continued to maintain a record of achievement as Salesperson of the Month and Salesperson of the Year for generated sales and margin of profit.

Should your schedule permit, I will be visiting the Rochester area next week and would love to meet with you. Your insight into the market and the future of the industry, as well as any specific advice or contact names you could provide, would be very helpful. I will call your office next Monday to see if we can find a convenient time to meet.

Thank you for your consideration, Ms. Cummings, and I hope to speak with you soon.

Sincerely,

Chris Smith

Enc. Resume

▶ Explaining reason for job search is optional.　　▶ Job descriptions emphasize candidate's accomplishments.

NETWORKING LETTER
(Bank Manager)

178 Green Street
St. Louis, MO 63130

June 8, 20--

Pat Cummings
Vice-President, Operations
Any Bank
1140 Main Street
Omaha, NE 68124

Dear Mr. Cummings:

Jennifer Mills, a colleague of mine at United Bank in St. Louis, suggested your name as an authority in the Midwest banking industry. Jennifer mentioned meeting you on a visit to your Omaha office last month, and was impressed by both the reputation and successful operations of your branches. I am writing to ascertain any information you can provide regarding banking opportunities in Nebraska, where I will be relocating next month.

As my enclosed resume indicates, I am a skilled professional with more than ten years of relevant experience. In addition to an M.B.A. degree (Executive Program—five years field representative experience required), and a B.A. degree in Economics and Finance, I have more than eighteen years of comprehensive banking experience. My expertise includes all aspects of banking and finance, credit administration, and management, including commercial lending and development, real estate loans, and end-to-end joint venture management. My experience also encompasses a successful term as Chief Financial Officer for a Japanese-American joint venture, and a term as Vice-President, Bank of St. Louis.

I will be visiting the Omaha area next week to begin my job search. Would your schedule permit a few moments to speak with me at this time? I would greatly appreciate any information or guidance you could provide, and my calendar is very flexible. Please contact me at the above address, or call (314) 555-5555 (early morning or evenings). Thank you for your time.

Sincerely,

Chris Smith

Enc. Resume

▶ Candidate immediately names referral.

▶ Letters stresses candidate's extensive experience and significant accomplishments.

NETWORKING LETTER
(Beverage Manager)

178 Green Street
Lexington, KY 40508
(606) 555-5555

April 10, 20--
Pat Cummings
Vice-President, Importing
Any Corporation
1140 Main Street
Philadelphia, PA 19130

Dear Ms. Cummings:

It was a pleasure skiing with you and Alex Park last month. Alex has been telling me for years how well we would get along, and it was a pleasure discovering that his instincts were correct. At that time, you urged me to forward a resume, so that you could inform me of suitable career opportunities at Any Corporation and other refreshment dealers.

During the past six years, I have been involved in customer service and operations management for a company that offers complete office beverage services to businesses and manufacturing plants throughout the United States. One of my responsibilities has been testing, evaluating, introducing, and promoting gourmet coffees and beverages to discriminating coffee drinkers. In addition, I managed key accounts and was involved in training personnel in methods of beverage brewing that would assure quality results.

Although my position has been challenging, I feel it is time for me to make a change to the primary segment of the coffee industry, importing and roasting, which I feel can offer me broader responsibilities and opportunities. I would like to apply my combined knowledge and experience in the office coffee service business to operations or sales to institutional accounts and resellers such as office beverage services.

I am pleased to see that Any Corporation is expanding its beverage services to the Midwest. I am confident, due to my years of experience, that I could be a key player in such a growth environment. May we meet to discuss?

Sincerely,

Chris Smith

Enc. Resume

▶ Candidate reminds networking contact of last encounter.

▶ Closing reiterates candidate's knowledge of organization.

NETWORKING LETTER
(Broadcast Manager)

178 Green Street
Menomonie, WI 53818

May 4, 20--
Pat Cummings
Deejay
Any Radio Station
1140 Main Street
Madison, WI 53715

Dear Mr. Cummings:

As you may recall, I am scheduled to graduate from the University of Wisconsin this month. The internship I completed at your station last spring has definitely confirmed my desire to seek a career in broadcasting, and I am writing to ask for your assistance in reaching this objective.

My desire is to participate in the management training program of a progressive broadcaster, studio, or agency seeking a highly motivated achiever who sees success in a ground-floor opportunity that offers enhanced potential for career growth and advancement based upon outstanding performance. As I prepare to graduate, I am attempting to gather contact names and information concerning major players in the industry. I hope to schedule some informational interviews while still in school to begin my job search.

Mr. Cummings, I recall from my time at the station that you are especially knowledgeable about the industry as a member of the Wisconsin Broadcasters Association. Any assistance you could provide in the way of referrals or general advice would be greatly appreciated. Would it be possible to get together for lunch one afternoon after your broadcast? If so, please contact me at (608) 555-5555 to arrange a mutually convenient time to meet. Thank you for your time.

I hope to hear from you soon.

Sincerely,

Chris Smith

Enc. Resume

▶ Candidate briefly reintroduces himself/herself to networking contact in opening.

▶ Candidate does not limit available opportunities by stating specific position desired.

NETWORKING LETTER
(Business Consultant)

178 Green Street
Price, UT 84501

February 21, 20--

Pat Cummings
Marketing Director
Any Catalog
1140 Main Street
Salt Lake City, UT 84130

Dear Ms. Cummings:

Congratulations! I recently read on the online network about the success of your new women's clothing catalog. You have certainly succeeded in broadening your market share while increasing your reputation and profit margin.

As you know, during the past twenty years, I launched and managed a unique mail-order collectible stamp business from product research and procurement to ultimate sale. Currently, I am looking for a new opportunity where I can utilize my advertising, market research, and sales and merchandising skills in flex-time, per diem, or project assignments. While I have thoroughly enjoyed running my own business, I am ready to slow down and focus my efforts on freelance or part-time work.

Ms. Cummings, I am writing to you as a colleague in the catalog business who is familiar with my experience. I would appreciate your assistance in referring me to any organization in need of a professional with my qualifications. I can offer a strong background in catalog development, media selection, and advertising design which has generated higher than normal returns. In addition, I have expertise with complex databases, inventory control systems, and forms design to simplify maintenance of mail-order, inventory, and international databases. I am capable of working effectively in a number of areas requiring creative, innovative thinking and have the ability to work independently or as a team member.

Enclosed please find several copies of my business profile. Should your organization have any openings, or should you know of a company in need, I would greatly appreciate your forwarding my materials to the appropriate contacts. Please don't hesitate to contact me at the above address or by phone at (801) 555-5555. Thank you.

Sincerely,

Chris Smith

Enc. Business profiles

▶ Candidate indicates type of employment desired.

▶ Candidate familiarizes networking contact with relevant skills and experiences.

NETWORKING LETTER
(Business Manager)

178 Green Street
St. Joseph, MO 64507
(816) 555-5555

October 5, 20--

Pat Cummings
Executive Vice-President
Any Corporation
1140 Main Street
St. Peters, MO 63376

Dear Mr. Cummings:

Thank you for taking the time out of your schedule to speak with me yesterday. It is always a pleasure to speak with a friend of David's. As I mentioned on the phone, I am seeking a new association with a company that can benefit from my experience in the development, implementation, and management of manufacturing and business information systems and networks.

As you know, I have devoted the past sixteen years to senior-level positions and played a key role in designing and managing systems that provide support to all facets of corporate functioning and strategic decision-making on domestic or international levels. To better acquaint you with my expertise and record of success in modern, automated management, manufacturing, and business information systems and control methods, I am enclosing a summary of my qualifications and accomplishments.

If you are aware of a firm in need of a professional with my qualifications, I would appreciate your forwarding my business profile for their review and further discussion.

Should you or a receptive firm require additional information, please contact me at the address cited above or by phone during the daytime at (816) 555-4444. If there is any assistance I can provide you, Pat, please do not hesitate to let me know.

With best regards,

Chris Smith

Enc. Business profile

▶ Candidate thanks addressee for time extended.

▶ Candidate requests that attached profile be forwarded.

NETWORKING LETTER
(Chief Financial Officer)

178 Green Street
El Paso, TX 79998
(915) 555-5555

June 25, 20--

Pat Cummings
President
Any Bank
1140 Main Street
Menomonie, WI 54751

Dear Ms. Cummings:

I am currently seeking a position as a Chief Financial Officer. Brad Peltser suggested that I contact you in order to focus my job search. I am exploring the Midwest as a site for relocation, and am anxious to learn more about the midwestern job market.

I have a record of outstanding success in the management of corporate financial operations for fast-paced manufacturing companies and associated commercial operations, in multilocation, multistate, and international environments.

My sixteen years of progressively responsible experience has encompassed management of all aspects of the financial and treasury functions, in a range from Cost Accounting Manager to Chief Financial Officer and Vice-President, Finance. This experience has fully encompassed the successful management of corporate real estate, human resources, and general operations areas. In addition to holding an M.B.A. in Finance, and a B.A. in Accounting, I have been a Certified Public Accountant since 20--.

May we meet? I am eager for your advice about the job market in the Midwest for senior-level officers.

Thank you for your consideration.

Sincerely,

Chris Smith

Enc. Resume

▶ Candidate immediately specifies type of position sought.

▶ Candidate quantifies extensive experience.

NETWORKING LETTER
(Commercial Real Estate Sales Executive)

178 Green Street
Honolulu, HI 96841

February 20, 20--

Pat Cummings
Staff Coordinator
Any Real Estate Company
1140 Main Street
San Francisco, CA 94111

Dear Mr. Cummings:

Are you in need of a well-organized, highly motivated, profit-oriented representative to market and sell acquired properties? Lee Yang, from your commercial sales division, felt that my qualifications would make me an excellent contribution to your staff.

During the past fifteen years, I have been actively involved in diverse industries with concentration on both residential and commercial properties. I have successfully managed and taken various businesses from foreclosure to profitable and salable properties. My ability to start up, set up, reorganize, and manage profitable business operations also applies to the management of major accounts or territories to increase market share.

Please find my resume enclosed. I would like to arrange a personal interview at your convenience. I am planning to relocate to your area, I am free to travel, and the compensation package is negotiable. Please contact me at the above address or by phone at (808) 555-5555.

I look forward to your return response.

Yours sincerely,

Chris Smith

Enc. Resume

▶ Introducing letter with a question draws attention to candidate.

▶ Candidate notifies networking contact of travel availability and/or compensation requirements.

NETWORKING LETTER
(Community Relations Specialist)

178 Green Street
Winchester, VA 22601
(703) 555-5555

August 21, 20--

Pat Cummings
Director, Community Planning
Any Organization
1140 Main Street
Virginia Beach, 23456

Dear Ms. Cummings:

I am writing at the suggestion of Barbara Winters, a fellow member of the Community Outreach Organization in Winchester. I am currently in search of a long-term association with an organization in the field of community relations. Barbara mentioned her frequent working relationship with Any Organization, and felt your office may be in need of a skilled professional with my qualifications.

During the past fifteen years, my experience has been concentrated in areas of community relations and government affairs working in public sector, university, and private industry settings. I have extensive experience working with various populations and divergent groups, and have been actively involved and successful in troubleshooting and problem-solving during the planning and decision-making processes pertaining to issues impacting communities.

I possess strong presentation, communication, and interpersonal skills, and I have trained, managed, and molded support staffs into efficient and productive teams. Based on my qualifications, I feel confident of my ability to make a significant contribution to your organization.

Although my resume provides a good summary of my background and experience, I would like to arrange a mutually convenient meeting, during which we can further discuss any availabilities within Any Organization. Please contact me at the above address or phone, or by fax at (703) 444-4444.

Thank you for your time.

Sincerely,

Chris Smith

Enc. Resume

▶ Professional membership shows candidate's commitment to his/her field.

▶ Including a fax number is optional in a cover letter.

NETWORKING LETTER
(Construction Engineer)

178 Green Street
Huntington, WV 25755

July 20, 20--

Pat Cummings
President
Any Construction Company
1140 Main Street
Montgomery, WV 25136

Dear Mr. Cummings:

    Jeff Fallon of B&D Construction forwarded me the name of your company as one that might be in need of an addition to its construction team. My desire is to find a challenging position in which to utilize my formal training and practical experience in the construction field.

    In addition to a Bachelor of Science degree with a concentration in Civil Engineering, I have two Associate degrees in related subjects, as well as eleven years of term and full-time employment in the construction industry. My knowledge includes the construction of schools, parking structures, museums, medical facilities, office buildings, and other structures. I am experienced in supervision, engineering layout, construction coordination, purchasing, and many aspects related to the organization and business of construction.

    After reviewing my resume, if you have a position in your organization for someone with training and experience who will work to a high standard of excellence, please contact me at the above address, or call (304) 555-5555. I would like to arrange a personal interview, during which we could further discuss my potential for service while in your employment.

    Thank you for your consideration.

Sincerely,

Chris Smith

Enc. Resume

▶ Letter highlights candidate's acquired professional and educational training.

▶ Networking letter establishes candidate's knowledge of his/her field.

NETWORKING LETTER
(Construction Manager)

178 Green Street
Newnan, GA 30264
(404) 555-5555

January 20, 20--

Pat Cummings
Project Manager
Any Construction Company
1140 Main Street
Macon, GA 31208

Dear Ms. Cummings:

It has been about two years since our last meeting, but I am sure you remember the work we completed together on the Independence Office Park in Macon. Since that time, I have continued my association with T&C Construction until cutbacks were instituted last week. Ms. Cummings, I would like to ask for your assistance as I begin my search for a new position.

Currently, I am seeking an association with a firm where I can utilize my knowledge and expertise in the area of project management, property management, field crew supervision, negotiations, purchasing, and construction office operation. I have supervised on-site crews on various commercial and residential projects, have good communication and negotiation skills, and work well with vendors, owners, management, office, and construction trades. I am a licensed Hydraulic Equipment Operator, hold a Class II license on heavy construction equipment, and have extensive experience in the operation of major, heavy construction, earth moving, and transportation equipment.

I wonder if we could get together at your convenience for a meeting. Any contact names or general advice you could provide would greatly assist me as I construct a job-hunting campaign. I would also very much like to get reacquainted and learn what has been going on at Any Construction Company over the last two years. I will call you soon to confirm a good time to meet.

Sincerely,

Chris Smith

Enc. Resume

▶ Letter solicits networking contact's advice rather than assistance with job placement.

▶ Candidate includes licensure relevant to his/her field.

NETWORKING LETTER
(Consultant)

178 Green Street
St. Charles, MO 63302
(314) 555-5555

November 6, 20--

Pat Cummings
President
Any Corporation
1140 Main Street
Chesterfield, MO 63017

Dear Mr. Cummings:

I obtained your company name from my client, Fred Mosley, President of ISS, Incorporated. My expertise is in working with small, nonprofit health care and human services organizations, such as ISS, that have problems meeting their commitments because of budget constraints. As an experienced independent consultant, I implement cost-effective techniques to put in place the systems, programs, and controls necessary to generate the dollars to meet and exceed fundraising goals.

During the past twenty years, I have played a key role in the management, planning, and successful execution of projects that require working with decision-makers, committees, volunteer groups, and community organizations on institutional/organizational development. I am qualified to handle such projects, from needs survey to achievement of projected funding objectives, and I am prepared to provide you, or any suitable corporation you are aware of, with this expertise on a per-assignment rather than full-time basis. Depending on your needs, my consulting fees will be quoted on a per-project or hourly rate.

If you are in the process of, or are planning, a campaign, please contact me so that we can arrange a meeting to discuss your requirements. I can be reached at the above address or phone, or by fax at (314) 444-4444. I will be glad to provide you with a client list and documentation of my achievements at that time.

Sincerely,

Chris Smith

Enc. Professional profile

▶ First paragraph introduces candidate to networking contact.

▶ Discussion details how candidate's qualifications will benefit potential employer.

NETWORKING LETTER
(Corporate Treasurer)

178 Green Street
Canyon, TX 79016
(806) 555-5555

June 4, 20--

Pat Cummings
Vice-President
Any Corporation
1140 Main Street
Cedar City, UT 84720

Dear Ms. Cummings:

At the suggestion of Tom Poudrier, I am submitting my resume for the Corporate Treasurer position. I have followed your company's rapid growth during the past two years, and read with much excitement your prediction for further expansion in the trade journal *Real Estates*. I wish to be a part of this exciting atmosphere.

During the past thirteen years, I have compiled a record of success as Vice-President/Treasurer of a multicorporate real estate development and management company, and I have ten years of additional experience as Corporate Treasurer and Controller with a nonprofit educational research firm and an electronic manufacturer.

I am pursuing a new opportunity utilizing my financial and management expertise. My interest is in working in a business or nonprofit environment where my associates and I share the common goal of profitable growth and mutual gain.

After reviewing my qualifications, I would appreciate your contacting me for a personal meeting. I can be reached at the above address, by phone, or a message may be left at (806) 555-4444. I appreciate your consideration.

Sincerely,

Chris Smith

Enc. Resume

▶ Specific company information illustrates candidate's commitment to his/her field.

▶ Candidate informs networking contact of work experience in field of interest.

NETWORKING LETTER
(Credit Officer)

178 Green Street
Baton Rouge, LA 70821
(504) 555-5555

May 25, 20--

Pat Cummings
Chief Loan Officer
Any Bank
1140 Main Street
LaPlace, LA 70069

Dear Mr. Cummings:

Pursuant to your recent conversation with my father, I am forwarding the attached resume for your evaluation. It is my desire to participate in a leading commercial credit training program as a first step in my commercial banking career. I understand that your loan officer development program is regarded as one of the finest in the industry.

Please note that in addition to receiving my recent Master of Business Administration degree in Finance and Management Policy with honors, I have a Bachelor of Arts degree in Economics and two years of progressively responsible experience working in diverse areas of operations and marketing support with McEllis Industries, Inc.

I would like to demonstrate my potential to succeed with your bank, working as an individual contributor or as a team member, to the achievement of mutual goals and objectives. For this reason, I welcome the opportunity to meet with you in order to further discuss your current or anticipated needs in terms of my qualifications and career objectives. I will contact your office on Wednesday, May 31 to schedule a convenient interview time.

Sincerely,

Chris Smith

Enc. Resume

▶ Basis for referral is immediately established. ▶ Educational honors indicate candidate's potential to excel.

NETWORKING LETTER
(Customer Support Representative)

178 Green Street
Scranton, PA 18510

April 1, 20--

Pat Cummings
Customer Support Manager
Any Corporation
1140 Main Street
Greenburg, PA 15601

Dear Ms. Cummings:

I am a former college classmate of your son Dennis, and have, since graduation, worked as a Customer Support Representative for a manufacturer of high-volume copier and reprographic equipment. Although my position has been challenging and fast-paced, at this point in my career, I am seeking a new, long-term association where my expertise and motivation can be more fully utilized.

I had lunch with Dennis last week while on a business trip to Pittsburgh, and he suggested that you might have an availability within the customer support department of your corporation. I have enclosed my resume as an expressed interest in applying for such an opening.

During the past three years, I have gained progressively responsible experience in providing sales support and training to new hires and end-users of major commercial, institutional, industrial, and government accounts on a national level. I am an effective representative and support individual with the ability to provide liaison between sales, service, customers, and corporate personnel.

I would love to meet with you to further outline my experiences and how I could contribute successfully to your firm. Please contact me when you have a free moment to schedule an interview. I can be reached at the above address or by phone at (717) 555-5555. I look forward to hearing from you.

Sincerely,

Chris Smith

Enc. Resume

▶ Networking letters may allow for personal discussion.

▶ Letter emphasizes valuable skills.

NETWORKING LETTER
(Director of College Development)

178 Green Street
Pittsburgh, PA 15217
(412) 555-5555

June 8, 20--
Pat Cummings
Alumni Development Director
Any University
1140 Main Street
New Haven, CT 06520

Dear Mr. Cummings:

I am glad we had the opportunity to meet at the Educational Development Symposium. I thoroughly enjoyed exchanging ideas about the interplay between the academic and the financial worlds. Your development ideas have enriched the scope of my knowledge and I hope our discussion benefited you as well. As you suggested, I have enclosed a resume to remind you of my background.

In addition to a Master of Education degree in Administration and Supervision and a Bachelor of Arts degree in Business Administration, I offer ten years of experience in positions ranging from Assistant Director of Alumni and Parent Relations with a four-year college, to my most recent position as Director of the Annual Fund with a college preparatory school.

My experience includes a full range of management responsibilities, including full knowledge of the institutional advancement field, public/client relations, development/fundraising, special event planning, marketing/sales, and promotion/advertising.

I am interested in exploring opportunities at other colleges. If you know of any openings, or have colleagues who may be aware of developmental opportunities at other universities, I would appreciate your passing the information along to me.

I hope to speak with you again soon.

Sincerely,

Chris Smith

Enc. Resume

▶ Candidate reminds networking contact of last encounter.

▶ Educational credentials accentuate candidate's qualifications.

NETWORKING LETTER
(Director of Information Services)

178 Green Street
Bellingham, WA 98226
(206) 555-5555

November 19, 20--

Pat Cummings
Director of Informational Services
Any Municipality
1140 Main Street
Bellingham, WA 98226

Dear Ms. Cummings:

After so many years of working in your department, it is with mixed emotions that I greet your departure. While I will regret your absence, I congratulate you on your retirement and the successful conclusion of your years of service.

At your retirement celebration, you said that you had recommended me to the search committee as your replacement. I would be honored to act in this position, and thank you for your recommendation. As you suggested, I hereby remind you of my career history.

During the past fourteen years, I have held positions as Manager of Systems Planning and Development, Principal Systems Analyst, and Manager of Computer Operations with Any Municipality. In this capacity, my responsibilities have included directing the operations of a data processing center serving numerous departments within the city hall complex. In keeping with numerous changes in municipal systems and procedures, my work in data processing has been increasingly complex and required extensive program development, systems analysis, troubleshooting and problem-solving, employee training, and supervision in computer operations.

Allow me to reiterate my interest in contributing my energy and skills to Any Municipality. I am confident that, given this opportunity, I can uphold your high standard of service which, as a result of your efforts, the city has come to expect.

Thank you for your kind consideration.

Sincerely,

Chris Smith

Enc. Resume

▶ Candidate familiarizes networking contact with relevant skills and experiences.

▶ Candidate chronicles career progression within firm.

NETWORKING LETTER
(Driver)

178 Green Street
Cookeville, TN 38505
(901) 555-5555

June 21, 20--

Pat Cummings
Shipping Services Manager
Any Corporation
1140 Main Street
Florence, MS 39703

Dear Mr. Cummings:

Last week I spoke with Brooke Breyfogle, who encouraged me to contact you. My desire to drive for Any Corporation has prompted me to forward the attached resume for your evaluation.

Please note that in addition to six years as a Package Car Driver for United States Shipping, I received intensive training in Diesel Mechanics while a member of the U.S. Marine Corps. I also managed a Marine auto hobby shop where I learned basic auto mechanics. In my current job, I have gained valuable insight into the task of working effectively while on a tight schedule, maintaining good customer relations, and interfacing regularly with employees and management.

I will contact your office on Monday to establish a mutually convenient time for a meeting, during which we may more fully discuss your current or anticipated driver needs in terms of my qualifications.

Thank you for your time and consideration.

Sincerely,

Chris Smith

Enc. Resume

▶ Candidate details how past military experience will benefit potential employer.

▶ In closing, candidate specifically requests interview.

NETWORKING LETTER
(Editor)

178 Green Street
Arlington, VA 22207
(703) 555-5555

December 9, 20--

Pat Cummings
Vice-President, Editorial Department
Any Corporation
1140 Main Street
Wise, VA 24293

Dear Ms. Cummings:

John Curran suggested that I contact you. He spoke very highly of your creative, market-sensitive approach to publishing and your tremendous success in publicizing your books. He also said that you might have plans to expand your editorial team. If so, I thought that my qualifications might be of interest to you.

I have seven years of experience as a Nonfiction Editor. For the past two years, I have acquired books for McDoogle's Professional Book Group. There, I worked with authors on books that address the wide range of challenges facing today's managers and small business owners—from cash management to business security. I also acquired books on personal business topics such as Margaret Miller's *Loving Your Job* for the career/self-help market. Scheduled for release in January 20--, Miller's book has already received a strong response from book clubs (20,000 copy advance order) and an enthusiastic endorsement from Michael Morin.

Earlier in my career, I acquired books on health, fitness, recreation, and other nonfiction topics for Stevens & Dunn. Although designed for the academic environment, these books had strong crossover appeal to the trade market. Also, I have procured many author contacts and book ideas I would like to pursue.

I would love to meet with you and find out more about Any Corporation's publishing program as well as possible ways in which we might work together. I will call you within a week to see if we can schedule an appointment soon. Thank you.

Sincerely,

Chris Smith

Enc. Resume

▶ Relevant work experience is emphasized while other positions are omitted.

▶ Candidate informs networking contact of his/her commitment to field of interest.

NETWORKING LETTER
(Electrical Engineer)

178 Green Street
Mt. Pleasant, MI 48859

July 18, 20--

Pat Cummings
Director, Products and Services
Any Corporation
1140 Main Street
Kalamazoo, MI 49007

Dear Mr. Cummings:

Thank you for taking the time to speak with me on the phone yesterday. I saw your nephew Brenden last night and sent your regards as you requested. Brenden hopes to see you soon, and confirms that he is, indeed, working hard to graduate.

As I mentioned on the phone, I am a candidate for a Bachelor of Science degree in Electrical Engineering, anticipating graduation in May 20--. I have enclosed my resume as per your request. Ideally, I would like to find a position in which I could contribute to a firm's technical products and services through my combined academic and practical experience.

I certainly do not expect that you will be able to provide me with a position, Mr. Cummings, but I would greatly appreciate any leads or contact names you may know of in the field. Additionally, would it be possible to meet? I would love to get your insight into the industry, as well as hear any advice you could provide for my search. Please contact me at the above address or by phone at (517) 555-5555 to arrange a mutually convenient time to get together.

I appreciate your time.

Sincerely,

Chris Smith

Enc. Resume

▶ Letter appeals to networking contact's knowledge of industry.

▶ Career objective gives focus without limiting candidate's opportunities.

NETWORKING LETTER
(Elementary Teacher)

178 Green Street
Medford, MA 02155
(617) 555-5555

July 18, 20--

Pat Cummings
President
Any Teachers' Association
1140 Main Street
Everett, MA 02149

Dear Ms. Cummings:

Hello! I hope that you are enjoying your new position at the Union. We certainly miss you at Medford Elementary. Many of the students still ask when you are returning, and the teacher's room has been so quiet without you. When are you coming back to visit us?

Pat, I am also writing on a business-related subject. Since the town lost its override appeal this month, I have found myself out of a job. I was hoping that, as Association President, you might know of a school system in need of an classroom veteran.

I am seeking a position that involves teaching and motivating children toward academic success and self-improvement, possibly one in which I can utilize my certification and six years of experience in special needs education. I am especially interested in a professional environment that caters to the development and well-being of children either in an educational or child-care setting.

If you could refer me to any leads you might be aware of, I would be grateful. I have enclosed my resume to assist you in the brainstorming process. I'll call you early next week to talk further.

Thank you for taking the time to assist me. I look forward to catching up soon!

With best regards,

Chris Smith

Enc. Resume

▶ Familiarity with networking contact allows for personalized writing style.

▶ Dedication to candidate's field of interest is emphasized.

NETWORKING LETTER
(Environmental Services Director)

178 Green Street
Provo, UT 84602
(801) 555-5555

November 22, 20--

Pat Cummings
Director
Any Corporation
1140 Main Street
Washington, PA 15301

Dear Mr. Cummings:

My desire to secure a position in the management of large-scale environmental services or related operations with an institution offering enhanced potential for career growth and development has prompted me to forward the attached resume for your evaluation. Mindy LeMouge suggested that you may be aware of such a position.

Please note that in addition to an Associate degree in Public Environmental Health, and intensive additional professional-level training in this area, I possess eighteen years of progressively responsible experience in the management of environmental services operations for commercial and institutional employers.

My experience encompasses all aspects of departmental management, including the development of policies and procedures, personnel hiring, training, supervision and evaluation, scheduling, customer and vendor negotiations and relations, cost estimation, budget development and management purchasing, payroll, management reporting, inventory control, scheduling, and wage and salary negotiation.

I would appreciate a chance to meet, in which we could discuss the environmental industry. Frankly, I would appreciate any advice you, with your vast experience in the field, could offer me regarding my current job search. I will call your office to schedule a mutually convenient time for such a meeting.

Sincerely,

Chris Smith

Enc. Resume

▶ Type of position desired is clearly stated.

▶ Letter highlights candidate's management skills.

NETWORKING LETTER
(Executive Nonprofit Director)

178 Green Street
Sedalia, MO 65301
(816) 555-5555

April 21, 20--

Pat Cummings
Chairperson
Any Foundation
1140 Main Street
Odessa, TX 79762

Dear Ms. Cummings:

Dean Wareham recently informed me of the open position of Executive Director at Any Foundation. Mr. Wareham suggested that I contact you directly before entering the general applicant pool.

During the past fifteen years, I have established a record of achievement in leadership positions with a nationally renowned, nonprofit organization. My positions as Development, Public Relations, and Telecommunications Director required the capability to handle multimillion-dollar budgets and development drives. In addition, I was responsible for all areas of public relations and marketing for multiple projects, the most recent being a $95 million retirement community that required extensive contact with the legal profession.

My expertise, as outlined in my resume, meets all the requirements essential to the position of Executive Director of Any Foundation, including monitoring responsibility, long- and short-term planning, and the implementation of policies and procedures for a well-run organization. Based on my qualifications, I feel that I can provide management and administrative expertise for positive direction and quality membership services.

I look forward to hearing from you.

Thank you for your time.

Sincerely,

Chris Smith

Enc. Resume

▶ Candidate immediately names referral.

▶ Closing reiterates candidate's qualifications for position.

NETWORKING LETTER
(Field Service Manager)

178 Green Street
Belleville, MI 48112

August 20, 20--

Pat Cummings
Human Resources Manager
Any Cancer Institute
1140 Main Street
Boston, MA 02118

Dear Mr. Cummings:

During a recent conversation with Dr. Elizabeth Bradley, a specialist in children's leukemia, I mentioned my interest in the human resources division of Any Cancer Institute, specifically for the Field Service Manager position advertised.

Dr. Bradley has firsthand knowledge of my organizational and management skills, as well as my comprehensive training and experience dealing with the day-to-day management of care control for children. She recommended that I contact you directly, to make you aware of my interest in the position and my conviction that I am capable of handling its inherent responsibilities in order to achieve the goals of Any Cancer Institute.

Although I have forwarded an application to your director of human resources, I am enclosing a copy of my resume for your review. I am planning to relocate permanently to the Boston area and hope to do so as an employee of your facility. Any assistance you can provide is appreciated.

Should you require additional information, please contact me at the above address or by phone at (313) 555-5555 or (313) 555-4444.

Yours sincerely,

Chris Smith

Enc. Resume

▶ Introduction states candidate's desire to join specific organization.

▶ Candidate informs networking contact of mutual acquaintance.

NETWORKING LETTER
(Finance Assistant)

178 Green Street
Zephyr Cove, NV 89448
(702) 555-5555

March 30, 20--

Pat Cummings
Senior Loan Administrator
Any Corporation
1140 Main Street
Chicago, IL 60605

Dear Ms. Cummings:

I truly enjoyed our conversation last week at the Racquet Ball Club. I hope you relish the remainder of your stay in Las Vegas.

As you may recall, I will be graduating from the University of Las Vegas in May with a degree in Finance. For the past three months, I have been interning at Marshall Howard Company. I have learned the auditing and payment coordination aspects of the business in-depth, gaining praise for my motivation, professionalism, and willingness to take on new tasks.

Currently, I am looking for an entry-level finance position with a dynamic company. I would greatly appreciate any assistance you could provide. Enclosed are my resume and a letter of recommendation for your review.

Thank you in advance for your help. It is greatly appreciated.

Sincerely,

Chris Smith

Enc. Resume, Letter of recommendation

▶ Internship experience is valuable for candidates with little job experience, particularly if it corresponds to the position sought.

▶ Candidate thanks networking candidate in advance for his/her assistance.

NETWORKING LETTER
(Finance Executive)

---

178 Green Street
Maryville, MO 64468
(816) 555-5555

May 14, 20--

Pat Cummings
Executive Vice-President
Any Corporation
1140 Main Street
Fulton, MO 65251

Dear Mr. Cummings:

    I received your name as a key figure in the Missouri banking industry from a mutual friend, Rebecca Meader. I understand that Rebecca is a fellow member of the Fulton Country Club and has often accompanied you on the golf course. She generously offered your services as a contact for my job-search campaign.

    For the past fifteen years, I have acted as a top producer in new business development, consumer lending, system implementation, personnel management and training, customer service, and financial counseling. Although my positions have been challenging, at this point in my career, I am exploring new opportunities in which to apply my extensive background and experience in banking and finance.

    Please note that in addition to formal education and a degree in Business Administration, I have undertaken advanced study in financial counseling and mortgage banking. I have worked in a $140 million credit union in the greater St. Louis area. I also have extensive customer support and technical coordination experience providing support and training to select client personnel on an IBM-automated ordering system.

    I would greatly appreciate your consideration of my enclosed resume for any suitable availabilities at Any Corporation, and would welcome the opportunity to speak with you in a personal meeting. Please feel free to contact me at the above address or phone, or by fax at (816) 555-4444. Thank you for your consideration, Mr. Cummings.

    I look forward to hearing from you.

Sincerely,

Chris Smith

Enc. Resume

▶ Candidate informs networking contact of work experience in field of interest.

▶ Including a fax number is optional in a cover letter.

NETWORKING LETTER
(Finance Manager)

---

178 Green Street
Downers Grove, IL 60515
(708) 555-5555

January 25, 20--

Pat Cummings
Human Resource Director
Any Bank
1140 Main Street
New York, NY 10128

Dear Ms. Cummings:

John Monroe, of First Avenue Bank, informed me that you might be expanding your staff. Based on my comprehensive experience in the field of finance, I can offer your firm a broad range of management and administrative skills in banking.

During the past twenty-five years, I have played a key role in the trust banking industry in positions ranging from Tax Officer to my current position as Chief Trust Officer. Because of my ability to adapt strategies to changing conditions, I was able to apply innovative approaches that increased productivity, accuracy, and profits. As a result, customer service, corporate visibility and image, and customer base were substantially improved.

I am confident I could contribute my expertise to the continued success of Any Bank, and would welcome the chance to discuss career opportunities. I will call your office to schedule an interview.

Thank you for your time.

Sincerely,

Chris Smith

Enc. Resume

▶ Candidate immediately introduces qualifications.

▶ Candidate immediately introduces purpose for writing.

NETWORKING LETTER
(Genetic Research Technician)

178 Green Street
Baton Rouge, LA 70821
(504) 555-5555

March 13, 20--

Pat Cummings
Director
Any Center
1140 Main Street
Lake Charles, LA 70602

Dear Mr. Cummings:

I am a good friend of Anne Connelly, whom I understand is a colleague of yours at Any Center. Anne thought that, as an experienced veteran in the field of biomedical research, you would be able to offer some valuable assistance with my job search.

I am currently seeking a challenging position as a Genetic Research Technician. In addition to a Bachelor's degree in Biology with a concentration in Genetics, which I received in 20--, I have hands-on laboratory experience as a lab assistant conducting studies related to neuropsychology. I have researched and written class papers on germ line therapy, genetic technology, legal aspects of genetics, and genetics testing in the workplace. I am a highly motivated, career-oriented individual who would like to contribute to an established facility by combining both my academic and practical experience, as outlined in the enclosed resume.

Would it be possible to meet? I would like to briefly solicit your advice and, possibly, gather any further names to contact in the field. I will call your office on Friday to confirm a time.

Thank you for your consideration.

Sincerely yours,

Chris Smith

Enc. Resume

▶ Letter appeals to networking contact's knowledge of industry.

▶ Valuable research experience is highlighted in detail.

NETWORKING LETTER
(Golf Instructor)

178 Green Street
Albuquerque, NM 87190
(505) 555-5555

February 14, 20--

Pat Cummings
Director
Any Golf Club
1140 Main Street
Las Cruces, NM 88003

Dear Ms. Cummings:

As a result of a recent referral from Mr. David Stefan regarding an entry-level opening for an instructor at Any Golf Club, I am submitting my resume for your review.

I possess eight years of education, training, coaching, and playing experience. My involvement with the game of golf began in high school and, since then, my skill level and affection for the sport have increased. Currently, I am seeking a career opportunity that will allow me to use my education and experience to make a positive contribution by maintaining high standards and a professional image within a club environment.

I am very interested in this opening. Could I perhaps schedule a personal interview with you at your convenience? I will contact your offices on Monday, February 20 to discuss an appropriate meeting time.

Sincerely,

Chris Smith

Enc. Resume

▶ Candidate informs networking contact of his/her commitment to field of interest.

▶ Phrasing request in question form is a strong closing.

NETWORKING LETTER
(Human Resources Manager)

178 Green Street
Rockford, IL 61108
(815) 555-5555

July 7, 20--

Pat Cummings
Division Manager
Any Corporation
1140 Main Street
Kankakee, IL 60901

Dear Mr. Cummings:

It was a real pleasure talking to you during the S.H.R.M. Conference & Exposition in St. Louis. I found our discussion both interesting and informative.

As I mentioned, I am currently in search of a new career opportunity in human resources management and would appreciate your assistance. My most recent assignments include the following:

- More than three years directing the human resources activities, systems, procedures, and programs for Yurof Supplies, Inc.
- Creating from scratch a full personnel administration system for Buttrick Tool & Die Co.
- Three years as Industrial Relations Manager for the Cancellare Group, supervising a department of eleven employees.

I do not expect that you would know of a suitable opening for me at this time. However, I would value any ideas or suggestions you may have that could help direct my job search.

The enclosed resume details my professional experience and some of my accomplishments. Should you hear of anything, or simply have a suggestion for me, please give me a call.

Thank you for your time and consideration. I hope to talk to you soon.

Sincerely,

Chris Smith

Enc. Resume

▶ Bullets in networking letter draw attention to candidate's accomplishments.

▶ Candidate immediately thanks addressee for previous meeting.

NETWORKING LETTER
(Insurance Manager)

178 Green Street
Wayne, NE 68787

October 7, 20--

Pat Cummings
Underwriter
Any Insurance Agency
1140 Main Street
York, NE 68467

Dear Ms. Cummings:

It was very nice speaking with you yesterday and learning about the changes taking place at Any Insurance Agency. As per your request, I am enclosing my business profile for your review.

My experience as an underwriter, account manager, and office manager has provided me with expertise in all facets of insurance agency operation. Once oriented to the policies of a new firm, I feel I have the knowledge and skill to assume responsibility for any of the above, or related, positions.

Any assistance you can provide in my search for a position would be much appreciated. Should you require additional information, please contact me at the address cited above or call me at (402) 555-5555.

Thank you for taking the time to assist me in my job search.

Yours sincerely,

Chris Smith

Enc. Business profile

▶ Letter is brief and concise.

▶ Letter solicits networking contact's advice rather than assistance with job placement.

NETWORKING LETTER
(International Controller)

178 Green Street
Kilgore, TX 75662
(903) 555-5555

January 16, 20--

Pat Cummings
Finance Manager
Any Corporation
1140 Main Street
Austin, TX 78713

Dear Mr. Cummings:

It was a pleasure meeting you last month while visiting Bob and Cheryl Maxmillian at their home in Austin. As you may recall, at that time I was working as an International Controller of Divinex, a multidivision manufacturer of automatic test equipment. Recent ownership changes have prompted me to seek another association in finance management. When I updated Bob on my search recently, he suggested I obtain your assistance.

I possess more than sixteen years of experience working with foreign manufacturing entities and sales/service subsidiaries, which has involved corporate financial planning and analysis, international reporting, treasury and tax management, and interactive MIS systems for both corporate and divisional financial operations. I am searching for a position that would allow me to utilize my diverse background while providing the opportunity for career growth.

Should you know of any corporations in the Austin area in need of someone with my qualifications, would you kindly forward my resume to the appropriate contacts? Also, I will be visiting Bob and Cheryl in two weeks' time, to meet with industry insiders and continue my search. If your schedule permits, I would like to meet, perhaps for lunch or dinner. I would greatly appreciate your input as a fellow professional in the field. I will contact you next week to find a time that works for you.

Thank you for your assistance. I hope to see you again soon.

Sincerely,

Chris Smith

Enc. Resume

▶ Explaining reason for job search is optional.

▶ Candidate details applicable work experience.

NETWORKING LETTER
(International Marketing Specialist)

---

178 Green Street
Stratford, CT 06497
(203) 555-5555

April 10, 20--

Pat Cummings
Senior Marketing Specialist
Any Corporation
1140 Main Street
Middlebury, CT 06762

Dear Mr. Cummings:

My uncle, Joe McGinness, a former Fiji fraternity brother of yours at Worcester Polytechnic Institute, suggested I contact you to explore career opportunities in our mutual field of interest, international marketing.

I graduated from Fairfield University in May 20--, with a Bachelor of Science in Textile Marketing. I feel that through my educational extracurricular programs and work experience, I have gained an outstanding business foundation upon which I can build my professional career. I consider myself to be a determined competitor. Setting high, yet realistic, goals for myself and seeing them through to their completion is something I pride myself on and which is a key ingredient in my success to date. I am ambitious and willing to devote the extra time that is almost always necessary for worthwhile achievements. Additionally, I would consider travel and/or relocation.

My past experiences have helped me sharpen my interpersonal skills. To me, the marketing field offers unlimited growth potential and a career in which one is directly rewarded for hard work and perseverance. Therefore, I believe marketing is the ideal profession for me, since I am willing to work long and hard to attain success.

I would appreciate a chance to meet with you, at your convenience, to discuss possible career opportunities within your firm or in others in your immediate area. I will call your office during the week of April 17 to confirm an interview time. Thank you for your consideration and for any efforts you may extend on my behalf.

Sincerely,

Chris Smith

Enc. Resume

▶ Discussion of personal qualities reiterates candidate's ability to contribute to potential employer.

▶ Letter focuses on acquired skills rather than detailing past employers.

NETWORKING LETTER
(Inventory Control Supervisor)

178 Green Street
Glassboro, NJ 08028

May 24, 20--

Pat Cummings
Inventory Control Coordinator
Any Corporation
1140 Main Street
New Brunswick, NJ 08903

Dear Mr. Cummings:

Beth Monaco, Director of Operations at Welman Industries, suggested I contact you with regard to employment opportunities.

I have enclosed my resume, which outlines my extensive experience in inventory maintenance and control. I am a self-motivated individual who can work well with people, grasp and expand on ideas, tackle and follow through on difficult projects, and achieve or exceed objectives. Although my positions have been fast-paced, challenging, and broad in scope, I feel it is time for a change. Currently, I am investigating new opportunities where my skills can be best utilized to the advantage of the organization.

I feel confident that I can make an immediate as well as long-term contribution to your organization, as I have for my past employers. I will call your office on Friday, June 2, to see if we can schedule a meeting for further discussion.

In the interim, if additional information is required, please contact me at the above address or by phone at (609) 555-5555.

Thank you for your consideration.

Sincerely,

Chris Smith

Enc. Resume

▶ Closing indicates specific date when candidate will follow up inquiry.

▶ Letter relies on action verbs rather than passive verbs for emphasis.

NETWORKING LETTER
(Legal Assistant)

178 Green Street
Johnson City, TN 37614

June 28, 20--

Pat Cummings
Assistant District Attorney
Any Office
1140 Main Street
Nashville, TN 37203

Dear Ms. Cummings:

Lee Ellis, Director of Career Services at East Tennessee State University, gave me your name as a valuable contact within the Nashville law enforcement field. I am a recent graduate of East Tennessee State, which I understand is your alma mater as well. During the past several years, I have been preparing myself for a career in law where I can utilize my dual degrees in Criminology and Psychology in the public or private sector.

As my enclosed resume reveals, in addition to my academic studies in these fields, I have experience as a student Investigative Assistant with the Memphis County District Attorney's office, where I was involved in a variety of investigations and other assigned duties dealing with law enforcement and legal issues. Based upon my performance in this position, I received the highest possible evaluation. I consider myself to be dependable, capable of rapid orientation and training, and skilled at assuming responsibility for assignments as an individual or as a team member.

I am considering attending law school in several years, and would love the opportunity to confirm my interest in law and law enforcement through a Legal Assistant position at an organization such as Any Office. I would greatly appreciate the opportunity to meet with you to discuss availabilities at your office or to receive any referrals you might find helpful. Would your schedule permit a few free moments next week? I will call on Monday to schedule a mutually convenient time.

Should you require additional information prior to our meeting, please contact me at the above address or by phone at (615) 555-5555.

Sincerely,

Chris Smith

Enc. Resume

▶ First paragraph introduces candidate to networking contact.

▶ Candidate's most recent position is outlined in detail.

NETWORKING LETTER
(Leisure Trainer)

178 Green Street
Lincroft, NJ 07738
(908) 555-5555

March 1, 20--

Pat Cummings
President
Any Travel Agency
1140 Main Street
Nyack, NJ 10960

Dear Mr. Cummings:

Anna Murphy, co-owner of Kannenberg Travel, suggested you as a top contact in the travel industry. I am confident that as an Educator and Staff Trainer with comprehensive experience in domestic and foreign travel, I have the qualifications necessary for the position of Leisure Trainer. Do you have a need for a person with my expertise?

During my seven years in travel, I have been involved in the development, sales, and marketing of travel products, agency management, and staff development. My experience encompasses diverse travel packages and customized leisure and educational travel.

Currently, I am seeking a new association within the travel industry where I can utilize my combined teaching and travel experience to train new agents in the nuances of providing clients with a quality travel experience and maintaining the agency's high standards. I am interested in Any Travel Agency because your company has committed itself to expanding into Asian travel markets, an area I was just beginning to explore in my last position.

I would like to speak with you. May we meet?

Sincerely,

Chris Smith

Enc. Resume

▶ Closing reiterates candidate's interest in specific corporation.

▶ Networking letter establishes candidate's knowledge of his/her field.

NETWORKING LETTER
(Maintenance Supervisor)

178 Green Street
New Castle, DE 19720
(302) 555-5555

April 3, 20--

Pat Cummings
Facilities Manager
Any Country Club
1140 Main Street
New Castle, DE 19720

Dear Ms. Cummings:

I enjoyed playing doubles with you and Brian Fee last week. With regard to the open Maintenance Supervisor position you mentioned, I am forwarding my career history. Pat, I am confident that I can provide your facility with top-notch care and maintenance.

My primary technical skills include plumbing, heating, and the general maintenance of residential and commercial properties. I have broad-based knowledge of and experience in construction and mechanical trades such as electrical work, roofing, painting, carpentry, and other areas essential to the cost-effective upkeep of a quality facility. Presently, I am interested in a position in property management where my skills in these areas can be best utilized.

Please contact me so that we may discuss how my experience can benefit your club. If the Maintenance Supervisor position has been filled, I would appreciate if you could forward my resume to other facility managers or other useful contacts.

Thank you for your time.

Sincerely,

Chris Smith

Enc. Resume

▶ Personalized tone reinforces candidate's familiarity with addressee.

▶ Candidate requests that attached resume be forwarded.

NETWORKING LETTER
(Marketing Assistant)

178 Green Street
Dazey, ND 58428
(701) 555-5555

June 2, 20--

Pat Cummings
Director of Marketing
Any Corporation
1140 Main Street
Chicago, IL 60605

Dear Mr. Cummings:

It was a pleasure talking with you during our flight to Rome this past April. I hope you enjoyed your trip.

As you may recall, I was a senior at Harvard University studying marketing and sales. You were kind enough to give me your business card with instructions to contact you once I was "liberated from the fetters of academia." Finally, that day has arrived.

Although I am a recent graduate, I have held several internships at major Boston corporations. As a result, I know how to buy and sell in an aggressive, no-holds-barred manner while retaining the diplomacy necessary to garner respect.

I have enclosed my resume for your reference and file. If you know of anyone seeking a fresh new addition to his or her marketing team, please let me know.

Thank you for your assistance.

Sincerely,

Chris Smith

Enc. Resume

▶ Internship experience demonstrates candidate's familiarity with field of work.

▶ Reminds networking contact of common experience.

NETWORKING LETTER
(Marketing Specialist)

178 Green Street
Youngstown, OH 44555
(216) 555-5555

March 27, 20--

Pat Cummings
Director, Sales and Marketing
Any Corporation
1140 Main Street
Largo, MD 20772

Dear Ms. Cummings:

Thank you for taking the time to speak with me briefly after your sales presentation on behalf of Any Corporation last Thursday. As you may recall, I am relocating to your area next month and I am interested in securing a marketing position within Any Corporation.

During the past five years, my experience in my present position as Marketing Specialist has been focused on product management, strategic planning, marketing, and the sale of equipment, systems, chemicals, and related products and services. Currently, I have responsibility for the worldwide marketing of bio-instrument chemicals sold to biotech markets, pharmaceutical markets, and research laboratories.

As my enclosed resume indicates, my success in product management, new business/market development, and the sales management of national and international markets has provided me with the qualifications I feel would contribute to the growth and profitability of your firm.

At your convenience, I would like to discuss, in detail, the mutual benefit of my joining your management team. I consider myself to be a persistent achiever, and feel confident that I can make a significant difference. I will call your office on April 3 to arrange a meeting time.

I appreciate your consideration and look forward to speaking with you.

Yours sincerely,

Chris Smith

Enc. Resume

▶ Closing reiterates candidate's qualifications for position.

▶ Letter focuses on functional skills applicable to potential employer.

NETWORKING LETTER
(Medical Sales Representative)

178 Green Street
Odenton, MD 21114
(301) 555-5555

April 20, 20--

Pat Cummings
Sales Director
Any Corporation
1140 Main Street
Emporia, KS 66801

Dear Mr. Cummings:

I write this letter to remind you of our conversation at the Innovex Medical Sales Trade Conference in California. As you urged me to forward a summary of my credentials, I have enclosed my resume.

During the past fifteen years, my positions have ranged from Sales Representative to Corporate Vice-President responsible for the sales management of diagnostic imaging equipment and consumables to a $70 million health care market. I have established and continue to maintain excellent contacts with physicians, material management directors, directors of purchasing, and other senior decision-makers. My expertise is in developing and managing key accounts in the medical industry, including major hospitals, imaging centers, HMOs, and group purchasing offices. Salary requirements are negotiable. In addition, I am willing to relocate, given a suitable opportunity.

I am confident that my skills qualify me for a range of senior-level sales positions. Are you aware of any avenues I might pursue to fully utilize my skills? I would appreciate the chance to talk with you. Please contact me in order to let me know when you can take a few moments out of your schedule for a face-to-face discussion.

It was a pleasure meeting you, and I look forward to speaking with you again.

Sincerely,

Chris Smith

Enc. Resume

▶ Discussion of experience clearly spells out candidate's area of expertise.

▶ Candidate notifies networking contact of travel availability and/or compensation requirements.

NETWORKING LETTER
(Microwave Technician)

178 Green Street
Manchester, NH 03105

January 14, 20--

Pat Cummings
Chief Technician
Any Corporation
1140 Main Street
Keene, NH 03431

Dear Ms. Cummings:

In a recent informational interview, Steven Hague of NewMark Industries referred me to your firm. I am interested in joining an organization where I can utilize my strong technical and leadership skills in microwave or related industries.

I have eleven years of experience in the microwave industry working with state-of-the-art microwave communications antennas. My expertise is in test setups for outdoor and indoor test ranges, as well as the design, manufacturing, and repair maintenance of microwave antennas. In addition, I have extensive experience working with customers and inspectors on final tests to FCC regulations. I am well qualified to assume responsibility for managing projects from initial design to final test and operation.

After you have reviewed my background, please contact me so that we may arrange a personal interview to further expand upon your requirements and my ability to meet them. I can be reached at the above address or at (603) 555-5555.

Thank you for your consideration. I await your response.

Sincerely,

Chris Smith

Enc. Resume

▶ Letter appeals to networking contact's knowledge of industry.

▶ Letter focuses on acquired skills relevant to field of interest.

NETWORKING LETTER
(Mortgage/Loan Officer)

178 Green Street
Conway, AR 72032
(501) 555-5555

April 4, 20--

Pat Cummings
Chief Loan Officer
Any Bank
1140 Main Street
Little Rock, AR 72203

Dear Mr. Cummings:

Recently, I ran into an old college roommate and friend, Ellen Barie. As I am currently considering a new association with a bank or corporation in a Mortgage/Loan Officer capacity, Ellen suggested I contact you. She mentioned that she had worked as a Teller at your Little Rock main branch, and thought you might be interested in someone with my qualifications.

As the enclosed resume indicates, my extensive loan experience has encompassed office supervision and general bookkeeping, with a concentration in credit and collections, within the mortgage, insurance, and banking industries. My current position as a Senior Collections Specialist has provided me with the opportunity to accomplish and exceed a set objective of reducing delinquent loans from $24 million to $10 million within six months. At this point, I feel I have successfully surpassed both company and personal goals, and am searching for new and greater challenges.

I am very interested in the opportunities available at Any Bank. Could we meet for a personal interview? I would be happy to make myself available at your convenience.

Sincerely,

Chris Smith

Enc. Resume

▶ Dollar amounts quantify candidate's accomplishments.

▶ Candidate informs networking contact of mutual acquaintance.

NETWORKING LETTER
(Nurse)

178 Green Street
Kingston, RI 02881
(401) 555-5555

November 19, 20--

Pat Cummings, R.N.
Nursing Director
Any Hospital
1140 Main Street
Bristol, RI 02809

Dear Ms. Cummings:

Are you in need of a nursing professional with extensive clinical, research, and teaching experience? Laura Fogerty, a nurse in your pediatric unit, suggested that I contact you regarding employment opportunities at Any Hospital.

I possess fifteen years of experience in clinical research and direct patient care with an emphasis on neuroscience intensive care, memory disorders, and brain and cognitive sciences. During the past three years, I have functioned as a Staff Nurse assigned to a neuro-intensive care unit.

I am well qualified to teach, counsel, conduct utilization reviews, and/or administer programs related to health care, equipment, or human services—all in appropriate settings. I am capable of making presentations to individuals and groups, skilled at conducting meetings and teaching classes, and have the required communication skills necessary to demonstrate as well as instruct medical professionals and support staffs.

Enclosed please find my business profile. I would be happy to make myself available for an interview to discuss possible openings matching my qualifications. Please feel free to contact me at the above address or daytime phone, or evenings at (401) 555-4444.

I look forward to your return response.

Sincerely,

Chris Smith, R.N.

Enc. Business profile

▶ After name, candidate includes professional title.

▶ Introductory question draws attention.

NETWORKING LETTER
(Paralegal)

---

178 Green Street
Toledo, OH 44501
(419) 555-5555

March 17, 20--

Pat Cummings
Principal
Any Law Firm
1140 Main Street
Beachwood, OH 44122

Dear Mr. Cummings:

The last time we spoke at the University Club, you urged me to contact you if you could be of assistance. My interest in pursuing and expanding my professional career as a paralegal has prompted me to forward the attached resume for your review and consideration.

Please note that I am a candidate for a certificate in Paralegal Studies, December 20--. While attending college and continuing postgraduate study, I have had hands-on experience in the preparation of litigation, probate, corporate, and real estate documents, as well as with computer system applications for the legal profession. In addition, I have developed strong coaching, training, and leadership skills to handle complex, people-oriented, and/or detailed assignments as an individual or a team member.

I would appreciate any information you can provide regarding the legal profession and the role that paralegals play in it. May we meet to discuss? I am eager to learn about the job market and career mobility, as well as about all aspects of the law. I will call your office within the next week or so to schedule a mutually convenient time to talk.

Thank you for your attention in this manner.

Sincerely,

Chris Smith

Enc. Resume

▶ Continuing education demonstrates candidate's dedication to his/her field.

▶ Candidate immediately specifies type of position sought.

NETWORKING LETTER
(Payroll Supervisor)

178 Green Street
Hayward, CA 94541

June 6, 20--

Pat Cummings
Office Manager
Any Corporation
1140 Main Street
Los Angeles, CA 90017

Dear Ms. Cummings:

I received your name as a contact for my job search from a mutual friend, Steve Herson. I was employed at Steve's bank several years ago, and worked closely with him on many projects. In a recent conversation, Steve mentioned that you might be in need of a professional with my qualifications.

As my enclosed resume indicates, in addition to a Bachelor of Arts degree in Economics, my background encompasses eleven years of progressively responsible and sophisticated hands-on experience ranging from Marketing Research Assistant to Union Benefits Coordinator and Human Resources Administrator. In my present position as Payroll Administrator with a special emphasis on the day-to-day details of financial operations and related areas, I have gained valuable experience and training in important organizational and operational areas of a company's general business operation.

I am very interested in investigating opportunities at Any Corporation and believe I could successfully contribute to your staff. Please contact me at the address cited above or call (415) 555-5555 to arrange a mutually convenient time for an interview.

Thank you for your consideration.

Sincerely,

Chris Smith

Enc. Resume

▶ Candidate thanks networking contact in advance for his/her assistance.

▶ Including a telephone number is essential in a cover letter.

NETWORKING LETTER
(Power Systems Designer)

178 Green Street
Mesa, AZ 85028
(602) 555-5555

August 22, 20--

Pat Cummings
Systems Designer
Any Corporation
1140 Main Street
Tempe, AZ 85284

Dear Mr. Cummings:

Debbie Swanson of Systems Powerphasing recommended I contact you concerning my interest in securing a position in the field of power systems design. I understand that your corporation leads the field in power-related emerging technologies. Debbie spoke highly of your work and thought you could provide me with some useful information.

My background includes seven years of experience in positions as Technical Sales Representative and Medical Equipment Technician with a medical equipment manufacturer, and Power Systems Engineer with a manufacturer of telecommunications earth stations. My most recent experience involves all phases of power systems design projects from proposal preparation and specification to on-site installations, customer training, and full operation.

I am very interested in continuing my career in power design with a new firm. I know that your expertise in the field and knowledge of the current trends would be very helpful in my search. Would it be possible to meet briefly? I can easily make myself available at your convenience, and will call you on Monday to see when we might get together.

Thank you for your generous consideration, Mr. Cummings.

Sincerely,

Chris Smith

Enc. Resume

▶ Introduction expresses candidate's knowledge of firm.

▶ Candidate informs networking contact of work experience in field of interest.

NETWORKING LETTER
(Production Manager)

178 Green Street
Arlington, VA 22229
(703) 555-5555

July 22, 20--

Pat Cummings
Director of Operations Management
Any Corporation
1140 Main Street
Macon, GA 31201

Dear Ms. Cummings:

As Alex Drumlins may have told you, I was caught in Timony's recent downsizing. I am writing to inquire if Any Corporation has any openings in production/operations, or if you can provide industry contacts that I may use in my job search.

My related experience extends throughout the last two decades. In addition to a Bachelor of Science degree in Management, I possess four years of supervisory and production management experience with a large Washington, D.C.–based corporation. While working my way through college, I experienced aspects of many other disciplines and gained valuable insights into corporate structure.

Thank you for your time and consideration. May I hear from you?

Sincerely,

Chris Smith

Enc. Resume

► Part-time work experience during school indicates candidate's strong work ethic.

► Explanation for unemployment is optional in a networking letter.

NETWORKING LETTER
(Program Coordinator)

178 Green Street
Walnut Creek, CA 94596
(510) 555-5555

July 3, 20--

Pat Cummings
Human Resources Manager
Any Corporation
1140 Main Street
Cupertino, CA 95014

Dear Mr. Cummings:

I write to remind you of our conversation at the Earth Now! Environmental Services Conference. At that time, you urged me to forward a summary of my credentials whenever I began a job search. Although still employed, I have begun to explore new opportunities. I would appreciate any assistance you can provide, be it informing me of positions in your company or forwarding my resume to other industry contacts.

During the past sixteen years, my experience has focused on environmental and pest control systems. My past four years as District Manager have encompassed P&L responsibility for sales, service, and public relations, as well as training and awareness programs affecting institutional and commercial markets, community environments, and related government legislation.

I wish to join a company that can benefit from my combined technical, sales/service, and management skills. I am most effective in directing in-house or field activities involving environmental programs for a company or its key accounts in the public or private sector.

I am confident that my experience distinguishes me as a top-notch environmental control systems executive. I look forward to discussing with you how and where I might best utilize my talents.

Thank you.

Sincerely,

Chris Smith

Enc. Resume

▶ Candidate briefly reintroduces himself/ herself to networking contact in opening.

▶ Letter immediately states candidate's purpose.

NETWORKING LETTER
(Project Manager)

178 Green Street
Northridge, CA 91324

November 27, 20--

Pat Cummings
Director
Any Institute
1140 Main Street
Los Angeles, CA 90053

Dear Ms. Cummings:

Pursuant to my conversation with Alex Franks on November 9, I am enclosing my resume as an expression of my interest in the position of Project Manager.

Through my education and experience in the transportation field, I have dealt with the public in an assistance capacity in both business and community service environments. In each position I have held, my initiative and ability have led to advancement and the assumption of greater responsibilities.

During the preparation of my recently completed thesis, I conducted extensive research on water transportation. (Enclosed please find an abstract from that thesis.) In addition, my current position involves transportation research and computer transportation modeling.

I feel that my skills, eagerness to learn, and motivation to succeed would contribute to a productive association with Any Institute. I would welcome an opportunity to meet with you to discuss ways in which my capabilities may suit your needs. Please consider the enclosed and direct your response to the above address, or phone me at (818) 555-5555.

Your time and consideration are appreciated. I look forward to hearing from you.

Sincerely,

Chris Smith

Enc. Resume, Thesis abstract

► Research projects illustrate candidate's initiative.

► Candidate immediately specifies type of position sought.

NETWORKING LETTER
(Promotions Representative)

178 Green Street
Bakerton, KY 42711
(606) 555-5555

March 16, 20--

Pat Cummings
Vice-President, Promotions
Any Corporation
1140 Main Street
Knoxville, TN 37902

Dear Mr. Cummings:

Susan Schlegal, Madison Corporation's Promotions Representative, recommended I contact you about the possibility of an opening with Any Corporation. Please accept the enclosed resume as an expression of my interest in joining your organization.

As you can see from my resume, my diverse experience includes administrative duties, telemarketing, coaching, and instructing gymnasts. Ideally, I would like to apply my enthusiasm for athletics, combined with my educational background and acquired business skills, to an organization where my capabilities could be utilized to accomplish mutually agreed upon goals. I feel strongly that Any Corporation is such an organization.

I am confident that my experience and education, coupled with an eagerness to learn and a motivation to succeed, would contribute to a productive association with your company. I would value an opportunity to discuss any current or long-term positions that may be available either at Any Corporation or within the field.

You may contact me at the address cited above, or I will contact you early next week, to arrange a meeting at your earliest convenience.

Your time and consideration are very much appreciated. I look forward to speaking with you in the near future.

Sincerely,

Chris Smith

Enc. Resume

▶ Candidate immediately names referral.   ▶ Letter focuses on filling employer's needs, not the job candidate's.

NETWORKING LETTER
(Property Manager)

178 Green Street
Cocoa Beach, FL 32932
(407) 555-5555

March 3, 20--

Pat Cummings
District Manager
Any Corporation
1140 Main Street
Stamford, CT 06904

Dear Ms. Cummings:

It was a pleasure to meet you last week at the Realtor's Association. Our conversation has prompted me to write to you. As indicated by the enclosed resume, I have progressively advanced from Property Manager to Senior Area Manager with multistate, multisite responsibility for full residency and profitability of major investment properties. At this point in my career, I am seeking a new and challenging opportunity where my qualifications can be utilized by a progressive investment property and/or property owner/management organization.

I have a record of cost-effective management for individual, client, and company-owned properties including high-rise luxury apartment buildings, multistructure condominiums converted from apartments, and subsidized housing. I am accustomed to working with government agencies and associated regulations.

My expertise in troubleshooting, problem-solving, turning serious rental losses into profitable operations, capital improvement plans, preventive maintenance, and maintenance management has enabled me to provide harmonious tenant, owner, and community relationships and trouble-free operation of properties.

If your organization or any of your colleagues can provide an opportunity for someone with my experience, I would like to explore that possibility in the hope of a mutually beneficial association. May we meet for discussion?

I look forward to talking to you soon.

Sincerely,

Chris Smith

Enc. Resume

► Candidate reminds networking contact of last encounter.

► Qualifications highlight candidate's problem-solving ability.

NETWORKING LETTER
(Publicist)

178 Green Street
Woodland Hills, CA 91367

July 9, 20--

Pat Cummings
Publicity Director
Any Corporation
1140 Main Street
Santa Ana, CA 92701

Dear Mr. Cummings:

Lee Cyndis suggested I write you with regards to support areas of advertising and public relations. I would appreciate any information or advice you can provide about how to search for a publicity-related support position. I have enclosed a resume to acquaint you with my background.

I possess comprehensive experience in the support of direct mail fundraising activity for a major university. My training and expertise also include areas of publicity and public relations, staff training and supervision, program coordination and budget management, market research and copyediting, and management and administration of related detail.

I have excellent writing skills, work well under pressure, and meet deadlines consistently. In addition, I have experience with streamlining operations for enhancing production efficiency at an optimum cost.

I would appreciate the chance to meet with you so that we may discuss how my abilities prepare me for a position in the advertising world. I can be reached at the above address or at (818) 555-5555.

I look forward to speaking with you at your earliest convenience. Thank you for your time.

Sincerely,

Chris Smith

Enc. Resume

▶ Candidate focuses on relevant functional skills.

▶ Letter solicits networking contact's advice rather than assistance with job placement.

NETWORKING LETTER
(Publishing Intern)

178 Green Street
Charleston, SC 29403
(803) 555-5555

April 28, 20--

Pat Cummings
Editor
Any Publishing Company
1140 Main Street
Boston, MA 02210

Dear Ms. Cummings:

    I will be graduating from the College of William and Mary in May 20--, and am searching for an avenue that will lead me to a career in publishing.

    Lee Jones, an Editorial Assistant at Any Publishing, suggested your company as a possible place to gain experience. I will be living in Massachusetts during June, July, and August and I am hoping that you will consider me for a summer internship. I would welcome the opportunity to work several days a week, full- or part-time, throughout the summer months in order to better understand the workings of a publishing house.

    As an intern, I could contribute excellent editing, researching, and writing skills. I am familiar with computers and the general library cataloging systems. Additionally, I am an eager and quick learner, and an observer with a creative eye for detail.

    My resume is enclosed; writing samples and references are available upon request. I look forward to hearing from you.

    Thank you for your consideration.

Sincerely,

Chris Smith

Enc. Resume

▶ Candidate requests addressee's return response.

▶ First paragraph introduces candidate to networking contact.

NETWORKING LETTER
(Quality Control Engineer)

178 Green Street
Daytona Beach, FL 32117
(904) 555-5555

January 24, 20--

Pat Cummings
Production/Operations Manager
Any Corporation
1140 Main Street
Long Grove, IL 60047

Dear Mr. Cummings:

I enjoyed talking with you on the plane from Denver. I only wish that we had met a little earlier, on the slopes of Winter Park. Enclosed is the resume you asked to see. I am very interested in discussing opportunities within Any Corporation.

As a Quality Control Engineer, I played a key role in the growth of Victor, Inc., where I interfaced with all departments including sales, purchasing, manufacturing, and inventory. I am knowledgeable in quality functions and have experience bringing product lines through the transitional stages from research/prototype to full production.

During the past seven years, I have implemented and audited clean room contamination control, electrostatic discharge, and internal auditing programs for semiconductor and engineering facilities.

I am interested in joining the professional staff of a firm where I can apply my experience in quality control engineering and manufacturing. I am innovative, productive, accurate, and work well as an individual or as a team member.

I will be in Chicago for a training conference from April 10 to April 14. I would enjoy meeting with you at that time to talk further. Please let me know if this would be a good time to schedule a meeting.

I look forward to hearing from you soon.

Sincerely,

Chris Smith

Enc. Resume

▶ Networking letter may allow for personal discussion.

▶ Discussion of personal qualities reiterates candidate's ability to contribute to potential employer.

NETWORKING LETTER
(Record Manager)

178 Green Street
Kent, OH 44243

October 15, 20--

Pat Cummings
Senior Vice-President, Artists and Repertoire
Any Record Company
1140 Main Street
Dayton, OH 45402

Dear Ms. Cummings:

It has come to my attention, via industry sources, that you have recently assumed the position of Senior Vice-President of the Artist and Repertoire Department for Any Record Company. As it is common practice for new administrators to acquire their own personnel, I am enclosing my resume for your consideration. I have been observing some very positive changes occurring within Any Record Company and I would very much like to become part of your team.

My experience includes the discovery and management of Escalator Rise (Islo), with which Steve Kline is acquainted, and co-management of Sligo Blue, with which Rick Mavan is quite familiar. I have also managed two independent labels, one of which originally signed Pain Cave (Addison). Accordingly, as I feel I have accumulated extensive experience in artist development and product management, I am confident I could become a valuable asset to your department.

Should you like to review a demo tape, please do not hesitate to contact me at (216) 555-5555. I would appreciate the opportunity to speak with you personally, at your earliest convenience.

Thank you for your time. I look forward to hearing from you in the near future.

With best regards,

Chris Smith

Enc. Resume

▶ Letter incorporates industry knowledge into discussion of qualifications.

▶ Candidate familiarizes networking contact with relevant skills and experiences.

NETWORKING LETTER
(Research Assistant)

---

178 Green Street
Elgin, IL 60123

July 20, 20--

Pat Cummings, M.D.
Director of Pharmaceutical Research
Any Hospital
1140 Main Street
Cicero, IL 60650

Dear Dr. Cummings:

Susan Burwen of your human resources department recently informed me of an opening for a Research Assistant (Allergic Diseases) in your pharmaceutical division. Susan and I have been longtime friends, and she felt that my qualifications as a Researcher would ideally match your job requirements. Although I have submitted my resume to Susan, I would like to introduce myself to you as well.

As a graduate of the Massachusetts College of Pharmacy and Allied Health Science, where I earned my Pharmacy degree, I have had the opportunity to perform research in laboratory facilities and have received both instruction and hands-on experience in the use of state-of-the-art research techniques and equipment. As a member of a family who, for generations, has been severely affected by allergic diseases, it has always been my professional objective to either research a cure or contribute to discovering a treatment that would alleviate the discomfort of allergy sufferers.

Given the opportunity to become a part of your pharmaceutical laboratory, I will apply my education, laboratory training, and technical skill toward the achievement of your research objectives dealing with gene regulation and allergic diseases. I would very much like the opportunity to meet with you for further discussion. I will call your office early next week to arrange a time that is convenient for you.

Should you require additional information, please feel free to contact Susan Burwen. Also, I can be reached at the address cited above or (705) 555-5555.

Thank you for your time.

Sincerely,

Chris Smith, Ph.D.

Enc. Resume

▶ Personal experience with industry strengthens candidacy.

▶ Closing invites addressee to inquire about additional information.

NETWORKING LETTER
(Restaurant Manager)

178 Green Street
Glen Burnie, MD 21060

April 26, 20--

Pat Cummings
Regional Manager
Any Restaurant Chain
1140 Main Street
Silver Spring, MD 20901

Dear Ms. Cummings:

    I am writing in response to a referral from a colleague of yours, Jim Murray. Jim was the Assistant Manager of your Baltimore location in 20--, when I worked there as a waitress. When I expressed my desire to return to your organization in a managerial position, Jim enthusiastically responded with several contact names, including yours.

    I have enclosed my resume as an expressed interest in exploring available management opportunities at Any Restaurants. In addition to an Associate degree in Hotel/Restaurant Management, I have five years of experience ranging from Roving Manager with a multiunit restaurant operation to General Manager of a full-service restaurant, lounge, and multiple function/banquet facility. My experience encompasses front- and back-of-the-house management, food and beverage preparation, and personnel training and supervision.

    I feel confident of my potential to make a significant contribution to your restaurant chain. My previous experience as a waitress not only provided specific insight into your management operations, but also was very rewarding personally.

    After you have reviewed my qualifications, please do not hesitate to contact me at the address cited above or call (301) 555-5555. I would like to arrange a mutually convenient time for a meeting to discuss your current or anticipated needs in terms of my qualifications.

    I greatly appreciate your consideration.

Sincerely,

Chris Smith

Enc. Resume

▶ Candidate's practical experience outweighs his/her education.

▶ Candidate immediately introduces purpose for writing.

NETWORKING LETTER
(Retail Sales Manager)

178 Green Street
Berkeley, CA 94710

May 7, 20--

Pat Cummings
Regional Manager
Any Corporation
1140 Main Street
Carson City, NV 89706

Dear Mr. Cummings:

I am currently considering a change of position and am launching a campaign to find a new opportunity in a growth-oriented retail company. At the suggestion of your colleague Maureen Dodge, I have enclosed my professional profile and would appreciate any assistance you may be able to provide.

My objective is to join the management staff of a medium-size retail chain that is at a stage in its growth where it needs experienced leaders to help it successfully reach new expansion goals. With my experience and successful achievements within domestic and international operations, I can provide the impetus to enhance the revenue stream and profit margins through staff development, product diversification, quality services, customer satisfaction, and cost control.

My professional experience with Martins Fashions and the entrepreneur-type environment of Dressing for Success is a valuable resource for moving a company through its next phase of growth. My successes in all aspects of operations further underscore the valuable contribution I could make to an innovative firm such as yours. Although my geographic preference is the West Coast, I will consider a move for an enterprising company that views experience and capabilities essential to achieving its goals.

Should you know of any organizations searching for a professional with my qualifications, please contact me at the address cited above or by phone at (510) 555-5555. As I have not yet discussed a potential move with my current employer, I would like to request your confidentiality in this matter.

Sincerely,

Chris Smith

Enc. Professional profile

▶ Candidate informs networking contact of all relevant information, including geographical preference.

▶ Closing informs addressee of need for confidentiality.

NETWORKING LETTER
(Sales Director)

178 Green Street
Sumas, WA 98295
(604) 555-5555

February 7, 20--

Pat Cummings
Eastern District Manager
Any Corporation
1140 Main Street
New York, NY 10028

Dear Ms. Cummings:

It was great to meet you at the DeLux Designer's conference. I hope we have the chance to speak again soon. As you may remember, I am looking for a new opportunity where my excellent sales skills, strong work ethic, and initiative would directly correlate to my growth, advancement, and future within a company.

During the past six years I have had experience in new business development, negotiations, proposal and contract preparation, and interfacing with banks and attorneys.

Throughout my career, I have worked well independently or as a member of a team. I possess sound knowledge of and experience with the sales of tangible and intangible products as indicated in the enclosed resume. I feel confident that I can be an asset to your company as I have for my present and past employers.

My strong interest in Any Corporation makes relocation feasible and salary issues negotiable.

I look forward to our next discussion.

Sincerely,

Chris Smith

Enc. Resume

▶ Reminds networking contact of common experience.

▶ Closing is straightforward and concise.

NETWORKING LETTER
(Sanitarian)

178 Green Street
Rockville, MD 20850

May 6, 20—

Pat Cummings
Director
Any Health Department
1140 Main Street
Baltimore, MD 21207

Dear Mr. Cummings:

As per your request when we spoke at last week's district meeting, I am enclosing my updated resume so that I may be considered for the position of Sanitarian with Any Health Department.

During the past seventeen years, I have been professionally associated in various capacities with private and public health care facilities and educational institutions. My activities have not only involved health care provider services, but also required extensive involvement with individuals and groups, both of which required direct interfacing with community, municipal, and public health agencies.

A prime interest for me is to work in an area where my recommendations can make a difference in the quality of care and in the environmental surroundings of people dependent on the decisions made by the staff of a municipal health department. I am equally effective working independently or as part of a team effort, and I hope to be able to apply my skills toward achieving the objectives of the department.

I want to thank you for the opportunity to be considered for the position. Should you require any additional information prior to a personal interview, please contact me at the above address or by phone at (301) 555-5555.

Yours sincerely,

Chris Smith

Enc. Resume

▶ Networking letter establishes candidate's knowledge of his/her field.

▶ Candidate thanks networking contact in advance for his/her assistance.

NETWORKING LETTER
(Secretary)

178 Green Street
Birmingham, AL 35294
(205) 555-5555

November 15, 20--

Pat Cummings
Personnel Director
Any Corporation
1140 Main Street
Mobile, AL 36630

Dear Ms. Cummings:

Maureen Deegan suggested I speak with you regarding a secretarial position with Any Corporation. Enclosed is my resume for your consideration. I hope, in reviewing my background, you will find that my qualifications suit your needs.

During the last five years with Stuart Photographers, my responsibilities included assisting on shoots, handling incoming calls, arranging appointments, and light typing. As Service Representative for the Dalton Corporation, I dealt with all customer inquiries and resolved problems in shipping and billing. I am accustomed to working closely with staff and management in a fast-paced environment and enjoy the satisfaction of doing a job well.

Also enclosed is my resume for your review. I am eager to join the staff of Any Corporation and would be glad to make myself available for an interview. I look forward to hearing from you at your earliest convenience.

Sincerely,

Chris Smith

Enc. Resume

▶ Letter focuses on candidate's most relevant qualifications.　　▶ Basis for referral is immediately established.

NETWORKING LETTER
(Special Agent)

178 Green Street
Wayne, NJ 07866

April 15, 20--

Pat Cummings
Special Agent
Any Bureau
1140 Main Street
Washington, DC 20036

Dear Mr. Cummings:

At the request of Ms. Morrow, Special Agent in Charge, I am enclosing my profile in consideration for a position as Special Agent with Any Bureau.

Prior to my recent tour of duty in Afghanistan, I had planned to separate from my position as Group Targeting Officer, attached to special forces, for a position with an investigations bureau. However, my direct involvement in the war on terror and related ongoing assignments have made it necessary for me to put my earlier plan, for a June 20-- transition, on hold. Unfortunately, I will not be able to attend the session at the Employment Release Force Center at Fort Dix on March 30, and ask that you review this application in my absence. At this writing, however, I hope to be able to accept a new position during the first quarter of 20--.

I am free to travel and relocate within the United States, as assignments require, and I am confident that I can provide the skills and quality of performance required of its Special Agents by Any Bureau. As soon as it is mutually convenient, I would like to arrange for a meeting to discuss bureau requirements and my ability to handle the responsibilities of the position.

Please contact me at the above address or leave a message by phone at (201) 555-5555 should you require additional information prior to our meeting.

I look forward to your return response.

Sincerely,

Chris Smith

Enc. Professional profile

▶ Candidate informs networking contact of mutual acquaintance.

▶ Candidate informs networking contact of all relevant information, including geographical preference.

NETWORKING LETTER
(Staff Accountant)

178 Green Street
Newport, RI 02840

November 15, 20--

Pat Cummings
Director, Career Services
Any College
1140 Main Street
Smithfield, RI 02917

Dear Ms. Cummings:

It was nice meeting you at the alumni luncheon on Monday. If you recall, at that time you offered your assistance in my job search. I would greatly appreciate any help you may be able to provide.

During the past three years, I have been employed as a Staff Accountant with a major corporation with responsibility for maintaining financial statements and monthly closings, and preparing financial reports using Microsoft Excel. During the prior four years, while attending college, I held positions of increasing responsibility in areas ranging from auditing to accounts payable in corporate and nonprofit environments.

These positions have been fast-paced and challenging, and the experience I gained is broad in scope. However, to further my career in accounting and finance, I am investigating new opportunities where I can apply my experience to benefit a company that offers room for advancement based on personal preference.

Should you know of any corporation in need of an experienced accountant, please do not hesitate to forward the attached resume. Also, if you have any questions or can provide any further guidance, I can be reached at (401) 555-5555 or (401) 555-4444.

I appreciate your time, Ms. Cummings.

Sincerely,

Chris Smith

Enc. Resume

▶ Candidate reminds networking contact of last encounter.

▶ Candidate requests that attached resume be forwarded.

NETWORKING LETTER
(Teacher: Secondary Level)

178 Green Street
Atlanta, GA 30303
(904) 555-5555

June 4, 20--

Pat Cummings
Headmaster
Any Academy
1140 Main Street
Sarasota, FL 34236

Dear Mr. Cummings:

    Diego Arrigo suggested I contact you in reference to teaching positions in the fields of history and social studies. I am not sure if openings currently exist within your school, but I would appreciate any advice or information you could provide about career opportunities in the academic world. As a recent graduate with a Master of Education degree in Secondary Education, and a Bachelor of Arts degree in History, my goal is to become associated with a university or private school where I can apply my education and experience in the field of education.

    From 20-- to June 20--, I worked as a permanent Substitute Teacher with responsibility for teaching various secondary-level courses, including history. I possess superior research, computer, leadership, and organizational skills, and I am capable of working independently or as a team member in an educational, administrative, or research environment.

    I would appreciate the chance to meet with you. As a young academic, I am interested to hear how your career has progressed to its current point. Please contact me at your convenience so that we may schedule a time to meet.

    I look forward to hearing from you.

Sincerely,

Chris Smith

Enc. Resume

▶ Letter appeals to networking contact's knowledge of industry.

▶ Educational credentials accentuate candidate's qualifications.

NETWORKING LETTER
(Telecommunications Specialist)

178 Green Street
Savage, MT 59262
(406) 555-5555

September 26, 20--

Pat Cummings
Telecommunications Consultant
Any Corporation
1140 Main Street
Chicago, IL 60605

Dear Ms. Cummings:

Several years ago, I was your son Dan's classmate at the University of Miami. When I bumped into him last week in Billings, Montana, of all places, he informed me that you deal closely with several leading specialists in the telecommunications field and suggested I contact you immediately.

I am interested in joining a company where I can contribute strong skills and education in communications. I offer:

- A Bachelor of Arts degree in Communications
- Familiarity with all areas of marketing, public relations, and advertising
- One year of experience as a promotions intern at a radio station
- Fluency in German

I would greatly appreciate any advice and/or referrals you might be able to give me. I will call you in a few days to follow up.

Thank you for your time.

Sincerely,

Chris Smith

Enc. Resume

► Bullets in networking letter draw attention to candidate's accomplishments.

► Candidate requests additional referrals from networking contact.

NETWORKING LETTER
(Telemarketer)

178 Green Street
Wooster, OH 44691
(216) 555-5555

December 4, 20--

Pat Cummings
Director, Telemarketing
Any Corporation
1140 Main Street
Columbus, OH 43216

Dear Mr. Cummings:

Your name was given to me by Leanne Marquis, who I understand has worked with you on several promotional projects. Leanne is a close friend of my mother's, and has been very helpful in assisting me obtain an entry-level position in the telemarketing field. Leanne felt that I would benefit from your extensive industry experience.

I possess four years of successful part- and full-time employment in sales administration and support, and have worked most recently in telemarketing, direct mail, marketing, and sales for a variety of product and/or service-orientated companies.

I would like to meet with you briefly to discuss your insights into the industry. Any referrals or advice you could provide as I prepare to launch my job search would be greatly appreciated. I will contact your office on Friday morning to see if we can schedule a few moments together at your convenience.

Thank you for your consideration.

Sincerely,

Chris Smith

Enc. Resume

▶ Closing suggests a meeting to follow letter.　　▶ Candidate immediately names referral.

NETWORKING LETTER
(Transportation Coordinator)

178 Green Street
Batesville, MS 38606
(601) 555-5555

January 11, 20--

Pat Cummings
Operations Manager
Any Campaign
1140 Main Street
Tupelo, MS 38802

Dear Ms. Cummings:

I recently completed an extended association with the campaign team to elect Congressman Bob Millis. Now that the election is over, Campaign Director Marsha Herns suggested I contact your office to offer my services as Transportation Coordinator.

I have spent the last eleven years owning and operating my own business—coordinating limousine and luxury car services for business professionals and politicians, entertainment celebrities, foreign dignitaries, and the general public. I have the stamina and enthusiasm to work long hours, possess the experience and ability to handle crisis situations, and am known to be responsible and innovative when it comes to getting the job done as planned and on schedule.

Enclosed please find my business profile. If you are need of a competent, experienced Transportation Coordinator, I would like to meet for further discussion. I could be available for an interview at your convenience, and would be happy to supply references at that time.

I look forward to hearing from you.

Sincerely,

Chris Smith

Enc. Business profile

▶ Candidate immediately specifies type of position sought.

▶ Candidate emphasizes how past business experience can benefit potential employer.

NETWORKING LETTER
(Victim Witness Advocate)

178 Green Street
Pawtucket, RI 02860

December 1, 20--

Pat Cummings
Bureau Chief
Any Agency
1140 Main Street
Providence, RI 02902

Dear Mr. Cummings:

In a recent telephone conversation, Marcie Waters of the Children's Protectorate Agency suggested I submit my resume for your review regarding the position of Victim Witness Advocate.

Please note that, in addition to a Bachelor of Arts degree in Psychology and fluency in English, Spanish, and French, my most recent experience has been as a Special Police Officer/Security Officer for Puttnicks Department Store. During my term of employment there, I have, on a daily basis, been called upon to employ skillful, sensitive interviewing and counseling techniques during the detention/arrest procedure, from initial apprehension through court appearances. In addition, for more than three years, I have had the opportunity to interact extensively with staff, customers, and families at all levels.

My experience has provided me with the ability to motivate others toward achieving personal objectives while promoting human dignity. I would welcome the chance to discuss available or anticipated professional opportunities within Any Agency. Should you require additional information, I can be reached at the above address or by phone at (401) 555-5555.

Thank you for your attention to this matter.

Sincerely,

Chris Smith

Enc. Resume

▶ Foreign language skills strengthen candidate's qualifications.

▶ Candidate informs networking contact of work experience in field of interest.

NETWORKING LETTER
(Writer/Reporter)

178 Green Street
Holdrege, NE 68949

April 9, 20--

Pat Cummings
Managing Editor
Any Newsletter
1140 Main Street
Omaha, NE 68102

Dear Ms. Cummings:

At the suggestion of a member of your staff, I am writing to express my interest in a position with your writing/reporting team.

As a recent college graduate, class of 20--, with a major in Political Science and a minor in English, I have extensive experience in researching, abstracting, and writing accurate, detailed papers on topical issues, using journalistic techniques.

Currently, I am seeking a career opportunity with a publication, such as *Any Newsletter*, where I can combine my writing skills with my keen interest in ecology to research and report on discoveries and events dealing with the environment on a local, regional, or international level. Also, based on my interest in providing effective pollution awareness materials to the general public, I consider myself to be a viable candidate for the position.

Enclosed are my resume and samples of my writing. I am confident of my ability to handle the responsibilities of the position offered. Should you wish to schedule a personal interview, please contact me by phone between 5:30 and 10 P.M. at (308) 555-5555.

I look forward to your return response.

Sincerely,

Chris Smith

Enc. Resume, Writing samples

▶ Candidate familiarizes networking contact with relevant skills and experiences.

▶ Closing cites specific times candidate may be reached.

NETWORKING LETTER
(X-Ray Technician)

---

178 Green Street
Allentown, PA 18105
(215) 555-5555
May 31, 20--

Pat Cummings, M.D.
Director of Radiology
Any Hospital
1140 Main Street
Philadelphia, PA 19106

Dear Dr. Cummings:

Your name comes highly recommended to me as an expert in the field of radiology from your associate, Dr. Richard Meyer of Northwest Hospital. Dr. Meyer has been gathering contacts to assist me in investigating employment opportunities, and informs me that you are seeking additional X-Ray Technicians for your team.

In addition to Associate degrees in Liberal Arts, May 20--, and Radio Technology, May 20--, I have two years of academic and clinical intern experience, covering a wide range of radiographic services including the operation of equipment, associated clinical materials and supplies, and radiographic procedures. I also gained experience with film processing, documentation, patient records, and patient relations.

The attached resume summarizes my background. I would greatly appreciate a personal interview in which I could further outline my potential to make a significant contribution to your facility.

If you will please contact me at the address or phone cited above, I would like to arrange a mutually convenient time for such a meeting.

Thank you for your consideration.

Yours sincerely,

Chris Smith

Enc. Resume

▶ Candidate informs networking contact of mutual acquaintance.

▶ Relevant internship bolsters otherwise limited work experience.

CHAPTER 17

BROADCAST LETTER

With a broadcast letter, well-qualified candidates can advertise their availability to top-level professionals in a particular field. The candidate attempts to entice the potential employer, in this case a top-level executive, to consider his or her impressive qualifications for available positions. Although the broadcast letter discusses a candidate's background in detail, a resume is usually included. Since this type of letter is used primarily by seasoned executives, its tone should reflect the candidate's experience, knowledge, and confidence in his or her capabilities.

A candidate using the broadcast letter format might begin, "Are you in need of a Management Accountant who, in her most recent association, contributed to productivity improvements resulting in an annual savings of $20 million?" This attention-grabbing opening is effective only if the reader understands the significance of such an accomplishment. For this reason, broadcast letters are not recommended for those candidates who are conducting broad-based job searches, where cover letters may end up in the human resources department, rather than in the hands of a fellow industry executive.

BROADCAST LETTER
(Account Executive)

178 Green Street
Knoxville, TN 37902

July 16, 20--

Pat Cummings
Managing Director
Any Theater
1140 Main Street
Nashville, TN 37203

RE: Account Executive

Dear Mr. Cummings:

Please note that I have ten years of progressively responsible experience, which includes management positions in hospitality services, marketing, promotion, corporate communications, and public and media relations. My focus has been on events planning, press relations, and the implementation of image-building, attention-getting public relations operations and events for several nationally recognized companies. My accomplishments include:

- Increased paid attendance for special events by more than 31 percent as Marketing and Promotions Coordinator.
- Development of city/corporate transportation programs that substantially increased employee participation.
- Prepared and made presentations as Public Relations Representative and Lecturer before Chambers of Commerce and Convention and Visitor Bureaus, as well as during group sales to private, professional corporate organizations.

My current responsibilities encompass hosting a weekly international program on TV Channel 38 and three out-of-state cable stations. My responsibility involves research, script preparation, on-site taping coordination, and on-air interviews.

I have enclosed my resume. My prime interest is in the challenge and personal satisfaction I will derive from achieving your company's objectives. The compensation package is negotiable. To arrange for a meeting, please contact me at the above address or call (615) 555-5555.

Sincerely,

Chris Smith

Enc. Resume

▶ Candidate limits experiences discussed to significant accomplishments.

▶ Candidate quantifies extensive experience.

BROADCAST LETTER
(Account Manager)

---

178 Green Street
Burlington, VT 05401
(802) 555-5555

January 18, 20--

Pat Cummings
Accounting Supervisor
Any Corporation
1140 Main Street
Montpelier, VT 05602

Dear Ms. Cummings:

Throughout my extensive experience in the field of accounting, I have been aware of, and impressed by, the growth and national reputation of Any Corporation. If your firm is in need of a qualified, seasoned Account Manager, I would welcome the opportunity to meet with you.

I offer more than twenty years of experience as a hands-on manager in all areas of accounting including general ledger, accounts payable, payroll, budgeting/forecasting/analysis, and management reporting. I possess a strong background in cost accounting, inventory control, and supervision. Some of my accomplishments include:

- Initiating a department analysis that increased productivity by 20 percent.
- Implementing a strong system of internal controls that resulted in a reduction of inventory write-offs from $300,000 per year to $0.
- Revising and implementing a revenue accounting system in support of the direct end customer sales of a European subsidiary, which resulted in a cost savings of $150,000 per year.
- Negotiating policy decisions regarding expenditures and investments across multiple businesses and disciplines.
- Writing policies to govern worldwide fiscal processes throughout the company.

Thank you for your consideration in this matter. I look forward to speaking with you further concerning possible openings at Any Corporation.

Sincerely,

Chris Smith

Enc. Resume

▶ Statistics and dollar amounts quantify candidate's accomplishments.

▶ Candidate customizes broadcast letter to meet needs of potential employer.

BROADCAST LETTER
(Chiropractor)

178 Green Street
Chicago, IL 60601
(312) 555-5555

April 9, 20--

Pat Cummings
Chairperson of the Board
Any Clinic
1140 Main Street
Chicago, IL 60601

Dear Mr. Cummings:

I am a certified Chiropractor currently exploring affiliations with established clinics. I have worked in the Chicago area for more than twenty years and, as a result, my reputation for quality care is well known.

Currently, I work as a Chiropractic Therapist with the Chicago Chiropractic Center, a position I have held for the past fifteen years. In this capacity I provide spinal manipulation and handle the musculoskeletal needs of sports injury patients, alleviate pain in elderly patients and those with work-related injuries, and help victims of industrial accidents regain their strength and stamina.

I am also an active member of the following associations:

- American Chiropractic Association
- Illinois Chiropractic Society
- Chicago Chiropractic Society
- Sports Injury Council of the American Chiropractic Association

If my qualifications are of interest to you, I can be reached at the phone number and address above.

Sincerely,

Chris Smith, D.C.

Enc. Resume

▶ Professional memberships show candidate's commitment to his/her field.

▶ Letter details how candidate's most recent experience will benefit potential employer.

BROADCAST LETTER
(Corporate Salesperson)

178 Green Street
Newberg, OR 97132
(503) 555-5555

February 9, 20--

Pat Cummings
Vice-President, Sales
Any Corporation
1140 Main Street
Portland, OR 97201

Dear Ms. Cummings:

For more than ten years, I have been instrumental in opening, selling to, and servicing accounts as well as establishing corporate accounts in a multistate region. Some of my accomplishments include:

- Opening and servicing accounts that resulted in an increase in volume from $50,000 to $500,000.
- Achieving successful sales exceeding 20 percent of entire account inventory.
- Increasing customer accounts by 10 percent in a six-month period.

Currently, I am seeking a new position with a company that can benefit from the efforts of a self-starter who has not only developed new approaches to sales and has experience with customer-controlled computer inventories, but who has also motivated individuals and groups to achieve desired objectives or quotas as both independent contributors and team producers.

I am a dedicated, highly productive, hard-working individual with the kind of persistence that gets results. I work best in a competitive environment and prefer working with an incentive package.

I would be happy to meet in a personal interview to provide you with more detail as to my qualifications and how they can best serve your company.

Thank you for your consideration and early response.

Sincerely,

Chris Smith

Enc. Resume

▶ Broadcast letter includes only experience most relevant to position sought.

▶ Bulleting draws attention to major accomplishments.

BROADCAST LETTER
(Credit Manager)

178 Green Street
Dickinson, ND 58601

May 10, 20--

Pat Cummings
President
Any Corporation
1140 Main Street
Jamestown, ND 58405

Dear Mr. Cummings:

My current position as Credit Manager with a $20 million manufacturing and distribution firm, has, during the past ten years, been both challenging and gratifying. In my association with this firm, I have successfully set up and enforced credit controls that resulted in reducing DSO from sixty to thirty-three days. I am continually involved in training personnel in credit/collection policies and procedures, troubleshooting and resolving sales/customer disputes, and making credit/collection decisions to reduce bad debt risk and increase cash flow.

However, it is time for me to make a change, and I am investigating new opportunities where my expertise can make a bottom-line difference. I can offer a firm, such as Any Corporation, twenty years of successful credit management experience. Based on my contribution to the credit profession, I received recognition, through NACM New England, as Credit Executive of the Year, 20--, and was elected the first woman President of the same professional credit association for the 20---20-- term.

I would appreciate scheduling a mutually convenient time to discuss your requirements for a truly competent Credit Manager and my ability to handle the responsibilities of that position.

My compensation requirement is in the $65,000–$75,000 range. Should you require additional information prior to our meeting, please contact me at the above address or by phone at (701) 555-5555.

I look forward to your return response.

Sincerely,

Chris Smith

Enc. Resume

▶ Impressive credentials and awards further enhance candidate's qualifications.

▶ Broadcast letters often suggest a salary range.

BROADCAST LETTER
(Entrepreneur)

178 Green Street
Washington, DC 20013
(202) 555-5555

June 26, 20--

Pat Cummings
Chief Executive Officer
Any Company
1140 Main Street
Arlington, VA 22234

Dear Ms. Cummings:

I am a successful entrepreneur with fifteen years of experience in areas that include planning, organization, setup, start-up, and management of unique and successful retail sales, product development, manufacturing, and marketing ventures.

Most recently, I have been involved in the launching of a gourmet food product within retail accounts and the hospitality industry. This new venture has given me the opportunity to participate, firsthand, in product formulation, development, and package design. And, under my direction, the product increased its distribution by 52 percent and averaged $150 million in sales.

Although my previous positions have been broad in scope, requiring the skills of a well-organized, innovative individual, I am seeking a new association that will afford me the opportunity to participate in high-level decision-making processes and to contribute to the company's growth and success.

I look forward to a new challenge. Please call with questions.

Sincerely,

Chris Smith

Enc. Resume

▶ Candidate selects only most impressive accomplishments to describe.

▶ Job descriptions indicate how candidate contributed to his/her previous employers.

BROADCAST LETTER
(Fashion Designer)

178 Green Street
Colorado Springs, CO 80903

May 13, 20--

Pat Cummings
Manager
Any Corporation
1140 Main Street
Jacksonville, FL 32231

Dear Mr. Cummings:

I am a veteran of the fashion industry seeking a position with an aggressive, cutting-edge design team. Any Corporation's recent, extensive marketing campaign has confirmed my interest in the company.

I possess three years of diverse experience as an Art Director and Fashion Designer working with a screen-printing company. In this capacity, my principal responsibility has been creating the art and fashion design of clothing lines for national mass markets.

I feel that my creative skills and experience in dealing with sales and buyers can be effectively utilized with a firm such as yours. If you have the need for a highly motivated achiever, then we have good reason to meet.

Please respond at the above address or by phone at (719) 555-5555 to arrange a mutually convenient time for a meeting to discuss my qualifications. A portfolio of my creative work is available for your review.

Thank you for your consideration.

Sincerely,

Chris Smith

Enc. Resume

▶ Letter incorporates company knowledge into discussion of qualifications.

▶ Stating that a portfolio is available on request is beneficial for certain positions.

BROADCAST LETTER
(Financial Consultant)

178 Green Street
Casper, WY 82604
(307) 555-5555

January 11, 20--

Pat Cummings
Communications Services Specialist
Any Corporation
1140 Main Street
Des Moines, IA 52401

Dear Ms. Cummings:

During the past fifteen years, I have held senior-level positions ranging from Senior Consultant with a Big-8 CPA firm, where I specialized in corporate financial planning and control, to my current activity as Chief Financial Officer/Consultant for investment banking and venture capital groups.

Although I am presently involved in interesting and challenging projects, I am ready for a change. I feel that my experience in financial management and administration can better be utilized in a firm that requires a high-energy, self-starter for its management team—in short, a professional who can impact a positive bottom line.

I have established a fine track record in financial and strategic planning that produced high-profit results and encompassed:

- Multimillion-dollar improvement in cash flow.
- Reduction in operating costs and increased profitability of a rapid growth service organization (from $15 million to $28 million within two years).
- Profit and business planning, financial evaluation, and long-range financial forecasting for a $140 million group of operating companies.
- Negotiation for public and private funding totaling $35 million.

I feel that a meeting to discuss both the opportunities available at Any Corporation, and my capabilities, would be mutually beneficial. For a phone interview, or to arrange for a meeting, please contact my office phone at (307) 444-4444.

Sincerely,

Chris Smith

Enc. Resume

▶ Bulleting the broadcast letter brings immediate attention to candidate's accomplishments.

▶ Including a business number is optional in a cover letter.

BROADCAST LETTER
(Fleet and Transportation Manager)

178 Green Street
Altus, OK 73521
(918) 555-5555

April 25, 20--

Pat Cummings
Executive Vice-President
Any Corporation
1140 Main Street
Tulsa, OK 74106

Dear Mr. Cummings:

If your firm can benefit from a committed professional with general, financial, fleet, and transportation management experience, then we have good reason to meet.

In addition to a Master's degree in Business Administration, summa cum laude, from Harvard University and advanced study in dealer management, I offer:

- More than sixteen years of senior-level management experience with P&L responsibility for a composite automotive dealership offering new and used car/truck sales, service, and rental/leasing operations.
- Eight years of additional experience in banking as an investment officer with investment analysis and portfolio management responsibility.
- Expertise in the design, implementation, and installation of computerized accounting systems, as well as extensive experience with financial analysis, budgets, and cost-effective corporate operations.
- Skill in the selection and development of management teams, incentives, and benefit programs to retain the most capable personnel.
- Knowledge of developing cash management and financial programs to provide funding for new or continuing operations to maximize returns on investment.
- Qualifications to function as controller, financial analyst, operations, or administrative manager where corporate management is interested in achieving its objectives of cost-effective operations and increased profitability.

I am in search of a fast-paced, aggressive company that could benefit from my ability to quickly increase growth and profitability. Relocation and travel would be considered. Thank you for your time.

Sincerely,

Chris Smith
Enc. Resume

▶ Educational honors are emphasized.　　　▶ Broadcast letter effectively highlights candidate's significant accomplishments.

BROADCAST LETTER
(Freight Supervisor)

178 Green Street
Raleigh, NC 27611

September 1, 20--

Pat Cummings
District Supervisor
Any Corporation
1140 Main Street
Fayetteville, NC 28302

Dear Ms. Cummings:

During the past thirteen years, I have been actively involved in positions as Field Manager of Contained Operations and Night Operations Supervisor of freight stations and service centers dealing with domestic and international freight deliveries.

In addition to the supervision of day-to-day operations, my experience encompasses hiring, training and supervision of drivers, office and support personnel, and the provision of cost-effective quality service within a multiple service network. I have sound knowledge of computer systems design for freight movement management, and am skilled in both troubleshooting and resolving problems relative to the movement or transfer of materials.

Although my present situation is challenging and diverse, I feel that it is time for me to make a change. I am looking for a new association with a firm that can benefit from my extensive experience with import/export traffic. Depending on the benefits package, salary is negotiable.

I would welcome the opportunity to discuss your requirements and to further outline my qualifications. Should you require additional information, please contact me at the above address or by phone at (919) 555-5555.

Thank you for your consideration.

Sincerely,

Chris Smith

Enc. Resume

▶ Specific contributions emphasize candidate's achievements and problem-solving abilities.

▶ Compensation requirements are often discussed in a broadcast letter.

BROADCAST LETTER
(Legal Associate)

178 Green Street
St. Louis, MO 63135

August 26, 20--

Pat Cummings
Attorney-at-Law
Any Law Firm
1140 Main Street
Detroit, MI 48221

Dear Mr. Cummings:

As a newly arrived St. Louis Attorney in the Detroit area, who is now a permanent resident of Michigan, I am interested in a position as a First Year Associate with a firm that has a need for strong legal support in the areas of litigation, trade regulation, corporate, or general practice of law.

During my three and a half years as a Legal Assistant with Murphy, Smith, and Murray, I was actively involved in researching and drafting memoranda in areas of trade regulations, copyrights, and trademarks. I managed the discovery process, handled the deposition process, and provided litigation support during trials.

My experience as Contract Consultant/Assistant to a Vice-President of Elliot Fashions involved extensive research, contract negotiations, and the review, from a legal perspective, of all print advertising and other written materials relative to nonapparel products for this international conglomerate. I have worked in close cooperation with all departments and prepared materials for final approval by the corporate legal department.

The enclosed resume is a summary of my experience for your review. I was admitted to the Missouri Bar, January 20--, and to further my legal career, I plan to sit for the Michigan Bar exam in February 20--.

I am anxious to discuss with you how my credentials might benefit your firm. Should you require additional information as to my ability and interests or can advise me concerning other possible avenues of employment in the legal profession, please contact me at the above address or by phone at (314) 555-5555.

Thank you in advance for your interest and assistance.

Sincerely,

Chris Smith

Enc. Resume

▶ Professional accreditation enhances candidate's qualifications.

▶ Relevant work experience is emphasized while other positions are omitted.

BROADCAST LETTER
(Marketing/Sales Executive)

178 Green Street
Cedar Rapids, IA 54201
(319) 555-5555

April 10, 20--

Pat Cummings
Chief Account Executive
Any Corporation
1140 Main Street
Wichita, KS 67202

Dear Ms. Cummings:

I am a seasoned Marketing/Sales Executive seeking an association with an aggressive, young firm such as Any Corporation. I offer extensive experience and achievements in marketing, business development, and product management at national and international levels.

During the past ten years, my successes have included:

- Development of sales programs and new businesses to increase penetration, market share, and revenue through advanced, technically sophisticated systems management services.
- Team participation in the development and marketing of new service products for a service business generating $3.7 billion worldwide.
- P & L responsibility for an added-value services business generating $90 million.
- Established record of achievement for producing positive bottom-line results in a high-tech service-oriented business with worldwide markets.

I am well qualified to direct areas that are key to achieving your business objectives. I am prepared to play an integral role in the profitable management of corporate programs designed to broaden your business opportunities on national and/or international levels.

My salary range is in the mid-$70,000 range. However, as my primary interest is in the challenge of the position and your goals, this figure is negotiable.

Sincerely,

Chris Smith

Enc. Resume

▶ Broadcast letter often separates major accomplishments for emphasis.

▶ Broadcast letter emphasizes candidate's strong record of success.

BROADCAST LETTER
(Multimedia Specialist)

178 Green Street
Chicago, IL 60611
(312) 555-5555

June 13, 20--

Pat Cummings
Executive Director
Any Corporation
1140 Main Street
Des Moines, IA 50309

Dear Mr. Cummings:

    During the past three years I have been actively involved in research, development, and demonstration projects that have focused on the introduction of interactive multimedia instructional methodologies into both corporate training programs and university curricula.

    My participation in these projects has been primarily in the areas of concept development and marketing, proposal writing, and project management. I offer experience in curriculum analysis and design, human factors research, instructional design, and media production. In addition, I am capable of operating a wide variety of authoring and development tools on both PC-compatible and Macintosh platforms.

    I am currently looking for an opportunity to work in an organization that is introducing, or developing plans to introduce, interactive multimedia instruction techniques as components of its corporate training program.

    I believe that my comprehensive knowledge of interactive multimedia technology, my vision for its application in corporate training, and my experience as a Senior Human Resources Manager offer a unique mix of credentials—all summarized in the enclosed resume.

    I would be delighted to discuss my qualifications with you at your convenience. Thank you for your consideration.

Sincerely,

Chris Smith

Enc. Resume

▶ Candidate refers to attached resume in closing.

▶ Letter details how candidate's most recent experience will benefit potential employer.

BROADCAST LETTER
(Program Manager)

178 Green Street
Tulsa, OK 74117
(918) 555-5555

August 12, 20--

Pat Cummings
Director
Any Company
1140 Main Street
Anadarko, OK 73005

Dear Ms. Cummings:

An article in the July issue of *Oklahoma Business Journal* featured Any Company's recent success and growth. As a Program Manager interested in establishing connections with a new, up-and-coming firm, I submit the enclosed resume for your review.

My qualifications include more than twelve years of managing experience with Ricochet Data. In this capacity I developed and coordinated short- and long-range plans for the design and introduction of four new microcomputer products. I also created master charts to track major milestones and critical path activities, directed a management task force to develop a set of work instructions for the introduction of outsourced products, and reduced product time to market by 25 percent.

My work in retail management might also be of interest to you. While employed at Lorenz Company, I generated gross annual sales in excess of $2 million for four consecutive years, managed a sales and service team of twenty people, and provided superior customer service and support.

Should my qualifications match your current or anticipated needs, I can be reached at the telephone number and address above.

Sincerely,

Chris Smith

Enc. Resume

▶ Candidate customizes broadcast letter to meet needs of potential employer.

▶ Qualifications highlight candidate's leadership skills.

BROADCAST LETTER
(Real Estate Executive)

178 Green Street
Appleton, WI 54912

December 14, 20--

Pat Cummings
President
Any Corporation
1140 Main Street
Madison, WI 53713

Dear Mr. Cummings:

During the past thirteen years, working with a full-service real estate and consulting firm, I have acted as:

- Director of Development for consulting services generating $1.8 million in fees.
- Project Manager overseeing major additions and renovations for corporate and institutional clients involving 1.2 million square feet.
- Property/Asset Manager of half a million square feet of company-developed, -owned, and -managed real estate.

My position has been one of diverse responsibilities and challenges. However, I feel it is time for me to make a change to a larger, more aggressive firm where my comprehensive experience in development, property/asset management, and related consulting skills can be better utilized.

In prior positions, as Regional Manager and Loan Officer, I gained broad experience and insight into residential and commercial financing with emphasis on the mortgage and mortgage insurance industries involving institutions and private investors. I am confident that this combination of varied and successful experience can be effectively applied to a firm competing against other major full-service real estate operations.

Should you require additional information, please contact me at the above address or by phone at (414) 555-5555. Since my present employer is not aware of my intent to make a change, I would appreciate your holding this correspondence in the strictest confidence. Thank you.

Sincerely,

Chris Smith

Enc. Resume

▶ Letter suggests discretion.

▶ Broadcast letter includes only experience most relevant to position sought.

BROADCAST LETTER
(Senior Vice-President)

---

178 Green Street
Bridgeton, MO 63044
(314) 555-5555

January 3, 20--

Pat Cummings
President
Any Bank
1140 Main Street
St. Louis, MO 63146

Dear Ms. Cummings:

I am currently the Senior Vice-President at Central St. Louis Bank where I have been for the past twenty-five years. Please note my credentials:

- Fifteen years of diverse experience ranging from Acting Branch Manager and District Manager to my present position as Vice-President.
- Supervised all internal departments including sales/account development, human resources, customer relations and customer service supervision, and product and sales support.
- Increased new business by 25 percent in one year through extensive interface with clients, decision-makers, and support personnel.

Although my present position is challenging, I am looking to associate myself with a progressive firm that addresses both national and international banking markets. I offer both experience and enthusiasm.

I look forward to hearing from you.

Sincerely,

Chris Smith

Enc. resume

▶ Broadcast letter often separates major accomplishments for emphasis.

▶ Closing reiterates candidate's interest in position.

BROADCAST LETTER
(Senior-Level MIS Operator)

178 Green Street
Birmingham, AL 35266

September 5, 20--

Pat Cummings
Controller
Any Corporation
1140 Main Street
Mobile, AL 36630

Dear Mr. Cummings:

I am currently seeking a position change and would like to meet with you to discuss senior-level opportunities within your firm's MIS department. I am interested in applying my combined technical knowledge and experience to create and implement innovative concepts for greater information systems efficiency.

I can offer your firm:

1. Seventeen years of experience with corporate information systems.
2. Experience in the operation and supervision of administrative functions of UNIX systems using AT&T System V operating software.
3. Skill in communicating with domestic/international networks, mainframes, and network system support.
4. Ability to work as a team member, team leader, and/or independent contributor working off-site via modem and data network, to assist users in sales, finance, manufacturing, and production.
5. Effective interface for mainframe/network and UNIX systems problems involving either hardware or software.
6. Techniques to teach the cost-effective utilization of multifunctioning systems from mainframe to PC, and instruct system operators in system problem identification and resolution.

This list summarizes my experience. However, during a comprehensive interview we could further discuss your requirements and expand on my ability to handle the responsibilities of the position under consideration. Please contact me at the above address or by phone at (205) 555-5555.

Yours sincerely,

Chris Smith

Enc. Resume
Internet: *csmith@service.com*

▶ Avoid technical jargon unless it is specific to candidate's field.

▶ Including an e-mail address may be advantageous for certain fields of work.

BROADCAST LETTER
(Vice-President of Administration)

178 Green Street
Dodge City, KS 67801
(316) 555-5555

July 26, 20--

Pat Cummings
Chief Executive Officer
Any Corporation
1140 Main Street
Wichita, KS 67226

Dear Ms. Cummings:

I have served as Vice-President of Administration and Finance at Third Bank of Kansas for the past eighteen years. Although this position has been very challenging, I am interested in a change and feel that my background might be of interest to you.

Please consider the following qualifications:

- Provided handling and record-keeping services for corporate, fiduciary, and personal custody accounts with assets totaling $20 billion.
- Managed administrative sales, which totaled more than $500,000.
- Directed administrative processes for 56 percent of the department's largest and most complex accounts.
- Analyzed new accounting systems to determine customers' needs.
- Developed and maintained strong securities operational knowledge.

In addition to my extensive experience, I am also a member and past president of the Securities Operations Association of the Heartland, speaker/panel member of the Kansas Bankers Association, and past president of the Bank of Heartland Supervisors' Association.

I look forward to hearing from you in the near future.

Sincerely,

Chris Smith

Enc. Resume

▶ Candidate selects only most impressive accomplishments to describe.

▶ Job-related affiliations demonstrate candidate's active participation in his/her field.

BROADCAST LETTER
(Warehouse Operator)

178 Green Street
Indianapolis, IN 46206

July 15, 20--

Pat Cummings
Controller
Any Corporation
1140 Main Street
South Bend, IN 46626

Dear Mr. Cummings:

My broad-based experience in state-of-the-art warehousing and distribution systems and procedures, with operations ranging from $7 million to $160 million, can be of immeasurable value to a company interested in cost-cutting, expansion, or greater efficiency and improved service.

My prior positions have been challenging and provided me with both responsibility for reorganizing, restructuring, and upgrading systems and controls for cost-effective, efficient, and productive warehousing operations. Currently, I am seeking a new position with a firm that can benefit from my experience.

Should you wish to discuss my credentials further, I can be reached during business hours at (317) 555-5555 or evenings at (317) 444-4444.

Your return response is appreciated.

Sincerely,

Chris Smith

Enc. Resume

▶ Broadcast letter emphasizes candidate's strong record of success.

▶ Including an evening telephone number is optional in a cover letter.

BROADCAST LETTER
(Zoologist)

178 Green Street
Lexington, KY 21345
(606) 555-5555

June 26, 20--

Pat Cummings
Director
Any Stable
1140 Main Street
New York, NY 10153

Dear Ms. Cummings:

I am a Zoologist with eight years of experience working primarily with racehorses. I am currently seeking a position in a stable where my expertise in genetics and breeding will contribute to the success of the organization. Perhaps my credentials will interest you.

First, my most recent experience includes work with the following:
- Center for DNA Research, Cambridge, MA; Spring 20--
- Truman Thoroughbred Stables, Hamilton, MA; Spring 20--
- Center for Genetic Research, New York, NY; Summer 20--

Currently I serve as Genetics/Breeding Specialist for the Uphill Thoroughbred Stables and Stud Farm. In this position, I work directly with doctors of veterinary medicine and racehorse trainers in breeding and grooming top-quality thoroughbreds for racing and dressage. I also investigate genetic factors, forecast crossbreeding, and evaluate artificial insemination considerations of specific mares and studs.

Although I am quite happy with my present employer and the work is challenging, I am interested in a position where I can conduct more intensive research in a laboratory environment. If my qualifications meet your needs, please call.

I look forward to hearing from you.

Sincerely,

Chris Smith, D.V.M.

Enc. Resume

▶ Valuable research experience is highlighted in detail.

▶ Broadcast letter effectively highlight candidate's extensive experience.

CHAPTER 18

RESUME LETTER

Suppose you've put together your resume to emphasize your sales experience and along comes a classified ad for a Computer Programmer, a position for which you also would be qualified. Do you shrug your shoulders and say "Oh well, my resume is all wrong for that one"? No. You roll up your sleeves and create a resume letter.

A resume letter is a nifty little job-searching tool, which lets you tailor your responses to the positions available by combining your cover letter and resume. Using a resume letter, you can customize your job application to meet the needs of a specific employer, position or industry. Just like a resume, your resume letter should include all relevant information pertaining to your background and qualifications, including education, work experience, and functional skills. Keep in mind, however that while the resume letter offers a convenient way to apply for a position, it doesn't take the place of a full-blown resume. You will still need one of those as the hiring process progresses.

RESUME LETTER
(Business Manager)

178 Green Street
Hillsboro, MO 63050
(314) 555-5555

January 12, 20--

Pat Cummings
President
Any Corporation
1140 Main Street
Columbia, MO 65211

Dear Mr. Cummings:

I am a seasoned professional offering more than twenty-one years of extensive experience in business and corporate administrative responsibilities in the following areas:

- Cost engineering and estimating
- Accounting and financial analysis
- Planning and scheduling
- Personal computers and microsystems
- Procurement and contact administration
- Claims preparation and pricing
- Documentation and negotiations
- Mainframe computers and systems

In addition to the experience cited above, I have worked with construction managers, project managers, project engineers, project accountants, discipline engineers and designers, as well as with quality assurance and other technical and support personnel. I am able to establish effective rapport with supervisors, colleagues, and subordinates and have hands-on knowledge of computer services and office procedures.

During seventeen years with Picciano & Houllahan Engineering, Inc., I have established a record of which I am quite proud. I have assumed positions of increasing responsibility, and I am now ready for a greater challenge. I believe you will agree that my record justifies my expectation for seeking a staff-level position with the opportunity to fully utilize my experience and potential for advancement to a line-management position.

On both a day-to-day and long-range basis, I have participated in the cost and scheduling activities of both large and small projects, and a number of various types: fuel, fossil, nuclear, process, pulp and paper, industrial, infrastructure, and environmental. My strengths include a strong background in project controls, budget forecasting and maintenance, staff supervision, and problem solving. I have the respect of colleagues and clients in terms of overall effectiveness, on-schedule and under-budget performance, and quality of final product and/or reports.

My goal is to join a firm that requires the immediate use of these skills to either increase a rate of established growth, or to effect a turnaround situation.

Within the next week or so, I will call to see whether you agree that our mutual interests would be served by exploring this matter further, and if so when your calendar might permit time for a personal interview.

Thank you for your time and consideration.

Sincerely,

Chris Smith

▶ Resume letter format combines cover letter and resume into one.

▶ Background summary accentuates candidate's acquired professional skills and impressive track record.

RESUME LETTER
(Cardiologist)

178 Green Street
Payne Gap, KY 41537
(606) 555-5555

April 30, 20--

Pat Cummings
Chief Administrator
Any Hospital
1140 Main Street
Sandy Springs, SC 29677

Dear Ms. Cummings:

I recently read about your need for a Cardiologist in the May edition of the bulletin published by the South Carolina Medical Association. Please accept the following summary of accomplishments as my application for this opportunity.

- Two years as Cardiology Fellow with extensive experience covering the full spectrum of clinical cardiology.
- Experience encompasses: cardiac catheterization and angioplasty, cardiac pacing and electrophysiology, echocardiography, exercise testing and nuclear imaging, in- and out-patient hospital care of cardiac patients.
- Two years of experience as a Clinical Instructor in Medicine at St. Martha's Hospital, teaching interns, residents, and medical students.
- Board certified—Internal Medicine, board eligible in Cardiology.

In my current position as Cardiology Fellow at St. Martha's, I have had the opportunity to utilize state-of-the-art systems, procedures, and techniques covering the full spectrum of clinical cardiology. I am also presently involved in research encompassing clinical evaluation of the bundeen cross-coronary stent, and have just completed a review article dealing with ventricular arrhythmias. Additionally, I received my Doctor of Medicine degree from the Boston College School of Medicine, and a Bachelor of Science degree in Preprofessional Studies from the University of Pennsylvania.

I am planning to move to South Carolina shortly, and I understand that you need a qualified Cardiologist to fill your vacancy. Would you have a few moments to speak with me next week during a scheduled visit to your area? I am sure I could convince you that I have the capabilities and the motivation to join your staff.

I will call your office on Friday to follow up on this inquiry.

Sincerely yours,

Chris Smith, M.D.

▶ Advanced degrees and varied clinical experience add weight to cover letter.

▶ After name, candidate includes professional title.

RESUME LETTER
(Community Center Director)

178 Green Street
West Chester, PA 19380
(800) 555-5555

February 29, 20--

Pat Cummings
President and Executive Director
Any Community Center
1140 Main Street
Philadelphia, PA 19114

Dear Mr. Cummings:

I was sorry to hear about your retirement in the article "Community Top Gun to Step Down" featured in the February 28 edition of the *Philadelphia Enquirer*. Your accomplishments as Executive Director at Any Community Center speak for themselves, and I am sure your dedication and vision will be sorely missed.

I understand from a statement you made in the article that you will be personally choosing your successor prior to retirement. As a seasoned Community Center Director myself, I would be honored if you would consider me worthy of continuing your work. Presently, I am working as the Associate Executive Director of the Westchester YMCA.

My responsibilities encompass all aspects of operations:

Supervision: Supervise seven full-time program directors and nonexempt administrative staff. Recruit, hire, train, and evaluate full- and part-time staff. Organize and conduct staff meetings and training events. Responsible for career development for full-time professional staff.

Management: Financial management of a $2 million multidepartment annual budget. Developed and projected new annual budget, balanced and allocated funds, and ensured branch departments met financial goals. Operations management of all program areas, member services, office administration, and facility maintenance. Administered safety and risk-management procedures for the branch.

Fundraising: Chaired 20-- Annual Support Campaign and Community Gifts Chair of the 20-- Annual Support Drive. Organized campaign activities, recruited and trained volunteers, managed telephone solicitations, developed prospects, and implemented related administrative procedures.

Programs/Services: Managed multiprogram areas, scheduling, enrollment, and member evaluations. Established program guidelines and criteria. Managed and supervised membership department and front desk area, program registration, and member services/relations.

Community Relations: Responsible for administration and allocation of scholarship/financial aid funds. Assisted in volunteer development program. Direct responsibility to branch board of directors and program committees. Responsible for public service announcements and public relations via presentations at various community organizations.

I would be very interested in talking with you about your requirements for the position. When would be a convenient time to meet?

Sincerely,

Chris Smith

▶ Categorizing qualifications adds strength to cover letter.

▶ Letter focuses on the needs of the employer, not the job candidate.

RESUME LETTER
(Construction Manager)

178 Green Street
Fort Worth, TX 76104
(817) 555-5555

June 16, 20--

Pat Cummings
Principal Engineer
Any Corporation
1140 Main Street
Arlington, TX 76004

Dear Ms. Cummings:

During the past eighteen years, I have developed the professional skills that are the essential building blocks for successful project and construction management. Currently, I am looking for a new position with a firm, such as yours, where I can apply these skills to increasingly complex and challenging projects with profitable bottom-line results.

After earning my Bachelor of Science degree in Civil Engineering from the University of Austin, Texas, and competing in the Olympics in 20--, I joined B.R. Rice, Inc. as a Construction Engineer managing construction on major power plant sites in Mexico, Texas, and California. From 20-- to 20--, I was responsible, as Senior Project Manager, for project engineering and design/build project management assignments in the power, environmental, and commercial process industries. This included both field and home office desk assignments for both public and private sector companies.

Since 2001, I have been the Director of Engineering and Principal Engineer for an engineering and environment consulting company. My responsibilities also include marketing, proposal preparation, and project management. I serve as a consultant to public and private sector clients in business planning, environmental permitting, financing, design/construction management, and start-up of environmental and waste management building projects.

To date, I have managed the design and construction of projects representing more than 32 million cubic feet of building volume, 200 megawatts of power, and nearly $275 million in financing.

My projects have been varied and complex. Some of my prior project management accomplishments include:

- Design and construction of a four-year, $52 million coal conversion project in Austin, Texas. Completed the project on schedule and $500,000 under budget.
- Process, site, and building designs—a $30 million portion of the largest waste-to-energy facility in the world, in Cincinnati, Ohio. Managed a $3.5 million design, field engineering, and a start-up assistance contract. Directed a project team that issued twenty-five individual construction contract bid packages, each one on schedule. Recommended $1 million in value engineering cost savings to the client, and closed out the contract $500,000 under budget.
- Provision of constructability review and pricing for an advanced energy research project for the U.S. Department of Energy and NASA.
- Direction of the development, planning, and implementation of a $1.3 billion, twenty-three-year engineering and construction program extending the lives of fourteen power plants for a large electric utility company.

As an Engineering Management Professional, I am technically proficient; apply creative solutions to complex problems; encourage team building among project participants; maintain constant communication both up and down the ladder; set and ensure achievement of total quality management objectives; and closely monitor resource allocations and expenditures, goal attainments, and project team performance.

I am keenly interested in suitable availabilities at Any Corporation and am immediately available pending adequate prior notice to my current employer. The reason for leaving my current employment is the desire to join a larger company where I can put all of my knowledge to use and be deeply involved in all phases of complex, construction projects.

I look forward to meeting with you, in confidence, to discuss my experience and the mutual benefits of my joining your company.

Sincerely,

Chris Smith, P.E.

▶ Two pages is an acceptable length for top positions.

▶ Letter emphasizes achievements and does not simply list job responsibilities.

RESUME LETTER
(Director of Information Services)

178 Green Street
Clearfield, UT 84016

November 5, 20--

Pat Cummings
Vice-President, Operations
Any Corporation
1140 Main Street
Salt Lake City, UT 84104

Dear Mr. Cummings:

I am interested in your advertisement for a Director of Information Services as published in the November edition of the *Salt Lake Tribune*. Several of the qualifications I could bring to this position include:

- Extensive experience in COBOL Programming.
- Proven managerial abilities.
- Self-motivation; able to set effective priorities to achieve immediate and long-term goals and meet operational deadlines.
- Development of interpersonal skills, having dealt with a diversity of professionals, clients, and staff members.
- Ability to function well in fast-paced, high-pressure atmosphere.

For the past eleven years I have had the opportunity to progress in positions of responsibility at my current employer from Programmer to Director of Information Services. In this capacity, I control programming and systems, computer operations, data entry, membership records, and membership promotion and retention departments. I have successfully implemented complete financial reporting systems, inventory, accounts receivable, computerized production of publications, and applications.

In addition to my work experiences, I hold both a Bachelor's and a Master's degree in Business Administration. I am proficient in Burroughs B-2900 computer systems, with various peripheral equipment and 35 online CRT terminals (COBOL).

I am very interested in learning more about your work at Any Corporation and how I might best apply my skills to your advantage. Please contact me at (801) 555-5555 to schedule a meeting.

Sincerely,

Chris Smith

▶ Including computer skills may be advantageous for certain fields of work.

▶ Letter's format outlines all relevant information to field of interest, including qualifications, achievements, and education.

RESUME LETTER
(District Manager)

178 Green Street
Long Beach, CA 90802

December 27, 20--

Pat Cummings
Vice-President, Pacific Region
Any Restaurant Chain
1140 Main Street
Los Angeles, CA 90010

Dear Ms. Cummings:

I would like to express my sincere interest in the District Manager position you advertised in the December 26 edition of the *Los Angeles Times*. I have taken the liberty of summarizing my background in the restaurant franchise industry for your consideration:

- Fifteen years of successful experience in the management of three franchise restaurants, including financing, contractual agreements, corporate and personnel relations, property management, facilities design and layout, advertising, promotion, and community relations.
- Experience also includes purchasing, inventory control and management, personnel hiring, training, scheduling and evaluation, security, policy and procedure.
- Proven record as top salesperson. Consistently awarded top sales manager honors.

For the past ten years, I have succeeded in increasingly responsible positions with the Pizza Palace franchise. In my current position as Branch Manager, I am responsible for managing a work force of more than 250 employees, while generating annual sales in excess of $3.5 million. I am actively involved in all aspects of successful business operations, including sales, finance, and personnel management, property maintenance, and associated aspects of administrative detail.

I would be happy to supply several excellent references at your request. Additionally, I would be available at your convenience to meet for an interview. Please contact me at (203) 555-5555, or evenings at (203) 444-4444.

I appreciate your consideration, Ms. Cummings.

Sincerely,

Chris Smith

▶ Career objective is supported by awards and accomplishments.

▶ Candidate tailors resume letter to his/her field of interest.

RESUME LETTER
(Hospital Administrator)

178 Green Street
Norwalk, CT 06856
(203) 555-555

August 11, 20--

Pat Cummings
Chairperson, Board of Directors
Any Hospital
1140 Main Street
Bridgeport, CT 06605

Dear Mr. Cummings:

Thank you for speaking with me this morning regarding the Hospital Administrator position available at Any Hospital. As per your request, please allow me to present several of my most relevant experiences and accomplishments in health care management/administration.

For the past year, I have been working as Acting Director of the Norwalk Medical Center. In this capacity, I am responsible for the supervision/coordination of all administrative services for the city's public health care program. This includes the health care and hospitalization for indigent, low-income, and welfare patients, consistent with care-afforded insurance and fee-for-service patients. In addition, I troubleshoot staff and general administration conflicts and resolve policy issues, as well as develop reports for budgeting proposals and expenditure control.

Previous to my current position, I spent six years as Central Administrator of Emergency Services for the same institution. I coordinated all administrative details of the department, prepared the department budget, and monitored expenditures. As Administrator, I also supervised ward secretaries, interpreters, and ancillary personnel. This same duty was performed in the position of Unit Manager, which I held from 20-- to 20--. This position gave me exposure to several aspects of administrative support, vendor relations, and inventory control.

My work experience is supported by a Master of Science degree in Health Service Administration, a certificate in Management Development from the Connecticut Hospital Association, and a Bachelor of Arts degree in English.

I am very eager to apply my acquired knowledge of health care administration to the position at Any Hospital. I hope my qualifications match your requirements, and that I will have the opportunity to speak with you again in a personal interview. Thank you for your consideration.

Sincerely,

Chris Smith

▶ Specific contributions emphasize candidate's achievements and problem-solving abilities.

▶ Resume letter format is particularly effective for top-level positions.

RESUME LETTER
(Manufacturing Manager)

178 Green Street
Lake City, FL 32056
(904) 555-5555

May 8, 20--

Pat Cummings
Chief Executive Officer
Any Corporation
1140 Main Street
Chicago, IL 60611

Dear Ms. Cummings:

I discovered Any Corporation through your listing in the *Chicago JobBank*. I am an experienced executive with a broad technical as well as management background in the machining and manufacturing fields. Next month, I will be moving permanently to Illinois, and would be very interested in learning of suitable management opportunities at your firm.

With more than sixteen years of training in the manufacturing industry, I possess a proven track record of accomplishment. Some of the experiences I could bring to Any Corporation include:

Manufacturing Manager; Gladstone Motor Company, Lake City, VT

- Oversaw modernization and reorganization of engine plant contracted for remanufacture of Dane Motor Company engines.
- Set up controls for workers in manufacturing departments and the machine shop, which included grinding, boring, and honing operations.
- Initiated an improved quality control system to meet Dane specifications for full-year warranty. System resulted in reduction of rejects to less than 4 percent on 500 to 600 engines completed monthly.
- Classified purchasing details on 80 different production engines; implemented inventory control; greatly improved ordering efficiencies; and set up effective marketing service policies.

Manufacturing Manager; P.I.L. Engineering Company, Tampa, FL

- Supervised the production of a machine shop that subcontracted to manufacture precision machine parts and assemblies for the electronic industry.
- Developed and implemented manufacturing, cost control, and quality control programs; successfully developed business to $8.2 million in annual sales.

General Manager; Ferou Maintenance, Tampa, FL
- Shouldered full responsibility for tractor-trailer maintenance company servicing the Shaw Line Hault Fleet consisting of 500 trailers and 200 tractors traveling between Florida and the mid-Atlantic states.
- Initiated many vehicle design changes that were adopted by the Stanza Motor Company.
- Designed unique field service trucks on which specifications were written for national application.

I will be in the Chicago area during the week of May 22 to 26, and would be very interested in meeting with you at that time regarding possible openings appropriate for my qualifications. Perhaps I could share several of my design and organizational ideas, which I feel might benefit operations at Any Corporation. I will contact you next week to schedule a mutually convenient meeting time.

Sincerely,

Chris Smith

▶ Resume letter includes all pertinent information that would appear on a resume.

▶ Candidate's work experience reads like a series of accomplishments, not just a list of job duties.

RESUME LETTER
(Real Estate Director)

178 Green Street
Hunt Valley, MD 21030
(301) 555-5555

March 3, 20--

Pat Cummings
President
Any Corporation
1140 Main Street
Landover, MD 20785

Dear Mr. Cummings:

Are you searching for an Executive Director to supervise operations, stimulate development, and increase your market share? As a seasoned professional in the field of real estate management, I have the ability to quickly and significantly contribute to Any Corporation in an executive capacity.

I have selected several career highlights to demonstrate my abilities:

- **Multidisciplined Professional:** Possess real estate background encompassing business development, strategic planning, marketing, and construction project management.
- **Marketing Edge:** While with current employer, Raze Realty and Construction Company, Inc., developed a vital network of business and industry contacts instrumental to the acquisition of key contracts with the China Society, Jen Bright, and Weld Corporations.
- **Technical Expertise:** Offer a Bachelor of Science in Mechanical Engineering from the Massachusetts Institute of Technology. Possess proven abilities to estimate costs, and design and install electrical, telecommunications, fire and safety, and related technological systems.
- **Project Executive:** Managed full profit and loss accountability for key client projects involving scheduling, cost accounting, cash flow analysis, purchasing, and professional relations.
- **Human Resources Management:** Able to recruit, assign, motivate, and evaluate management and support staff. Developed and implemented progressive policies for 500 employees.
- **Cost Conscious:** Developed innovative cost-savings programs including cellular telephone service and Raze T-Bar Systems.

- **Sales Achiever:** Reputation for excellent sales presentations. Closed the largest single sale within Meyer for an infrared lighting control system.
- **Skilled Negotiator:** Deal successfully with U.S. and Asian corporate representatives. Handled contractor negotiations, secured an equity position with RSSO for Raze's 1,500-room Manhattan Ritz Hotel.

Let's get together to further discuss your needs in terms of my qualifications. Please contact me with a tentative interview time that is convenient for you.
I look forward to your response.

Sincerely,

Chris Smith

▶ Candidate carefully details all relevant experience, accomplishments, and educational credentials.

▶ Closing is straightforward and concise.

RESUME LETTER
(Vice-President, Sales and Marketing)

178 Green Street
Pigeon Forge, TN 37868
(615) 555-5555

October 14, 20--

Pat Cummings
Chief Executive Officer
Any Corporation
1140 Main Street
Nashville, TN 37211

Dear Ms. Cummings:

In a phone conversation on Friday, my neighbor and your Senior Sales Representative, Milton Farley, informed me of the newly vacant position of Vice-President, Sales and Marketing at Any Corporation. Milton felt that my extensive experience as an executive in this area would make me an excellent candidate for this opportunity. In this regard, please allow me to describe my background.

Experience:
Vice-President; Littleton and Shelley, Nashville, TN

Company is a $10 million, industry-leading producer of toys and related items manufactured and sold internationally. Started as Purchasing Manager, assuming additional responsibilities for outside sales, and, on basis of outstanding success in the development and handling of key accounts and general operations, advanced to current position of Vice-President in charge of sales and product development.

Accomplishments:
- Personal sales in excess of $4 million a year, while managing/working with network of more than 46 sales organizations employing 150 sales representatives.
- Managed development, sourcing, manufacturing, and importation of total doll and doll accessory product lines from Far East and Europe. Reduced cost of manufacture by 15 percent.
- Added $350,000 at significant margin to gross sales through establishment of new division marketing line of doll accessories. Developed new fashions projected at $600,000 first-year sales.

- Developed new sales accounts, through establishment of national representative/distributor organization, from annual sales of $250,000 to current volume of $850,000.

Although my time at Littleton and Shelley has provided me with a great deal of challenge and satisfaction, I would like to apply my experience to a new environment. I am familiar with your products and services, and am confident I could provide innovative and cost-effective supervision of your sales and marketing team. Based on my experience, my compensation requirements are between $100,000-$115,000.

Could we meet for further discussion?

Sincerely,

Chris Smith

▶ Statistics and dollar amounts quantify candidate's accomplishments.

▶ Resume letter often includes salary range.

CHAPTER 19

COVER LETTERS FOR SPECIAL SITUATIONS

Writing a cover letter can seem like an even more formidable task when you find yourself in what we call "special situations." Perhaps you lack paid job experience, have taken a break from the workplace in order to raise children, are concerned about possible discrimination due to age or disability, or are trying to enter a field in which you have no practical experience. Not to worry! The key to improving your cover letter in these special situations is to emphasize your strengths. Focus on your marketable skills (whether they were acquired in the workplace or elsewhere), and highlight impressive achievements, relevant education and training, and/or related interests. And, of course, you should take care to downplay or eliminate any information that may be construed as a negative or weakness.

For example, if you are a "displaced homemaker" (a homemaker entering the job market for the first time), you might structure your cover letter to highlight the special skills you've acquired over years of multitasking as a wife and mother while downplaying your lack of paid experience. If you are an older job candidate, use your age as a selling point. Emphasize the depth of your experience, your maturity, your sense of responsibility, and your positive outlook. Changing careers? No problem! Instead of focusing on your job history, you should emphasize the marketable skills you've acquired that are considered valuable in the position you are seeking. For example, let's say your career has been in real estate and, in your spare time, you like to run marathons. Recently, you heard about an opening in the sales and marketing department at an athletic shoe manufacturer. What you need to do is emphasize the skills you have that the employer is looking for. Not only do you have strong sales experience, you're familiar with the needs of the company's market, and that's a powerful combination!

Throughout this chapter you'll find creative solutions for even the most daunting career obstacles. Use them as a guideline for creating your own job-winning cover letters.

50-PLUS JOB CANDIDATE
(Product Manager)

---

178 Green Street
Fort Worth, TX 76111
(817) 555-5555

April 11, 20--

Pat Cummings
Vice-President
Any Corporation
1140 Main Street
Fort Worth, TX 76101

Dear Mr. Cummings:

Is your corporation in need of a motivated professional with comprehensive product management experience? If so, I would like to present my qualifications for your consideration.

In my vast experience, I have gained valuable insight into all aspects of product/protocol development and management to obtain FDA product approval. As Product Manager for Estrade, Inc., I provided extensive coordination of all product development activities for a large medical supply corporation. This acquired knowledge of clinical research would be especially beneficial to your development team.

I have consistently maintained a strong motivation for developing innovative product design and management, as well as a flexibility toward new approaches and marketing techniques. I am thoroughly proficient in most major computer applications, including Microsoft Word and Excel; I can navigate the Internet with ease. Much of my work has necessitated collaboration with systems consultants on the design and implementation of data management systems, including remote access.

I would be happy to further outline my skills during the course of a personal interview. After you have reviewed my qualifications, please contact me to schedule a time that is convenient for you to meet.

I appreciate your consideration and look forward to speaking with you.

Sincerely,

Chris Smith

Enc. Resume

▶ Summary of experience accentuates candidate's acquired professional skills and impressive track record.

▶ Valuable computer skills are highlighted.

50-PLUS JOB CANDIDATE
(Director of Marketing: Higher Education)

178 Green Street
Olathe, KS 66062

October 9, 20--

Pat Cummings
President
Any Community College
1140 Main Street
Kansas City, MO 64105

Dear Ms. Cummings:

    In response to your ad for a Director of Marketing, which appeared in yesterday's edition of the *Kansas City Star*, I am pleased to enclose a copy of my resume. I believe that my talents and skills are an ideal match to the job requirements you stated in your ad. More specifically...

YOU REQUIRE:
- Innovation and creativity
- Strategic leadership
- Strong technical skills
- Demonstrated abilities in personnel management and fiscal responsibility

I OFFER:
- More than 25 years of experience in the successful promotion of community colleges and vocational training programs
- A proven track record of boosting enrollment and endowments
- Demonstrated abilities to manage multiple projects and people in a deadline-sensitive environment
- An established reputation for always being on time and under budget
- The right combination of strong academic credentials and practical, real-world know-how

    Would you like to know more? Then let's get together to discuss how I can put my energy and experience to the task of creating a positive public image for Any Community College. I may be reached anytime at (913) 555-5555. I look forward to your call.

Sincerely,

Chris Smith

Enc. Resume

▶ Bullets draw attention to key points.

▶ Candidate emphasizes lengthy work experience and availability without calling attention to age.

ALL EMPLOYMENT AT ONE COMPANY
(Inventory Control Manager)

178 Green Street
Minot, ND 58702
(701) 555-5555

April 4, 20--

Pat Cummings
President
Any Corporation
1140 Main Street
Grand Forks, ND 58201

Dear Ms. Cummings:

I am currently searching for a position in inventory control and administration, and would like to inquire about suitable opportunities at Any Corporation.

As a member of your staff, I would offer more than twelve years of experience in inventory control management, in positions ranging from Office Manager to Vice-President of Inventory Management/Administrative Services. I possess a strong background in customer service, excellent interpersonal skills, and a strong motivation to successfully complete any task put before me. These qualifications are supported by a Master of Business Administration degree, and a Bachelor of Science in Management.

If given the chance, I am confident I could cost-effectively direct your inventory control. Please contact me at your convenience to schedule a meeting. The opportunity to further prove my capabilities is of great interest to me.

I look forward to your reply.

Sincerely,

Chris Smith

Enc. Resume

► Letter outlines series of promotions.

► Candidate's highest educational achievement is shown before other less significant degrees.

ALL EMPLOYMENT AT ONE COMPANY
(Materials Manager)

178 Green Street
Daytona Beach, FL 32115

August 18, 20--

Pat Cummings
Vice-President, Fiscal Affairs
Any Hospital
1140 Main Street
Orlando, FL 32816

Dear Mr. Cummings:

During the past eighteen years, I have progressed rapidly in positions of responsibility from Supervisor of Patient Transportation to Manager of Warehousing/Distribution to my current position as Senior Buyer and Manager of Inventory Control.

Although my prior associations have been growing and challenging experiences, I would like to make a position change and move into materials management within the health care field. I am in search of an opportunity in which I can use my skills to achieve the same meaningful results, but in a broader scope of responsibility.

Through cost-effective negotiations, purchasing, and control, I have been able to reduce the expenditures of all in-house medical and nonmedical supplies substantially each year as Manager of Inventory Control. In addition, I played a key role in automating inventories and providing a functional layout for warehouse locations, which effectively reduced the selection and distribution process for warehoused materials. This also enabled me to provide more stringent controls, thereby reducing shrinkage, damage, and obsolescence—common problems causing great concern in the health care field.

Enclosed is my resume. I would very much like to schedule a mutually convenient interview time. I can be reached at the address cited above or by phone at (904) 555-5555. The opportunity to join your management team is of great interest to me, and I look forward to meeting with you for further discussion.

Sincerely,

Chris Smith

Enc. Resume

▶ Candidate omits past employer's name.

▶ Letter indicates how candidate contributed to previous employer.

APPLICATION FOR IN-HOUSE POSITION
(District Supervisor)

178 Green Street
Big Stone Gap, VA 24219
(703) 555-5555

September 17, 20--

Pat Cummings
Personnel Director
Any Gas Company
1140 Main Street
Norfolk, VA 23510

RE: Management Job Posting
District Supervisor (Grade 25)

Dear Ms. Cummings:

In keeping with the management job posting for the above position, I am enclosing my resume, which summarizes my experience with Any Gas Company, as well as with other employers in the gas distribution-related industry.

All of these positions required my ability to provide technical support, retain personnel, and supervise outside contractors, and work with developers and public officials during joint work programs and projects. I am extremely well organized, manage time efficiently, and have the technical capability to work with and direct company and contractor personnel on all phases of gas distribution systems, from new construction to replacement and operation.

In addition, I believe my previous accomplishments with Any Gas attest to my strong communication skills and my ability to work harmoniously with people at all levels of responsibility within departments. During my five years of service, I feel that I have succeeded in making a substantial contribution. The position of District Supervisor would offer me the opportunity to extend that contribution, and I feel well prepared to handle its challenges and responsibilities.

I look forward to meeting with you in a personal interview to discuss my interest in this position. Thank you for your consideration.

Sincerely,

Chris Smith

Enc. Resume

▶ Candidate chronicles career progression within firm.

▶ Four short paragraphs is the ideal length for a cover letter.

AT-HOME PARENT REENTERING THE WORK FORCE
(Graphic Designer)

178 Green Street
Mountain View, CA 92715
(415) 555-5555

July 23, 20--

Pat Cummings
Director
Any Advertising Agency
1140 Main Street
Sausalito, CA 94966

Dear Mr. Cummings:

I am very interested in a freelance or part-time position in graphic design or advertising production. I forward the attached resume for your evaluation.

Please note that in addition to a Bachelor of Arts degree and current enrollment in the Massachusetts College of Art's Graphic Design Certificate Program, I offer more than seven years of valuable experience in the production and traffic areas of print and graphic design, and in related fields including fundraising and direct and mass mailings.

As you can see from my resume, I left the field three years ago with excellent references to raise a family and manage a household. Now, with my family well established, I am highly motivated to return to the work force and contribute the valuable experience gained before and during my hiatus.

I would like the opportunity to make a significant contribution to the success of Any Advertising Agency. I am available at the above address and phone number should you have any further questions.

I look forward to hearing from you.

Sincerely,

Chris Smith

Enc. Resume

▶ Letter focuses on candidate's past job experience while incorporating functional qualifications.

▶ Continuing education demonstrates candidate's dedication to his/her field.

AT-HOME PARENT REENTERING THE WORK FORCE
(Salesperson)

178 Green Street
Fort Collins, CO 80525
(303) 555-5555

August 14, 20--

Pat Cummings
Department Manager
Any Store
1140 Main Street
Aurora, CO 80012

Dear Ms. Cummings:

Emmett Puffin recently informed me that you are seeking a full-time addition to your children's department sales staff. I have been observing some very positive changes at Any Store, especially your new campaign to promote back-to-school sportswear. I am anxious to join such a successful sales team.

As my resume indicates, I possess more than three years of experience within the retail and wholesale arenas. I am committed to quality sales and service standards and am eager to continue my record of success with Any Store. As your newest Sales Associate, I would contribute strong interpersonal skills and an enthusiastic selling approach.

I will contact you on Friday to schedule a personal interview. I look forward to discussing how my capabilities could be guided to suit your needs.

Thank you for your time and consideration.

Sincerely,

Chris Smith

Enc. Resume

▶ Letter omits mention of employment gaps. ▶ Candidate expresses interest in returning to full-time employment.

BILINGUAL APPLICANT
(Medical Receptionist)

178 Green Street
Palm Harbor, FL 34683
(727) 555-5555

April 24, 20--

Pat Cummings, M.D.
Any Pediatric Clinic
1140 Main Street
Tampa, FL 33614

Dear Dr. Cummings:

In response to your ad in Sunday's *Tampa Tribune* for a medical reception-ist, I am pleased to enclose my resume for your consideration. A graduate of Plant High School, I have completed courses in medical terminology, billing, and transcription at Hillsborough Community College. For the last two years, I have worked as a receptionist and clerk typist in the Admitting Department at Tampa General Hospital. I am knowledgeable in a variety of software programs, includ-ing Microsoft Office, Word, and Excel. My typing speed is 60 wpm.

While I am sure that, like me, most of the applicants for this position can offer a pleasing telephone voice, professional demeanor, and exceptional orga-nizational skills, I bring one competency that few of them probably have—I am fluent in both English and Spanish. A visit to the doctor is stressful enough for children and their parents, but for those who do not speak the language, it is dou-bly so. I will be able to immediately put them at ease and to help them complete the necessary paperwork as well as assist you and your staff with your translation needs during examinations and treatment.

I believe I could make a positive contribution to your practice and I would welcome the opportunity for an interview. Thank you for your consideration and I look forward to hearing from you.

Sincerely,

Chris Smith

Enc. Resume

▶ Relevant work experience and education are described.

▶ Candidate's bilingual ability sets her apart from other applicants.

CAREER CHANGER
(Advertising Assistant)

178 Green Street
Daytona Beach, FL 32115
(904) 555-5555

August 18, 20--
Pat Cummings
Hiring Manager
Any Advertising Agency
1140 Main Street
Orlando, FL 32816

Dear Mr. Cummings:

I am very interested in pursuing my career in the advertising industry at Any Advertising Agency. While researching area firms, I read an exciting piece in *Ad World* about your recent campaign for Homeloving soups. Congratulations on receiving a Clio Award for your efforts.

I would love to join your winning team in an entry-level, administrative position. I can offer more than eight years of administration, promotion, and communication experience. The following achievements would be especially beneficial to your firm:

Administration: Recordkeeping and file maintenance. Data processing and computer operations, accounts receivable, accounts payable, accounting research and reports. Order fulfillment, inventory control, and customer relations. Scheduling, office management, and telephone reception.

Promotion: Composing, editing, and proofreading correspondence and PR materials for own housecleaning service.

Communication: Instruction, curriculum and lesson planning, student evaluation, parent-teacher conferences, development of educational materials. Training and supervising clerks.

Computer Skills: Proficient in Microsoft Word, Lotus 1-2-3, Excel, Filemaker Pro, and ADDS Accounting System.

I would like to request a personal interview to further outline my skills, and how they could be immediately applicable to an administrative position at Any Advertising Agency. I will call your office on August 23 to schedule a convenient meeting time.

Thank you, Mr. Cummings. I look forward to our conversation.

Sincerely,

Chris Smith
Enc. Resume

▶ Categorizing qualifications adds strength to cover letter.

▶ Introduction expresses candidate's knowledge of firm.

CAREER CHANGER
(Business Consultant)

178 Green Street
Arkadelphia, AR 71999
(501) 555-5555

March 12, 20--

Pat Cummings
Human Resources Director
Any Corporation
1140 Main Street
Pine Bluff, AR 71601

Dear Ms. Cummings:

I am responding to your recent request in the *Arkansas Democratic-Gazette* for a Business Consultant.

Currently, I am a faculty member in the Department of Management and Aviation Science at Henderson State University. I am also engaged in several temporary assignments involving the installation, conversion, and maintenance of automated accounting systems, troubleshooting, and training. I have working knowledge of, and have taught, several applications and operating systems. This includes, but is not limited to, the use of electronic spreadsheets (1-2-3, Excel, Quatro, etc.), and word processing and accounting (Peachtree, AccPac, Great Plains, MYOB, Quicken, Quickbooks, One-Write Plus, etc.) in Windows, Mac, and traditional DOS (PC) environments.

In strategic market development, the ability to assess customer needs relative to overall market conditions and to respond to them rapidly is critical for successful business development. Let me provide you with innovative approaches to getting the job done.

I would like the opportunity to help you increase your value-added services and profitability. I look forward to discussing this further.

Sincerely,

Chris Smith

Enc. Resume

▶ Related work experience is accentuated. ▶ Computer experience calls attention to candidate's technical knowledge.

CAREER CHANGER
(Casino Dealer)

178 Green Street
Carson City, NV 89706

August 26, 20--

Pat Cummings
Hiring Manager
Any Casino
1140 Main Street
Las Vegas, NV 89109

Dear Mr. Cummings:

Although I have spent the past two years as a medical student and my work experience has been focused in medical research and direct patient care, I am interested in a career change. I am in search of a position where I can use my skills to deal effectively with people, in an exciting and fast-paced environment such as Any Casino.

My work experience and educational discipline have provided me with the ability to rapidly learn new skills and produce solid returns with minimal instruction or supervision. I realize that to become a competent Casino Dealer requires training and experience, and I am willing to devote the time and effort necessary to become a professional in the field.

My professional profile is enclosed. I would like to convince you that I am qualified and strongly dedicated to becoming an effective Dealer for your casino. Can we schedule an interview?

Should you require additional information, please contact me at the above address or by phone at (702) 555-5555. May I hear from you?

Yours sincerely,

Chris Smith

Enc. Professional profile

▶ Letter emphasizes qualifications pertaining to candidate's job objective.

▶ Phrasing request in question form is a strong closing.

CAREER CHANGER
(Computer Programmer)

178 Green Street
Yankton, SD 57078
(605) 555-5555

February 2, 20--

Pat Cummings
Director of Information Systems
Any Corporation
1140 Main Street
Sioux Falls, SD 57117

Dear Ms. Cummings:

After eighteen years in a successful practice of general dentistry, I have decided on a career change. To make the transition into computer programming, I sold my practice and have spent the last four years preparing as both a full-time student of computer programming and a Customer Service Representative and computer operator with the products division of CMZ Incorporated.

Although my present position is interesting and has provided me with the opportunity to apply my technical and computer skills, I am looking for a position with room for merit advancement based on my personal performance and contribution to the cost-effective efficiency of your systems.

The enclosed resume summarizes my background and experience. I am available to discuss my qualifications in a personal meeting. I can be reached at the above address or by phone at (605) 555-5555.

Sincerely,

Chris Smith

Enc. Resume

▶ Unrelated work experience is omitted.　　▶ Continuing education indicates candidate's ongoing commitment to his/her field.

CAREER CHANGER
(Credit Analyst)

178 Green Street
Laie, HI 96762
(808) 555-5555

April 6, 20--

Pat Cummings
Credit Supervisor
Any Corporation
1140 Main Street
Honolulu, HI 96816

Dear Mr. Cummings:

Please accept the enclosed resume as an expressed interest in joining Any Corporation to contribute and develop my skills.

My experience lies in customer service and sales, where I have dealt with the public in a sales and assistance capacity in a financial environment. I would now like to expand and advance my career by applying my developed skills to a position as a Credit Analyst. Relevant skills and experience include:

- Bachelor of Science degree in Business Administration.
- Extensive experience in researching, compiling, and analyzing financial reports.
- Exclusively responsible for customer service for more than 1,000 accounts.
- Opened and serviced 85 new accounts over a one-year period.

I would welcome the opportunity to meet with you to discuss ways in which my capabilities might suit your needs. Please consider my application and direct your response to the address cited above.

Your time and consideration is very much appreciated. I look forward to hearing from you.

Sincerely,

Chris Smith

Enc. Resume

▶ Letter emphasizes qualifications pertaining to candidate's job objective.

▶ Bullets make cover letter easy to read.

CAREER CHANGER
(Marketing Executive)

178 Green Street
Boise, ID 83725
(208) 555-5555

August 5, 20--

Pat Cummings
Vice-President
Any Corporation
1140 Main Street
Chicago, IL 60605

Dear Ms. Cummings:

I am forwarding my resume with regard to the opening in your marketing department as advertised in the August 6 edition of the *Chicago Tribune*.

Although I am currently employed in a management position, I am interested in a career change, especially one that would allow me to combine a thorough knowledge of boating with my sales, marketing, and communication skills. I am an imaginative, well-organized self-starter with a strong interest in boating. As a semiprofessional sailboat racer, I twice won national honors and participated in the races at Cape Cod. In addition, I have made lasting contacts with owners and officials.

After you have had the chance to review my resume, please contact me so that we can further discuss the possibility of my joining your staff. I am confident that my business background and knowledge of boats will enable me to have a favorable impact on both your sales and image.

Thank you for your attention, and I look forward to speaking with you again to learn more about this opportunity.

Sincerely yours,

Chris Smith

Enc. Resume

▶ Awards draw attention to candidate's significant accomplishments.

▶ Candidate expresses knowledge in his/her field of interest.

CAREER CHANGER
(Nurse)

178 Green Street
Statesboro, GA 30460

February 22, 20--

Pat Cummings
Nursing Supervisor
Any Hospital
1140 Main Street
Gainesville, GA 30503

Dear Mr. Cummings:

Six years ago, I started a career in nursing. I subsequently left to enter business, and later opted to resign from a lucrative position to pursue my first career, nursing.

During the past four years, I have been employed as a Patient Care Technician while concurrently completing my degree requirements and all associated clinical rotations at the Medway, City Veteran's, and St. Luke's Hospitals. I will receive my Associate degree in Nursing, May 20--, and I am interested in joining a professional nursing staff where I can continue to develop my clinical experience in order to advance within the profession.

The enclosed resume is a brief summary of my education, clinical training, and experience. However, the opportunity to meet with you will enable me to further detail my qualifications and dedication to quality patient care. Should you require additional information prior to our meeting, please contact me at the address cited above or by phone at (912) 555-5555. I am interested in available opportunities with your hospital and look forward to hearing from you.

Yours sincerely,

Chris Smith

Enc. Resume

▶ Only relevant educational training is included.

▶ Candidate tailors letter to his/her field of interest.

CAREER CHANGER
(Product and Services Developer)

178 Green Street
Wichita, KS 67202

February 1, 20--

Pat Cummings
Vice-President
Any Bank
1140 Main Street
Topeka, KS 66607

Dear Ms. Cummings:

During the past eight years, I have been actively involved as Vice-President and Director of Operations of an established, quality, $1.4 million function/recreation complex with total responsibility for creating effective sales programs and assuring the quality of services provided.

Currently, I am seeking a career change and opportunity to associate with a progressive bank where I can effectively apply my creative and innovative talents and capability for developing or increasing new service products.

I am flexible, highly energetic, and adept at initiating promotional advertising and marketing programs that will stimulate growth and profits. I am not afraid of the risk or extra time required to gain valuable banking experience at Any Bank, and I would welcome the challenge.

The enclosed resume summarizes my background and experience. Should you require additional information, please contact me at the above address or phone me at (316) 555-5555. I will contact your office next week to schedule a mutually convenient time to meet.

I appreciate your consideration.

Yours sincerely,

Chris Smith

Enc. Resume

▶ Powerful adjectives, when used sparingly, ensure maximum impact.

▶ Interest in new field is emphasized.

CAREER CHANGER
(Real Estate Developer)

178 Green Street
Norfolk, VA 23529
(804) 555-5555

July 20, 20--

Pat Cummings
Director of Real Estate Development
Any Corporation
1140 Main Street
Alexandria, VA 22312

Dear Mr. Cummings:

After several years of diverse and successful experience as a Municipal Bond Broker, I decided to pursue a career encompassing a broader scope of real estate development. To achieve this objective and establish myself as a professional in the field of real estate development, I have spent the past year completing a comprehensive graduate program and earned a Master's degree in Real Estate Development from the University of Virginia.

Presently, I am investigating career opportunities with a progressive developer emphasizing the financial and field aspects of project management. My experience, prior to entering said graduate program, required extensive involvement in the purchase and sale of bonds for financing public and private developments. These included private and public construction developments and business ventures that required the ability to work with decision makers and financial/investment professionals in the field of real estate development.

I am a dedicated, energetic self-starter who can recognize opportunities and has always been willing to devote the time necessary to complete any task thoroughly. With this attitude, I feel confident that I can readily become a valuable asset as a member of your management team.

I am presently available for an interview, and will be glad to meet with you at a mutually convenient time. My resume is enclosed for your review.

I appreciate your consideration.

Yours sincerely,

Chris Smith

Enc. Resume

▶ Impressive educational background strengthens cover letter.

▶ Closing informs addressee that resume is enclosed.

CAREER CHANGER
(Sales Representative)

178 Green Street
Belle, WV 25015

February 24, 20--

Pat Cummings
Sales Manager
Any Corporation
1140 Main Street
Clarksburg, WV 26302

Dear Ms. Cummings:

If you are in need of a highly motivated achiever skilled in selling products and services and developing client relationships and new business, then we have good reason to meet.

During the past six years, I have owned and operated a photography studio and photo-processing laboratory, both of which require the ability to manage inside production while generating enough outside sales to keep the business profitable. Since accomplishing my objective, I am interested in associating with a firm, such as Any Corporation, that can benefit from my ability to sell, manage, and train others to do a quality job.

I am confident of my ability to handle a sales position requiring innovative thinking for positive results. I would welcome the opportunity to convince you of my enthusiasm and skill in a personal interview. When would be a good time for us to meet?

I can be reached at the address cited or by phone at (304) 555-5555.

Sincerely,

Chris Smith

Enc. Business profile

▶ Related work experience is accentuated.　　▶ Closing reiterates candidate's qualifications for position.

DISPLACED HOMEMAKER
(Administrator)

178 Green Street
Solon, OH 44139

February 25, 20--

Pat Cummings
Human Resources Director
Any Corporation
1140 Main Street
Cleveland, OH 44111

Dear Mr. Cummings:

I would like to offer my skills and experience for your consideration regarding administrative positions available at Any Corporation.

As an addition to your staff, I would bring extensive, varied experience in administration, including staff supervision, meeting planning and direction, and activities scheduling. I have the ability to speak effectively before groups, and communicate well through phone contact or the written word. Additionally, my skills include fundraising, promotion, and bookkeeping.

I am very interested in contributing to the continued success at Any Corporation, and am sure I would meet your expectations. Could we get together for further discussion? Please contact me at the address cited above or by phone at (216) 555-5555.

Thank you for your time.

Sincerely,

Chris Smith

Enc. Resume

▶ Letter focuses on the needs of the employer, not the job candidate.

▶ Letter emphasizes qualifications pertaining to candidate's job objective.

FIRED/LAID OFF
(Recruiter)

178 Green Street
Pennsauken, NJ 08110
(609) 555-5555

July 23, 20--

Pat Cummings
President
Any Executive Search Firm
1140 Main Street
Pleasantville, NJ 08232

Dear Ms. Cummings:

My interest in applying for a position as Recruiter at your firm has prompted me to forward the attached professional profile for your consideration.

Over the past seven years I recruited high technology, support staff, and marketing personnel. Much of this experience involved extensive travel, training program development, and networking with prospective clients. I possess valuable contacts within the management information systems, software development, and engineering industries that could prove to be a valuable asset to your client base.

I would very much like to apply my skills and knowledge as a member of your recruiting staff. I believe that, in a very short time, I could significantly contribute to your success.

I will follow up this inquiry with a phone call within a few days. Thank you for your time.

Sincerely,

Chris Smith

Enc. Professional profile

▶ Letter omits reason for departure from last job.

▶ Unrelated work experience is omitted.

FIRED/LAID OFF
(Sales Director)

178 Green Street
Provo, UT 84603
(801) 555-5555

November 19, 20--

Pat Cummings
Chief Executive Officer
Any Corporation
1140 Main Street
Salt Lake City, UT 84110

Dear Mr. Cummings:

Todd Duncan, of your operations department, suggested I contact you concerning employment opportunities. Todd mentioned that you were considering expanding your sales staff, and thought you might benefit from a professional with my qualifications.

I offer more than twenty years of progressively responsible experience in sales, culminating in my most recent position as Director of Sales and Pricing with a $750 million, 120-store chain. As a senior-level manager, I have been responsible for all aspects of store operations, including merchandising management, buying, strategic planning, marketing, and staff development and management.

Although I have thoroughly enjoyed my present position, corporate downsizing has prompted me to search for a new position. I feel that my years of successful management experience can be more advantageously utilized by a growing and diversifying firm such as Any Corporation.

If you are looking for a well-organized, innovative individual with the ability to garner results, please contact me. I would be happy to meet with you at your convenience.

Sincerely,

Chris Smith

Enc. Resume

▶ Letter briefly suggests reason for departure and emphasizes skills and accomplishments.

▶ Candidate immediately introduces purpose for writing.

FORMER SMALL BUSINESS OWNER
(Environmental Advocate)

178 Green Street
Cambridge, MA 02142

May 18, 20--

Pat Cummings
Director
Any Agency
1140 Main Street
Boston, MA 02118

Dear Ms. Cummings:

    I am seeking a challenging position in the promotion of environmental awareness. I read about your agency in the May edition of *Save Our Earth*, and was impressed by your Stop and Think! campaign to educate Boston in the way of environmentally safe alternatives for everyday living. I would like to become a part of your dedicated team.

    I possess both a passion for environmental concerns and experience in the practical application of related programs. For the past four years, I have been operating my own business, Recycling Renegades, in Cambridge. To begin, I successfully acquired the first recycling permit in the city of Cambridge for ferrous and non-ferrous metal, aluminum, high-grade paper, and plastic. As Owner and Manager, I conducted research, developed pilot programs, formulated networks for voluntary recycling, picked up and processed materials, and distributed proceeds to community associations.

    Although still extremely committed to recycling efforts, I feel it is time to shift to a wider focus. I would like to apply my skills to developing innovative programs for the promotion of all environmental concerns.

    Would it be possible to meet for a personal interview? I have several fresh ideas I would like to share with you. Please contact me at (617) 555-5555 at your earliest convenience.

Sincerely,

Chris Smith

Enc. Resume

▶ Candidate emphasizes how past business experience can benefit potential employer.

▶ Introduction states candidate's desire to join specific organization.

FREELANCER
(Production Assistant)

178 Green Street
Miami, FL 33132

September 21, 20--

Pat Cummings
Executive Producer
Any Production Company
1140 Main Street
Hialeah, FL 33012

Dear Mr. Cummings:

I am writing to express my keen interest in the Production Assistant position, as advertised in the September 20 edition of the *Miami Herald*.

I possess extensive experience in all aspects of video production, including positions as Writer, Researcher, Director, and Editor. For the past three years, I have been a freelance Production Assistant working on several commercial and documentary pieces. As Chief Assistant on "Milk Carton Kids: An American Crisis," I assisted in preliminary research/writing, scheduling location shooting, and screening potential interview candidates. I also helped in the completion of two public service announcements for Miami Child Services, where my duties also involved camera operation and heavy editing work.

My freelance experience has been diverse and rewarding, and yet, I would like a permanent production position where my skills can be utilized to a greater advantage. I have admired Any Production Company's work for some time, and attended your screening of "Silent Victims" at the Miami Rape Awareness Convention last month. I would like the opportunity to contribute to such remarkable work.

Please contact me at (305) 555-5555 or (305) 444-4444 evenings, if you need any additional information or if you would like to arrange a meeting.

I look forward to hearing from you.

Sincerely,

Chris Smith

Enc. Resume

▶ Candidate clearly indicates type of position desired.

▶ Candidate's most relevant work experience is prioritized.

FREELANCER
(Writer)

178 Green Street
Oklahoma City, OK 73125
(918) 555-5555

January 6, 20--

Pat Cummings
Publisher
Any Publishing Company
1140 Main Street
Toledo, OH 43660

Dear Ms. Cummings:

I am a Freelance Writer well versed in educational and reference materials for college students and adults. I am particularly experienced in the areas of careers, self-help, and parenting. I have noticed that several books on these subjects published by Any Publishing Company have appeared on the bestseller lists, and I am interested in learning more about your freelance needs.

Over the past ten years I have developed a writing style that is precise, clear, and accurate. Whether creating textbook materials, teacher apparatuses, or ancillary activities and worksheets, I am capable of tailoring tone and approach to a variety of purposes and audiences. I have become quite adept at synthesizing information and conveying it in a creative and well-organized manner.

I am sure that our mutual interests will be served by discussing your projects in greater detail. I would be happy to provide writing samples and references testifying to the quality of my work.

Thank you for your consideration. I look forward to hearing from you.

Sincerely,

Chris Smith

Enc. Resume

▶ Letter emphasizes candidate's strong work history.

▶ Letter incorporates company knowledge into discussion of qualifications.

FREQUENT JOB CHANGER
(Marketing Assistant)

178 Green Street
El Segundo, CA 90245
(213) 555-5555

December 14, 20--

Pat Cummings
Director of Marketing
Any Corporation
1140 Main Street
Los Angeles, CA 90089

Dear Mr. Cummings:

I am currently seeking an entry-level opportunity in a successful marketing department, and have learned about Any Corporation through the *L.A. Top Sellers Guide*. Congratulations on such an outstanding year.

As you can see from the enclosed resume, since completion of my Bachelor of Science degree, my professional associations have been extensive and diverse. Throughout my experiences, I have developed several important skills that I believe could benefit your marketing department. I possess solid communication skills, both in person and by phone. I am proficient with Macintosh, PC, and spreadsheet applications, and I can effectively manage all aspects of daily business operations, including inventory management and account maintenance. Above all, I possess a strong work ethic and enthusiasm to learn.

Last month I took an intensive seminar entitled "Marketing for Success!" This investment conclusively confirmed my desire to pursue marketing as a career. I know that, if given the chance, I could quickly prove my worth as a member of your staff. Would you permit me that chance?

I look forward to your response.

Sincerely,

Chris Smith

Enc. Resume

▶ Letter expresses commitment to field of interest.

▶ Letter focuses on acquired skills rather than detailing past employers.

GAPS IN EMPLOYMENT HISTORY
(Assistant Curator)

178 Green Street
Tallassee, AL 36078

June 3, 20--

Pat Cummings
Curator
Any Museum
1140 Main Street
Mobile, AL 36633

Dear Ms. Cummings:

If you are in need of a skilled individual to assist you in museum operations, I would like to offer the enclosed resume for your consideration. I am currently seeking a full-time position in which I can apply both my museum and gallery experience and keen interest in fine art.

As you will note from my resume, I have completed two extensive internships for successful art galleries elsewhere in Alabama. In each position, I was exposed to all aspects of operations, from sales to clerical duties. My responsibilities also included assisting customers, setting up displays, and completing mailings for exhibitions. I also possess a Bachelor of Art degree in Art History, and have participated in several related seminars.

In addition, I have spent the last year traveling extensively through Europe, visiting some of the finest museums in the world. This experience has greatly intensified my interest in securing a position in the art world.

I would be available for an interview at your convenience to discuss my qualifications further. Please contact me at the address cited above or by phone at (205) 555-5555.

Sincerely,

Chris Smith

Enc. Resume

▶ Candidate expresses interest in returning to full-time employment.

▶ Letter briefly explains reason for employment gaps.

GAPS IN EMPLOYMENT HISTORY
(Editor)

178 Green Street
Seymour, CT 06483
(203) 555-5555

August 21, 20--

Pat Cummings
Executive Editor
Any Magazine
1140 Main Street
Shelton, CT 06484

Dear Mr. Cummings:

During a recent telephone conversation, Ellen Marquis, Editor of *On The Town*, recommended that I contact you regarding employment opportunities. I am an experienced Editor interested in continuing a successful career in the field of magazine publishing. A summary of my qualifications includes:

- More than ten years of combined experience in writing and editing.
- Adept at managing multiple responsibilities simultaneously.
- Experienced at delegating authority and motivating others to ensure efficiency and productivity.
- Computer knowledge, including Lotus 1-2-3, Microsoft Word, WordPerfect, and PageMaker.

Specifically in the area of magazine publishing, my responsibilities have included selecting submissions, assisting in layout and design, recruiting writers, and writing headlines. I possess a Bachelor of Arts degree in English and additional coursework completion in Desktop Publishing and Feature Writing.

I would welcome the opportunity to meet with you in a personal interview to discuss my qualifications in relation to your needs. I will call you on Monday, August 28, to follow up on this inquiry.

I appreciate your time, Mr. Cummings.

Sincerely yours,

Chris Smith

Enc. Resume

▶ Letter omits mention of employment gaps.　　▶ Continuing education demonstrates candidate's dedication to his/her field.

IMMIGRANT
(Accountant)

178 Green Street
Eagan, MN 55122
(612) 555-5555

September 12, 20--

Pat Cummings
Senior Accountant
Any Corporation
1140 Main Street
Bloomington, MN 55438

Dear Ms. Cummings:

I am currently searching for an accounting position in which I may contribute my financial expertise as well as my ability to interface effectively with the business community on an international scale.

I offer more than twelve years of comprehensive accounting experience, in both public and private firms. My skills include audits, Chapter 11 filings and bank reconciliation, preparation of financial reports, and accounts payable/receivable. In my most recent position as Senior Accountant, I was solely responsible for the setup and modification of a new computer system, and for leading a steering committee to select the general ledger package, which is currently in use.

As you will note from my resume, the majority of my work experience has been focused in Madrid, Spain. Last year, I made the decision to permanently move to the United States with my family, and am very interested in securing a long-term association with a firm such as Any Corporation. Please be assured that although English is my second language, I have been speaking it fluently for more than twenty years. As a Staff Accountant at your firm, I could provide translation services to your international department if needed, and an extensive knowledge of European financial dealings.

I would very much like to meet with you for further discussion. I will call your office next week to confirm a meeting time that fits your schedule. In the interim, please contact me if I can provide you with any additional information.

Sincerely,

Chris Smith

Enc. Resume

▶ Work permit information is optional in a cover letter.

▶ Foreign language skills strengthen candidate's qualifications.

MILITARY BACKGROUND
(Electronics Supervisor)

178 Green Street
Laramie, WY 82071
(307) 555-5555

March 23, 20--

Pat Cummings
Personnel Supervisor
Any Corporation
1140 Main Street
Whitewater, WI 53190

Dear Mr. Cummings:

For eighteen years, I have been actively involved in electronic communication operations, equipment maintenance and documentation, and personnel training and supervision with the United States Navy.

I am currently investigating opportunities in the civilian electronics industry to which I can apply this training and experience. I am especially interested in joining an organization that has a need for an experienced supervisor. My strongest assets include achieving full manpower utilization, working cooperation, and a high degree of employee morale and productivity through better management techniques.

My experience extends itself to civilian as well as military personnel and encompasses human resources management and other personnel programs. My experience in line-supervision involved large technical as well as clerical stages of the operation and maintenance of highly complex equipment and communication systems.

My qualifications are broad and can be effectively utilized in the management of personnel programs, human resources management instruction, and/or line supervision. I am confident that my joining Any Corporation in any of these areas of responsibility would be mutually beneficial. I will call you next week to discuss further your needs in relation to my qualifications.

I am willing to relocate, and future compensation packages are negotiable.

I appreciate your consideration.

Sincerely,

Chris Smith

Enc. Resume

▶ Including a military record can be advantageous if it relates to candidate's job objective.

▶ Willingness to relocate can be advantageous.

MILITARY BACKGROUND
(Transportation Operator)

178 Green Street
Provo, UT 84602
(801) 555-5555

January 10, 20--

Pat Cummings
Controller
Any Corporation
1140 Main Street
Provo, UT 84602

Dear Ms. Cummings:

During the past twelve years, my experience has been focused on transportation and sales, and seven of these were spent with the United States Army. Although my recent experience has been in the sale of intangibles, I am interested in resuming a civilian career in transportation operations or in the sale of products or equipment allied to the transportation field.

I have a Bachelor of Science degree, and I am a graduate officer of the U.S. Army Transportation School—the equivalent of a graduate school. In addition to managing all phases of complete civilian and tactical transportation operations (vehicles from two-and-one-half-ton cargo trucks to ten-ton tractor trailers and petroleum tankers), I have taught courses and have trained troops in the total transportation cycle in the United States and abroad.

The enclosed resume summarizes my educational background and experience in the areas I have cited above. I feel confident that with my qualifications in the transportation field, I can contribute substantially toward the efficient operation of an in-house traffic, transportation, and distribution function, and/or commercial transportation depot.

I would appreciate the opportunity to further discuss my qualifications in the transportation field and the immediate and long-term contribution I could make to Any Corporation.

If my qualifications interest you, please contact me. I will be glad to furnish any additional information you require.

Sincerely,

Chris Smith

Enc. Resume

▶ Qualifications call attention to candidate's relevant supervisory and administrative experience.

▶ Candidate details how past military experience will benefit potential employer.

NO CLEAR CAREER PATH
(Account Manager)

178 Green Street
Gallup, NM 87301
(505) 555-5555

July 21, 20--

Pat Cummings
Hiring Manager
Any Accounting Firm
1140 Main Street
Albuquerque, NM 87103

Dear Mr. Cummings:

I am seeking an entry-level position in accounting that will allow me to apply my expertise in both financial management and customer service. While researching area firms, I became very interested in Any Accounting Firm's esteemed training and development program. To such a program, I would bring:

- Bachelor of Science degree, cum laude, in Finance.
- Four years of collections experience.
- Successful collection of 90 percent of company's overdue accounts.
- Experience in accounts payable and accounts receivable.
- Computer skills: Lotus 1-2-3, Microsoft Word, and MASS-11.
- Knowledge of spreadsheets and accounting software.
- Excellent interpersonal skills.
- Strong leadership qualities.

I am a highly motivated self-starter who has the ability and drive to make a significant contribution to your firm. My resume is enclosed for your review. Would your schedule permit a meeting next week to further discuss my desire to join Any Accounting Firm's staff? I will call you on Friday, July 28, to follow up on this inquiry.

Thank you for your consideration. I look forward to speaking with you.

Sincerely,

Chris Smith

Enc. Resume

▶ Letter focuses on functional skills applicable to potential employer.

▶ Educational honors indicate candidate's potential to excel.

OVERSEAS EMPLOYMENT HISTORY
(Marketing Assistant)

178 Rue Vert
Paris, France
011-331-45-55-55

January 7, 20--

Pat Cummings
Director of Human Resources
Any Corporation
1140 Main Street
New York, NY 10028

Dear Ms. Cummings:

    I am looking for a new association with an international service-oriented organization that can benefit from my multilingual and organizational skills in a marketing position.

    I have a Bachelor of Arts degree in French (summa cum laude), am fluent in French and Italian, and have strong proficiency in Spanish. In addition, I have experience as an Interpreter and Translator working on international market research with the International Marketing Department at the University of Paris. I concurrently worked as an Administrative Assistant to professors and business executives.

    Since 20--, I have been tutoring individuals in foreign languages and English as a Second Language. I am familiar with various cultures and work well with multilingual, multicultural individuals and groups.

    The enclosed resume summarizes my experience. I will be in New York from February 14 through February 28 to secure permanent housing arrangements. I would appreciate the opportunity to meet during that time so that we may discuss the mutual benefits of my joining your firm.

    I will call your office the week of February 6 to confirm receipt of my application and to schedule an interview. Thank you for your time.

Sincerely,

Chris Smith

Enc. Resume

▶ Candidate emphasizes international work experience and how it might benefit potential employer.

▶ Candidate indicates time frame for follow-up contact.

PART-TIME EMPLOYMENT HISTORY
(Art Instructor)

178 Green Street
Marysville, OH 43040
(513) 555-5555

January 28, 20--

Pat Cummings
Principal
Any Elementary School
1140 Main Street
Dayton, OH 45404

Dear Mr. Cummings:

I would like to express my interest in applying for the part-time Art Instructor position advertised in the *Dayton Daily News*.

I am a trained Elementary Art Instructor with expertise in arts and crafts instruction as well as program conception and coordination. For four years, I taught art classes on a part-time basis for the Roosevelt School in Marysville. In addition to my teaching and program management activities, I arranged field excursions and produced an annual district-wide arts competition. Also, I hold a State of Ohio Elementary Education Certificate in Art, and a Bachelor of Fine Arts degree in Art Education.

For the past year, I have been spending weekends as Arts and Crafts Program Director for the Dayton Parks and Recreational Association. I create and facilitate programs for children, control a budget, select and purchase supplies, and supervise aides in various duties. Since this work is restricted to weekends, my weeks would be completely open to fulfill my responsibilities as your Art Instructor. I am confident that I could create and maintain an exciting program at Any Elementary School.

My resume is enclosed for your review. I would welcome the opportunity to discuss my relevant experience further in a personal interview. At such a time, I could provide you with several excellent references attesting to my skills, as well as a portfolio of past programs I have implemented.

I look forward to hearing from you.

Sincerely,

Chris Smith

Enc. Resume

▶ Candidate indicates type of employment desired.

▶ Part-time employment history indicates candidate's ability to handle multiple responsibilities.

PART-TIME EMPLOYMENT HISTORY
(Store Manager)

178 Green Street
Brooklyn, NY 11735
(516) 555-5555

April 30, 20--

Pat Cummings
District Manager
Any Retail Chain
1140 Main Street
New York, NY 10016

Dear Ms. Cummings:

My interest in joining your dynamic staff in a full-time management position has prompted me to forward the enclosed resume for your consideration.

During the past seven years, I have held progressively responsible positions in retail sales, from Salesperson to Manager. In my most recent position as Store Manager for Raintree Designs, I assumed responsibility for boosting branch sales from $.5 to $1.2 million in one year. I possess hands-on experience in sales, inventory control, and product promotion. As Assistant Manager for Rips, Inc. in Brooklyn, I supervised a staff of twelve, oversaw the production of a promotional video, and assisted in the selection of chain-wide promotion techniques.

As my resume reveals, the majority of my retail management experience has been on a part-time basis. At this point in my career, I am ready to apply my acquired skills to a long-term, more permanent association. As an employee of Any Retail Chain, I would extend every effort to increase sales and promotion, and to assure smooth store operations.

After you have had the opportunity to review my qualifications, I would appreciate hearing from you to schedule a personal interview. I would like to learn more about your needs, and discuss my ability to contribute to your goals.

Thank you for your time.

Sincerely,

Chris Smith

Enc. Resume

▶ Part-time experience is relevant to full-time employment.

▶ Specifically citing number of personnel supervised draws attention to candidate's leadership abilities.

PHYSICALLY CHALLENGED
(Meeting Planner)

178 Green Street
Mukilteo, WA 98275
(206) 555-5555

October 3, 20--

Pat Cummings
Director of Human Resources
Any Corporation
1140 Main Street
St. Charles, MO 63302

Dear Mr. Cummings:

I recently learned from your Vice-President of Operations, Marsha Ponnif, that you might be in need of a Meeting Planner to join your management structure. I am submitting the enclosed business profile for your review.

During the past sixteen years, I have successfully demonstrated solid troubleshooting and problem resolution skills in management, marketing, and sales. My progressively responsible experience includes:

- Corporate/institutional meeting planning.
- Hospitality service coordination.
- Destination management/program coordination.
- Employee/client incentive programs.
- Sales/customer service.

Although my positions have been fast-paced and broad in scope, I would like to make a change and am very impressed by the products and services offered by Any Corporation. Could we meet for an interview? I will contact you next week to schedule a convenient time for further discussion.

Thank you, Mr. Cummings. I look forward to our next conversation.

Sincerely,

Chris Smith

Enc. Business profile

▶ Unless it is immediately relevant to a candidate's job objective, indicating a physical handicap is unnecessary.

▶ Basis for referral is immediately established.

PHYSICALLY CHALLENGED
(Telemarketer)

178 Green Street
West Lafayette, IN 47906
(317) 555-5555

March 14, 20--

Pat Cummings
Telemarketing Director
Any Corporation
1140 Main Street
Lafayette, IN 47902

Dear Ms. Cummings:

I am writing to inquire about possible telemarketing opportunities available at Any Corporation.

During the past five years of direct telemarketing experience, I have acquired a proven track record of outstanding selling and closing capabilities. In my recent position at EPS Telecommunications, I consistently achieved at least 10 percent of total sales records through cold-calling techniques. I am an excellent listener who is patient and sensitive to clients' needs, and I am calm under pressure.

Although I have enjoyed my past positions, my true desire has always been to enter the realm of sports-related telemarketing. I have maintained a wide general knowledge of, as well as active participation in, sports activities. Each year I participate in the Indiana State Marathon, and last year placed fourth in the Wheelchair Division.

I am confident of my ability to apply this combined interest and capability to successfully meet all sales quotas at Any Corporation. Please contact me after you have had a chance to review my enclosed resume. I would be very interested in talking with you further regarding suitable telemarketing opportunities.

Thank you for your time.

Sincerely,

Chris Smith

Enc. Resume

▶ Job descriptions emphasize candidate's accomplishments.

▶ Interest in new field is emphasized.

RECENT GRADUATE
(Airline Caterer)

178 Green Street
Providence, RI 02902
(401) 555-5555

October 4, 20--

Pat Cummings
College Relations Representative
Any Service
1140 Main Street
Hartford, CT 06115

Dear Mr. Cummings:

I am enclosing my resume to apprise you of my interest in working for your airline catering service.

I will receive my Bachelor of Science degree in Food Service from Johnson and Wales University in January. In addition to studying such valuable courses as Chemical Science, Organic Chemistry, Nutrition, and Food Service Administration, I have learned a great deal about the food industry as an active member of the Student Association for Agricultural Science. Further, I offer solid experience in the food industry through working as an Assistant Manager for two summers at a local yogurt shop.

I would be very interested in securing an entry-level position with Any Service. If you feel that my qualifications might meet your needs, please contact me at (401) 444-4444. A message may also be left at the phone number listed above.

Thank you for your attention, and I look forward to your response.

Sincerely,

Chris Smith

Enc. Resume

▶ Letter includes coursework that corresponds to position desired.

▶ College activities are related to candidate's field of study and career objective.

RECENT GRADUATE
(Assistant Museum Director)

178 Green Street
Vermillion, SD 57069

June 26, 20--

Pat Cummings
Museum Director
Any Museum
1140 Main Street
Rapid City, SD 57701

Dear Ms. Cummings:

    I am a recent graduate of the University of South Dakota with a well-rounded art history background. I would like to put my skills and knowledge to use in an entry-level position at your prestigious museum, perhaps as an Assistant Director to the Curator.

    As my resume indicates, I participated in an exclusive summer program for art history majors at the Louvre in Paris. There, I studied some of the most significant works of European art and attended a very interesting seminar about the workings of the Louvre itself. I also worked for two summers at the Metropolitan Museum of Art in New York City, where I served as a Museum Assistant at the information booth. My coursework in African-American art, modern art, and museum science has also prepared me well for an entry-level position in a fine arts museum.

    I have long been a lover of art and art museums. I have been visiting your museum since I was a small child and would be thrilled at the opportunity to become a part of your excellent staff.

    Enclosed is my resume for your consideration. I may be reached at (605) 555-5555 after 3 P.M. on weekdays and anytime on weekends. I hope to hear from you soon.

Sincerely,

Chris Smith

Enc. Resume

▶ Letter conveys polite enthusiasm.

▶ Applicable coursework, workshops, and seminars are highlighted.

RECENT GRADUATE
(English Teacher)

178 Green Street
Plymouth, MA 02360
(508) 555-5555
April 8, 20--

Pat Cummings
Human Resources Manager
Any School District
1140 Main Street
Newton, MA 02164

Dear Mr. Cummings:

In response to last week's advertisement for an English Teacher in the *New England Journal of Higher Education*, I have enclosed my resume for your consideration.

I have recently graduated from Boston College with a Bachelor's degree in Secondary Education. I am certified to teach both English and Special Education. In addition to fulfilling my practice teaching requirement in your district, I participated in a volunteer literacy program to tutor both youths and adults struggling with reading difficulties. I also organized and performed in a variety show at Newton High School that benefited special needs students.

As I fulfilled my practice teaching requirement in District 5, I was continually impressed by its high educational standards and its long-standing record of graduating students whose SAT scores are among the highest in the nation. I would consider it a great honor to be invited to teach in such an accomplished district.

I will be calling you on Monday, April 10, to confirm that you have received my resume and to answer any questions you may have. I look forward to speaking with you.

Sincerely,

Chris Smith

Enc. Resume

▶ Position applied for is clearly and immediately defined.

▶ Volunteer experience gives candidate a competitive edge.

RECENT GRADUATE
(Environmental Campaigner)

178 Green Street
New London, CT 06320

July 17, 20--

Pat Cummings
Regional Program Director
Any Environmental Campaign
1140 Main Street
Danbury, CT 06810

Dear Ms. Cummings:

As a recent graduate of Tufts University Environmental Leadership Training Program and a 20-- graduate of Mesa State College with a degree in Biology, I am currently launching my career as an Environmental Campaigner in areas of concern that affect local, national, or world communities.

For the past several years, my elective studies concentrated on biology, chemistry, and the scientific, management, and political issues associated with the environment. In addition, I have organized recycling programs in my hometown and on college campuses. Now I aim to make environmental campaigning my full-time profession. I am anxious to devote my energy to Any Environmental Campaign, and am confident I can make a significant contribution.

I can be reached at the address cited above or by phone at (203) 555-5555.

Looking forward to your return response for a better world.

Sincerely,

Chris Smith

Enc. Resume

▶ Activities highlight candidate's involvement in local community.

▶ Relevant coursework adds depth to candidate's educational background.

RECENT GRADUATE
(Forester)

178 Green Street
Los Angeles, CA 90053
(213) 555-5555

July 30, 20--

Pat Cummings
Director
Any Bureau
1140 Main Street
Oakland, CA 94612

Dear Mr. Cummings:

I am a recent college graduate with a degree in Earth Science and Forestry and am seeking a position in Forestry in the Pacific states.

In June, I graduated from the University of Southern California with a Bachelor's degree in Earth Science and Forestry. I have studied many relevant courses including Forest Economics, Range Management, Ecology, Soil Science, Hydrology, Wildlife, and Agronomy. In 20--, I was recognized for outstanding achievement in the natural sciences when I was awarded the prestigious Lukestrom Badge.

I also offer on-site work experience, having interned last summer for the California State Soil Conservation Service. In this position, I was exposed to all aspects of applied soil science. I provided technical assistance primarily to farmers and ranchers to promote the conservation of soil, water, and related natural resources. Equally important, I helped to develop programs to combat soil erosion and maximize land productivity without damaging the environment.

I gained valuable experience in forestry when I attended Southern California University's Field Camp in Walgreen Falls. I planted and maintained trees and rare natural vegetation and recorded and charted their growth. In addition to testing soil and water samples, I tracked wildlife and worked to preserve natural habitats for endangered species.

If you feel that I am suited for a position with Any Bureau, I would greatly appreciate an interview. I may be reached at the number listing above during the morning hours. Thank you for your consideration.

Sincerely,

Chris Smith

Enc. Resume

▶ Relevant internship bolsters otherwise limited work experience.

▶ Extracurricular and school-related awards add weight to candidate's letter.

RECENT GRADUATE
(Gerontologist)

178 Green Street
Worcester, MA 01610
(508) 555-5555

June 23, 20--

Pat Cummings
Director
Any Agency
1140 Main Street
Salem, MA 01970

Dear Ms. Cummings:

Thank you for taking the time to speak with me today. As I mentioned on the phone, I am interested in beginning a career in the field of gerontology.

I am currently a senior at the College of the Holy Cross, majoring in Sociology. I have studied a variety of subjects including gerontology, which is how I first became interested in this field. Other related courses I have taken include Poverty and Crisis, the Political Economy of Health Care in the United States, Race Relations, and Women in Society. My current grade point average is 3.64 and I am a member of the Phi Beta Kappa honor society.

In addition to my schoolwork, I am an active member of the student-run Volunteers for a Better World Program. Some of the experiences I have gained through this organization include serving Thanksgiving dinner to the homeless at a local soup kitchen, tutoring underprivileged junior high school students in math and English, and co-directing a very successful annual campus food drive. As a contributing writer for the *Angora*, I wrote many articles and editorials concerning various social issues, including the plight of the elderly.

As a result of my classroom studies and my volunteer experience, I feel that I have an excellent grasp of the social and political issues that affect older adults in the United States. I feel that, at your agency, I could make a real difference in the lives of older people.

I have enclosed my resume and a sample article for your perusal. Thank you for your attention to this matter and I look forward to your response.

Sincerely,

Chris Smith

Enc. Resume
Writing sample

▶ Educational honors are emphasized.

▶ Personal interests and activities are relevant to candidate's field of interest.

RECENT GRADUATE
(Legal Assistant)

178 Green Street
Aston, PA 19014
(215) 555-5555

April 4, 20--

Pat Cummings
Attorney-at-Law
Any Firm
1140 Main Street
Erie, PA 16563

Dear Mr. Cummings:

Justice Ellen Malone of Allentown Courthouse suggested that I contact you regarding an opening you may soon have for a Legal Assistant.

I will be graduating this May from Temple University with a Bachelor of Arts degree in African-American Studies. In addition to my core studies, I have studied in a variety of areas including business administration and computer applications. In 20--, I was awarded the prestigious Lieberman Scholarship.

I also offer a strong background in law, having worked in a variety of legal settings throughout my college years. I was a volunteer for Temple's Student Legal Aid, helping students with a variety of legal problems. I worked part-time over the past three years as a Volunteer Probation Officer for the Allentown juvenile court. And in addition to being an Outside Media Contact for an Aston Outreach Unified Neighborhood Team, I spent one summer as a Research Assistant for the Chief County Clerk of Allentown.

All of these positions have given me a strong sense of the law and extensive knowledge about the American legal system. Moreover, this experience has convinced me that I would like to pursue law as a career. Justice Malone highly recommends your firm as one that might be a good match for my goals and qualifications.

Enclosed is my resume. I will contact you within the week to further discuss the possibility of securing this position. Thank you for your time.

Sincerely,

Chris Smith

Enc. Resume
Writing sample

▶ Part-time work experience during school indicates candidate's strong work ethic.

▶ Impressive credentials and awards further enhance candidate's qualifications.

RECENT GRADUATE
(Physicist)

178 Green Street
White Plains, NY 10604
(914) 555-5555

March 16, 20--

Pat Cummings
Professional Recruiter
Any Photographic Institute
1140 Main Street
Long Island, NY 11747

Dear Ms. Cummings:

Perhaps you are seeking an addition to your excellent team of physicists? A new person can provide innovative approaches and ideas to the challenges of research and development.

As you can see from my resume, I will be graduating in June from New York University (NYU) with a Bachelor's degree in Physics. I also have studied related fields such as chemical engineering, mathematics, and systems applications, all of which I am sure would help me as a physicist with Any Photographic Institute. I offer solid experience, having worked for two summers for the physics department at NYU, both as an intern and a laboratory technician.

Additionally, I have a personal interest in photography, having been an avid amateur photographer for many years. I built my own darkroom and have won several awards for my photographs. Because of this, I feel that Any Photographic Institute is an especially good match for my skills and interests.

Please advise me of any positions that may become available. Your consideration of my credentials is greatly appreciated.

Sincerely,

Chris Smith

Enc. Resume

▶ Use of concrete examples highlights candidate's achievements.

▶ Internships strengthen candidate's short work history.

RECENT GRADUATE
(Set Designer)

178 Green Street
Columbia, SC 29202
(803) 555-5555

August 14, 20--

Pat Cummings
Stage Director
Any Production Company
1140 Main Street
Columbia, SC 29202

Dear Mr. Cummings:

Lynne Winchester recently indicated that you may have an opening for a Set Designer and suggested that I contact you. I seek a creative position involving stage design in television.

I graduated last December from Clemson University with a Bachelor of Arts degree in Theatre Arts and a concentration in Studio Art. In addition to modern drama, and music and sound in theatre, I completed courses in set creation and design, intermediate painting, and woodworking. As a member of the drama club, I designed and helped create props for numerous campus productions including *The Tempest* and *Marco Polo Sings a Solo*.

As for my work experience, I co-designed and co-created the props and decorations for a new miniature golf course with a tropical island theme, which turned out to be a big hit. I also gained valuable skills working as an apprentice to a busy carpenter and painting houses for a large company.

Enclosed is my resume as well as some photographs of my work. I have some great ideas for the sets of "Trivia Tunes" and "Videos after Dark" which I would like to discuss with you in a personal interview. I may be reached at the above listed number before 1 P.M. on weekdays. Thank you for your consideration of my application.

Sincerely,

Chris Smith

Enc. Resume, Photographs

▶ Courses listed are related to candidate's field of interest.

▶ Enclosure line refers to all attached materials.

RECENT GRADUATE
(Translator)

178 Green Street
Chicago Heights, IL 60411
(708) 555-5555

July 5, 20--

Pat Cummings
Director
Any Council
1140 Main Street
Denver, CO 80204

Dear Ms. Cummings:

I am writing with the hope that you will consider me for the position of Translator as advertised in today's *Rocky Mountain News*.

I graduated last month with a Bachelor of Arts degree in International Relations and French Language from Northwestern University. Consistently on the dean's list and graduating one year early with honors and advanced standing, I have been recognized throughout my career for excellent scholarship. I was also very active in many extracurricular events and organizations, including a residential honors program studying ethics and politics. By my junior year, I had become a Model United Nations Advisor, an Alumni Ambassador, and President of the International Affairs Society.

In addition, I have work experience in the field of international affairs, having served as an interpreter and translator for a Parisian film corporation. In this position, I interpreted during negotiations regarding film co-productions and translated agreements, film scripts, scenarios, and foreign correspondence. I also worked as the Assistant to the Parisian Correspondent for Desliases Associates, a prestigious import/export company.

I feel confident that an interview would determine that my expertise in international affairs and the French language and culture makes me well qualified for this position. I am not limited by location and would enjoy the opportunity to live and work in Denver for Any Council.

I look forward to meeting you, Ms. Cummings, and will give you a call to follow up on this letter toward the end of next week.

Sincerely,

Chris Smith

Enc. Resume

▶ For recent graduates, extracurricular activities demonstrate potential for productivity.

▶ Educational honors indicate candidate's potential to excel.

RETIREE REENTERING THE WORK FORCE
(Insurance Sales Representative)

178 Green Street
Apollo Beach, FL 33572
(813) 555-5555

June 23, 20--

Pat Cummings
Owner
Any Insurance Agency
1140 Main Street
Tampa, FL 33606

Dear Mr. Cummings:

Are you looking for a knowledgeable sales rep who isn't afraid to roll up his sleeves and put in a full day's worth of honest work? Who'll labor tirelessly to ferret out leads on his own, instead of waiting for you to supply them? If so, then we need to talk.

In an insurance sales career spanning more than thirty-five years, I established myself as a consistent, self-motivated top producer selling a broad range of insurance and investment products to businesses, individuals, and families. In 20--, I retired from the industry, thinking it was time to kick back and relax. I planned to do a little fishing, play a game of golf now and then, and spend time with my grandkids. But here it is three years later and I'm just plain bored. I'm itching to get back into the insurance business and I'm hoping you'd like to have me on your team.

With that in mind, I've enclosed my resume for your consideration. Once you've had a chance to look it over, let's get together to discuss how my credentials might contribute to your firm's profitability and help increase customer satisfaction. Please contact me at your earliest convenience at the number cited above so that we can set up a mutually convenient time to meet. I am eager to start selling again.

Sincerely,

Chris Smith

Enc. Resume

▶ Opening a cover letter with a question is an attention-grabber.

▶ Candidate's upbeat, energetic tone should dispel any worries about hiring a retiree.

RETIREE REENTERING THE WORK FORCE
(Math Instructor)

178 Green Street
Bartow, FL 33830
(813) 555-5555

August 2, 20--

Pat Cummings
Principal
Any Junior High School
1140 Main Street
St. Petersburg, FL 33716

Dear Mr. Cummings:

Recently I bumped into long-time friend and colleague, Harry Nestor, Superintendent of St. Petersburg Schools. Harry tells me that Any High School is currently searching for a part-time Math Instructor for the upcoming school year. I would like to express my interest in assuming such a position.

As my enclosed professional profile reflects, I possess more than thirty-three years of experience in junior high and high school education. Before assuming my most recent position as Principal of Sacred Heart Junior High School in St. Petersburg, I taught math and science courses to middle school children for thirteen years. My expertise ranges from remedial math to precalculus for advanced students. In addition to my Master's degree in Education, I hold a Florida State Teacher Certification.

Although retired for more than two years, I feel I still have much to offer in the field of education, and would once again like to apply my skills to the personal and intellectual advancement of all students.

I look forward to hearing from you further regarding this position.

Sincerely yours,

Chris Smith

Enc. Professional profile

▶ Candidate explains how extensive experience will benefit potential employer.

▶ Professional certification and strong educational background add strength to cover letter.

TEMPORARY EMPLOYMENT HISTORY
(Administrative Assistant)

178 Green Street
Van Nuys, CA 91411

October 1, 20--

Pat Cummings
Director
Any Temporary Agency
1140 Main Street
Van Nuys, CA 91411

Dear Ms. Cummings:

I am forwarding the enclosed resume for your consideration regarding suitable temporary assignments.

My five years of consecutive temporary assignment work have provided me with skills and qualifications applicable to many different fields. In short, I would offer a potential employer:

- Three years of accounting, financial, and administrative experience.
- Computer knowledge, including PC, Macintosh, and Honeywell systems.
- Proficiency in several word processing programs and spreadsheet applications.
- Outstanding communication and organizational skills.

Should you require any additional information after reviewing my qualifications, please do not hesitate to contact me at the above address or by phone at (818) 555-5555. I would prefer to receive an assignment in the Van Nuys area, and compensation requirements are negotiable.

Sincerely,

Chris Smith

Enc. Resume

▶ Candidate informs agency contact of all relevant information, including travel availability and salary requirements.

▶ Letter focuses on acquired skills relevant to field of interest.

TEMPORARY EMPLOYMENT HISTORY
(Publisher's Assistant)

178 Green Street
Wilmington, DE 19899
(302) 555-5555

February 22, 20--

Pat Cummings
Editor
Any Publishing Company
1140 Main Street
New Castle, DE 19720

Dear Mr. Cummings:

I would like to take this opportunity to express my interest in the Publisher's Assistant position advertised in the February 21 edition of the *News-Journal*.

I am a 20-- graduate of Johns Hopkins University, with a Bachelor of Arts degree in English. Since my graduation, I have accepted several temporary positions with area businesses in order to gain a wide range of skills with the ultimate goal of securing an entry-level position in publishing. While at Curran, Moylan, and Hudson, I developed strong written and interpersonal communication skills. My responsibilities included sorting mail, interfacing with management and clients, and data input. As a temporary Marketing Assistant at Finner and Grant Publishers, I assisted in special project work in the editorial department and with administrative responsibilities.

Each of my experiences has provided me with excellent computer and general office skills, which I could apply to the position of Publisher's Assistant. I would appreciate the chance to discuss my qualifications with you, and to learn more about current projects at Any Publishing Company. I plan to call you within the next several days to arrange a meeting.

Thank you for your consideration.

Sincerely,

Chris Smith

Enc. Resume

▶ Candidate immediately specifies position being applied for.

▶ Temporary experience is relevant to full-time employment.

WEAK EDUCATIONAL BACKGROUND
(Parking Supervisor)

178 Green Street
Scottsdale, AZ 85254
(602) 555-5555

May 13, 20--

Pat Cummings
Manager of Operations
Any Airport
1140 Main Street
Phoenix, AR 85021

Dear Ms. Cummings:

I am currently investigating opportunities to which I can apply my knowledge of, and extensive experience in, the management of large parking facilities.

In my most recent position at Parkinson Hotel, my proven abilities and tireless work ethic resulted in rapid advancement to a management position after only one year of service as a Parking Attendant. As Supervisor of Parking Facilities, I oversaw all financial collections, maintained customer service standards, effectively troubleshot, and managed a large staff. Additionally, I administered work schedules and payroll, assigned duties, and interfaced with hotel management.

I am a self-motivated, people-oriented, responsible individual capable of meeting your expectations for quality supervision. I look forward to a personal interview to further discuss how I can contribute to your parking staff.

Sincerely,

Chris Smith

Enc. Resume

▶ Listing educational background is optional if candidate possesses extensive work experience.

▶ Qualifications highlight candidate's problem-solving ability.

WEAK EMPLOYMENT BACKGROUND
(Finance Broker)

178 Green Street
Irving, TX 75038
(803) 555-5555

December 14, 20--

Pat Cummings
Broker
Any Corporation
1140 Main Street
El Paso, TX 79998

Dear Mr. Cummings:

During the past seven years, I have held positions ranging from Supervisor of field operations to Sales and Marketing Manager of jewelry and specialty products, and am comfortable in both wholesale and retail markets.

Currently, I am seeking a change that will allow me to utilize my experience in telemarketing, inside sales management, and dealings with commodity brokers in sales with an established security brokerage or related financial service.

During the course of my research into the field, I was impressed by the innovative sales techniques and increasing market share held by Any Corporation. I would love to begin a long-term association with your firm, and I am willing to start at entry level and participate in your formal registered-representative training program. I am confident that I have the ability to quickly establish contact with customers and develop sales-producing accounts.

The enclosed resume summarizes my background and experience in the areas I have cited above. I would welcome the chance to discuss the possibility of joining your team. I will call you next Tuesday to schedule a mutually convenient time to meet.

Thank you, Mr. Cummings, for your consideration. I look forward to speaking with you.

Sincerely yours,

Chris Smith

Enc. Resume

► Letter emphasizes valuable skills.

► Candidate's practical experience outweighs his/her education.

WEAK EMPLOYMENT BACKGROUND
(Sales Manager)

178 Green Street
Kalamazoo, MI 49006
(616) 555-5555

June 20, 20--

Pat Cummings
On-Site Sales Manager
Any Corporation
1140 Main Street
Roscommon, MI 48653

Dear Ms. Cummings:

If your company is looking for a self-motivated person who can work well with people, grasp and expand on new ideas, tackle and follow through on difficult projects, and achieve set objectives, then I feel we have good reason to meet.

Confident in my ability to succeed, I offer you a Bachelor of Science degree in Economics (cum laude), a graduate degree in Urban Affairs, experience in sales, and the desire to apply all or part of this background to a structured management training program in your firm.

The enclosed resume summarizes my background. I am not afraid of hard work, can work under pressure, and honestly feel that within a short time I could be contributing a profitable return on your company's training investment. I am available any time to learn more about Any Corporation and convince you of my desire to join your ranks.

I look forward to meeting with you. Thank you for your time.

Sincerely,

Chris Smith

Enc. Resume

▶ Impressive educational experience and qualifications helps compensate for candidate's short employment history.

▶ Candidate refers to attached resume in closing.

CHAPTER 20

ELECTRONIC COVER LETTERS (E-MAIL FORMAT)

In this age of ubiquitous technology, there's a pretty good chance that you'll be making a lot of your job applications online. E-mail has usurped traditional correspondence as the preferred mode of delivery for written communication; even classified ads in newspapers these days ask for resumes by e-mail. And as we have pointed out more than once in this book, every resume you send, online or otherwise, must be accompanied by a cover letter.

Electronic cover letters are not so very different from their hard copy cousins. You still need to "sell" yourself in a way that is confident but not overly boastful. And your primary object still needs to be getting yourself to the next stage in the application process—a personal interview. The major difference between cover letters that travel through cyberspace and those that go by land is length. You only have about half the space to say what you need to say. While hard copy cover letters are typically four paragraphs long, those that you send by e-mail are more likely to be no longer than two. There's no room to ramble; you must make every word count. And don't forget to include your address and phone number!

In addition to making "cold" contacts with employers and responding to "help wanted" ads, you can use e-mail for several other activities related to your job-search, including networking, requests for information and notifying prospective employers of address and phone number changes. For the sake of good manners, however, you should continue to send your thank-you letters by "snail mail." It's a nice touch that will make you stand out from the rest of the applicants who probably don't know any better.

ELECTRONIC COVER LETTER: RESPONSE TO PRINT CLASSIFIED AD
(Assistant Editor)

To: *patcummings@anybooks.com*
From: *chrissmith@bluepencil.com*
Subj: Assistant Editor position

Dear Ms. Cummings:

I am pleased to attach my resume in response to your recent advertisement in the *Boston Globe* for an Assistant Editor. I believe that my strong written and verbal communication skills, as well as my proficiency in both Microsoft Word and WordPerfect and several desktop publishing programs, including Page-Maker, make me the ideal candidate for this position. For the last two years, I have worked as a reporter and copyeditor for a weekly newspaper; previously, I was features editor, graphic artist, and reporter for various college publications.

I would welcome the opportunity to meet with you to further discuss my abilities as they relate to your specific needs. May we schedule an appointment soon? I look forward to hearing from you.

Sincerely,

Chris Smith

178 Green Street
Worcester, MA 01610
(508) 555-5555
chrissmith@bluepencil.com

▶ Candidate cites source of information re: position available.

▶ Applicable work experience and competencies are briefly described.

ELECTRONIC COVER LETTER: RESPONSE TO PRINT CLASSIFIED AD
(Payroll Supervisor)

To: *patcummings@anycompany.com*
From: *chrissmith@addemup.com*
Subj: Payroll Supervisor position, *Richmond Times-Dispatch,* June 4, 20--

Dear Mr. Cummings:

    With more than ten years of progressively responsible hands-on business experience and a Bachelor of Arts degree in Economics, I am confident that I am the qualified candidate you seek for the position of Payroll Supervisor. As the attached resume reveals, my background includes positions as a Marketing Research Assistant, Union Benefits Consultant, and Human Resources Administrator. Presently, I am employed as Payroll Administrator at a midsize manufacturing firm, where I oversee day-to-day financial operations and supervise a staff of six. I am well-organized, detail-oriented, and committed to serving your corporation in an efficient and productive way.

    I am eager to learn more about this position and how I can contribute to your company's overall success. Please contact me by e-mail at the address above or phone (703) 555-5555 to arrange a mutually convenient time for a meeting. I look forward to hearing from you.

Sincerely,

Chris Smith

178 Green Street
Big Stone Gap, VA 24219
(703) 555-5555
chrissmith@addemup.com

▶ Candidate focuses on filling employer's needs, not hers.

▶ Subject line is used to cite source information.

ELECTRONIC COVER LETTER: "COLD" CONTACT
(Civil Engineer)

To: *patcummings@anyfirm.com*
From: *chrissmith@digsdirt.com*
Subj: Civil Engineering opportunities

Dear Ms. Cummings:

I have more than ten years of progressively responsible experience acquired during roadway, civil, site, hazardous waste, and waterfront projects, as well as Certification in Surveying Technology and a Bachelor of Science degree in Forest Resource Management. At present, I am investigating new and broader career opportunities that would allow me to put my extensive technical and supervisory skills to work for a progressive firm such as yours.

The attached resume describes my qualifications and accomplishments in greater detail. I am confident of my ability to make a positive and immediate contribution to Any Firm and would welcome the opportunity to personally discuss your current or anticipated staffing requirements face-to-face. I can be reached by e-mail at the address above or by phone at (401) 555-5555. I await your reply.

Sincerely,

Chris Smith

178 Green Street
Providence, RI 02903
(401) 555-5555
chrissmith@digsdirt.com

▶ Professional certification and strong educational background add strength to cover letter.

▶ Addressee is referred to attached resume for details on applicant's qualifications.

ELECTRONIC COVER LETTER: "COLD" CONTACT
(Plant Manager)

To: *patcummings@anycorporation.com*
From: *chrissmith@smoothoperations.com*
Subj: Plant management position

Dear Mr. Cummings:

Are you looking for a competent plant manager who will effectively handle all aspects involved in the smooth operation of your organization? If so, I have attached my confidential resume for your consideration. In addition to more than five years of vocational training and hands-on experience with automated, semiautomated, and mechanical plant equipment and systems, I have been involved in quality control, purchasing, and labor negotiations. Although I enjoy my present position with ABC Manufacturing, I am ready to make the change to a new environment that will offer me greater challenge and increased potential for growth.

I will call your office on April 12 to schedule a personal interview at your convenience. Thank you for your time and consideration.

Sincerely,

Chris Smith

178 Green Street
Little Rock, AR 72204
(501) 555-5555
chrissmith@smoothoperations.com

▶ Candidate immediately describes his/her qualifications   ▶ Letter suggests discretion

ELECTRONIC COVER LETTER: INFORMATION REQUEST
(Membership Directory)

To: *patcummings@anyzoologyassociation.com*
From: *chrissmith@infosearch.com*
Subj: Membership directory

Dear Mr. Cummings:

    I am currently conducting a search for job availabilities in the field of zoology within the Midwest and would appreciate any assistance you may be able to provide with regard to the members of your association. Do you publish a membership directory that I might use in my job-search efforts, and if so, how may I go about obtaining a copy?

    Thank you for your time. I look forward to your return response.

Sincerely,

Chris Smith

178 Green Street
Tempe, AZ 85285
(602) 555-555
chrissmith@infosearch.com

▶ Information request is direct and concise.　　▶ Candidate immediately states purpose of request.

ELECTRONIC COVER LETTER: ADDRESS/PHONE NUMBER CHANGE
(Laboratory Assistant)

To: *patcummings@anymedicalassociation.com*
From: *chrissmith@continuedinterest.com*
Subj: New address/phone number

Dear Ms. Cummings:
    I am writing to inform you of a change in my address and phone number. Effective July 1, you may reach me at:

178 Green Street
Shawnee Hills OH 43965
(216) 555-5555

    For your convenience, I have attached an updated copy of my resume. I continue to look forward to hearing from you with regard to any Laboratory Assistant positions you may have available. Thank you for your consideration.

Sincerely,

Chris Smith
chrissmith@continuedinterest.com

▶ Address-change letter is accompanied by updated resume.

▶ New information is set apart from the body of the letter for emphasis.

ELECTRONIC COVER LETTER: NETWORKING
(Chief Financial Officer)

To: patcummings@anybank.com
From: chrissmith@needsomehelp.com
Subj: Job opportunities—referred by Brad Peltser

Dear Mr. Cummings:

    I am exploring the Midwestern job market in the hopes of securing a position as a Chief Financial Officer. Brad Peltser suggested you might be able to offer me some advice with regard to senior-level officer availabilities in Wisconsin and Illinois. During sixteen years of progressively responsible positions encompassing all aspects of the financial and treasury functions, I have built a record of outstanding success in the management of corporate financial operations for fast-paced manufacturing companies and associated commercial operations, in multilocation, multistate, and international environments. In addition, I hold an M.B.A. in Finance and a B.A. in accounting; I have been a Certified Public Accountant since 20--.

    The attached resume summarizes my qualifications and experience. Could be meet to discuss suitable opportunities in your region and where I might best direct my job-search efforts? I am eager for your ideas and insight.

Sincerely,

Chris Smith

178 Green Street
El Paso, TX 79998
(915) 555-555
chrissmith@needsomehelp.com

▶ Candidate immediately specifies type of position sought.

▶ Candidate quantifies extensive experience.

CHAPTER 21

FOLLOW-UP LETTER (AFTER TELEPHONE CONVERSATION)

Immediately after a telephone conversation with a potential employer, you should send a letter expressing your gratitude for his or her time. Use this opportunity to reiterate your qualifications and continued interest in the position. Be sure to send your resume along with the letter. Doug B., an Accountant, followed his initial inquiry with a phone call and was lucky enough to speak with the Accounting Manager. After discussing the position for several minutes, Doug was able to schedule an interview. Immediately after the call, he sent a polite thank-you letter that reiterated his qualifications and confirmed their meeting time. Doug's letter set him apart from the competition.

FOLLOW-UP LETTER (AFTER TELEPHONE CONVERSATION)
(Acquisitions Manager)

178 Green Street
Brookings, SD 57006

July 2, 20--

Pat Cummings
Land Acquisitions Supervisor
Any Corporation
1140 Main Street
Yankton, SD 57078

Dear Mr. Cummings:

The opportunity to talk with you yesterday on a one-on-one basis gave me a positive feeling about the caliber of your company and its managers, and increased my interest in joining your firm. As per your request, I am enclosing my resume which briefly outlines my qualifications for a position involving right-of-way and land acquisition transactions.

I offer eleven years of progressively responsible experience acquired during roadway, civil, site, hazardous waste, and waterfront projects. This is supported by a Bachelor of Science degree in Forest Resource Management, certification as Land Surveyor-in-Training, and the challenge of Hazardous Site Activities courses. As a Surveyor, I have broad experience in researching deeds, and land and legal descriptions for commercial, industrial, and residential applications.

Currently, I am investigating new opportunities where my technical and supervisory skills can be effectively utilized and expanded upon. I am not opposed to learning new systems and procedures or accepting a support position leading to advancement within the company. If relocation is a requirement, then I am ready to make that commitment to achieve my career objectives.

I am confident of my ability to make a positive and immediate contribution to Any Corporation, and would welcome the opportunity to meet with you at your convenience. I can be reached at the above address or by phone at (605) 555-5555. Thank you for the chance to discuss available opportunities. I anticipate your response.

Yours sincerely,

Chris Smith

Enc. Resume

▶ Date of telephone conversation is noted immediately.

▶ Introduction refers to attached resume.

FOLLOW-UP LETTER (AFTER TELEPHONE CONVERSATION)
(Arbitrator)

178 Green Street
Yorktown Heights, NY 10598
(914) 555-5555

September 24, 20--

Pat Cummings
Director of Regional Administration
Any Corporation
1140 Main Street
Port Chester, NY 10573

Dear Ms. Cummings:

As per our conversation and your request, I am enclosing my business profile for your review in consideration for the position of Arbitrator with Any Organization.

In addition to a Bachelor of Arts degree and extensive study in arbitration, I have been actively involved as an Arbitrator for the Better Business Bureau for the past four years. My activities during the past thirteen years, as a licensed Auctioneer and Night Club Manager, have consistently involved skill in new business development, negotiating, listening, weighing facts, and making decisions to resolve disputes in the best interest of all parties concerned.

I have successfully arbitrated cases involving manufacturers, vendors, and customers, chaired arbitration panels, and established a reputation for being able to make fair decisions under stressful conditions.

The enclosed document summarizes my experience. If you feel that my qualifications match your needs, I would like to speak with you further in an interview. I can be reached at the above address and phone, or you may leave a telephone message at (914) 555-4444.

Thank you for your consideration of my application. I look forward to your return response.

Yours sincerely,

Chris Smith

Enc. Business profile

▶ Letter allows candidate opportunity to suggest personal interview as next step.

▶ Qualifications highlight candidate's problem-solving ability.

FOLLOW-UP LETTER (AFTER TELEPHONE CONVERSATION)
(Assistant Engineer)

178 Green Street
Rogers, AR 72757
(501) 555-5555

September 18, 20--

Pat Cummings
Executive Assistant
Any Shipbuilder
1140 Main Street
Little Rock, AR 72203

Dear Mr. Cummings:

Thank you for extending your time to me this morning over the phone. I am glad to hear that Mr. Gulesarian is still looking for an Assistant Engineer. I understand the expertise you are in search of, and I believe I possess it. To this position, I would bring:

- More than five years of progressively responsible, hands-on, management experience in the maintenance, repair, modification, overhaul, and installation of heavy marine equipment and machinery.
- Expertise with electrical, water, fuel, lubrication, hydraulic, power plant, motor control, and related systems and major components.
- Experience that includes AC/DC light and power systems, generators, controllers, starters, transformers, communications systems, general electronics, consoles, and computers.

I would be able to provide further testimony of my skills during the course of a meeting with Mr. Gulesarian. I will call his office late next week to see when his schedule would allow him a few moments to speak with me. In the interim, I have enclosed a professional profile for his consideration.

Again, I enjoyed our conversation and hope to speak with you again as the hiring process continues.

Sincerely,

Chris Smith

Enc. Professional profile

► Candidate expresses gratitude for addressee's consideration.

► Letter tailors experience and skills to position applied for.

FOLLOW-UP LETTER (AFTER TELEPHONE CONVERSATION)
(Assistant Portfolio Manager)

178 Green Street
Parsippany, NJ 07054
(201) 555-5555

March 28, 20--

Pat Cummings
Director of Finance
Any Firm
1140 Main Street
Morristown, NJ 08057

Dear Ms. Cummings:

Our phone conversation yesterday was both informative and valuable for my job search. Thank you for your help. As you know, I am very interested in joining Any Firm, whose progressive approach to financial planning and management has prompted me to forward the enclosed resume.

As I mentioned while speaking with you, I offer considerable work experience ranging from Promotional Sales Representative, Assistant Campaign Manager, and Assistant Budget Analyst to my present position as Assistant Portfolio Manager. I would like to meet and discuss further my qualifications and the opportunities you may have available.

Thank you again for your time. I look forward to your reply.

Sincerely,

Chris Smith

Enc. Resume

▶ Follow-up letter briefly reiterates relevant experience.

▶ In closing, candidate specifically requests interview.

FOLLOW-UP LETTER (AFTER TELEPHONE CONVERSATION)
(Associate Editor)

178 Green Street
Marylhurst, OR 97036
(503) 555-5555

January 4, 20--

Pat Cummings
Managing Editor
Any Corporation
1140 Main Street
Portland, OR 97201

Dear Mr. Cummings:

Thank you for taking the time to speak with me on the phone yesterday. As requested, I am sending my resume for your review.

As previously mentioned, I am currently an Editorial Intern at the Portland State University Press. My career goal is to become a Managing Editor. I proofread and copyedit on a regular basis at work using *The Chicago Manual of Style,* and recently completed a course in copyediting. I also help our Production Editor prepare manuscripts for turnover to the production department. I am eager to apply my knowledge, develop new skills, and contribute to a growing company.

I plan to contact you again before the summer, when you predicted there might be job openings. In the meantime, I hope that 20-- is a successful year for you and your growing company.

Sincerely,

Chris Smith

Enc. Resume

▶ Internship experience is valuable for candidates with little job experience, particularly if it corresponds to the position sought.

▶ Candidate expresses gratitude for addressee's consideration.

FOLLOW-UP LETTER (AFTER TELEPHONE CONVERSATION)
(COBOL Programmer)

178 Green Street
Norfolk, VA 23510
(703) 555-5555

February 12, 20--

Pat Cummings
Director of Human Resources
Any Corporation
1140 Main Street
Casper, WY 82604

Dear Ms. Cummings:

Thank you for taking the time from your schedule on Friday to speak with me regarding available COBOL Programmer positions with your clients. Please accept the enclosed resume as an expressed interest in joining your organization to contribute and develop my skills and abilities.

As you can see from my resume, my hardware exposure has included Suzuki and HyTech, and I have had substantial experience in implementing both batch and online computer systems using COBOL. Initiative and ability in each position I have held has led to advancement and the assumption of greater responsibilities.

I feel that I have acquired valuable experience and education and the skills that I have developed, coupled with an eagerness to learn and a motivation to succeed, would contribute to a productive association with your company.

I would welcome the opportunity to meet with you to discuss ways in which my capabilities may suit your needs or those of your clients. I would also like to reiterate my willingness to relocate, given a suitable opportunity. Please consider the enclosed resume and direct your response to the above address.

I appreciate your time and consideration. I look forward to hearing from you.

Sincerely,

Chris Smith

Enc. Resume

▶ Willingness to relocate can be advantageous.

▶ Technical language is acceptable when it relates to candidate's field.

FOLLOW-UP LETTER (AFTER TELEPHONE CONVERSATION)
(Concierge)

178 Green Street
Warren, MI 48091
(313) 555-5555

July 23, 20--

Pat Cummings
Executive Manager
Any Hotel
1140 Main Street
Port Huron, MI 48060

Dear Mr. Cummings:

I appreciate the time you took yesterday to speak with me concerning the Concierge position at Any Hotel. Your description of the position and its responsibilities was most helpful. I would like to take this opportunity to review my qualifications:

- Promoted to establish concierge department in 350-room luxury hotel.
- Responsible for setting tone and image of hotel as a result of providing guest services, including tourist information, tour arrangements, and hotel and airline reservations.
- Presently supervise and manage 40-person hotel staff, including concierge department assistants, mail and information clerks, bell staff, doormen, valet parking and hotel garage staff, and telephone operators.
- Diplomatically and effectively resolve guests' grievances/problems; compose responses and make follow-up phone contact.

In addition to the outlined experience, I would bring to the position an intimate knowledge of the area and its offerings and the ability to work well under pressure. My formal education includes dual degrees in Restaurant and Hotel Management and in French from Marquette University, as well as a year of study at the Sorbonne University, Paris.

After you have reviewed the enclosed resume, I would appreciate the opportunity to continue our phone conversation in person. Thank you.

Sincerely,

Chris Smith

Enc. Resume

▶ International exposure, in exchange programs, internships, or educational study are valuable assets in today's global marketplace.
▶ Candidate reiterates qualifications discussed in telephone conversation.

FOLLOW-UP LETTER (AFTER TELEPHONE CONVERSATION)
(Department Manager)

178 Green Street
Tacoma, WA 98416
(206) 555-5555

February 10, 20--

Pat Cummings
Chief Administrator
Any Hospital
1140 Main Street
Spokane, WA 99201

Dear Ms. Cummings:

It was a pleasure speaking with you today in connection with your search for a Department Manager. I feel my experience and achievements are well within the required qualifications set forth in your detailed job description, and I am confident of my ability to provide your department with the same dedication and capability I exercise in my present position.

As outlined in my resume, I have extensive administrative and fiscal management experience working with all departments on nonmedical aspects in a health care environment. The challenges associated with the available position at Any Hospital are of great interest to me and I would like the opportunity to meet with you, at your convenience, to further discuss my candidacy for this position.

Yours sincerely,

Chris Smith

Enc. Resume

► Closing reiterates candidate's interest in position.

► Candidate immediately reviews circumstances of most recent contact.

FOLLOW-UP LETTER (AFTER TELEPHONE CONVERSATION)
(Executive Marketing Director)

178 Green Street
Boise, ID 83725
(208) 555-5555

August 3, 20--

Pat Cummings
Vice-President
Any Corporation
1140 Main Street
Chicago, IL 60605

Dear Mr. Cummings:

I am forwarding my resume with regard to the opening in your marketing department that we discussed yesterday by phone.

Although I am currently employed in a management position, I am interested in a career change, especially one that would allow me to combine a thorough knowledge of boating with my sales, marketing, and communication skills. I am an imaginative, well-organized self-starter with a strong interest in boating. As a semi-professional sailboat racer, I twice won national honors and participated in the races at Cape Cod. In addition, I have made lasting contacts with owners and officials.

After you have had the chance to review the enclosed resume, please contact me so that we can further discuss the possibility of my joining your staff. I am confident that my business background and knowledge of boats will enable me to have a favorable impact on both your sales and image.

Thank you for your attention, and I look forward to speaking with you again to learn more about this opportunity.

Sincerely yours,

Chris Smith

Enc. Resume

▶ Career objective is supported by awards and accomplishments.

▶ Candidate expresses knowledge of his/her field of interest.

FOLLOW-UP LETTER (AFTER TELEPHONE CONVERSATION)
(Export Manager)

178 Green Street
New York, NY 10027
(212) 555-5555

July 1, 20--

Pat Cummings
Controller
Any Corporation
1140 Main Street
Chicago, IL 60605

Dear Ms. Cummings:

Thank you for taking time out of your busy schedule to speak with me yesterday regarding the Export Manager position. My interest in this position and in Any Corporation is stronger than ever, particularly because it would afford me the opportunity to become less desk-bound—an occupational hazard in my most recent employment.

Pursuant to our conversation, I have compiled a supplement to my resume, detailing my experience relevant to the position of Export Manager. As I explained to you, my family has been involved in the fashion industry for most of my life. I have actively assisted/advised both my mother and my uncle with their European outlets, acquiring considerable expertise and knowledge of the fashion accessory and perfume industries.

With regard to salary requirements, I did a brief cost survey of the Chicago area and happily discovered a favorable difference between that area and where I reside in New York. I would, therefore, be able to consider a salary somewhat lower than we discussed—perhaps in the low sixties—since my living expenses would be so significantly decreased.

I am very enthusiastic about the prospect of re-entering a field where my interpersonal skills and familiarity with European culture and fashion will be more fully utilized. I look forward to hearing from you again in the near future.

Sincerely,

Chris Smith

Enc. Resume

▶ Letter expresses commitment to field of interest.

▶ Including compensation requirements is optional.

FOLLOW-UP LETTER (AFTER TELEPHONE CONVERSATION)
(Flight Attendant)

178 Green Street
Mountain View, CA 94039

February 5, 20--

Pat Cummings
Director of Human Resources
Any Airline
1140 Main Street
San Francisco, CA 94104

Dear Mr. Cummings:

I appreciate the time you took to speak with me today regarding the Flight Attendant opening advertised in the *San Francisco Chronicle*. After considering the requirements you outlined, I am even more confident of my ability to meet your needs:

You require:
- Communication skills
- Customer service aptitude
- Specialized training

I offer:
- A Bachelor of Arts degree in Communications.
- Highly developed interpersonal skills, having dealt with a diversity of professionals, clients, and associates.
- Fluency in Spanish; a knowledge of German.
- More than five years of experience in retail/sales, dealing with a wide variety of clients.
- Skill at handling customer complaints and problem-solving.
- Flight Attendant certification.
- CPR training.
- Participation in three-day intensive seminar, "Reacting in an Emergency."

I have enclosed a resume for your review. I would welcome the chance to address my skills and enthusiasm for this position in a personal meeting. Please contact me at the above address or (415) 555-5555.

Sincerely,

Chris Smith

Enc. Resume

▶ Format is neat and professional.   ▶ Continuing education indicates candidate's ongoing commitment to his/her field.

FOLLOW-UP LETTER (AFTER TELEPHONE CONVERSATION)
(Head Coach)

178 Green Street
Rutland, VT 05701

September 27, 20--

Pat Cummings
Athletic Director
Any High School
1140 Main Street
Bennington, VT 05201

Dear Ms. Cummings:

As per your suggestion during our telephone discussion this morning, I am enclosing my updated resume as a means of expressing my continued interest in the position of Head Varsity Baseball Coach at Any High School.

As I stated during our discussion, I have successfully established myself as a winning coach in a comprehensive seasonal sports program encompassing six major sports and numerous minor sports in a co-ed environment. In baseball, I have consistently built highly competitive winning teams that have achieved championship status.

I consider myself to be a dedicated coach who has the ability to recognize young talent and develop a player's natural abilities and competitive spirit for the makings of a winning team. I would like to bring my coaching skills to Any High School, and hope you will consider my qualifications in keeping with your expectations for the position.

Should you wish to arrange a meeting for further discussion, please call me at my home, (802) 555-5555, or write me at the above address. I enjoyed talking with you and look forward to the opportunity to work with you at Any High School.

Sincerely,

Chris Smith

Enc. Resume

▶ Follow-up letter confirms candidate's enthusiasm for desired position.

▶ Experiences are tailored to employer's needs.

FOLLOW-UP LETTER (AFTER TELEPHONE CONVERSATION)
(Laboratory Technician)

178 Green Street
Weymouth, MA 02190
(617) 555-5555

September 12, 20--

Pat Cummings
Human Resources Director
Any Corporation
1140 Main Street
Chicago, IL 60605

Dear Mr. Cummings:

It was nice talking with you again today. As requested, I am enclosing my resume for your consideration.

In addition to a Bachelor of Science degree in Biology, I have five years of experience in a laboratory setting. This includes preparation and performance of experiments, as well as analysis, writing, and presentation of results.

Currently, I am investigating new opportunities where I can continue to develop my skills and apply my knowledge toward broader responsibilities and advancement. I look forward to our meeting on Monday, September 18, and learning more about the industry's forecast.

Again, thank you for taking time out of your busy schedule to aid me in my job search. Your confidence in my abilities is greatly appreciated.

Sincerely,

Chris Smith

Enc. Resume

▶ Candidate confirms meeting time established during previous telephone conversation.

▶ Including a telephone number is essential in a cover letter.

FOLLOW-UP LETTER (AFTER TELEPHONE CONVERSATION)
(Magazine Publishing Intern)

---

178 Green Street
Phoenix, AZ 85004
(602) 555-5555

March 28, 20--

Pat Cummings
Editor-in-Chief
Any Magazine
1140 Main Street
Little Rock, AR 72203

Dear Ms. Cummings:

Thank you for your time and courtesy during our telephone conversation on Friday, March 24 As I mentioned to you, I am very interested in the summer internship at *Any Magazine*.

I am currently participating in a senior-year internship at a Tucson-based publishing firm, Baker Communications Group. After my graduation in May, I want to expand my experience in the publishing and public relations fields. I feel the *Any Magazine* internship provides that opportunity, and that I can make a valuable contribution as a summer Intern.

I am most interested in discussing the possibility of working for *Any Magazine* this summer. I have enclosed my resume for your review, and I look forward to hearing from you.

Sincerely,

Chris Smith

Enc. Resume

▶ Relevant internship bolster otherwise limited work experience.

▶ Date of telephone conversation is noted immediately.

FOLLOW-UP LETTER (AFTER TELEPHONE CONVERSATION)
(Mailroom Supervisor)

178 Green Street
Carey, OH 43316
(419) 555-5555

March 23, 20--

Pat Cummings
Director of Human Resources
Any Corporation
1140 Main Street
Galion, OH 44833

Dear Mr. Cummings:

I enjoyed speaking with you over the phone yesterday and appreciate your consideration of my resume for the Mailroom Supervisor position.

I believe I possess the specific experience you require for this position. As I mentioned during our conversation, I have direct experience in mailroom management. In my current position at O'Keefe and Murphy, my responsibilities include:

- Coordinating all incoming mail, dispersing inter-building correspondence, managing courier services, and shipping/receiving.
- Researching and accounting for certified, registered, and express mail.
- Administering employee evaluations/appraisals, and scheduling hours.
- Obtaining/maintaining lease agreements for electronic machinery and equipment.

I am very interested in applying my skills as your new Mailroom Supervisor. Could we meet for a personal interview? Please contact me when your schedule permits a meeting.

Thank you for your courtesy yesterday. I look forward to speaking with you further.

Sincerely,

Chris Smith

Enc. Resume

▶ Type of position desired is clearly stated. ▶ Candidate expresses gratitude for addressee's consideration.

FOLLOW-UP LETTER (AFTER TELEPHONE CONVERSATION)
(Manager of Patient Services)

---

178 Green Street
Miami, FL 33054

September 15, 20--

Pat Cummings
Director of Patient Services
Any Hospital
1140 Main Street
Princeton, NJ 08540

Dear Ms. Cummings:

Thank you for a most interesting and enlightening discussion during our recent telephone interview pertaining to the position of Manager of Patient Services at Any Hospital. I am gratified to hear that Kelly Merke, currently interim Manager of Patient Services, was so thoughtful as to recommend me for this position.

As I previously mentioned, my interest is in the clinical aspect of the health care profession—an area in which my education, training, and experience is comprehensive. I am a skilled, dedicated professional with the ability to supervise a cost-effective clinical, patient, or support services activity.

My present position is diverse and represents the broad scope of clinical responsibility I am capable of handling. However, I am planning to relocate soon and I am seeking a new position, with a hospital such as Any Hospital, where I can continue to apply my clinical and supervisory expertise toward providing cost-effective, quality health care.

The enclosed resume summarizes my background and experience. After you have reviewed my qualifications, I would appreciate hearing from you so that we may discuss travel arrangements and a mutually convenient time for our one-on-one meeting. I can be reached by phone at (305) 555-5555 weekdays between 9 A.M. and 2 P.M.

Thanks again for the opportunity to discuss the position, and I hope to hear from you soon.

Yours sincerely,

Chris Smith

Enc. Resume

▶ Candidate discusses pertinent information received during telephone conversation.

▶ Candidate expresses best time of day to be reached in closing.

FOLLOW-UP LETTER (AFTER TELEPHONE CONVERSATION)
(Nanny)

178 Green Street
Boise, ID 83730
(208) 555-5555

July 6, 20--

Pat Cummings
1140 Main Street
Boise, ID 83757

Dear Mr. Cummings:

As per your request during our recent phone conversation, I have enclosed several references attesting to my abilities as a Nanny.

Also attached is a professional profile listing relevant activities that might be of interest to you. In addition to my experience as a private day-care provider, I have taught in infant, toddler, and preschool programs, where I was involved in planning curriculums, organizing activities, and communicating regularly with parents and staff.

I have made children's growth and development my career, and would very much like to apply my skills as your Nanny. I would appreciate the opportunity to speak with you further after you have verified my references, and would love to meet your children.

I hope to hear from you soon.

Sincerely,

Chris Smith

Enc. Professional profile, References

▶ Enclosure line refers to all enclosed materials.

▶ Dedication to candidate's field of interest is emphasized.

FOLLOW-UP LETTER (AFTER TELEPHONE CONVERSATION)
(Precision Inspector)

178 Green Street
Horsham, PA 19044
(215) 555-5555

October 16, 20--

Pat Cummings
Vice-President
Any Corporation
1140 Main Street
Reading, PA 19612

Dear Ms. Cummings:

   As per our phone conversation this morning, I would like to confirm our interview time of 9 A.M., Wednesday, October 18, for the Precision Inspector position.

   In preparation for our meeting, I would like to reiterate my qualifications for this position. I offer more than ten years of experience in:

- First-piece, in-process, and other phases of precision inspection.
- A wide variety of production manufacturing departments shops and associated inspection areas.
- Inspection procedures and methods pertaining to machined and fabricated complex parts from in-plant and vendors.
- Working to industrial and government specifications, and interpreted drawings.
- Making complicated setups and using tools and techniques to inspect finished goods with a maximum amount of efficiency and minimum supervision.

   I look forward to our interview and the opportunity to discuss the mutual benefit of our working together.

Sincerely,

Chris Smith

Enc. Resume

▶ Candidate confirms meeting time established during previous telephone conversation.

▶ Closing is brief and to the point.

FOLLOW-UP LETTER (AFTER TELEPHONE CONVERSATION)
(Principal)

---

178 Green Street
Atlanta, GA 30378
(404) 555-5555

February 6, 20--

Pat Cummings
Superintendent
Any School System
1140 Main Street
Mobile, GA 31776

Dear Mr. Cummings:

Thank you very much for taking the time to speak with me today regarding the Principal position available in your district. As you requested, I have enclosed a resume for your consideration.

I would be very interested in meeting with you and learning more about the position and its requirements. Should you need any additional information, please do not hesitate to contact me.

I look forward to pursuing the next step in the application process.

Sincerely,

Chris Smith

Enc. Resume

▶ Closing suggests a meeting to follow letter.   ▶ Introduction refers to enclosed resume.

FOLLOW-UP LETTER (AFTER TELEPHONE CONVERSATION)
(Production Assistant)

178 Green Street
Tulsa, OK 74103
(918) 555-5555

January 24, 20--

Pat Cummings
Human Resources Director
Any Publishing Company
1140 Main Street
Philadelphia, PA 19130

Dear Ms. Cummings:

Thank you for taking the time to talk with me on Friday, January 20 about your firm's opening for a Production Assistant. I am very interested in this position and believe it would be an appropriate place to learn more about the publishing field.

I enjoyed our conversation and look forward to hearing more about this opportunity. Thank you for your time and consideration.

Sincerely,

Chris Smith

Enc. Resume

▶ Follow-up letter confirms candidate's enthusiasm for desired position.

▶ Letter uses short sentences and common words.

FOLLOW-UP LETTER (AFTER TELEPHONE CONVERSATION)
(Protection Professional)

178 Green Street
Boulder, CO 80301
(303) 555-5555

May 1, 20--

Pat Cummings
Human Resources Director
Any Corporation
1140 Main Street
Englewood, CO 80112

Dear Mr. Cummings:

As you requested during our recent conversation, I am enclosing a summary of my education, training, and experience in security services management. Thank you for taking the time to discuss your requirements for the Certified Protection Professional position. I am very interested in applying my skills to meet your needs.

As I briefly explained, my experience in industry is with a multisite, 2,800-person division of a high-tech firm requiring strict adherence pertaining to security as well as physical accountability, safety, and environmental concerns. During the past seven years, I have played a key role in developing and installing cost-effective internal and off-site systems and controls essential for sophisticated, high-risk industries.

I feel that I have much to offer Any Corporation relative to directing a safe and secure environment. After you have reviewed my qualifications, I would like to arrange a personal meeting for further discussion. Please call me at your convenience.

Sincerely,

Chris Smith

Enc. Professional profile

▶ Candidate reiterates qualifications discussed in telephone conversation.

▶ Letter allows candidate opportunity to suggest personal interview as next step.

FOLLOW-UP LETTER (AFTER TELEPHONE CONVERSATION)
(Psychiatric Nurse)

178 Green Street
Racine, WI 53406
(414) 555-5555

May 2, 20--

Pat Cummings
Director of Human Resources
Any Hospital
1140 Main Street
Milwaukee, WI 53203

Dear Ms. Cummings:

Thank you for taking the time yesterday to discuss the Psychiatric Nursing position. I am excited about the opportunity and I am confident that I could make a positive contribution.

As mentioned during our phone conversation, some of my relevant experiences include:

- Work in diverse hospital and human service environments in a range of units from pediatric and medical/surgical, as well as handling mixed adults/adolescents with bipolar or borderline/acute personality disorders.
- Crisis intervention,and case management as related to patients suffering from conduct disorders, sexual and physical abuse, acute or chronic psychiatric distress, substance abuse, and physical challenges.
- Supervising three nurses and associated staff, assigning patients for evaluation, working with social service representatives and patients' families and/or guardians, distributing medications, providing emergency medical assistance, and handling associated details of medical administration.

I would like the opportunity to continue our discussion in person. Perhaps we could arrange a mutually convenient time to meet. I will contact your office on Monday, May 8, to set up an appointment.

Sincerely,

Chris Smith

Enc. Resume

▶ Bullets provide a clear and crisp presentation.

▶ Letter allows candidate follow-up opportunity to discuss his/her skills and accomplishments.

FOLLOW-UP LETTER (AFTER TELEPHONE CONVERSATION)
(Purchasing Agent)

178 Green Street
Carlsbad, NM 88220
(505) 555-5555

December 5, 20--

Pat Cummings
Supervisor, Order Entry Department
Any Store
1140 Main Street
Albuquerque, NM 87106

Dear Mr. Cummings:

As you requested during our recent discussion, I am enclosing my resume for you to review and distribute to the administration services department. My interest is in a position in which I can utilize, and the company can benefit from, my strong purchasing and inventory skills.

Although my present position is diverse and secure, there seems to be little room for further growth within the company and I think it is time for a change. I would like the opportunity to rejoin Any Store and I feel that my diverse purchasing, inventory, and traffic skills can be well utilized within the new administration services department.

I want to thank you in advance for your interest and your time, and look forward to a meeting with you to further discuss opportunities with Any Store. Should you require additional information or want to set up an interview, please contact me at the telephone number listed above. I have enjoyed working at Any Store in the past in part-time positions and would welcome the opportunity to join the company on a full-time basis.

Thanks again for your interest and assistance.

Sincerely,

Chris Smith

Enc. Resume

▶ Personalized tone reinforces candidate's familiarity with addressee.

▶ Candidate indicates type of employment desired.

FOLLOW-UP LETTER (AFTER TELEPHONE CONVERSATION)
(Regional Sales/Product Trainer)

178 Green Street
West Bend, IN 53095

June 3, 20--

Pat Cummings
National Sales Trainer
Any Corporation
1140 Main Street
Green Bay, WI 54307

Dear Ms. Cummings:

As per your request during our recent phone conversation, I am enclosing my resume for your review and to initiate a meeting to discuss the position of Regional Sales/Product Trainer for Any Corporation.

Audiovisual equipment and systems have been an integral part of my life as both a vocation and avocation. Based on my experience and accomplishments as a top producer in conceptual sales and technical training management, I am confident of my ability to contribute, through dealer training and motivation, to a substantial increase in sales of your product line. I feel that the combination of my knowledge of, and belief in, the quality of your products can only assist me in an exceptional performance for Any Corporation.

I would welcome a personal interview in which we would have the opportunity to discuss, in detail, your requirements and my ability to handle the responsibilities of the Regional Sales/ Product Trainer position.

Should you have any further questions, please do not hesitate to contact me at the above address or by phone at (414) 555-5555.

I look forward to your return response.

Sincerely,

Chris Smith

Enc. Resume

▶ Candidate highlights areas of expertise. ▶ Follow-up letter briefly reiterates relevant experience.

FOLLOW-UP LETTER (AFTER TELEPHONE CONVERSATION)
(Teacher)

178 Green Street
Akron, OH 44316

August 5, 20--

Pat Cummings, M.D.
Director
Any School for the Deaf
1140 Main Street
Dayton, OH 45404

Dear Dr. Cummings:

Thank you for the opportunity, during our recent phone conversation, to discuss the teaching position available at Any School for the Deaf. As you requested, I am enclosing my resume which reflects my dedication to teaching and counseling hearing-impaired children.

In addition to a Bachelor of Arts degree in Human Development, which includes coursework in child development, psychology of learning, and counseling theories, I have four years of experience working with the severely handicapped. This background, combined with my many years of personal experience as a hard-of-hearing person, can be successfully applied in a teaching capacity to motivate and benefit hearing-impaired children at your institution.

After you have reviewed my qualifications, I would appreciate meeting with you to further explain my interest in, and qualifications for, working within the deaf community. I feel I have the expertise, willingness for further personal development, interest, and patience required to work with your students.

Should you require additional information prior to our meeting, I can be reached at the above address or by phone at (216) 555-5555. I plan to make a follow-up call within a few days.

Once again, thank you for your courtesy.

Sincerely,

Chris Smith

Enc. Resume

▶ Courses listed are related to candidate's field of interest.

▶ Candidate immediately reviews circumstances of most recent contact.

CHAPTER 22

FOLLOW-UP LETTER (AFTER JOB INTERVIEW)

Presumably, if your initial cover letter is well written, it will open the door for future communication with a potential employer. Ideally, you would land a job interview! Should you reach this stage, it is courteous to send a follow-up letter within one day of your conversation. Not only will you appear thoughtful and detail-orientated, but your follow-up letter can give you a considerable edge over candidates who neglect this important step in the job-hunting process.

A follow-up letter expresses thanks to the employer for his or her time, and emphasizes your continued interest in the available position. Follow-up letters can also provide a convenient opportunity to reinforce your unique qualifications for the position. Simply stating something like, "I would like to reiterate my strong interest in this position. I believe that it would be an exciting opportunity, and I feel that my track record shows I would be a successful candidate," can enhance your candidacy dramatically.

FOLLOW-UP LETTER (AFTER JOB INTERVIEW)
(Administrative Assistant)

178 Green Street
Neptune, NJ 07754
(908) 555-5555

January 22, 20--

Pat Cummings
Hiring Officer
Any Corporation
1140 Main Street
Passaic, NJ 07055

Dear Ms. Cummings:

Thank you for interviewing me for the Administrative Assistant position on Friday. Our meeting was as informative as it was enjoyable.

I was impressed with your product lines and position in the marketplace, as well as your vitality and commitment to growth, and I hope to contribute to the continued growth of Any Corporation.

To this end, I would like to meet Richard Griffin to discuss how I may be of assistance. Organization and administration are two of my strongest skills, and I believe my experience in these areas would be beneficial to your company.

Thank you again for your time and consideration. I look forward to hearing from you.

Sincerely,

Chris Smith

▶ Letter immediately expresses candidate's gratitude for the interview.

▶ Candidate clearly expresses eagerness to work for specific employer.

FOLLOW-UP LETTER (AFTER JOB INTERVIEW)
(Assistant Editor)

178 Green Street
Fargo, ND 58102

June 22, 20--

Pat Cummings
Editor
Any Publication
1140 Main Street
Nashua, NH 03061

Dear Mr. Cummings:

I want to thank you for interviewing me yesterday with regard to the Assistant Editor position. I enjoyed meeting you and learning more about your company.

My enthusiasm for the position and my interest in working for *Any Publication* were strengthened as a result of our meeting. I am confident that my education and experience fit nicely with the job requirements, and I am sure I could make a significant contribution to the company over time. In short, you offer the opportunity I seek.

I am still planning on relocating to the Northeast. If, in the interim, I can provide you with any additional information, please feel free to contact me at (701) 555-5555.

Again, thank you for the interview and for your consideration.

Sincerely,

Chris Smith

▶ Letter immediately restates position candidate interviewed for.

▶ Candidate highlights pertinent information discussed during interview.

FOLLOW-UP LETTER (AFTER JOB INTERVIEW)
(Bank Manager)

178 Green Street
Pullman, WA 99164
(509) 555-5555

June 20, 20--

Pat Cummings
Vice-President, Northwest Region
Any Bank
1140 Main Street
Sumas, WA 98295

Dear Ms. Cummings:

Thank you for the quality time you extended me during our meeting on June 16 to discuss management opportunities with Any Bank.

I want to express my appreciation to you for providing an overview of the various responsibilities associated with management positions in Any Bank's northwest division. I am confident of my ability to meet your requirements for efficient and quality performance in any position for which I am considered.

Management opportunities with Any Bank are of great interest to me, and I look forward to hearing from your human resources representative for further discussion.

Thanks again for a most pleasant and informative interview.

Sincerely,

Chris Smith

▶ Candidate refers to information received during interview.

▶ Candidate uses opportunity to restate his/her interest in position.

FOLLOW-UP LETTER (AFTER JOB INTERVIEW)
(Business Manager)

178 Green Street
Hickory, NC 28603
(704) 555-5555

July 12, 20--

Pat Cummings, M.D.
Director of Retinopathy
Any Hospital
1140 Main Street
Raleigh, NC 27607

Dear Dr. Cummings:

Thank you for the time you took out of your busy schedule on Tuesday to discuss the requirements of the position of Business Manager. I hope I was able to convince you of my capability to cost-effectively execute the responsibilities of the position.

I would like to stress that my experience with Blue Cross/Blue Shield has involved interfacing and dealing with all operations and administrative departments on matters pertaining to financial and business reporting. As previously stated, I have broad experience with Microsoft Excel as well as with several other sophisticated programs designed for the health care industry. This knowledge and experience are essential requirements of the position under discussion.

From my initial interview on July 2 with Douglas Antonucci of your human resources department through my final interview with you yesterday, my interest in the position of Business Manager has strengthened. I sincerely feel that I am right for the job and hope that you and your associates have come to the same conclusion.

Thank you again for the time and courtesies extended to me by you, Dr. Martins, and Ms. D'Isidori. I look forward to joining your management team.

Sincerely,

Chris Smith
cc: Douglas Antonucci

▶ Candidate refers to all employees involved in the interview process.

▶ Computer experience calls attention to candidate's technical knowledge.

FOLLOW-UP LETTER (AFTER JOB INTERVIEW)
(Computer Operator)

178 Green Street
Baldwyn, MS 38824
(601) 555-5555

August 28, 20--

Pat Cummings
Manager, Billing Department
Any Corporation
1140 Main Street
Jackson, MS 39217

Dear Mr. Cummings:

Thank you for a most enjoyable interview in reference to the Computer Operator position at Any Corporation. It was a pleasure meeting you and Robert Richmond and learning more about the operations of your billings department.

I am very interested in contributing my seven years of experience operating computer systems to the success of your firm. As per your suggestion, I will call your office next week to check the status of the hiring process.

Again, thank you for your time and consideration.

Sincerely,

Chris Smith
cc: Robert Richmond

▶ Candidate establishes when follow-up contact will take place.

▶ Letter is easy and quick to read, and only relevant details are included.

FOLLOW-UP LETTER (AFTER JOB INTERVIEW)
(Conference Coordinator)

178 Green Street
Fort Smith, AR 72902
(501) 555-5555

August 5, 20--

Pat Cummings
Executive Director
Any Corporation
1140 Main Street
Little Rock, AR 72219

Dear Ms. Cummings:

Thank you for allowing me the opportunity to interview for the Conference Coordinator position. As the result of our informative discussion, my interest in the position has strengthened substantially.

As I mentioned during our interview, I can bring eight years of diverse part-time and full-time experience in positions which required flexibility and the ability to accept and follow through on new assignments and responsibilities. I have had the opportunity to deal with people on all levels in the workplace as an Instructor and Events Coordinator in hospitality and related businesses.

Based on my past work experience, as well as my Master's degree in Administration, I feel confident that I have the qualifications for the position under discussion. Please let me know if there is anything I can do to assist you further in your hiring process.

Thank you again for a most enjoyable interview.

Sincerely,

Chris Smith

▶ Letter highlights candidate's acquired professional and educational training.

▶ Candidate expresses his/her continued interest in desired position.

FOLLOW-UP LETTER (AFTER JOB INTERVIEW)
(Distribution Coordinator)

178 Green Street
Flint, MI 48501
(313) 555-5555

December 4, 20--

Pat Cummings
Vice-President, Operations
Any Corporation
1140 Main Street
East Lansing, MI 48824

Dear Mr. Cummings:

    It is not often that a candidate hears a company and job responsibilities presented as clearly as you did during our conversation last Friday. The Distribution Coordinator position sounds like an ideal opportunity for which I consider myself to be well-qualified. I appreciated the opportunity to discuss my credentials with you in so much detail.

    As we discussed, I possess seven years of experience managing a successful and profitable wholesale seafood company which has expanded into retail seafood sales and seafood restaurant operations. In addition, I have since been involved in multistate, retail operations that require cost-effective management of sales and operational activities from development of start-up locations to multistate distribution using all forms of transportation.

    My combined experience with fresh seafood, distribution, planning, and scheduling can be successfully applied to areas of interest to you and to the benefit of Any Corporation. I am excited about the challenge this position presents, and I look forward to your return response.

    Thank you again for the gracious invitation to your offices. I enjoyed my stay and I hope to return soon.

Yours sincerely,

Chris Smith

▶ Experience reinforces candidate's professional objective.

▶ Candidate uses opportunity to reiterate qualifications.

FOLLOW-UP LETTER (AFTER JOB INTERVIEW)
(District Sales Supervisor)

178 Green Street
Wicomico, VA 23184
(804) 555-5555

July 4, 20--

Pat Cummings
Human Resources Director
Any Corporation
1140 Main Street
Chicago, IL 60605

Dear Ms. Cummings:

I enjoyed meeting with you yesterday. Thank you for taking the time out of your busy schedule to talk with me about the Sales Supervisor position you have available at Any Corporation.

I would like to stress my interest in this position. The prospect of having the freedom to run a sales territory like my own business is exciting and appealing to me.

As I mentioned yesterday, my background includes extensive team selling, and I would like to emphasize that all decisions regarding the structure of presentations, targets, and general selling strategy within the downtown Lynchburg territory were principally my responsibility. I had the freedom to set pricing structure and to tailor product packages as I saw fit to best make the sale. I thrived on that freedom and was successful.

As a follow-up to our meeting, I will write a rough business plan, as we discussed, and I will contact Jordan Banks for further insight into the position.

Thank you again for your time. I look forward to meeting with you again in August at the Chicago office.

Sincerely,

Chris Smith
cc: J. Banks

▶ Letter highlights candidate's significant accomplishments.

▶ Letter avoids abbreviations and slang.

FOLLOW-UP LETTER (AFTER JOB INTERVIEW)
(Doctor)

178 Green Street
Luna, NM 87824
(505) 555-5555

December 2, 20--

Pat Cummings, M.D.
Director, Emergency Medicine Fellowship Program
Any Hospital
1140 Main Street
Chicago, IL 60605

Dear Dr. Cummings:

Thank you for allowing me to interview for the fellowship position in your department at Any Hospital. I appreciated the opportunity to meet with the faculty and the staff; everyone was most hospitable.

I was impressed with the program and in particular the thought that has gone into the fellowship curriculum development and research guidance. I came away very enthusiastic about the position.

Please extend my thanks to Dr. Lee, Dr. Murphy, and Dr. Sloat for a thoughtful discussion relative to the Emergency Medicine Fellowship Program. Being part of such a team is, indeed, an enticing prospect.

If you have any further questions please do not hesitate to contact me. I look forward to hearing from you.

Sincerely,

Chris Smith, M.D.
cc: Joan Lee, M.D.
Brian Murphy, M.D.
Susan Sloat, M.D.

▶ Candidate highlights pertinent information discussed during interview.

▶ Follow-up letter thanks all those involved in the interview process for an enjoyable experience.

FOLLOW-UP LETTER (AFTER JOB INTERVIEW)
(Editorial Assistant)

178 Green Street
Kingston, MA 02364

July 1, 20--

Pat Cummings
Editor
Any Publishing Company
1140 Main Street
Boston, MA 02106

Dear Mr. Cummings:

I want to thank you for interviewing me yesterday for the Editorial Assistant position you have available. I enjoyed meeting you and learning more about Any Publishing Company and your work on the *Internet Primer.*

This position offers an incredible opportunity to learn the entire editorial and production processes involved in creating a book. I think my education as well as my written and editorial skills are an idea match to the job requirements you outlined. Above all, I am very eager to learn and I know that I could make a significant contribution to your organizaton.

I would like to reiterate my strong interest in this position and in working with you and Daniel Connelly. This is the ideal opportunity I seek. Please feel free to call me at (617) 555-5555 if I can provide you with any additional information.

Again, thank you for the interview and your consideration.

Sincerely,

Chris Smith
cc: Daniel Connelly

▶ Follow-up letter further illustrates candidate's suitability for available position.

▶ Closing reiterates candidate's interest in position.

FOLLOW-UP LETTER (AFTER JOB INTERVIEW)
(Engineering Consultant)

178 Green Street
Geismar, LA 70734
(504) 555-5555

January 18, 20--

Ms. Pat Cummings
Vice-President
Any Corporation
1140 Main Street
Lafayette, LA 70504

Dear Ms. Cummings:

It was a sincere pleasure making your acquaintance on Tuesday regarding the position of Engineering Consultant. The personal dynamics that you exude, the predicted corporate growth, and the position's promised personal fulfillment, have left me very enthused.

Thank you for your consideration. I look forward to meeting with you again in the near future.

Sincerely,

Chris Smith

▶ Day of interview is generally included in follow-up letter.

▶ Letter is brief and to the point.

FOLLOW-UP LETTER (AFTER JOB INTERVIEW)
(Executive Assistant)

178 Green Street
West Hazelton, PA 18201
(717) 555-5555

July 18, 20--

Pat Cummings
Hiring Manager
Any Corporation
1140 Main Street
Pittsburgh, PA 15222

Dear Mr. Cummings:

It was a pleasure meeting you and Joyce Duncan last Friday and learning more about the products and services provided by Any Corporation. The Executive Assistant position sounds like the ideal opportunity to apply my administrative and organizational skills to the overall operations of your firm.

The qualifications I would bring to the position include:

- Nine years of experience handling all office functions, including preparing and generating letters and reports, payroll, accounts payable/receivable, and customer service.
- Organizational proficiency with Quicksilver Metro, Inc., reflected in my revamping of a records storage system to reduce records access time by more than 60 percent from the previous system.
- A scrupulous attention to detail which led me to discover and correct more than $125,000 in duplicated and incorrectly assigned labor charges.
- Experience working with a variety of both PC and Macintosh applications, including Microsoft Word, WordPerfect, Excel, and Lotus 1-2-3.

I am confident these skills could be successfully applied in the position of Executive Assistant. Thank you for considering my candidacy. I look forward to meeting with you.

Sincerely,

Chris Smith
cc: Joyce Duncan

Enc. Resume

▶ Letter highlights candidate's significant accomplishments.

▶ Computer skills listed are related to candidate's field of interest.

FOLLOW-UP LETTER (AFTER JOB INTERVIEW)
(Export Manager)

178 Green Street
Mill Valley, CA 94941
(414) 555-5555

March 22, 20--

Pat Cummings
Vice-President, Exports
Any Corporation
1140 Main Street
Minneapolis, MN 55404

Dear Ms. Cummings:

Thank you for taking time out of your schedule to speak with me yesterday regarding the position of Export Manager. My interest in this position, and in Any Corporation, is stronger than ever, particularly because it would afford me the opportunity to become less desk-bound—an occupational hazard in my most recent employment.

I will contact your offices on March 29 to determine the next stage in the application process. In the interim, any questions you have may be addressed to my business phone, (414) 444-4444, or fax, (414) 333-3333.

Sincerely,

Chris Smith

▶ Candidate indicates time frame for follow-up contact.

▶ Including a fax number is optional in a cover letter.

FOLLOW-UP LETTER (AFTER JOB INTERVIEW)
(Finance Executive)

178 Green Street
Casper, WY 82604

November 15, 20--

Pat Cummings
Hiring Manager
Any Corporation
1140 Main Street
Charleston, WV 25301

Dear Mr. Cummings:

Thank you for a most informative and enjoyable discussion during our meeting on Monday. The knowledge I gained during the interview has certainly enhanced my interest in joining Any Corporation.

With my expertise in strategic planning, international finance, marketing, and general management, I feel confident that I can meet your expectations and significantly contribute to your company's objectives as a member of your management staff.

I want to thank you again for the time and courtesy you extended to me. I look forward to meeting with you again for a continued discussion of marketing opportunities available with your company.

Should you require additional information prior to a second meeting, please contact me at the above address or by phone at (307) 555-5555.

Sincerely,

Chris Smith

▶ Candidate reminds addressee of how his/her qualifications will benefit potential employer.

▶ Language is straightforward and understandable.

FOLLOW-UP LETTER (AFTER JOB INTERVIEW)
(Fund Raiser)

178 Green Street
Baltimore, MD 21217

November 9, 20--

Pat Cummings
Vice-President
Any Organization
1140 Main Street
Silver Spring, MD 20910

Dear Ms. Cummings:

I wish to thank you and Shannon Rickle for the opportunity to discuss the fund raiser position advertised by your firm. As you requested, I am enclosing a writing sample for your review, and I would like to emphasize that the orientation and purpose of the campaign, as I understand it, is of great interest to me.

I feel that my experience, as outlined below, ideally matches your needs:

Requirements of the position:
- Extensive service and administrative experience.
- Ability to effectively manage personnel.
- Specific fundraising accomplishments.

My qualifications:
- More than eighteen years of strategic planning, administrative, and sales experience in a major service-intensive industry.
- As Director of Agencies, National Sales Trainer, Sales Manager, and Administrator, my responsibilities encompassed the development and management of personnel recruitment, orientation, training, telemarketing, data collection, and motivational programs, seminars, and workshops that generated dedicated, highly productive teams.
- During the three years I served as Vice-President of Wing Industries, I was responsible for the organization and planning of fundraising campaigns which successfully generated in excess of $800,000 for the reconstruction of a $1.2 million auditorium that had been destroyed by arson.

Based on this background, I feel confident that I have the principal qualifications necessary to manage and administer programs and provide meaningful support to fundraising campaigns that require strong organizational and motivational skills. If I can provide any additional information to assist you in your decision, please do not hesitate to contact me at (301) 555-5555.

Thank you again for a most enjoyable interview. I look forward to hearing from you.

Sincerely,

Chris Smith
cc: Shannon Rickle

Enc. Writing sample

▶ Unique format demonstrates candidate's ability to meet advertised job requirements

▶ Summary of experience highlights candidate's achievements.

FOLLOW-UP LETTER (AFTER JOB INTERVIEW)
(Hotel Manager)

178 Green Street
Fort Wayne, IN 46803
(219) 555-5555

January 23, 20--

Pat Cummings
Executive Director
Any Hotel Chain
1140 Main Street
Chicago, IL 60605

Dear Mr. Cummings:

I would like to thank you for meeting with me on Friday regarding the Hotel Manager availability. I enjoyed learning more about this opportunity and Any Hotel Chain.

I would also like to reiterate my interest in the position. I feel that it would be an exciting opportunity and believe my track record shows I would be a successful candidate.

I am looking forward to hearing your final decision. Thank you again.

Sincerely,

Chris Smith

▶ Follow-up letter should be no longer than one page.

▶ Candidate thanks addressee for continued consideration.

FOLLOW-UP LETTER (AFTER JOB INTERVIEW)
(Human Resources Representative)

178 Green Street
Gardner, MA 01440
(508) 555-5555

November 15, 20--

Pat Cummings
Director of Human Resources
Any Corporation
1140 Main Street
Winchester, MA 01890

Dear Ms. Cummings:

    I would like to thank you for extending your time to interview me yesterday for the HR Representative position. I was very impressed by the size of your staff, and I certainly understand how demanding such a position would prove to be.

    Ms. Cummings, after speaking with you, I am even more eager to join the ranks of your qualified representatives. I believe my education, training, and strong motivation would assist me in successfully completing all aspects of the position.

    Thank you again for meeting with me. I hope your hiring decision will result in our meeting again.

Yours sincerely,

Chris Smith

▶ Closing reiterates candidate's gratitude to interviewer.

▶ Letter immediately restates position candidate interviewed for.

FOLLOW-UP LETTER (AFTER JOB INTERVIEW)
(Inventory Control Analyst)

178 Green Street
Little Rock, AK 72203
(501) 555-5555

November 17, 20--

Pat Cummings
President
Any Corporation
1140 Main Street
Chicago, IL 60605

Dear Mr. Cummings:

    It was a pleasure meeting you today. I appreciate your taking the time from your hectic schedule to speak with me about your opening for an Inventory Control Analyst.

    The position is exciting and seems to encompass a number of diverse responsibilities. I believe that with my experience and skills, I would be able to contribute significantly to your organization.

    I look forward to hearing from you in the near future. If you need further information, please feel free to call me.

Sincerely,

Chris Smith

▶ Follow-up letter thanks addressee for enjoyable interview.

▶ Letter uses short sentences and common words.

FOLLOW-UP LETTER (AFTER JOB INTERVIEW)
(Legal Intern)

178 Green Street
Boston, MA 02215
(617) 555-5555

April 21, 20--

Pat Cummings, J.D.
Principal
Any Law Firm
1140 Main Street
Woodland Hills, CA 91367

Dear Ms. Cummings:

    Thank you for taking the time to interview me on Thursday. I enjoyed meeting with you to discuss the internship at Any Law Firm. I also enjoyed the tour of the office, which I found to be interesting and informative.

    Thank you again for your time and consideration. If you have any questions, I would be happy to provide whatever additional information you need. I look forward to hearing from you soon.

Sincerely,

Chris Smith

▶ Day of interview is generally included in follow-up letter.

▶ Candidate thanks addressee for continued consideration.

FOLLOW-UP LETTER (AFTER JOB INTERVIEW)
(Materials Manager)

178 Green Street
Chicago, IL 60605
(312) 555-5555

August 5, 20--

Pat Cummings
Vice-President of Operations
Any Corporation
1140 Main Street
Chicago, IL 60605

Dear Mr. Cummings:

I greatly enjoyed our meeting yesterday. I would like to reiterate my interest in Any Corporation's opening for a Materials Manager.

As I explained during our conversation, I feel confident that my qualifications match the requirements of the position. I offer twelve years of experience working as Manager of Warehousing and Distribution and as Senior Buyer for a large metropolitan hospital. Briefly, my accomplishments include:

- Reducing expenditures of all in-house medical and nonmedical supplies by 20 percent through cost-effective negotiations, purchasing, and control.
- Automating inventories, which increased efficiency and decreased costly errors, thus saving more than $10,000 annually.
- Designing a functional warehouse layout, which effectively reduced the selection and distribution process for warehoused materials and provided more stringent controls.
- Reducing shrinkage, damage, and obsolescence of inventory by 33 percent.

Thank you for the time and courtesy you and your associates extended to me. I look forward to hearing from you.

Sincerely,

Chris Smith

▶ Separating major accomplishments from body provides emphasis.

▶ Candidate's most relevant work experience is prioritized.

FOLLOW-UP LETTER (AFTER JOB INTERVIEW)
(Personal Secretary)

---

178 Green Street
Nashua, NH 03060
(603) 555-5555

July 14, 20--

Pat Cummings
President
Any Corporation
1140 Main Street
Manchester, NH 03103

Dear Ms. Cummings:

I found our interview this morning to be most refreshing. Your staff was hospitable, your facilities impressive, and our discussion informative. I am very interested in becoming your Personal Secretary.

You mentioned during our meeting that you are looking for an assistant with extensive knowledge of computer systems and applications. My computer literacy includes proficiency in Microsoft Word, WordPerfect, Lotus 1-2-3, dBase 111, DOS, Windows, DisplayWrite, and desktop publishing. I also have experience with spreadsheets inventory management.

I believe I have much to offer your company, and I hope I will receive the opportunity to prove my worth to you. Thank you for extending me your time, Ms. Cummings.

Sincerely,

Chris Smith

▶ First paragraph is short and hard-hitting.　　▶ Valuable computer skills are highlighted.

FOLLOW-UP LETTER (AFTER JOB INTERVIEW)
(Personnel Manager)

---

178 Green Street
Halifax, MA 02338
(617) 555-5555

March 10, 20--

Pat Cummings
President
Any Corporation
1140 Main Street
Lynn, MA 01903

Dear Mr. Cummings:

I am grateful for the time you took this morning to interview me for the Personnel Manager position. Any Corporation sounds like an exciting, fast-growing firm; I would very much like to apply my skills to your continued success.

During our conversation, you mentioned that you were looking for a professional who could adjust human resources policy to the needs of an expanding company. I believe I possess just the qualifications necessary to do this. My prior positions in human resources management have provided me with extensive experience in all aspects of policy conception and implementation. My skills range from training and program development to budget management and employee relations.

If given the chance, I am confident I can restructure your department to meet and exceed your expectations. I hope I will be offered that chance.

Thank you again for a most enjoyable interview.

Sincerely,

Chris Smith

▶ Follow-up letter demonstrates candidate's acquired company knowledge.

▶ Candidate highlights pertinent information discussed during interview.

FOLLOW-UP LETTER (AFTER JOB INTERVIEW)
(Product Design Engineer)

178 Green Street
Clarkston, MI 48346
(313) 555-5555

January 31, 20--

Pat Cummings
Chief Engineer
Any Corporation
1140 Main Street
Huron, MI 48060

Dear Ms. Cummings:

I would like to thank you for extending your time to interview me yesterday. Any Corporation is an impressive, innovative manufacturing site, one which I would be very interested in joining as a Product Design Engineer.

Please be assured of my abilities to perform the responsibilities of the position as you outlined them:

Your requirements:
1. Oversee product design and assembly.
2. Prepare and monitor expense and capital budgets.
3. Monitor product safety.
4. Generate product revenue.

My relevant experiences:
1. Oversaw design engineering for more than 200 consumer and PC products, both in assembled and kit form.
2. Managed $600,000 in expense budget, plus $2 to $9 million in preproduction engineering prototypes per year.
3. Regularly monitored product safety and regulatory compliance.
4. Responsible for adding $9 million worth of new product revenue out of $90 million in total business.

I look forward to hearing your hiring decision. Thank you again for considering my qualifications.

Sincerely,

Chris Smith

▶ Candidate reminds addressee of how his/her qualifications will benefit potential employer.

▶ Statistics and dollar amounts quantify candidate's accomplishments.

FOLLOW-UP LETTER (AFTER JOB INTERVIEW)
(Production Assistant)

178 Green Street
Rapid City, SD 57709

September 9, 20--

Pat Cummings
Station Manager
Any Television Station
1140 Main Street
Sioux Falls, ND 57117

Dear Mr. Cummings:

Thank you for meeting with me yesterday. I appreciate your thorough explanation of the Production Assistant position and, now that I know exactly what the it entails, I am confident that I can make a positive contribution to the station.

I want to reemphasize my strong interest in joining your team. I believe my degree in Mass Communications, my internship experience, and my winning attitude make me a suitable candidate for this position.

Please feel free to contact me at (605) 555-5555 with any questions, and I look forward to your reply.

Sincerely,

Chris Smith

▶ Letter immediately expresses candidate's gratitude for the interview.

▶ Candidate expresses his/her continued interest in desired position.

FOLLOW-UP LETTER (AFTER JOB INTERVIEW)
(Public Records Analyst)

178 Green Street
Long Beach, CA 90840
(310) 555-5555

May 28, 20--

Pat Cummings
Senior Analyst
Any Corporation
1140 Main Street
Thousand Oaks, CA 91362

Dear Ms. Cummings:

Thank you for speaking with me on Friday regarding the Public Records Analyst position. I am convinced my experience and training would benefit a progressive firm such as yours.

Please let me reiterate my qualifications:

- Twelve years of professional experience as a Marine Information Specialist and Public Records Analyst.
- Skilled in working with automated and manual record management systems.
- Increased corporation's efficiency by 84 percent with development of broad-based management programs for electronic records.
- Regarded as a specialist in records management systems analysis.
- Conducted workshops and seminars explaining records management and all phases of its practices.

Again, I appreciate your time and consideration. Please contact me at the above address or phone number with any further questions. I look forward to your reply.

Sincerely,

Chris Smith

▶ Letter highlights candidate's significant accomplishments.

▶ Letter highlights candidate's management skills.

FOLLOW-UP LETTER (AFTER JOB INTERVIEW)
(Publisher's Assistant)

178 Green Street
Albuquerque, NM 87109
(505) 555-5555

January 20, 20--

Pat Cummings
Human Resources Director
Any Publication
1140 Main Street
Albuquerque, NM 87109

Dear Mr. Cummings:

I very much enjoyed talking with you today about the position of Publisher's Assistant. I was particularly interested in the position's variety of tasks, which would make the day's work challenging. My experience at Malkmus Press is an excellent foundation for the work required at *Any Publication*.

I was glad to be able to meet Mr. Poska, and have no doubt that I would be an excellent assistant to him. I recognize the importance of making his day more productive; I know I could help to do that.

I am looking forward to hearing from you next week. Thank you for taking the time out of your busy schedule to talk with me. I found it to be a rewarding afternoon.

Sincerely,

Chris Smith
cc: Mr. Poska

▶ Follow-up letter further illustrates candidate's suitability for available position.

▶ Closing reiterates candidate's gratitude to interviewer.

FOLLOW-UP LETTER (AFTER JOB INTERVIEW)
(Real Estate Salesperson)

178 Green Street
Camden, SC 29020

June 19, 20--

Pat Cummings
General Manager
Any Corporation
1140 Main Street
Hilton Head, SC 29928

Dear Ms. Cummings:

It is not very often that a job interview is a relaxing and pleasant experience, but I found our discussion to be precisely that. It has increased my interest in and enthusiasm for a position in real estate sales, as well as my confidence that I can do an outstanding job for Any Corporation.

As I explained, I have several years of successful experience in promoting and selling high-priced commercial properties to clients in the upper income bracket. I consider the sale of exclusive, residential properties to require the same capability as making effective presentations, conversing, and negotiating with decision-makers in upper economic levels. I am sure that I will, through my persistent efforts, meet mutual sales objectives.

Once again, my thanks for a fine interview and I hope that you feel as I do—that I am the right person for the position. Please contact me at the above address or at (803) 555-5555.

Sincerely,

Chris Smith

▶ Candidate uses opportunity to restate his/her interest in position.

▶ Follow-up letter should be no longer than one page.

FOLLOW-UP LETTER (AFTER JOB INTERVIEW)
(Recycling Manager)

178 Green Street
Warsaw, IN 46580
(219) 555-5555

December 10, 20--

Pat Cummings
Director
Any Corporation
1140 Main Street
Crane, IN 47522

Dear Mr. Cummings:

My time spent at Any Corporation yesterday was thoroughly enjoyable. Thank you for taking the time to discuss the position of Recycling Manager with me. After carefully reviewing its requirements, I have composed a brief list of my matching qualifications:

- Sixteen years of broad experience in recycling programs, recyclable materials, and spinoff industries using materials to manufacture products for industrial and consumer markets.
- Solid experience in sales, customer service, and customer relations.
- Ability to promote and/or market products or services provided or produced by related recycling industries.
- Skill as an accomplished communicator who can effectively work with individuals and groups in educational and/or sales environments.

I am very interested in joining Any Corporation in this capacity. I know I can meet and exceed your expectations.

I look forward to learning of your decision.

Yours sincerely,

Chris Smith

▶ Candidate uses opportunity to reiterate qualifications.

▶ Letter emphasizes achievements, and does not simply list job responsibilities.

FOLLOW-UP LETTER (AFTER JOB INTERVIEW)
(Restaurant Manager)

---

178 Green Street
Mobile, AL 35202
(205) 555-5555

August 17, 20--

Pat Cummings
Chief Executive Officer
Any Restaurant Franchise
1140 Main Street
Birmingham, AL 35201

Dear Ms. Cummings:
 I enjoyed speaking with you earlier this week. You were most helpful in describing the opportunities available at Any Company. And, as promised, an additional copy of my resume is enclosed for your consideration.
 As I mentioned during our conversation, I am confident my seventeen years of experience owning and operating a string of franchise restaurants would contribute substantially to the success and growth of your company. I offer a strong professional background that encompasses the full range of financial, legal, and operational responsibilities including personnel, property, and general operations management, advertising and promotion, community and public relations, and the financial details of administrative management.
 Again, thank you for the time and courtesy you and your associates extended toward me. On Tuesday, August 22, I will contact your office to review my candidacy.

Sincerely,

Chris Smith

Enc. Resume

▶ Candidate indicates time frame for follow-up contact.

▶ Enclosure line suggests candidate is a meticulous, detail-oriented professional.

FOLLOW-UP LETTER (AFTER JOB INTERVIEW)
(Retail Sales Associate)

178 Green Street
Gary, IN 46402
(219) 555-5555

February 1, 20--

Pat Cummings
Retail Sales Manager
Any Store
1140 Main Street
South Bend, IN 46626

Dear Mr. Cummings:

I want to thank you for meeting with me on January 27 regarding the position of Sales Associate. I enjoyed the opportunity to learn more about the responsibilities and opportunities available at Any Store.

I also want to reiterate my interest in the position. I feel confident that my seven years of acquired sales experience, combined with well-seasoned communication and interpersonal skills, would make me an ideal candidate for this position.

Thank you again. I look forward to hearing your final decision.

Sincerely,

Chris Smith

▶ Letter is short and to the point.

▶ Follow-up letter briefly reiterates relevant experience.

FOLLOW-UP LETTER (AFTER JOB INTERVIEW)
(Sales Representative)

178 Green Street
Metairie, LA 70001
(504) 555-5555

January 5, 20--

Pat Cummings
Regional Sales Supervisor
Any Airline
1140 Main Street
Baton Rouge, LA 70803

Dear Ms. Cummings:

I appreciate you taking the time to interview me for the position of Sales Representative with your organization. I found your discussion of the operational procedures at Any Airline, as well as your expectations of the sales staff, to be very informative and interesting. I am confident that, as a Sales Representative, I would make a strong contribution to your staff by increasing profits and expanding your market.

I would like to reiterate the qualifications I possess that would contribute directly to your organization:

- More than twelve years of broad-based experience in travel, hospitality, and retail environment industries.
- Positions in Air Travel ranging from Customer Service Representative to Director of Regional Sales.
- Extensive responsibility handling major corporate accounts on both domestic and international levels.

Again, thank you for taking the time to consider my candidacy. I look forward to learning of your final decision.

Sincerely,

Chris Smith

▶ Candidate refers to information received during interview.

▶ Letter focuses attention on candidate's major skills and accomplishments.

FOLLOW-UP LETTER (AFTER JOB INTERVIEW)
(Staff Accountant)

178 Green Street
Eugene, OR 97401
(503) 555-5555

July 24, 20--

Pat Cummings
Human Resource Manager
Any Corporation
1140 Main Street
Portland, OR 97204

Dear Mr. Cummings:

I would like to thank you for meeting with me on Friday regarding the Staff Accountant position. After considering your needs, as we discussed, I am even more convinced of my ability to make a valuable contribution to your firm.

For your consideration, I have taken the liberty of matching my qualifications with the requirements of the position offered:

Solid Accounting Background:
Experience in excess of five years with all facets of accounting, including financial statements, budgeting, payroll, and accounts receivable.

Business Office Operation:
Broad experience supervising personnel at all levels. Maintained excellent banking relationships.

Computer Experience:
Broad knowledge of accounting software and PC-based applications including Excel and Lotus 1-2-3. Experience with mainframe systems and payroll services.

If I can be of additional assistance, please do not hesitate to contact me. I am very eager to apply my skills to the successful ranks of your accounting team, and I look forward to learning of your final decision.

Yours truly,

Chris Smith

▶ Letter allows candidate follow-up opportunity to discuss his/her skills and accomplishments.

▶ Closing emphasizes candidate's enthusiasm for desired position.

FOLLOW-UP LETTER (AFTER JOB INTERVIEW)
(Talent Agent)

---

178 Green Street
Chandler, AZ 85244
(602) 555-5555

March 12, 20--

Pat Cummings
Personal Manager
Any Talent Agency
1140 Main Street
Carefree, AZ 85377

Dear Ms. Cummings:

Thank you for the courtesy you extended to me during a most pleasant meeting, and for the time you took, on my behalf, to arrange a meeting with Roger Fallings. I came away feeling that both sessions were most interesting and informative.

My discussion with Mr. Fallings was quite enlightening and, as I expressed in my recent letter to him, I was very impressed not only with the portfolio of artists/label signings he outlined but also the professional image of Any Talent Agency as a marketing firm.

Based on this information and the materials I came away with, it is quite evident to me that your firm can provide the challenging environment in which I function best, and I, in turn, would like to provide the experience and skills necessary to achieve our mutual goals.

Once again, my thanks for your assistance in setting up a most productive meeting. I am certainly interested in exploring the position of Talent Agent further.

With best regards,

Chris Smith
cc: Roger Fallings

▶ Follow-up letter demonstrates candidate's acquired company knowledge.

▶ Powerful adjectives, when used sparingly, ensure maximum impact.

FOLLOW-UP LETTER (AFTER JOB INTERVIEW)
(Teacher)

178 Green Street
Loganville, GA 30249
(404) 555-5555

April 23, 20--

Pat Cummings
Principal
Any Elementary School
1140 Main Street
Norcross, GA 30071

Dear Mr. Cummings:

I thoroughly enjoyed my afternoon at Any Elementary School and our interview for the sixth grade teaching position. Thank you for taking time out of your day to speak with me.

It was also a pleasure to meet Richard Morrison and to observe his classroom for an hour. His dedication to the children he teaches is evident, and I would be honored to instruct room 160 during his leave of absence.

Thank you again for inviting me to your school. I hope that your hiring decision will result in my returning to Any Elementary in the fall.

Sincerely,

Chris Smith
cc: Richard Morrison

▶ Candidate immediately reviews circumstances of most recent contact,

▶ Letter immediately expresses candidate's gratitude for the interview.

FOLLOW-UP LETTER (AFTER JOB INTERVIEW)
(Writer/Researcher)

---

178 Green Street
Middletown, CT 06457
(203) 555-5555

January 16, 20--

Pat Cummings
Staff Writer
Any Publications
1140 Main Street
Waterbury, CT 06723

Dear Ms. Cummings:

Thank you for the opportunity to meet with you again today. It was a pleasure to learn more about the position you have available and your goals for continuing the success of the *Inside Connecticut* publications.

I am very excited about the potential the Writer/Researcher position has to offer. I am confident that my skills, abilities, and interest would contribute to enhance the productivity of this publication.

I hope that you find me a qualified candidate for this position, and I would enjoy the opportunity to contribute to your organization. Thank you for your consideration, and I look forward to hearing your decision.

Sincerely,

Chris Smith

▶ Letter immediately restates position candidate interviewed for.

▶ Candidate uses opportunity to reiterate qualifications.

CHAPTER 23

INFORMATION REQUEST

Requests for information are formal requests directed to organizations or potential employers for assistance in your job-hunting research. Common inquiries include requests for membership listings, annual reports, company brochures, and alumni data. When writing an information request, job seekers should be brief and to the point.

In your cover letter, simply state who you are and ask politely for the information you are requesting. For example, "I am an experienced Paralegal searching for a list of firms specializing in international law," is sufficient. To ensure a timely reply, always enclose a self-addressed stamped envelope, if possible.

INFORMATION REQUEST
(Alumni Network)

178 Green Street
Jackson Center, OH 45334
(513) 555-5555

August 10, 20--

Pat Cummings
Director of Career Planning
Any University
1140 Main Street
Richmond, VA 23298

Dear Mr. Cummings:

I am a 20-- graduate of Any University, who has been employed in the social services industry for the last six years. Budgetary cuts within my local youth services agency have prompted me to begin searching for a new position in case management.

Does the University provide a network of alumni in my field? Or perhaps there is a local chapter of graduates I can contact? Gaining several new contacts in Ohio in particular would be a valuable asset to my job-hunting research.

Please forward a directory of names, or information on how to contact other professionals in social services. I have enclosed a self-addressed stamped envelope for your convenience. Thank you for your assistance.

Sincerely,

Chris Smith

▶ Candidate briefly introduces himself/herself to addressee.

▶ Citing reason for job search is optional.

INFORMATION REQUEST
(Annual Report)

178 Green Street
San Jose, CA 95134
(408) 555-5555

January 27, 20--

Pat Cummings
Director, Public Relations
Any Corporation
1140 Main Street
San Francisco, CA 94120

Dear Ms. Cummings:

I am currently investigating career opportunities in the San Francisco area. In the course of my research, I found Any Corporation to be an industry leader in accounting and financial planning.

Could you send me information concerning your services? I would be especially interested in an annual report and company roster. I have enclosed a self-addressed stamped envelope for your convenience.

I appreciate your attention to my request.

Sincerely,

Chris Smith

▶ Candidate briefly introduces himself/herself to addressee.

▶ Citing reason for job search is optional.

INFORMATION REQUEST
(Career Planning Services)

178 Green Street
Arlington Heights, IL 60004
(708) 555-5555

November 7, 20--

Pat Cummings
Director
Any Woman's Bureau
1140 Main Street
Chicago, IL 60603

Dear Mr. Cummings:

    I am an accomplished loan officer who is finding it very difficult to obtain gainful employment in my field. My resources in the Chicago area have been exhausted and relocation is not an option. In this respect, I would like to ask for your help.

    I would be very eager to participate in any career planning or placement services you might offer. Could you please send any relevant information concerning your programs and services to the above address? I have enclosed a self-addressed stamped envelope for your convenience.

    Many thanks for your assistance. I look forward to hearing from you.

Sincerely,

Chris Smith

▶ Candidate includes all information necessary for response.

▶ Candidate thanks addressee in advance for his/her assistance.

INFORMATION REQUEST
(Company Catalog)

---

178 Green Street
Washington, DC 20071
(202) 555-5555

March 25, 20--

Pat Cummings
Publisher's Assistant
Any Publisher
1140 Main Street
New York, NY 10108

Dear Ms. Cummings:

I am writing to inquire about Any Publisher. Please send me information regarding your company size and target markets, as well a catalog of your most recent publications.

I have enclosed a self-addressed stamped envelope for your convenience. Thank you for your attention.

Sincerely,

Chris Smith

▶ Letter briefly inquires about desired information.

▶ Candidate immediately states letter's purpose.

INFORMATION REQUEST
(Course Registration)

178 Green Street
Olympia, WA 98507
(206) 555-5555

May 30, 20--

Pat Cummings
Director, Continuing Education
Any Community College
1140 Main Street
Seattle, WA 98119

Dear Mr. Cummings:

A friend of mine recently completed a course at your college focusing on career planning and job-hunting techniques. I have been unemployed for several months and feel that I could benefit greatly from such instruction.

Is such a course being offered during the upcoming semester? Please send me information on enrollment costs, course dates and times, and whatever application materials need to be completed. I have enclosed a self-addressed stamped envelope for your convenience.

Thank you for your kind assistance.

Sincerely,

Chris Smith

▶ Candidate names basis for referral.　　　　▶ Information request is direct and concise.

INFORMATION REQUEST
(Grants Listing)

---

178 Green Street
Worcester, MA 01610
(508) 555-5555

April 13, 20--

Pat Cummings
Director
Any Research Agency
1140 Main Street
New York, NY 10017

Dear Ms. Cummings:

    I would like to request information on research projects currently being conducted at your agency in the area of molecular biology.

    I will complete a Doctor of Physiological Chemistry degree from Worcester Polytechnic Institute in May and am searching for a new research association. My doctoral thesis focused on DNA sequence analysis and S1 mapping.

    Do you possess a listing of all grants conferred in related areas within the last two years? Any information you could provide would greatly assist me in my search. For your convenience, I have enclosed a self-addressed stamped envelope.

    Thank you.

Sincerely,

Chris Smith

▶ Candidate briefly introduces himself/herself to addressee.

▶ Candidate thanks addressee in advance for his/her assistance.

INFORMATION REQUEST
(Industry Directory)

178 Green Street
Heston, KS 67062
(316) 555-5555

September 25, 20--

Pat Cummings
President
Chamber of Commerce
1140 Main Street
Topeka, KS 66612

Dear Mr. Cummings:

I am currently conducting a job search in greater Kansas and would appreciate any assistance you could provide me.

My interest is in the field of computer programming, and I am wondering if you publish a Directory of Members, especially listing the major employers in the technology industry.

If so, could you possibly send me this information? I have enclosed a self-addressed stamped envelope for your convenience.

Sincerely,

Chris Smith

▶ Candidate specifies geographic preference for job-search assistance.

▶ Candidate includes all information necessary for response.

INFORMATION REQUEST
(Industry Newsletter)

178 Green Street
St. Louis, MO 63146
(314) 555-5555

October 11, 20--

Pat Cummings
Executive Officer
Any Association of Legal Services
1140 Main Street
Dallas, TX 75201

Dear Ms. Cummings:

I am in the process of conducting a job search in the greater Dallas area, to which I will be relocating next month.

Does your association publish a newsletter listing employment opportunities for legal professionals? If so, I would appreciate a copy and have enclosed a self-addressed stamped envelope for your convenience. I would also be interested in any type of placement service you provide to members, and the application process for membership.

Thank you for your assistance. I look forward to learning more about the services your association offers.

Sincerely,

Chris Smith

▶ Citing reason for job search is optional.

▶ Candidate courteously includes a self-addressed stamped envelope.

INFORMATION REQUEST
(Membership Listing)

178 Green Street
Tempe, AZ 85285
(602) 555-5555

July 18, 20--

Pat Cummings
Director
Any Association of Zoologists
1140 Main Street
Denver, CO 80205

Dear Mr. Cummings:

I am writing to inquire if your association provides a mailing list of members.

I am currently conducting a job search within the Midwest, and would appreciate any assistance you could provide regarding member names, their titles, organizations, addresses, and other relevant information.

Please forward any appropriate materials to the above address in the self-addressed stamped envelope I have provided for your convenience.

I look forward to your return response.

Sincerely,

Chris Smith

▶ Information request is direct and concise.   ▶ Candidate immediately states letter's purpose.

INFORMATION REQUEST
(Subscription Information)

178 Green Street
Everett, MA 02149
(617) 555-5555
February 5, 20--

Pat Cummings
Subscription Manager
Careers in Psychology
1140 Main Street
Boston, MA 02118

Dear Ms. Cummings:

I heard about your publication through the National Association of Psychologists. I understand that *Careers in Psychology* publishes an "Advertised Openings" section at the close of each edition. Could you possibly send me information on subscription prices and an order form?

I have enclosed a self-addressed stamped envelope for your convenience. Thank you.

Sincerely,

Chris Smith

▶ Candidate names basis for referral.

▶ Letter briefly inquires about desired information.

CHAPTER 24

ADDRESS/PHONE NUMBER CHANGE

In today's tough market, the job-search process is often lengthy. If your personal situation has changed since your last correspondence (i.e., a geographical move, and/or phone number change), you must always inform a potential employer. Keep your correspondence brief. This is a courtesy letter, not a full-page reiteration of your qualifications.

To begin, remind the employer of the position you applied for, and when. State the change in your circumstances and thank the reader for his or her continued consideration. Be sure to send along another, updated copy of your resume for the employer's convenience. Remember that this letter is not optional. If you want to remain in the running, you must stay in touch. An employer will not waste time trying to track you down!

ADDRESS/PHONE NUMBER CHANGE
(Laboratory Assistant)

178 Green Street
Shawnee Hills, OH 43965
(216) 555-5555

May 31, 20--

Pat Cummings
Research Scientist
Any Medical Association
1140 Main Street
Chicago, IL 60605

Dear Mr. Cummings:

I am writing to inform you that I have moved to the above address and telephone listing. Enclosed is an updated copy of my resume for your files. I am looking forward to hearing more about any Laboratory Assistant positions you may have available.

Thank you for your time.

Sincerely,

Chris Smith

Enc. Resume

▶ Address-change letter is accompanied by updated resume.

▶ Letter immediately states candidate's purpose.

ADDRESS/PHONE NUMBER CHANGE
(Musician)

178 Green Street
Winston-Salem, NC 27113

July 21, 20--

Pat Cummings
Agent
Any Production Studio
1140 Main Street
Durham, NC 27702

Dear Ms. Cummings:

I recently received your kind letter in response to my audition for the lead guitarist position. Since you mentioned that you would be keeping my resume and demo tape on file, I wanted to let you know that, effective August 1, my address will change to the address listed above. My new phone number is (919) 555-5555.

Until August 1, you can reach me at (708) 444-4444 in Aurora, IL.

I am still very interested in the position, and look forward to hearing from you soon.

Sincerely,

Chris Smith

Enc. Resume

▶ Candidate uses opportunity to restate his/ her interest in position.

▶ Candidate notifies addressee of specific date when changes will go into effect.

ADDRESS/PHONE NUMBER CHANGE
(Pet Groomer)

178 Green Street
Baltimore, MD 21210
(410) 555-5555

September 21, 20--

Pat Cummings
Owner
Any Pet Salon
1140 Main Street
College Park, MD 20742

Dear Mr. Cummings:

Thank you for meeting with me last week regarding the Pet Groomer position. I remain very interested in this opportunity and, for this reason, wanted to alert you to my address change. Effective October 1, I can be reached at the address and telephone number shown above.

I look forward to hearing from you.

Sincerely,

Chris Smith

Enc. Resume

▶ Candidate is careful to specify date of address change.

▶ Candidate expresses gratitude for addressee's consideration.

ADDRESS/PHONE NUMBER CHANGE
(Staff Nutritionist)

178 Green Street
Tampa, FL 33681
(813) 555-5555

April 6, 20--

Pat Cummings
Human Resources Manager
Any Hospital
1140 Main Street
Ocala, FL 32674

Dear Ms. Cummings:

Last month, I sent my resume in response to your advertisement in the Monday, March 13, edition of the *Tampa Tribune* for Staff Nutritionist. I am still very interested in this or similar openings at Any Hospital.

For this reason, I would like to make you aware of an address change from my previous inquiry. I have since moved from Jacksonville to the address listed above. I have enclosed an updated resume for your convenience.

Thank you. I look forward to hearing from you in the future.

Sincerely,

Chris Smith

Enc. Resume

▶ Address-change letter should be brief and direct.

▶ Letter cites advertisement's specific publication and date.

ADDRESS/PHONE NUMBER CHANGE
(Wholesale Buyer)

178 Green Street
Greenbelt, MD 20770

February 23, 20--

Pat Cummings
Senior Buyer
Any Corporation
1140 Main Street
Landover, MD 20785

Dear Mr. Cummings:

I want to thank you for a pleasant and informative interview last week in reference to the Wholesale Buyer position. I enjoyed meeting with you and Richard Mayes and learning more about your department's successful track record of commercial negotiations.

I would now like to alert you to a change in my phone number. The new listing is (301) 555-5555. My address remains the same.

Please be assured of my continued interest. I have enclosed an updated copy of my resume and look forward to hearing your decision.

Sincerely,

Chris Smith
cc: Richard Mayes

Enc. Resume

▶ In addition to including address change, candidate reiterates interest in position.

▶ Candidate refers to all employees involved in interview process.

CHAPTER 25

THANK-YOU LETTER (FOR GOOD REFERENCE)

During the course of your job search it may be necessary to call upon personal and professional references to support your credentials. These people are are taking their time to do a favor for you and deserve your written thanks. In additional to acknowledging their kind assistance, thank-you letters allow you to stay in touch with important contacts. When Rick R. requested a reference from a former employer, he sent a timely letter of thanks. Six months later, when Rick needed another reference, that same employer was more than happy to help him out.

When writing your letter, you may want to remind the person why you needed the reference and the outcome of his or her efforts. Keep your comments brief and your tone polite.

THANK-YOU LETTER (FOR GOOD REFERENCE)
(Biomedical Researcher)

178 Green Street
Hanover, NH 03755
(603) 555-5555

March 4, 20--

Pat Cummings, Ph.D.
Department Head, Biology
Any University
1140 Main Street
Florham Park, NJ 07932

Dear Dr. Cummings:

   I understand that you recently provided Helmut Industries with a reference attesting to my research abilities. During my interview this morning, Fredrick Jonns praised my senior thesis as you described it. Thank you so much for your enthusiasm regarding my work.

   I believe that my interview at Helmut went well, and I will keep you posted when a decision is reached. I hope all is going well at the lab.

Sincerely,

Chris Smith

▶ Candidate begins letter by thanking addressee for good reference.

▶ Personalized tone reinforces candidate's familiarity with addressee.

THANK-YOU LETTER (FOR GOOD REFERENCE)
(Bookkeeper)

---

178 Green Street
Washington, DC 20016
(202) 555-5555

November 11, 20--

Pat Cummings
Bookkeeper
Any Corporation
1140 Main Street
Washington, DC 20001

Dear Mr. Cummings:

    Thank you so much for your great reference regarding my application for the Bookkeeping position at The Baldwin Company.

    I am pleased to report that I have been offered, and have accepted, the position. I appreciate your efforts on my behalf.

Sincerely,

Chris Smith

▶ Candidate informs addressee of application's outcome.

▶ Letter uses short sentences and common words.

THANK-YOU LETTER (FOR GOOD REFERENCE)
(Broker)

178 Green Street
Sidney, MT 59270
(406) 555-5555

April 26, 20--

Pat Cummings
Investment Broker
Any Corporation
1140 Main Street
Missoula, MT 59807

Dear Ms. Cummings:

I want to thank you for the excellent reference you provided Denmark Associates. With your generous help, I was offered a position as a Broker.

I am excited about this opportunity and I appreciate your assistance. I look forward to returning the favor.

Sincerely,

Chris Smith

▶ In closing, candidate offers to reciprocate addressee's generosity.

▶ Including telephone number is necessary in a cover letter.

THANK-YOU LETTER (FOR GOOD REFERENCE)
(Fashion Designer)

178 Green Street
Sandy, UT 84070
(801) 555-5555

February 23, 20--

Pat Cummings
Designer
The Brittney Collection
1140 Main Street
Ogden, UT 84401

Dear Mr. Cummings:

I would like to thank you for speaking to the design staff at Edge Fashions on my behalf. I appreciate your support of my work in fashion design.

I hope that the new spring collection is going well. I am very interested in seeing its premiere in late February.

Thank you again. I promise to keep in contact as my job search continues.

Sincerely,

Chris Smith

▶ In closing, candidate promises to keep addressee informed of job search progress.

▶ Candidate thanks addressee for his/her assistance in job search.

THANK-YOU LETTER (FOR GOOD REFERENCE)
(Government Intern)

---

178 Green Street
Albany, GA 31701
(912) 555-5555

November 29, 20--

Pat Cummings
Assistant to the President
Any University
1140 Main Street
Doraville, GA 30340

Dear Ms. Cummings:

    I am writing to express my thanks for your kind reference regarding my summer internship application. The selection committee at the State House informs me that you were contacted, and that you spoke highly of my work in the President's office.

    I will contact you in early January when my application is processed and I hear of the outcome. Once again, I am very grateful for your help.

Best wishes,

Chris Smith

▶ Candidate begins letter by thanking addressee for good reference.

▶ Candidate establishes when follow-up contact will take place.

THANK-YOU LETTER (FOR GOOD REFERENCE)
(Nurse)

178 Green Street
Mount Vernon, NY 10550
(914) 555-5555

April 14, 20--

Pat Cummings, R. N.
Nursing Administrator
Any Hospital
1140 Main Street
New York, NY 10001

Dear Mr. Cummings:

Kathy Mohagan at West Side Hospital mentioned that she contacted you as a reference and that you spoke highly of my work at Any Hospital.

Thanks so much for your assistance, Pat. Please let me know if I can do anything in return.

With best regards,

Chris Smith

▶ Good reference letter sometimes assumes an informal tone.

▶ Candidate includes only relevant information.

THANK-YOU LETTER (FOR GOOD REFERENCE)
(Retail Store Manager)

---

178 Green Street
Golden, CO 80401
(303) 555-5555

July 21, 20--

Pat Cummings
Manager
Any Clothing Store
1140 Main Street
Ft. Lauderdale, Fl 33310

Dear Ms. Cummings:

    I am happy to say that my job search has come to an end! Delightful Duds, the retail clothing chain headquartered in Colorado, has offered me a position as Assistant Branch Manager. I am arranging for a move to Golden within the next two weeks.

    Ms. Cummings, thank you so much for offering to act as a reference for my job search, and for all the assistance that you provided. Your support is greatly appreciated.

    Please keep in touch and let me know how things are going at the store. I have listed my new address and phone number above.

    I hope to hear from you soon.

Sincerely,

Chris Smith

▶ Candidate informs addressee of application's outcome.

▶ Closing encourages reader to respond to letter.

THANK-YOU LETTER (FOR GOOD REFERENCE)
(Surgeon)

---

178 Green Street
Santa Clara, CA 95054
(408) 555-5555

June 11, 20--

Pat Cummings, M.D.
General Surgeon
Any Hospital
1140 Main Street
Palo Alto, CA 94304

Dear Dr. Cummings:

Thank you for speaking to Dr. Griffin in support of my credentials. As you know, getting established in the medical community is not easy and I appreciate the confidence you have in my abilities.

I have since been called back to interview with the Board of Directors. I will keep you updated on my progress.

Thank you again for all your help.

Sincerely,

Chris Smith

▶ In closing, candidate promises to keep addressee informed of job search progress.

▶ Closing is brief and to the point.

THANK-YOU LETTER (FOR GOOD REFERENCE)
(Teacher)

178 Green Street
Triangle Park, NC 27709
(919) 555-5555

May 29, 20--

Pat Cummings
Principal
Any High School
1140 Main Street
Raleigh, NC 27695

Dear Mr. Cummings:

Thank you for agreeing to act as a reference for my teaching application at Martin Luther King High School. I greatly appreciated your assistance, Pat.

I have been offered the position, and have gladly accepted. I will be teaching two sections of remedial English and one special topics course in journalism. The principal has also asked me to act as faculty moderator for the school newspaper. My year should be very busy, yet also very enjoyable.

Enjoy the remainder of your summer vacation. I hope to see you at association meetings in the fall.

Sincerely,

Chris Smith

▶ Candidate thanks addressee for his/her assistance in job search.

▶ Good reference letter sometimes assumes an informal tone.

THANK-YOU LETTER (FOR GOOD REFERENCE)
(Technical Writer)

178 Green Street
Marshalltown, IA 50158
(515) 555-5555

January 3, 20--

Pat Cummings
Editor/Technical Writer
Any Corporation
1140 Main Street
Des Moines, IA 50303

Dear Ms. Cummings:

    While interviewing at McErney Associates yesterday, I was informed that you provided an excellent reference for me.

    Thank you for your kind words. My interview for the Technical Writer position with McErney resulted in an invitation for a second meeting, this time with the vice president of the company.

    I appreciate your assistance. Would you let me know when I may return the favor?

With best regards,

Chris Smith

▶ In closing, candidate offers to reciprocate addressee's generosity.

▶ Candidate includes only relevant information.

CHAPTER 26

THANK-YOU LETTER (FOR LETTER OF RECOMMENDATION)

Potential employers sometimes require written letters of recommendation to complete the application process. These letters may be written by previous employers or, for those with little professional experience, by college professors. Since this person gave of his or her time to assist you in your job search efforts, it is only courteous that you offer your written thanks. As a result, he or she may be more likely to remember you and to be willing to provide further assistance in the future should you require it.

Kim W., a recent college graduate, submitted a letter of recommendation from an English professor when applying for a proofreading position. Despite her lack of experience, Kim's letter attested to her superior writing and editing skills and greatly improved her candidacy.

THANK-YOU LETTER (FOR LETTER OF RECOMMENDATION)
(Accountant)

---

178 Green Street
Hobbs, NM 88240
(505) 555-5555

May 31, 20--

Pat Cummings
Account Manager
Any Corporation
1140 Main Street
Santa Fe, NM 87504

Dear Mr. Cummings:

    I appreciate the kind letter of recommendation you wrote to assist me in my job search. Yesterday, I received an offer to begin work as a Staff Accountant with Enstel and Yang. Your praise of my internship work at Any Corporation definitely contributed to my success.

    If there is anything I can do in return, please don't hesitate to contact me. Thank you again.

Sincerely,

Chris Smith

▶ Candidate begins letter by thanking addressee for recommendation.

▶ Candidate informs addressee of application's outcome.

THANK-YOU LETTER (FOR LETTER OF RECOMMENDATION)
(Art History Student)

178 Green Street
Washington, DC 20007
(202) 555-5555

September 6, 20--

Pat Cummings
Professor of Art History
Any College
1140 Main Street
Worcester, MA 01610

Dear Dr. Cummings:

    Knowing how busy you are with different projects, I really appreciate the time you took to write a recommendation for my graduate school applications. I have since received three letters of acceptance and I am confident that your letter contributed to my success.

    Again, thank you for your continued support. I will be sure to keep in touch as I pursue my degree.

Sincerely,

Chris Smith

▶ Recommendation letters are not restricted to job-search process.

▶ Letter is easy and quick to read, and only relevant details are included.

THANK-YOU LETTER (FOR LETTER OF RECOMMENDATION)
(Chemical Engineer)

---

178 Green Street
Medford, WI 54451
(715) 555-5555

October 29, 20--

Pat Cummings
Distinguished Professor of Chemistry
Any University
1140 Main Street
West Bend, MI 53095

Dear Dr. Cummings:

Thank you for your excellent recommendation for my job-search applications. I feel confident that your acknowledgment of my abilities will contribute to the strength of my candidacy.

I will keep you informed as the selection process comes to a close next week.

Sincerely,

Chris Smith

▶ Candidate begins letter by thanking addressee for recommendation.

▶ Candidate indicates time frame for follow-up contact.

THANK-YOU LETTER (FOR LETTER OF RECOMMENDATION)
(Human Resources Representative)

178 Green Street
Hesston, KS 67062
(316) 555-5555

April 3, 20--

Pat Cummings
Assistant Director, Career Services
Any University
1140 Main Street
Topeka, KS 66612

Dear Mr. Cummings:

    I received your letter of recommendation in this morning's mail. Thank you for your kind words, and the effort you extended to mail it to me before my interview on April 12.

    I am sure that your letter will greatly assist me in presenting myself as a qualified candidate for the Human Resources Representative position with Any Corporation. I will be sure to inform you of the outcome of my interview.

    Thank you again.

Sincerely,

Chris Smith

▶ Candidate confirms receipt of recommendation letter.

▶ Letter avoids abbreviations and slang.

THANK-YOU LETTER (FOR LETTER OF RECOMMENDATION)
(Restaurant Manager)

178 Green Street
Augusta, ME 04336
(207) 555-5555

July 1, 20--

Pat Cummings
Manager
Any Restaurant
1140 Main Street
Kennebunk, ME 04043

Dear Ms. Cummings:

Thank you so much for taking the time to write me a letter of recommendation for my job search. As you know, I had an interview for the Management Training Program with Fat Dickie's restaurant chain last week.

I have since been asked back for a second interview. I will keep you posted as to the outcome of my application.

Thank you again, Pat. I hope that everything is going well at the restaurant.

Sincerely,

Chris Smith

▶ Candidate thanks addressee for his/her assistance in job search.

▶ Personalized tone reinforces candidate's familiarity with addressee.

CHAPTER 27

THANK-YOU LETTER (FOR REFERRAL)

As we mentioned in Chapter 8, many jobs are found with the assistance of a networking contact or referral. Throughout your job search keep track of all your referrals, and be sure to send each one a personalized thank-you note for his or her assistance. In your letter, briefly express sincere gratitude for the referral's help on your behalf. If his or her efforts directly led to a positive outcome for you, let the person know. It may be advantageous to offer your return assistance. In any event, sending a thoughtful thank-you letter is an invaluable career move. If you take the time to acknowledge someone's assistance on your behalf, he or she may be more likely to help you again in the future.

THANK-YOU LETTER (FOR REFERRAL)
(Acquisitions Editor)

178 Green Street
Twodot, MT 59085
(406) 555-5555

October 14, 20--

Pat Cummings
Managing Editor
Any Press
1140 Main Street
Chicago, IL 60605

Dear Ms. Cummings:

    I am happy to inform you that I have just accepted an offer for employment as an Acquisitions Editor at Dandelion Publishing Group. I should begin work there the first week of November.

    I would like to thank you for all of your help during my job search, specifically for putting me in touch with Ninona Punder at Dandelion's billings office.

    If there is ever anything that I can do for you, please do not hesitate to contact me. Yours was a favor I shall not soon forget.

    Again, many thanks and best wishes.

Sincerely,

Chris Smith

▶ Candidate indicates willingness to return favor.

▶ Letter demonstrates referral's positive results.

THANK-YOU LETTER (FOR REFERRAL)
(Bank Manager)

178 Green Street
Tacoma, WA 98477
(206) 555-5555

June 4, 20--

Pat Cummings
Assistant Vice-President
Any Savings Bank
1140 Main Street
Spokane, WA 99201

Dear Mr. Cummings:

I received your letter dated June 2, regarding my initial inquiry for job placement assistance. Thank you so much for providing several names for contact purposes.

I have enclosed another copy of my resume. Please feel free to pass it on to any colleagues searching for a new Branch Manager.

Once again, your assistance is greatly appreciated.

Sincerely,

Chris Smith

Enc. Resume

▶ Candidate requests that attached resume be forwarded.

▶ Candidate expresses appreciation to addressee for referral.

THANK-YOU LETTER (FOR REFERRAL)
(Computer Application Programmer)

178 Green Street
Lamar, CO 81052
(719) 555-5555

March 5, 20--

Pat Cummings
Vice-President of Human Resources
Any Corporation
1140 Main Street
Englewood, CO 80111

Dear Ms. Cummings:

Thank you for taking several moments to assist me with my job search last week. Although you indicated there were no vacancies at Any Corporation, the referrals you provided have been extremely useful.

In fact, I have been able to schedule two informational interviews with computer applications programmers at EMP and Stide and Huston. I hope to learn more about specific projects and innovations to keep me updated on industry trends.

Thank you again for your time. I am still very interested in pursuing opportunities at Any Corporation. I have enclosed another resume for your review should you anticipate a need for someone with my qualifications.

With best regards,

Chris Smith

Enc. Resume

▶ Closing informs addressee that resume is enclosed.

▶ Candidate informs addressee of referral's outcome.

THANK-YOU LETTER (FOR REFERRAL)
(Fitness Instructor)

---

178 Green Street
Van Nuys, CA 91411
(818) 555-5555

February 16, 20--

Pat Cummings
General Manager
Any Fitness Center
1140 Main Street
Van Nuys, CA 91411

Dear Mr. Cummings:

I am writing to thank you for your wonderful referral to Dani Johnson at Body Beautiful. When I called Ms. Johnson two weeks ago while on a visit to California, she invited me to interview for a Fitness Instructor position. Yesterday, she called to offer me the job!

Thank you so much for your assistance. If there is ever anything I can do in return, please do not hesitate to contact me. I have listed my new address and phone number above, effective March 1.

With best regards,

Chris Smith

▶ Candidate is careful to specify date of address change.

▶ Letter expresses usefulness of referral.

THANK-YOU LETTER (FOR REFERRAL)
(Medical Assistant)

178 Green Street
Richardson, TX 75083
(214) 555-5555

September 19, 20--

Pat Cummings, M.D.
Ophthalmologist
Any Hospital
1140 Main Street
Irving, TX 75038

Dear Dr. Cummings:

Although I regret that you did not have the need for an Assistant, I would like to thank you for referring me to Dr. Wilson in Richardson. In my meeting with him on Tuesday, I received several other contact names.

Should you become aware of any opportunities for a Medical Assistant, please let me know. I am still very interested in gaining hands-on experience before I begin graduate study in the field.

I hope to speak with you in the future.

Sincerely,

Chris Smith

▶ Candidate indicates specific referral who assisted him/her in job search.

▶ Candidate asks for addressee's further job-search assistance.

THANK-YOU LETTER (FOR REFERRAL)
(Nurse)

---

178 Green Street
Ketchikan, AK 99901
(907) 555-5555

August 26, 20--

Pat Cummings, R.N.
Nursing Administrator
Any Hospital
1140 Main Street
Anchorage, AK 99515

Dear Mr. Cummings:

Thank you for the wonderful referrals you provided for my job search. I called Michelle Peters as you suggested yesterday and was invited to interview for a nursing position.

Several of the other contacts you gave me very graciously offered their personal insight and/or further referrals.

I will keep you informed as my search for a position progresses. Thank you again.

Sincerely,

Chris Smith, R.N.

▶ Candidate indicates specific referral who assisted him/her in job search.

▶ After name, candidate includes professional title.

THANK-YOU LETTER (FOR REFERRAL)
(Photographer)

---

178 Green Street
Monroe, LA 71209
(318) 555-5555

November 1, 20--

Pat Cummings
Director
Any Corporation
1140 Main Street
New Orleans, LA 70130

Dear Ms. Cummings:

    Thank you for referring me to the resources available at the New Orleans Photography Center and especially to its Director, Peter O'Sullivan. The job listings he provided have been invaluable for my career search. I have since made numerous contacts and have scheduled two interviews.

    Thank you again and I would appreciate any assistance you might provide in the future.

Sincerely,

Chris Smith

▶ Candidate shares the results of a referral.

▶ Candidate asks for addressee's further job-search assistance.

THANK-YOU LETTER (FOR REFERRAL)
(Publicist)

---

178 Green Street
Anniston, AL 36202
(205) 555-5555

March 4, 20--

Pat Cummings
Director of Public Relations
Any Heart Association
1140 Main Street
Montgomery, AL 36102

Dear Mr. Cummings:

I enjoyed meeting with you on Friday at your Montgomery headquarters. Your work for the Heart Association seems very rewarding.

I would also like to thank you for referring me to Beth Holmes at the Committee on Social Awareness. My discussions with both Ms. Holmes and yourself have definitely confirmed my interest in public relations work for a non-profit organization.

Good luck with your new television campaign.

Sincerely,

Chris Smith

▶ Candidate immediately thanks addressee for pleasurable meeting.

▶ Candidate refers to information received during interview.

THANK-YOU LETTER (FOR REFERRAL)
(Software Technician)

---

178 Green Street
El Segundo, CA 90245
(310) 555-5555

December 22, 20--

Pat Cummings
Software Engineer
Any Corporation
1140 Main Street
Chicago, IL 60605

Dear Ms. Cummings:

    I am pleased to inform you that my job search has come to a successful conclusion. Yesterday, I was offered a position with L. GWA PO Inc., a Japanese software conglomerate that has recently opened a branch office in Los Angeles. I am delighted to be able to participate once again in the fast-paced world of computer technology.

    I would like to extend my warmest thanks to you for your encouragement and the excellent referrals you provided for my job search. The next time you visit Los Angeles, please be sure to let me know.

    Happy holidays and best wishes for the New Year.

Sincerely,

Chris Smith

▶ Letter demonstrates referral's positive results.

▶ Candidate indicates willingness to return a favor.

THANK-YOU LETTER (FOR REFERRAL)
(Teacher)

178 Green Street
Wilmington, DE 19803
(302) 555-5555

January 4, 20--

Pat Cummings
Principal
Any School
1140 Main Street
New Castle, DE 19720

Dear Mr. Cummings:

Thank you for putting me in touch with Steven Simons and the Wilmington School District. A number of opportunities were available there and I was fortunate enough to be offered a fourth-grade teaching position.

Again, I appreciate your assistance.

Sincerely,

Chris Smith

▶ Candidate informs addressee of referral's outcome.

▶ Candidate expresses appreciation to addressee for referral.

CHAPTER 28

THANK-YOU LETTER (AFTER INFORMATIONAL INTERVIEW)

Thank-you letters need not be restricted to potential employers. Everyone who assists you in any way during the course of your job search deserves written thanks for his or her efforts. Even in the case of an informational interview, a letter is required. Although you are not asking for a job, you have taken a person's time and should thank that person accordingly.

Consider Susan B., who wrote a timely thank-you letter to an industry executive with whom she met for an informational interview. The executive heard about an appropriate employment opportunity several weeks later and, impressed by Susan's considerate attention to detail, recommended her for the job!

THANK-YOU LETTER (AFTER INFORMATIONAL INTERVIEW)
(Art Designer)

178 Green Street
Radnor, PA 19087
(215) 555-5555

March 25, 20--

Pat Cummings
Art Director
Any Advertising Agency
1140 Main Street
York, PA 17402

Dear Ms. Cummings:

It was a pleasure meeting with you on Tuesday and learning about your work at Any Agency. I especially enjoyed watching you design the promotional sample for Smithe and Resin's new copier.

After spending the day with an art team at an advertising agency, I am sure that I want to pursue a career in art design. I will be sure to contact you upon graduation to follow up on your offer of placement assistance.

Good luck in your future endeavors at Any Agency, and thank you again for your kindness.

Sincerely,

Chris Smith

▶ Letter outlines candidate's course of action resulting from informational interview.

▶ Candidate establishes when follow-up contact will take place.

THANK-YOU LETTER (AFTER INFORMATIONAL INTERVIEW)
(Benefits Coordinator)

178 Green Street
Doraville, GA 30340
(404) 555-5555

March 21, 20--

Pat Cummings
Director
Any Corporation
1140 Main Street
Bainbridge, GA 31717

Dear Mr. Cummings:

The information you offered me yesterday concerning opportunities for Benefits Coordinator was most helpful. Thank you for the time you took to meet with me.

Prior to our discussion, I had no idea of the diverse opportunities someone with my experience could explore. I have already begun to research some of the companies you suggested and I am hopeful that I will find a position in the near future.

Again, thank you. Your assistance was most helpful.

Sincerely,

Chris Smith

▶ Candidate expresses gratitude for new knowledge obtained during informational interview.

▶ Letter clarifies candidate's career goals.

THANK-YOU LETTER (AFTER INFORMATIONAL INTERVIEW)
(Child Psychologist)

178 Green Street
Toast, NC 27049
(919) 555-5555

July 26, 20--

Pat Cummings
Associate Professor of Psychology
Any University
1140 Main Street
Chicago, IL 60605

Dear Ms. Cummings:

It was a pleasure seeing you again today. I appreciate the time you found in your busy schedule to meet with me.

It was interesting to learn about the use of interactive toys and models in child psychology. I have already been to the library to borrow the book by Leonard Finn that you recommended so highly. I am looking forward to reading about his ideas on child's play before the latency period.

As per your suggestion, I will be contacting Mr. Hayden within the next few days to set up an appointment. I will let you know how everything is progressing after I have met with him.

Again, thank you for your assistance. You will hear from me soon.

Sincerely,

Chris Smith

▶ Candidate highlights pertinent information discussed during interview.

▶ Letter expresses candidate's continued commitment to field of interest.

THANK-YOU LETTER (AFTER INFORMATIONAL INTERVIEW)
(High School Administrator)

178 Green Street
Grand Forks, ND 58201
(701) 555-5555

January 18, 20--

Pat Cummings
Assistant Superintendent
Any School System
1140 Main Street
Fargo, ND 58107

Dear Mr. Cummings:

I wish to thank you for speaking with me yesterday concerning my interest in obtaining a high school administration position. I have revised my resume according to your suggestions, and have enclosed a copy for your review.

I am planning to contact Daniel Conner as you suggested, and have already scheduled a meeting with Stephanie Birch with Bismarck Public Schools. I am sure these meetings will prove to be as insightful and enjoyable as our discussion.

I will keep you informed as my search progresses. If you think of any additional information that might be helpful, or contacts with whom I should speak, please do not hesitate to give me a call. Thank you again.

Sincerely,

Chris Smith

Enc. Revised resume

▶ Letter refers to updated resume attached.

▶ In closing, candidate promises to keep addressee informed of job search progress.

THANK-YOU LETTER (AFTER INFORMATIONAL INTERVIEW)
(Hotel Clerk)

178 Green Street
Newark, DE 19713
(302) 555-5555

September 18, 20--

Pat Cummings
General Manager
Any Inn
1140 Main Street
Wilmington DE 19801

Dear Ms. Cummings:

Thank you for being so gracious with your time on Friday. I found your description of current trends in hospitality very enlightening.

I appreciate the suggestions you made regarding my resume. I think the new version is much improved. I have enclosed a copy in the hope that you will feel free to make any further comments or to share it with anyone in the industry you feel might be interested in someone with my qualifications.

As per your suggestion, I will contact James Moller with Daylight Hotels this week. Again, thank you for all of your assistance.

Sincerely,

Chris Smith

Enc. Revised resume

▶ Candidate requests addressee's future consideration for available opportunities.

▶ Candidate expresses appreciation to addressee for referral.

THANK-YOU LETTER (AFTER INFORMATIONAL INTERVIEW)
(Marketing Assistant)

178 Green Street
Exeter, NH 03833
(603) 555-5555

December 5, 20--

Pat Cummings
Director, Marketing
Any Corporation
1140 Main Street
Keene, NH 03431

Dear Mr. Cummings:

I appreciate your taking a few moments to meet with me yesterday. I realize that, as Marketing Director of a large support staff, your time is very valuable.

After visiting Any Corporation and hearing about your experiences, I am even more confident that I would like to pursue a career in marketing upon my graduation next year. In the meantime, I will follow your advice on course selection and summer employment.

Thank you again for your time, Mr. Cummings. I plan to keep in touch throughout the year, as my job-hunting strategy becomes more focused.

Sincerely,

Chris Smith

▶ Candidate highlights aspects of informational interview that were especially helpful.

▶ Letter is short and to the point.

THANK-YOU LETTER (AFTER INFORMATIONAL INTERVIEW)
(Mechanical Engineer)

178 Green Street
Norman, OK 73019
(405) 555-5555

November 4, 20--

Pat Cummings
Mechanical Engineer
Any Corporation
1140 Main Street
Tulsa, OK 74102

Dear Ms. Cummings:

    Thank you for speaking with me yesterday regarding your work at Any Corporation. Your new design plans for coal-fired boilers sound very exciting. I wish you much success.

    As you know, I have been considering a shift in focus within the field of mechanical engineering. Although I have enjoyed my training in costing and standards, my greatest interest has always been transportation. I am sure your insight will help me determine the smoothest transition into this new line of design.

    As you requested, I will keep in contact as I pursue new opportunities.

Sincerely,

Chris Smith

▶ Interest in new field is emphasized.

▶ Letter refers to specific topics discussed during informational meeting.

THANK-YOU LETTER (AFTER INFORMATIONAL INTERVIEW)
(Meteorologist)

178 Green Street
New Rochelle, NY 10801
(914) 555-5555

April 22, 20--

Pat Cummings
Meteorologist
Any Television Station
1140 Main Street
Dobbs Ferry, NY 10522

Dear Mr. Cummings:

I thoroughly enjoyed my day at Any Television Station. Thank you for allowing me to assist you as you tracked the day's weather.

As a result of our time together, I now have a much better understanding of the immense time and skill necessary to interpret even the smallest piece of data. I certainly agree that broadcast forecasting is not just a "glamorous" profession.

I am still very interested in pursuing a career as a Meteorologist. I am sure the knowledge I gained from observing you at work will prove valuable in my studies.

Best of luck in your future endeavors.

Sincerely,

Chris Smith

▶ Candidate immediately thanks addressee for pleasurable meeting.

▶ Candidate cites specific information covered during the interview.

THANK-YOU LETTER (AFTER INFORMATIONAL INTERVIEW)
(Occupational Therapist)

---

178 Green Street
Downers Grove, IL 60515
(708) 555-5555

May 14, 20--

Pat Cummings
Occupational Therapist
Any Rehabilitation Center
1140 Main Street
Evanston, IL 60201

Dear Ms. Cummings:

Thank you for taking the time to meet with me on Friday. I enjoyed meeting you and learning about the programs offered at Any Rehabilitation Center.

Our discussion definitely strengthened my interest in occupational therapy as a career path. I am planning to take your advice and enroll in a graduate program in September. In the interim, I will contact the referrals you provided to inquire about summer internship possibilities.

Thank you again for your assistance.

Sincerely,

Chris Smith

▶ Candidate thanks addressee for time extended.

▶ Candidate confirms his/her commitment to field of interest.

THANK-YOU LETTER (AFTER INFORMATIONAL INTERVIEW)
(Social Worker)

178 Green Street
Jacksonville, FL 32256
(904) 555-5555

February 22, 20--

Pat Cummings
Social Worker
Any Agency
1140 Main Street
Clearwater, FL 34625

Dear Mr. Cummings:

Speaking with you yesterday was very helpful. Thank you for rearranging your busy schedule to offer your advice and experience.

Although I am considering a career in social work, I had not given thought to working exclusively with young adults until I visited your offices. The Early Intervention Program you direct is an amazing venture and I am now very interested in becoming involved with an agency that targets at-risk youth.

Currently, I am applying for an internship with the Jacksonville Teen Clinic. I will keep you updated on the status of my application.

Thank you again for the interest you expressed in my career search. I appreciate your help.

Sincerely,

Chris Smith

▶ Letter outlines candidate's course of action resulting from informational interview.

▶ Candidate confirms his/her commitment to field of interest.

CHAPTER 29

RESURRECTION LETTER

If several weeks or even months have passed since you mailed your initial inquiry and you have not received a response, your candidacy may be in need of a jump start. Sending a resurrection letter informs an employer of your continued interest in, and suitability for, a desired position. Begin by reminding the employer of your initial reason for writing. Next, reiterate your most relevant qualifications, and stress your desire to join the employer's organization. Be sure to close your letter by clearly stating how and when you can be reached, and enclose another resume for the employer's convenience.

Writing for a response to your application can be frustrating sometimes. But even if you feel this way, don't let it show in your resurrection letter. A hiring manager is more likely to respond to a polite, upbeat letter.

RESURRECTION LETTER
(Advertising Assistant)

178 Green Street
Parsippany, NJ 07054
(201) 555-5555

July 18, 20--

Pat Cummings
Senior Vice-President
Any Advertising Agency
1140 Main Street
Ridgefield Park, NJ 07660

Dear Ms. Cummings:

Congratulations on your recent write-up in the *Advertising Advantage*. Your innovative marketing campaign for Hi-land Products sounds very intriguing. I have no doubt it will be a huge success.

I am writing to inquire about joining your talented staff. You may recall that I sent a resume in response to the position of Advertising Assistant that appeared in the *New York Times* on May 28, 20--. Although I did not receive a response, I continue to believe that I would make a valuable addition to Any Advertising Agency. If any additional entry-level openings occur, I hope you will again consider my qualifications. I have enclosed a copy of my resume for your convenience.

Sincerely,

Chris Smith

Enc. Resume

▶ Introduction expresses candidate's knowledge of firm.

▶ Resurrection letters generally include another copy of the applicant's resume.

RESURRECTION LETTER
(Assistant Regional Manager)

178 Green Street
Beaverton, OR 97005

July 22, 20--
Pat Cummings
Hiring Director
Any Retail Chain
1140 Main Street
Portland, OR 97204

Dear Mr. Cummings:

   Since first sending my application materials in response to your advertisement for an Assistant Regional Manager, my interest in the position has continued to strengthen. In an effort to convince you of my capability to handle its responsibilities, I have prepared a comparison of my qualifications and the requirements you outlined in the July 14 edition of the *Oregonian*:

Your requirements:

 * At least five years' experience in retail management.
 * Ability to effectively deal with employees at all levels.
 * Extensive experience in problem resolution.
 * Knowledge of all aspects involved in retail operations.

My qualifications:

 * More than ten years working in all areas of store management for several nationally recognized chains.
 * Selection by current management for a highly sensitive headquarters position that requires the ability to deal with field and management personnel.
 * As Problem Resolution/Communication Coordinator, my responsibilities encompass troubleshooting and conflict resolution in field operations affecting a 500-unit retail chain and several distribution centers.
 * Experience handling issues pertaining to sales, distribution, personnel performance, corporate communications, customer satisfaction, and corporate image.

   I am a well-organized, innovative assistant capable of providing management with efficient follow-through and skillful support. My interest in contributing to the growth of Any Retail Chain is sincere, and I look forward to hearing from you regarding my candidacy. I can be contacted either at home at (503) 555-5555, or confidentially at my current employer at (503) 444-4444.

Sincerely,
Chris Smith
Enc. Resume

▶ Specific contributions emphasize candidate's achievements and problem-solving abilities.

▶ Candidate assures potential employer that his/her interest in position has strengthened since first inquiry.

RESURRECTION LETTER
(Bank Administrator)

178 Green Street
Knoxville, TN 37921

May 27, 20--

Pat Cummings
Division Head, Banking
Any Corporation
1140 Main Street
Memphis, TN 38103

Dear Ms. Cummings:

Approximately two weeks ago, I submitted a resume for your review and consideration. As I have yet to receive a response, I am enclosing a second copy of my resume in the event that my previous correspondence did not reach your desk.

As I previously indicated, I am interested in securing a new position with a company where I can apply the knowledge I have acquired during my employment and academic endeavors, along with my exceptional management and administrative skills, to a career in the banking industry.

I have seven years of experience in the marketing and management divisions of two banks, where I have been involved in every aspect of the administration, planning, and direction necessary for success. Accordingly, I feel I could become a valuable asset to your company.

I would appreciate the opportunity for a personal interview at your convenience. Please contact me at (615) 555-5555 during the day or at (615) 444-4444 during evening hours.

Thank you for your time. I look forward to hearing from you soon.

With best regards,

Chris Smith
Enc. Resume

▶ Candidate immediately states date of initial application.

▶ Candidate uses closing to suggest possibility of interview.

RESURRECTION LETTER
(Billings Clerk)

178 Green Street
Elko, NV 89801

July 27, 20--

Pat Cummings
Billings Supervisor
Any Corporation
1140 Main Street
St. Louis, MO 63121

Dear Mr. Cummings:

Thank you for considering my resume. Your time is greatly appreciated.

I wanted to inform you that I will be relocating to Missouri in the near future. My plans are to further my career in the accounting and finance industry in the St. Louis area. As an added note, I am taking a computer spreadsheet course, which should further enhance my skills in the field.

I am still very interested in progressing my career at Any Corporation and would ask for your consideration regarding any future availabilities. Until my move to St. Louis on August 28, I can be reached by phone at (702) 555-5555. I will call again in six weeks' time.

Thank you again. I look forward to speaking with you.

Sincerely,

Chris Smith
Enc. Resume

▶ Letter details continuing education completed since initial application.

▶ Candidate establishes when follow-up contact will take place.

RESURRECTION LETTER
(Business Manager)

178 Green Street
Dunnellon, FL 34433
(813) 555-5555

November 14, 20--

Pat Cummings
President
Any Corporation
1140 Main Street
Fort Lauderdale, FL 33301

Dear Ms. Cummings:

In a letter dated October 23, David Kipler, Group Vice-President of your company, indicated that my resume and cover letter regarding employment with Any Corporation were being forwarded to you for review.

To date, I have not received a response from you and so I am enclosing the attached resume to reiterate my interest in becoming a member of your firm.

I offer seven years of experience and the qualifications that could be well utilized in a managerial position with Any Corporation. In addition to a Master's degree in Business Administration, I offer experience in relevant positions ranging from Product Management Trainee to Clinical Service Manager of five company-operated, out-patient treatment centers.

I am very much interested in the opportunity to join Any Corporation and look forward to hearing from you.

Sincerely,

Chris Smith
cc: David Kipler

Enc. Resume

▶ Resurrection letter is often used to reiterate candidate's qualifications.

▶ Four short paragraphs is the ideal length for a resurrection letter.

RESURRECTION LETTER
(Commercial Photographer)

178 Green Street
Baltimore, MD 21214
(301) 555-5555

April 20, 20--

Pat Cummings
Hiring Manager
Any Advertising Agency
1140 Main Street
Wheaton, MD 20902

Dear Mr. Cummings:

After speaking with your colleague Michael Hicks yesterday, I understand that your search for a Commercial Photographer is still on. Please allow me to express my continued interest in the position, and to reiterate my qualifications.

In addition to having graduated from the two-year program in all aspects of professional photography offered at the Ziegler School of Photography, I have additional training in graphic and liberal arts, as well as in related areas of advertising and promotion. Examples of my work are currently on exhibit in London, Toronto, New York, Miami, and Los Angeles. My experience also includes diverse aspects of both large and small business operations, which is of great value in selecting subjects and backgrounds appropriate to commercial advertising and promotion, or personnel and public relations.

I have assembled a portfolio of relevant work that I think would be of interest to you. Will you be scheduling interviews soon? I would like to show you my work and express my sincere interest in producing quality products for Any Advertising Agency.

I will follow up this inquiry with a phone call next week. In the interim, I have enclosed another copy of my resume for your review. Thank you very much for your time.

Sincerely,

Chris Smith
cc: Michael Hicks

Enc. Resume

▶ Candidate includes training pertinent to his/her field of interest.

▶ Stating that a portfolio is available on request is beneficial for certain positions.

RESURRECTION LETTER
(Computer Programmer)

178 Green Street
St. Paul, MN 55164
(612) 555-5555

September 2, 20--

Pat Cummings
Systems Programmer
Any Corporation
1140 Main Street
Minnetonka, MN 55343

Dear Ms. Cummings:

Thank you for taking the time to speak with me in late May regarding entry-level computer programming positions at Any Corporation. Although you indicated that a hiring freeze is in effect at your firm for the immediate future, I would like to update you on several newly acquired skills I think you might find of interest.

During the past summer at the University of Minnesota's Studio, I worked as both a Programmer and Research Assistant, successfully meeting a variety of technical and intellectual challenges. As a Programmer, I learned Windows programming and implemented improvements to ConStats, a Windows-based package of educational software designed to teach introductory statistics. As a Research Assistant, I used the SAS statistical language to produce analyses regarding how ConStats was being used by students. This work resulted in a published journal article, an excerpt of which I have enclosed.

I am very interested in applying my newly acquired skills to your organization and would appreciate the opportunity to talk with you in a personal interview. Thank you for your time and consideration.

Sincerely,

Chris Smith

Enc. Resume
Excerpt from *Computer Programmer*, December 20--

▶ In effort to improve his/her candidacy, applicant mentions newly acquired skills.

▶ Technical language is acceptable when it relates to candidate's field.

RESURRECTION LETTER
(Correctional Officer)

178 Green Street
Butte, MT 59404
(406) 555-5555

January 18, 20--

Pat Cummings
Director of Security
Any State Prison
1140 Main Street
Billings, MT 59104

Dear Mr. Cummings:

    This letter regards a resume I faxed to your offices on Thursday, January 4. I have yet to hear if the Correctional Officer position has been filled, and I want you to know that I remain very interested in this opportunity. Please feel free to contact me with any additional questions concerning my qualifications.

    An additional copy of my resume is enclosed for your review.

Sincerely,

Chris Smith

Enc. Resume

▶ Candidate indicates date and nature of initial inquiry.

▶ Closing informs addressee that resume is enclosed.

RESURRECTION LETTER
(Field Engineer)

178 Green Street
Jacksonville, FL 32207
(904) 555-5555

March 17, 20--

Pat Cummings
Vice-President, Field Engineering
Any Corporation
1140 Main Street
Ocala, FL 32672

Dear Ms. Cummings:

Thank you very much for talking with me regarding the Field Engineer position for which I applied on March 4. I am glad to hear that the position is still available.

I would like to ask that you keep me in mind when considering candidates for the position. To that end, I have highlighted several of my most relevant experiences and accomplishments:

- More than six years of experience with an internationally recognized field engineering corporation.
- Maintenance and operation of UNIVAC and special purpose computers.
- Implementation of various cost-reduction programs resulting in savings of more than $150,000 in the form of reduced labor and material costs.
- Supervision and coordination of all field engineering functions.

I look forward to hearing from you to schedule an interview. Thank you for your time.

Sincerely,

Chris Smith

Enc. Resume

▶ In a resurrection letter, bullets provide a unique way to restate relevant qualifications.

▶ Closing encourages reader to respond to letter.

RESURRECTION LETTER
(Foreign Language Teacher)

178 Green Street
Hapeville, GA 30354
(404) 555-5555

May 20, 20--

Pat Cummings
Principal
Any High School
1140 Main Street
Warner Robins, GA 31088

Dear Mr. Cummings:

On May 6, I wrote to you regarding your anticipated opening for a Foreign Language Teacher to be filled in the 20-- school year.

In the event that my original application has gone astray, I have enclosed a packet containing an additional professional profile, proof of certification, and letters of recommendation.

I would appreciate the opportunity to sit down with you face-to-face to further discuss my qualifications and enthusiasm for this or other available positions. I will follow up this letter with a phone call in a few days.

Sincerely,

Chris Smith

Enc. Professional profile
Proof of certification
Letters of recommendation

▶ Candidate encloses all pertinent information, in the event that first inquiry was not received.

▶ In addition to initial position sought, candidate expresses willingness to fill other suitable positions.

RESURRECTION LETTER
(Freelance Copyeditor)

178 Green Street
Shawnee, OK 74801

November 21, 20--

Pat Cummings
Vice-President, Editorial
Any Publishing Company
1140 Main Street
Oklahoma City, OK 73125

Dear Ms. Cummings:

Please allow me to update my previous letter to Any Publishing Company with regard to your search for a Freelance Copyeditor. You will notice my resume has been revised to include more relevant experience.

My most recent assignment for Southwestern Publications involved copyediting material intended for educational television and geared for a high school audience. Many of my line corrections, as well as my editorial suggestions for improvements, were used in final versions. My work was found to be thorough, precise, and consistent.

I also edited a Master's thesis in Business Administration for a Langston University student. The text needed many corrections in spelling, grammar, usage, and style. I offered suggestions for improving content as well. The feedback on my work was quite good.

You may also recall that I am proficient in desktop publishing. I print high-quality resumes, essays, and formal letters for clients who contract for my services. I apply strict standards to all of my work and operate in a thoroughly professional manner.

Thank you again, Ms. Cummings, for considering me as a potential freelancer for Any Publishing Company. I will be following up this letter with a phone call in the next few weeks. Should you wish to contact me sooner, my phone number is (405) 555-5555. I look forward to communicating with you in the near future.

Sincerely,

Chris Smith

Enc. Resume

▶ In a resurrection letter, candidate restates relevant skills and accomplishments regarding position.

▶ Telephone number included in closing is omitted in return address.

RESURRECTION LETTER
(Fundraising Coordinator)

178 Green Street
Idaho Falls, ID 83415
(208) 555-5555

August 15, 20--

Pat Cummings
Senior Vice-President
Any Corporation
1140 Main Street
Boise, ID 83706

Dear Mr. Cummings:

I am very much interested in becoming your new Fundraising Coordinator.

In the weeks since I mailed my original application, I have given much thought to how closely my skills meet your requirements. I am confident that I could make a significant contribution to your corporation.

Knowing that you prefer not to take telephone inquiries, and that mail sometimes does not reach its destination, I am taking this opportunity to provide you with an additional copy of my resume, and to ask for your continued consideration of my candidacy.

If you have questions regarding my resume or the skills I would bring to this position, I would appreciate an opportunity to talk with you.

Sincerely,

Chris Smith

Enc. Resume

▶ Candidate assures potential employer that his/her interest in position has strengthened since first inquiry.

▶ Position applied for is clearly and immediately defined.

RESURRECTION LETTER
(Jewelry Designer)

178 Green Street
Norman, OK 73019
(405) 555-5555

August 7, 20--

Pat Cummings
Owner
Any Jewelry Maker
1140 Main Street
Edmond, OK 73034

Dear Ms. Cummings:

On July 12, I sent a resume and small portfolio of samples as my application for a position as a Designer for your jewelry line. Since I have not received a response, I can only assume that you did not have any suitable vacancies at that time. Please allow me to highlight my qualifications again, as I remain very interested in joining your design team:

- Eight years of experience as a model maker and designer for several prominent competitors in the jewelry industry.
- Honors graduate of the National School of Jewelry Design, including an award for outstanding achievement.
- Three years of additional, diverse experience as a Customer Service Representative in the jewelry industry.

Would it be possible to meet with you next week to discuss your needs and present several examples of my past design work? I will call you on Friday to schedule a time that is convenient for you.

Thank you for your continued consideration. I hope that our future discussions will result in our working together.

Sincerely,

Chris Smith

Enc. Resume

▶ Phrasing request in question form is a strong closing.

▶ Candidate immediately states date of initial application.

RESURRECTION LETTER
(Physical Therapist)

178 Green Street
Somerville, MA 02145
(617) 555-5555

November 16, 20--

Pat Cummings
Rehabilitation Coordinator
Any Clinic
1140 Main Street
Mansfield, MA 02048

Dear Mr. Cummings:

In a letter dated August 12, I expressed my interest in securing a staff position as a Physical Therapist at Any Clinic. Although I realize that there may not have been any suitable availabilities at that time, I have enclosed a second resume for continued consideration.

Since my initial application, I have been working on an independent research project while continuing my job search. My study evaluated back and shoulder strength of athletes suffering from tendinitis and bursitis. Last week, my results were accepted for publication with the *National Journal of Rehabilitation*.

I have enclosed an excerpt of my article for your review. I hope this strengthens my candidacy for a position at Any Clinic. I would welcome the chance to meet with you should any opportunities for a Physical Therapist become available.

Sincerely,

Chris Smith

Enc. Resume
Excerpt from journal article manuscript

▶ Publications are impressive and add weight to cover letter.

▶ Letter provides additional information not stated in initial inquiry.

RESURRECTION LETTER
(Purchasing Agent)

178 Green Street
Peoria, IL 61643
February 22, 20--

Human Resource Director
Any Corporation
P.O. Box 7777
Alton, IL 62002

Dear Human Resources Director:

    I am writing this letter to follow up on the resume I sent you on February 7. I am very interested in talking with you about the Purchasing Agent position. If you have any questions please do not hesitate to call me anytime at (309) 555-5555.

    I have enclosed another resume for your consideration.

    Thank you for your time.

Sincerely,

Chris Smith

Enc. Resume

▶ Candidate indicates date and nature of initial inquiry.

▶ Candidate invites addressee to respond to inquiry since specific employer is unknown.

RESURRECTION LETTER
(Radio Announcer)

178 Green Street
New Rochelle, NY 10801
January 4, 20--

Pat Cummings
Production Manager
Any Radio Station
1140 Main Street
Garden City, NY 11530

Dear Mr. Cummings:

Last week, I spoke with your assistant, Linda McMillian, regarding the initial resume and demo tape I sent as application for the On-Air Announcer position you have available. Although Ms. McMillian could not confirm whether you had had the chance to review my materials, she did inform me that the position is still available.

I would like to take this opportunity to express my continued interest in becoming an Announcer at Any Radio Station. Since I moved to New York three years ago, I have listened to and admired your station's broadcasts. I would love to contribute to the success of what Radio NY considers to be "Westchester's Best News Station."

As your newest Announcer, I would bring almost thirteen years of experience in diverse areas of AM and FM announcing, newscasting, and audio production, including current responsibility for a regular on-air shift with WJBF AM (1170), New Rochelle, New York.

I have enclosed another copy of my resume and tape. After you have reviewed these materials, I would like to arrange a meeting to further discuss the position. I can be reached at (914) 555-5555.

I look forward to speaking with you.

Sincerely,

Chris Smith

Enc. Resume
Demo tape

▶ Letter incorporates company knowledge into discussion of qualifications.

▶ In a resurrection letter, candidate restates relevant skills and accomplishments regarding position.

RESURRECTION LETTER
(Sales Representative)

---

178 Green Street
Yuma, AZ 85365
(602) 555-5555

November 7, 20--

Pat Cummings
Vice-President of Industrial Relations
Any Corporation
1140 Main Street
Helena, MT 59601

Dear Ms. Cummings:

On October 3, I sent you a letter expressing my interest in a position in professional sales and enclosed my resume for your review. As of today, I have not received a response and I am writing again to reiterate my interest in becoming a member of your sales staff.

My objective is to remain in the health care field with a company that is consistently developing, marketing, and promoting products to help those with chronic diseases. I would like to re-emphasize my education, clinical experience as a medical student, and practical experience in both medical research and direct patient care. Each of these experiences has given me the skills and sincerity to introduce and sell health care products, equipment, instruments, and services to medical professionals and administrators.

I have taken the liberty of enclosing a second copy of my resume. I am free to relocate and/or travel. I hope to hear from you so that I will have the opportunity to convince you that I have the qualifications and motivation to effectively represent your company.

Thank you again for reviewing my application materials. I look forward to your return response.

Sincerely,

Chris Smith

Enc. Resume

▶ Candidate thanks potential employer for consideration of initial inquiry.

▶ Discussion details how candidate's qualifications will benefit potential employer.

RESURRECTION LETTER
(Sanitation Inspector)

178 Green Street
Conshohocken, PA 19428
(215) 555-5555
May 23, 20--

Pat Cummings
Chief Inspector
Any Office
1140 Main Street
Lewisburg, PA 17837

Dear Mr. Cummings:

I am writing to express my continued interest in the position of Sanitation Inspector advertised in the May 8 edition of the *Express-Times*.

In the event that you did not receive my original mailing, I have enclosed a second copy of my resume for your consideration. I feel that this position provides the ideal opportunity to apply my thirteen years of experience in the public health and safety industry. I am confident that, given the opportunity, I would be readily able to effectively maintain your strict inspection standards.

I would be happy to further discuss my qualifications for this position in a personal interview. I am available at your convenience, and look forward to hearing from you.

In the interim, be assured of my enthusiasm and competence.

Sincerely,

Chris Smith

Enc. Resume

▶ Resurrection letters generally include an additional resume.

▶ Follow-up letter confirms candidate's enthusiasm for desired position.

RESURRECTION LETTER
(Shipping/Receiving Expediter)

178 Green Street
Anchorage, AK 99502
(907) 555-5555

April 17, 20--

Pat Cummings
Supervisor
Any Company
1140 Main Street
Fairbanks, AK 99701

Dear Ms. Cummings:

This letter follows a resume I mailed to your offices last Monday. I am very interested in the Shipping/Receiving Expediter position you advertised in the Sunday, April 9, edition of the *Anchorage Daily News*.

Please note that I offer twelve years of experience with The Alpha Corporation as an Expediter. In this capacity I enter packing slips, invoices, and other material control information into a highly specialized computer system, identify package contents and compare them to packing slips, schedule daily deliveries of incoming traffic, and create and implement an inventory system.

I am confident I can make an immediate contribution to Any Company. If you have any questions, I can be reached at the address and telephone number above.

Thank you for your consideration and I look forward to hearing from you.

Sincerely,

Chris Smith

Enc. Resume

▶ Resurrection letter is often used to reiterate candidate's qualifications.

▶ Closing invites addressee to inquire about additional information.

RESURRECTION LETTER
(Social Worker)

178 Green Street
Baltimore, MD 21218
(301) 555-5555

June 1, 20--

Pat Cummings
Director
Any Agency
1140 Main Street
Landover, MD 20785

Dear Mr. Cummings:

Please accept this updated version of my application materials for the Social Worker position. I remain very interested in this opportunity and my revised resume is enclosed for your consideration.

Recently, I worked as an Intern at the Baltimore Community Center. My responsibilities included intake, evaluation, and treatment of individuals, couples, and families in a medical and social service setting. The experience also entailed volunteering at the Andrew T. Ferris Children's Clinic two days a week, where my primary duties included the diagnostic evaluation and treatment of children, adolescents, adults, and families, as well as investigation of care and protection petitions within a multidisciplinary team.

I hope these experiences strengthen my candidacy for the position. I look forward to your reply.

Sincerely,

Chris Smith

Enc. Resume

▶ Letter provides additional information not stated in initial inquiry.

▶ Activities highlight candidate's involvement in local community.

RESURRECTION LETTER
(Staff Accountant)

178 Green Street
Parsippany, NJ 07054

August 4, 20--

Pat Cummings
Director of Human Resources
Any Corporation
1140 Main Street
New York, NY 10019

Dear Ms. Cummings:

Last year I spoke with Susan Rutter, the Director of Human Resources with your Chicago office, about the possibility of working within that division of Any Corporation as a Staff Accountant.

Since that conversation, I have relocated to the New York area. Consequently, I would like to continue my application process with Any Corporation through your office. I have enclosed a resume for your consideration.

I graduated from the University of Chicago in May with a Bachelor's degree in Accounting and Economics. Both my education and my internship at Gunn and Millstreet have adequately prepared me to begin a career in the corporate arena, and I am very eager to apply this experience to a position at Any Corporation.

I would be happy to further outline my capabilities and learn more about your prestigious training program during the course of a personal interview. I can be reached at the above address or by phone at (201) 555-5555. I look forward to your reply.

Sincerely,

Chris Smith

Enc. Resume

▶ Letter details continuing education completed since initial application and follows up on a previous contact in another office of the same firm.
▶ Candidate clearly expresses eagerness to work for specific employer.

RESURRECTION LETTER
(Systems Analyst)

178 Green Street
Schenectady, NY 12305

March 2, 20--

Pat Cummings
Supervisor
Any Company
1140 Main Street
Olympia, WA 98505

Dear Mr. Cummings:

Last week I interviewed with Matthew Pratt at Pisces Data Systems, Inc. for a Systems Analyst position. While there were no such positions available with his firm at this time, Mr. Pratt knew of several openings at Any Corporation and he therefore took the liberty of faxing my resume to your attention. I am unsure if you actually received the information so I have enclosed an additional copy. I am very interested in opportunities at Any Company.

Allow me to review my qualifications:
- Set up the interfacing of a mini-computer to a PC in order to archive daily receipts onto optical disks.
- Created a device driver for a new disk system, and developed a new operating system to handle the new driver.
- Qualified all of Devlin software onto a new computer system.
- Built a new method of handling orders within the system.
- Rewrote accounts receivable program system to handle long-term notes.

I will contact your offices this coming Wednesday (March 8) to discuss how my skills can benefit your company. If you have any further questions before this time, please feel free to call me at (508) 555-5555.

Sincerely,

Chris Smith

Enc. Resume

▶ In a resurrection letter, bullets provide a unique way to restate relevant qualifications.

▶ Candidate encloses all pertinent information, in the event that first inquiry was not received.

RESURRECTION LETTER
(Telemarketer)

---

178 Green Street
Grace City, OH 58445
(216) 555-5555

February 19, 20--

Hiring Manager
P.O. Box 7777
Kent, OH 44242

RE: Advertisement in the February 2 edition of the *Sun Newspaper*

Dear Hiring Manager:

    Please consider this letter as a follow-up inquiry regarding my resume sent on February 4, 20-- with regard to the telemarketing position.

    Should the advertised position still be available, I would be very interested in discussing my qualifications with you in a personal interview. As the enclosed copy of my resume reflects, I have a proven track record of selling and closing capabilities as a Telemarketer. Last year, I independently generated more than $1.5 million in sales for my employer through cold-calling techniques. I would like to apply the same successful telemarketing abilities to your firm.

    When can we meet for an interview?

Sincerely,

Chris Smith

Enc. Resume

▶ Job descriptions indicate how candidate contributed to his/her previous employers.

▶ In closing, candidate specifically requests interview.

RESURRECTION LETTER
(Translator)

---

178 Green Street
New Haven, CT 06511
(203) 555-5555

May 23, 20--

Pat Cummings
Director
Any Program
1140 Main Street
Meriden, CT 06450

Dear Mr. Cummings:

Three months ago, I applied for a Translator position with Any Program. I am aware that you hire sporadically depending on the needs of your clients and, for this reason, I am enclosing an updated resume for your review. If any positions are currently available, I hope you will consider my qualifications.

As you may recall, I have a working knowledge of written and spoken Japanese, as well as the following relevant experience:

- Served as liaison between Japanese diplomats and the Japanese-American relations group, and with the Japanese press during the prime minister's visit to New England in September 20--.
- Translated correspondence and filed inquiries from the Japanese population in the Hartford business community.
- Designed and circulated posters, banners, and invitations in order to introduce the Japanese community to New England.
- Organized travel itineraries for Japanese officials visiting the New England area.

I would welcome the opportunity to discuss how my background can benefit your program. I will contact your offices early next week to arrange a mutually convenient meeting time.

Thank you for your consideration.

Sincerely,

Chris Smith

Enc. Resume

▶ Letter stresses candidate's foreign language skills and international exposure.

▶ In addition to initial position sought, candidate expresses willingness to fill other suitable positions.

RESURRECTION LETTER
(Typist)

178 Green Street
Gaithersburg, MD 20879
(301) 555-5555

March 3, 20--

Pat Cummings
Executive Hiring Officer
Any Corporation
1140 Main Street
Potomac, MD 20854

Dear Ms. Cummings:

On February 15, I faxed my resume to your office. To date, I have not received a response, but I want you to know that I remain very interested in the typing position. If it has not been filled, I would welcome the opportunity to discuss this job opportunity with you. If, however, the position has been filled, I would appreciate your input as to how I might further my job search with Any Corporation. I have enclosed a SASE for your convenience.

I am also enclosing another copy of my resume with references, in the hopes I might be considered for any other opportunities that may become available in the future.

Thank you for your time.

Sincerely,

Chris Smith

Enc. Resume
References
SASE

▶ Candidate encloses all pertinent information, in the event that first inquiry was not received.

▶ Closing is straightforward and concise.

CHAPTER 30

RESPONSE TO REJECTION

A well-written thank-you note, mailed within one or two days of receiving notice of rejection, makes a positive statement. Admittedly, this technique is less widely used than other thank-you letters, but it can be equally effective as a means of opening doors to other opportunities. When Danny P. was turned down for a position as Publicity Director, he quickly wrote his interviewer a letter which expressed his disappointment at not being offered the job, but also his thanks for the company's consideration of his qualifications. Impressed by his initiative, the interviewer provided Danny with several contact names to assist in his ongoing job search.

When writing your letter, be sure to emphasize your continuing interest in being considered for future openings, and always be careful to use an upbeat tone. Although you may be disappointed at not receiving an offer and still consider yourself the best candidate for the job, you should never imply that you don't respect the employer's hiring decision.

RESPONSE TO REJECTION
(Administrative Assistant)

178 Green Street
Shawnee, OK 74801
(405) 555-5555

February 27, 20--

Pat Cummings
President
Any Corporation
1140 Main Street
Oklahoma City, OK 73101

Dear Mr. Cummings:

Thanks to you and your enthusiastic staff for all the help offered me while visiting your offices last week. Although I was not selected for the Administrative Assistant position, I would appreciate detailed feedback on how to improve my candidacy for future openings at Any Corporation. Yours is a team I hope to someday join. I hope you will let me know what I can do to achieve this goal.

Again, thank you for your consideration. I look forward to your response.

Sincerely,

Chris Smith

▶ Letter expresses candidate's continued interest in working for the company.

▶ Candidate requests addressee's return response.

RESPONSE TO REJECTION
(Architect)

178 Green Street
Middletown, RI 02840
(401) 555-5555

July 10, 20--

Pat Cummings
President
Any Firm
1140 Main Street
Providence, RI 02912

Dear Ms. Cummings:

Again, thank you for meeting with me last week to discuss the opportunities for Architects at Any Firm. I admire the innovative work you and your staff produce and, although I was not chosen for the position, I would like to be considered for upcoming projects.

I have enclosed an additional copy of my resume for your files. Thank you for your attention and I hope to hear from you in the near future.

Sincerely,

Chris Smith

Enc. Resume

▶ Candidate refers to attached resume in closing.

▶ Candidate recalls enjoyable interview process.

RESPONSE TO REJECTION
(Assistant Editor)

178 Green Street
White Plains, NY 10604
(914) 555-5555

July 1, 20--

Pat Cummings
Editor
Any Publication
1140 West 43rd Street
New York, NY 10036

Dear Mr. Cummings:

Once again, I would like to thank you for affording me the chance to interview for the Assistant Editor position with *Any Publication*. Although I am disappointed I was not selected for the position, I enjoyed meeting with you and your staff and learning more about your company.

I am still interested in opportunities with *Any Publication* and would appreciate it if you would keep me in mind for future openings in either your magazine or book divisions. Thank you again for your consideration.

Sincerely,

Chris Smith

▶ Candidate begins letter by thanking addressee for previous consideration.

▶ Closing thanks addressee in advance for attention.

RESPONSE TO REJECTION
(Counselor)

178 Green Street
Wadesboro, NC 28170
(704) 555-5555

September 5, 20--

Pat Cummings
Head Counselor
Any Center
1140 Main Street
Charlotte, NC 27706

Dear Ms. Cummings:

Thank you for meeting with me last Friday regarding your current vacancy. Although I regret not being chosen for the Counselor position, I found the interview process very informative.

Please note that I have applied for a Master's degree in Social Work program to begin in January of 20--. I would be very interested in pursuing the field work required for my M.S.W. degree in a counseling capacity at Any Center.

I will contact you again in the future to inquire about suitable opportunities.

Thank you again for your consideration.

Sincerely,

Chris Smith

▶ Letter provides additional information not stated in initial inquiry.

▶ Type of position desired is clearly stated.

RESPONSE TO REJECTION
(Telemarketer)

---

178 Green Street
Ontario, OR 97914
(503) 555-5555

March 3, 20--

Pat Cummings
Human Resources Director
Any Corporation
1140 Main Street
Albany, OR 97321

Dear Mr. Cummings:

As per receipt of your letter dated March 1, I understand that your search for a Telemarketing Professional has come to an end. Although I am disappointed that I was not chosen for the position, I appreciate your taking the time to interview me. I was impressed by both Any Corporation's products and its friendly staff.

I am still very interested in applying for any current or anticipated availabilities at Any Corporation. I have enclosed another copy of my resume for your convenience. I hope you will consider my qualifications in the future.

I look forward to speaking with you again.

Sincerely,

Chris Smith

Enc. Resume

▶ Candidate relays enthusiasm for future opportunities.

▶ Candidate refers to information received during interview.

CHAPTER 31

WITHDRAWAL FROM CONSIDERATION

If you must withdraw your application from consideration at any point in the hiring process, it is best to inform the employer in writing. This will establish you as a courteous individual worthy of consideration should you reapply for a position in the future. In general, a withdrawal letter should be concise. You may or may not choose to include the reason for your withdrawal, but if you do, phrase it briefly and in positive terms.

WITHDRAWAL FROM CONSIDERATION
(Coach)

178 Green Street
Orono, ME 04473
(207) 555-5555

October 12, 20--

Pat Cummings
Head Coach
Any High School
1140 Main Street
Portland, ME 04104

Dear Ms. Cummings:

Thank you for the time you spent with me last week discussing coaching opportunities. I enjoyed meeting both you and the players. You have a great team.

As we discussed, my most recent experience has been with college-level teams and yesterday I was offered an excellent opportunity at the University of Maine. Although I am confident I would have enjoyed working with your players, I must withdraw from consideration.

Again, thank you and best of luck in the upcoming season.

Sincerely,

Chris Smith

▶ Candidate may include a brief explication when withdrawing from consideration.

▶ Candidate immediately thanks addressee for pleasurable meeting.

WITHDRAWAL FROM CONSIDERATION
(Firefighter)

178 Green Street
Decatur, IL
(217) 555-5555

December 12, 20--

Pat Cummings
Captain
Any Fire Department
1140 Main Street
Palos Heights, IL 60455

Dear Mr. Cummings:

Last week I met with you to discuss your opening for a Firefighter. I was very impressed by the team of people working at Any Fire Department and the facility itself was one of the most technologically advanced I have seen.

Although I am convinced I would have enjoyed the position, I must withdraw my candidacy. My family and I have decided to relocate and the move will take us out of state.

Thank you again and best wishes.

Sincerely,

Chris Smith

▶ Withdrawal letter is brief and to the point.

▶ Language is straightforward and understandable.

WITHDRAWAL FROM CONSIDERATION
(Freelance Textbook Editor)

178 Green Street
Boca Raton, FL 33486
(407) 555-5555

August 22, 20--

Pat Cummings
Vice-President, Promotion
Any Corporation
1140 Main Street
Pensacola, FL 32520

Dear Ms. Cummings:

On August 8, I responded to your advertisement in the *Florida Times-Union* for a Freelance Textbook Editor.

I am not aware whether this position has been filled, but I would like to inform you that I no longer wish to be considered. I have accepted an offer from Holden Press to work as Project Manager on a new series of elementary grammar textbooks.

This new position was offered on a contractual basis, to last three months. At the end of that period, I will no doubt be seeking other freelance opportunities. Should your company need a freelance editor for similar projects in the future, I would appreciate your consideration.

Sincerely,

Chris Smith

▶ Candidate indicates date and nature of initial inquiry.

▶ Letter expresses candidate's continued interest in working for the company.

WITHDRAWAL FROM CONSIDERATION
(Hairstylist)

178 Green Street
Carthage, MS 39051
(601) 555-5555

June 4, 20--

Pat Cummings
Owner
Any Boutique
1140 Main Street
Jackson, MS 39205

Dear Mr. Cummings:

I would like to express my appreciation for the time you extended to me during our interview on May 30 for the Hairstylist position. I have rarely seen such a friendly and enthusiastic staff, and your customers certainly seem satisfied with your work!

Although the position sounds wonderful, I am writing to withdraw my name from consideration. Since our meeting, my current employer has offered me a promotion that I cannot turn down. I hope my decision does not hinder your hiring process; I know that whomever you chose will prove to be an excellent Hairstylist.

Once again, thank you for your consideration.

Sincerely,

Chris Smith

▶ Follow-up letter thanks addressee for enjoyable interview.

▶ Candidate apologizes for inconvenience to potential employer.

WITHDRAWAL FROM CONSIDERATION
(Legal Assistant)

178 Green Street
Ann Arbor, MI 48108
(313) 555-5555

October 9, 20--

Pat Cummings
Principal
Any Law Firm
1140 Main Street
Sterling Heights, MI 48314

Dear Ms. Cummings:

I enjoyed meeting with you over lunch on Friday to discuss the possibility of my working as a part-time Legal Assistant with your firm. Your knowledge about the legal field and description of your own experiences were very insightful. Any Law Firm sounds like an ideal environment in which to gain the kind of experience I am looking for.

Unfortunately, I must withdraw my candidacy to assist you this fall. As you know, I am completing my law degree, and my schedule next semester does not permit the flexibility that the position would demand.

Thank you for the assistance you graciously extended. I hope that we can work together in the future.

Sincerely,

Chris Smith

▶ Letter expresses candidate's appreciation for addressee's consideration.

▶ Candidate refers to information received during interview.

WITHDRAWAL FROM CONSIDERATION
(Nurse's Aide)

178 Green Street
Denver, CO 80239
(303) 555-5555

March 11, 20--

Pat Cummings, R.N.
Nursing Director
Any Hospital
1140 Main Street
Stratford, CT 06497

Dear Mr. Cummings:

I regret to inform you that I am withdrawing my application from the pool of applicants for the Nurse's Aide position. An abrupt change in my personal situation has made relocation to your area impossible at the present time.

I wish you the best of luck as your search continues.

Sincerely,

Chris Smith

▶ When withdrawing from consideration, providing a specific reason is optional.

▶ Letter immediately states candidate's purpose.

WITHDRAWAL FROM CONSIDERATION
(Preschool Instructor)

178 Green Street
Newnan, GA 30265
(404) 555-5555

December 12, 20--

Pat Cummings
Owner
Any Preschool
1140 Main Street
Macon, GA 31297

Dear Ms. Cummings:

I would like to thank you for taking the time to interview me last Thursday for the part-time Preschool Instructor position. It was a pleasure meeting you and Jennifer Hedge, as well as the wonderful children you have the opportunity to work with.

As I mentioned during our conversation on Thursday, my prime interest is in obtaining full-time teaching work. Therefore, I have decided to accept a position as a Pre-Kindergarten Teacher in an elementary school near my home. Although I would have enjoyed working with your fine staff, I feel that this position provides an ideal opportunity for me to pursue my goals.

I have no doubt that you will find a qualified instructor to fill your vacancy, as you manage an excellent developmental facility for children. Thank you again for considering my candidacy.

Best of luck in your future endeavors.

Sincerely,

Chris Smith
cc: Jennifer Hedge

▶ Candidate may include a brief explication when withdrawing from consideration.

▶ Candidate refers to all employees involved in interview process.

WITHDRAWAL FROM CONSIDERATION
(Regional Sales Manager)

178 Green Street
Kennelworth, NJ 07033
(201) 555-5555

July 1, 20--

Pat Cummings
Human Resources Director
Any Corporation
1140 Main Street
New Brunswick, NJ 08933

Dear Mr. Cummings:

   As you may recall, I spoke with you over the phone several weeks ago regarding the status of my application for the Regional Sales Manager position. Thank you for the time you extended to inform me of the hiring process.

   While I understand that you are still in the process of sorting through resumes, I wanted to notify you that I no longer wish to be considered as an applicant. I have just accepted another offer for a similar position.

   I wish you the best of luck in your search for a qualified candidate.

Sincerely yours,

Chris Smith

▶ Letter expresses candidate's appreciation for addressee's consideration.

▶ Follow-up letter confirms candidate's enthusiasm for desired position.

WITHDRAWAL FROM CONSIDERATION
(Systems Analyst)

---

178 Green Street
Melville, NY 11754
(516) 555-5555

February 13, 20--

Pat Cummings
Custom Products Engineer
Any Corporation
1140 Main Street
Cleveland, OH 44112

Dear Ms. Cummings:

It was a pleasure meeting with you and touring your corporate headquarters last week. Thank you for extending me the invitation to fly out to Ohio; I thoroughly enjoyed my first stay in Cleveland.

During my visit, I was continually impressed by your innovations in product development and testing. Your organization's reputation is certainly well deserved.

Unfortunately, I feel I must withdraw from further consideration for the Systems Analyst position. After thoroughly weighing my options, I have decided that it is not in the best interest of my family to relocate at this time. I apologize for the seemingly sudden nature of my decision; I hope that I have not caused too much inconvenience.

Congratulations on your continued success. I wish you all the best in the future.

Sincerely,

Chris Smith

▶ Candidate apologizes for inconvenience to potential employer.

▶ Follow-up letter demonstrates candidate's acquired company knowledge.

WITHDRAWAL FROM CONSIDERATION
(Travel Agent)

178 Green Street
Lexington, MA 02173
(617) 555-5555

December 12, 20--

Pat Cummings
President
Any Travel Agency
1140 Main Street
Allston, MA 02134

Dear Mr. Cummings:

I enjoyed meeting with you yesterday to discuss the Travel Agent position. The prospect of working with you and your staff in such a fast-paced environment was very exciting.

However, after much thought, I have decided to withdraw my candidacy. The extensive travel the position involves is not well suited to my present situation.

Again, thank you for your consideration and best of luck with your search.

Sincerely,

Chris Smith

▶ When withdrawing from consideration, providing a specific reason is optional.

▶ Withdrawal letter is brief and to the point.

CHAPTER 32

REJECTION OF OFFER

If you decide to reject an employment offer, it is always a good idea to inform the employer in writing. Even if you rejected the offer over the phone, you should confirm your decision with a formal letter. Begin by thanking the interviewer for both the offer and the time extended to your candidacy. Stating a reason for your rejection is optional. Above all, keep your letter upbeat—you never know if you might have reason to reapply to this company in the future!

REJECTION OF OFFER
(Archivist)

178 Green Street
Rogers, AR 72757
(501) 555-5555

May 22, 20--

Pat Cummings
Executive Director
Any University Library
1140 Main Street
Little Rock, AR 72211

Dear Ms. Cummings:

I received your letter dated May 20, and would like to thank you for offering me the Archivist position at Any University Library.

Although the prospect of working with such a prestigious reference collection is very enticing, I must decline your offer. I have accepted a position assisting a local historian on a book project. Since this opportunity requires only a part-time commitment, I feel it is better suited to my personal situation.

You manage a wonderful facility, Ms. Cummings. I am confident that you will have no trouble finding a professional eager to join your staff.

Best regards,

Chris Smith

▶ When rejecting an offer, providing a reason is optional.

▶ Candidate indicates type of employment desired.

REJECTION OF OFFER
(Assistant Art Director)

178 Green Street
Rupert, ID 83350
(208) 555-5555

May 15, 20--

Pat Cummings
Art Director
Any Corporation
1140 Main Street
Chicago, IL 60605

Dear Mr. Cummings:

I would like to use this opportunity to thank you for taking the time to meet with me last week.

However, after careful thought and consideration, I must decline your tempting offer for the position of Assistant Art Director. I have decided that my interests and career goals lie elsewhere at this point in my life. Perhaps our needs will coincide at a later date.

Thank you again. Best wishes for your continued success.

Sincerely,

Chris Smith

▶ Letter clarifies candidate's career goals and leaves the door open for future contacts.

▶ Candidate's explication of rejection is concise.

REJECTION OF OFFER
(Dental Hygienist)

178 Green Street
Terre Haute, IN 47804
(812) 555-5555

May 12, 20--

Pat Cummings, D.M.D.
Any Dental Center
1140 Main Street
Wayne, IN 46802

Dear Dr. Cummings:

I received your letter of May 8, offering me the Dental Hygienist position at Any Dental Center. The compensation and benefits sound very tempting, and I am confident I would enjoy working with your staff.

However, shortly before receiving your letter, I was offered, another position, which I have accepted. Thank you for your time and consideration of my candidacy.

Best wishes,

Chris Smith, R.D.H.

▶ Letter confirms candidate's receipt of offer.　　▶ Letter uses short sentences and common words.

REJECTION OF OFFER
(Editor)

178 Green Street
Bartow, FL 33830
(813) 555-5555

September 17, 20--

Pat Cummings
Senior Editor
Any Publishing Company
1140 Main Street
Miami, FL 33173

Dear Mr. Cummings:

Thank you so much for your generous offer of employment, and for your confidence in my abilities as an Editor.

As I explained in our phone conversation, a newly arisen personal situation has caused me to rethink my plans to relocate to Miami. After much deliberation, I have decided that I must postpone my plans. I apologize for informing you of this change on such short notice, and I regret not being able to seize the opportunity to work for such a distinguished organization.

I hope that we will be able to join forces at some point in the future.

Sincerely,

Chris Smith

▶ Letter's tone is both courteous and appreciative.

▶ Candidate begins letter by thanking addressee for previous consideration.

REJECTION OF OFFER
(Law Enforcement Officer)

178 Green Street
Chalmette, LA 70043
(504) 555-5555

January 5, 20--

Pat Cummings
Police Chief
Any Police Department
1140 Main Street
Broussard, LA 70518

Dear Ms. Cummings:

I would like to extend my thanks to you and your squad for meeting with me about the Law Enforcement Officer position. I enjoyed the time I spent at the station. You have a great group of people working with you.

Although I know I would be proud to serve on your team, I must decline your generous offer. I have accepted a position in a neighboring town.

Thank you again and best of luck for a safe New Year.

Sincerely,

Chris Smith

▶ Candidate expresses gratitude for addressee's consideration.

▶ Candidate recalls enjoyable interview process.

REJECTION OF OFFER
(Marine Biologist)

178 Green Street
Tacoma, WA 98411
(206) 555-5555

November 4, 20--

Pat Cummings
Environmental Scientist
Any Corporation
1140 Main Street
Seattle, WA 98188

Dear Mr. Cummings:

I want to thank you for considering me qualified to represent your organization in the development and testing of aquatic toxicity. I consider Any Corporation to be a leader in the field of environmental testing, and am continually impressed by your work.

While I have enjoyed my work in toxicity, at this point in my career, I have decided to shift focus and so I must decline your generous offer. I have accepted a position researching aquaculture survival techniques in the Pacific Ocean. I feel this position will ideally lend itself to my career goals.

Thank you again for your confidence in my abilities as a Marine Biologist. Best of luck with your current aquatic testing project.

Sincerely,

Chris Smith

▶ Candidate closes letter on a positive note.

▶ Dedication to candidate's field of interest is emphasized.

REJECTION OF OFFER
(Paralegal)

178 Green Street
Woodbridge, NJ 07095
(908) 555-5555

March 4, 20--

Pat Cummings
Hiring Manager
Any Law Firm
1140 Main Street
Cherry Hill, NJ 08034

Dear Ms. Cummings:

Thank you very much for offering me the chance to work as a full-time Paralegal at Any Law Firm next fall. I realize what a challenging and gainful experience this opportunity represents.

As I explained in our interview on February 28, I had also submitted law school applications for the upcoming year. Early this week, I received notification of my acceptance at Fordham University.

After weighing my choices, I realized that the best decision would be to begin law school without delay. However, I sincerely wish to thank you for your trust in my skills.

Should you need a summer intern or part-time Law Clerk within the next three years, I would welcome the opportunity to work for your firm.

Sincerely,

Chris Smith

▶ Candidate relays enthusiasm for future opportunities.

▶ When rejecting an offer, providing a reason is optional.

REJECTION OF OFFER
(Production Assistant)

178 Green Street
Belair, TX 77401
(713) 555-5555

May 27, 20--

Pat Cummings
Producer
Any Production Company
1140 Main Street
Dallas, TX 75227

Dear Mr. Cummings:

It was a pleasure meeting with you last week and learning more about the current film projects underway at Any Production Company. I was pleased to receive your generous offer to assist you on a part-time basis as a Production Assistant.

Since our meeting, however, I have received an opportunity to pursue a documentary film project of my own. As you may recall, I was waiting for a decision on a grant proposal; on Thursday, I received word that I have been granted the necessary funding.

I am afraid this project will consume my energies on a full-time basis, so I must decline the opportunity to work with you on your new film. I admire your work greatly, Mr. Cummings, and know that I would have enjoyed assisting you.

Good luck on your project!

Sincerely,

Chris Smith

▶ Letter confirms candidate's receipt of offer.   ▶ One page is standard length for cover letters.

REJECTION OF OFFER
(Program Coordinator)

178 Green Street
Carlsbad, NM 88220
(505) 555-5555

April 5, 20--

Pat Cummings
Resort Director
Any Resort
1140 Main Street
Albuquerque, NM 87121

Dear Ms. Cummings:

Thank you very much for your employment offer extended during our meeting on April 3. I appreciate your confidence in my ability to perform the duties of Program Coordinator.

After careful deliberation, however, I must decline the position. As I previously mentioned, I have been considering a career in the hospitality industry for some time, and thought that the Program Coordinator position would provide exactly the type of entry-level experience I needed. I now realize that my true ambition is to follow in your footsteps; I want to become a Resort Director. Therefore, I have enrolled in a graduate program in Hospitality Management which begins later this month.

I wish you continued success at Any Resort. I was very impressed by your property and would like to apologize for any inconvenience my decision may cause.

Sincerely,

Chris Smith

▶ Candidate thanks addressee for employment offer.

▶ Letter provides additional information not stated in initial inquiry.

REJECTION OF OFFER
(Publishing Intern)

178 Green Street
Youngstown, OH 44501
(216) 555-5555

July 24, 20--

Pat Cummings
Editor
Any Publishing Company
1140 Main Street
Easton, PA 18044

Dear Mr. Cummings:

I would like to thank you for taking the time to talk to me about Any Publishing Company and for offering me an internship position. I enjoyed meeting both you and Lee Jones and was very enthusiastic about the type of company Any Publishing appears to be. Being able to participate in the editorial as well as the production side of publishing is quite appealing to me, and I realize how unique this opportunity is. I feel that the internship position and I would have been a perfect fit.

As you know, an abrupt change in my personal circumstances necessitated my turning down your offer. I want you to know that I sincerely regret this, as I know it would have been a both pleasure and a challenging experience to work for you. I hope I have not inconvenienced you. Thank you again for your time.

Sincerely,

Chris Smith
cc: Lee Jones

▶ Candidate apologizes for inconvenience to potential employer.

▶ Candidate's explanation of rejection is concise.

REJECTION OF OFFER
(Researcher)

178 Green Street
Winterthur, DE 19735
(302) 555-5555

February 14, 20--

Pat Cummings
Vice-President, Research and Development
Any Corporation
1140 Main Street
Chicago, IL 60605

Dear Ms. Cummings:

Thank you for taking the time to meet with me on Friday to discuss the opportunities for employment within your research and development department.

While I appreciate your generous offer, I have decided to decline the position. I have accepted a job elsewhere which I feel is better suited to my long-term needs.

Again, many thanks for your time. I wish you the best of luck in your future endeavors at Any Corporation.

Sincerely,

Chris Smith

▶ Candidate closes letter on a positive note.

▶ Letter expresses candidate's appreciation for addressee's consideration.

REJECTION OF OFFER
(Sales Representative)

178 Green Street
Menomonee Falls, WI 53051
(414) 555-5555

January 30, 20--

Pat Cummings
Vice-President, Sales
Any Corporation
1140 Main Street
Milwaukee, WI 53202

Dear Mr. Cummings:

I truly enjoyed our meeting on Friday to discuss the possibility of my joining Any Corporation in a sales position. Your staff seems very enthusiastic, and I was impressed by your semiannual sales record. That is quite an achievement.

Although I greatly appreciate your confidence in my abilities, I must decline your employment offer. I realize that in order to generate the quantity of sales necessary to reach mutual goals, I would have to invest a great deal of time in travel. At this point, that is not an allowance I am able to make.

Once again, thank you for your consideration. Best of luck in the future.

Sincerely,

Chris Smith

▶ Candidate highlights pertinent information discussed during interview.

▶ Letter's tone is both courteous and appreciative.

REJECTION OF OFFER
(Systems Representative)

178 Green Street
Newnan, GA 30265
(404) 555-5555

July 5, 20--

Pat Cummings
Director of Information Services
Any Corporation
1140 Main Street
Houston, TX 77030

Dear Ms. Cummings:

It was a pleasure talking with you on Monday concerning the Systems Representative position. I appreciated the opportunity to meet and talk with several members of your staff; everyone was very courteous and helpful.

I would also like to thank you for offering me employment at that meeting. However, I have decided to accept another position more in keeping with my specific career goals. Please accept my apology for having to decline your invitation.

I wish you the best of luck in the future.

Sincerely,

Chris Smith

▶ Candidate expresses gratitude for addressee's consideration.

▶ Day of interview is generally included in follow-up letter.

REJECTION OF OFFER
(Teacher)

178 Green Street
Canton, MA 02024
(617) 555-5555

June 19, 20--

Pat Cummings
Principal
Any Elementary School
1140 Main Street
Billerica, MA 01821

Dear Mr. Cummings:

    Thank you for taking the time to meet with me regarding teaching positions at Any Elementary School, and for offering me the opportunity to fill the vacancy in your fourth-grade classroom.

    As you know, my prime interest is in securing a position where I may apply my newly acquired skills in ESL instruction. I understand that budgetary constraints will not allow you to offer that type of position for the upcoming school year. However, I feel that this is where my interests and abilities best lie.

    I appreciate your offer, and although I cannot join your school at this time, I hope that our paths will cross in the future.

Sincerely,

Chris Smith

▶ Candidate thanks addressee for employment offer.

▶ Candidate confirms his/her commitment to field of interest.

REJECTION OF OFFER
(Veterinary Assistant)

178 Green Street
Kingston, RI 02881
(401) 555-5555

December 5, 20--

Pat Cummings, D.V.M.
Veterinarian
1140 Main Street
Warwick, RI 02888

Dear Dr. Cummings:

Thank you very much for offering me the opportunity to intern at your office for the upcoming semester.

Unfortunately, I have not been able to come to an agreement with the internship coordinator's office at the University of Rhode Island to work the twenty hours per week the position would demand. The University strictly adheres to its maximum commitment of fifteen hours per week.

I truly regret not being able to work with you. I hope that, in the future, circumstances will allow me to be of your assistance.

Again, my thanks for your generous offer.

Sincerely,

Chris Smith

▶ Letter is brief and concise.

▶ Candidate requests addressee's future consideration for available opportunities.

CHAPTER 33

RESIGNATION LETTER

Always send a formal resignation letter at least two weeks prior to terminating your present employment. Many resignation letters simply state your last day of employment and a willingness to assist in the transition process. Other letters may personally thank the employer and/or explain your reasons for departure. Whatever the circumstances may be, take care to phrase your resignation letter in a positive way. This is neither the time nor the place to lay out grievances. Your past employer may be called upon to provide a reference for you in the future.

RESIGNATION LETTER
(Architect)

178 Green Street
Greenwich, CT 06830
(203) 555-5555

March 24, 20--

Pat Cummings
Head Architect
Any Corporation
1140 Main Street
Hartford, CT 06106

Dear Ms. Cummings:

Effective April 7, 20--, I will be terminating my employment with Any Corporation. I have allowed two weeks prior to my departure for assisting in the transition process.

I have recently accepted a position as Head Architect with a local office in the public sector. I feel that this new opportunity is well suited to my long-term career goals.

I would be happy to train and assist my replacement, as well as complete any other organizational matters that need my attention.

Sincerely,

Chris Smith

▶ Letter indicates employee's willingness to help with departure preparations.

▶ Employee immediately specifies last date of employment.

RESIGNATION LETTER
(Environmental Consultant)

178 Green Street
Southfield, MI 48075
(313) 555-5555

April 7, 20--

Pat Cummings
Vice-President of Environmental Affairs
Any Corporation
1140 Main Street
Detroit, MI 48208

Dear Ms. Cummings:

I am writing to inform you that I will be leaving Any Corporation permanently on April 21, 20--. After much deliberation, I have decided to leave the State of Michigan.

Thank you for allowing me the opportunity to work with and learn from such an outstanding staff. The knowledge I have gained in my year at Any Corporation will surely aid me in my future endeavors. I am especially grateful for your close and patient supervision of my training. Your kind encouragement assured me of my ability to handle all aspects of the environmental consulting business.

If there is anything I can do to make my departure easier, please let me know.

Sincerely,

Chris Smith

▶ Letter indicates employee's willingness to help with departure preparations.

▶ Resignation letter should be dated two weeks prior to departure.

RESIGNATION LETTER
(Forester)

178 Green Street
Cheyenne, WY 82001
(504) 555-5555

February 15, 20--

Pat Cummings
Executive Director
Any State Park
1140 Main Street
Cheyenne, WY 82001

Dear Mr. Cummings:

As of March 6, I will be terminating my employment at Any State Park.

As you know, my goal has always been to work full-time as an advocate for forestry preservation. Recently, I have been offered, and accepted, a year's appointment with the International Forestry Preservation Corps in Brasilia, Brazil. The chance to work and live among the rain forests of Brazil is a unique and exciting opportunity that I could not turn down.

I have thoroughly enjoyed my time at Any State Park, and regret having to abandon my work here. Please be assured that I will extend every effort to make my departure as smooth as possible.

I appreciate your understanding.

Sincerely,

Chris Smith

▶ Letter briefly describes reason for departure.   ▶ Tone is both polite and somewhat formal.

RESIGNATION LETTER
(Hotel Manager)

178 Green Street
London, NWI 4SA UK
(44) 71 555 55 55

October 20, 20--

Pat Cummings
Vice-President, International Division
Any Corporation
1140 Main Street
Los Angeles, CA 90071

Dear Ms. Cummings:

I am writing to inform you that I have decided to return to the United States or Canada to establish a more permanent base for my family as of November 10.

I regret leaving Any Corporation, but as you know, I have asked several times, without success, for relocation to a position in the North American division. I had enjoyed working for Any Corporation and would have liked to continue. However, I have established an excellent reputation and the credentials for quality and profitability in both food and beverage and general hotel operations over the years, and I am confident these will assist me in securing a new position within the industry.

Once again, I regret having to resign from my position. I wish you much success in the future.

Sincerely,

Chris Smith

▶ In a rejection letter, stating reason for departure is optional.

▶ Letter's purpose is immediately stated.

RESIGNATION LETTER
(Marketing Director)

178 Green Street
Houston, TX 75217
(713) 555-5555

March 17, 20--

Pat Cummings
President
Any Company
1140 Main Street
Addison, TX 75001

Dear Mr. Cummings:

Regretfully, I must offer you my resignation effective March 31. Although I have enjoyed watching Any Company grow from its beginnings to its present, formidable size in my capacity as your Marketing Director, my ability to contribute to its future success is past. For this reason, I have accepted a position with a smaller company that offers the potential for growth.

I am grateful for the experience you allowed me. If there is anything I can do to make my departure a smooth one, please let me know.

Sincerely,

Chris Smith

▶ Employee expresses regret for departure.

▶ Resignation letters are generally short and to the point.

RESIGNATION LETTER
(Medical Technologist)

178 Green Street
West Fargo, ND 58078
(701) 555-5555

May 31, 20--

Pat Cummings
Senior Medical Technologist
Any Hospital
1140 Main Street
West Fargo, ND 5878

Dear Ms. Cummings:

Friday, June 16, will be my last day of employment at Any Hospital.

I have accepted a research position in a private laboratory setting. While I have enjoyed working as a member of your staff, my new employment will allow me to pursue hematology, which is, as you know, an area of real interest for me.

Please let me know if there is anything I can do to assist you in locating a replacement.

Sincerely yours,

Chris Smith

▶ Resignation letter should be dated two weeks prior to departure.

▶ Employee offers his/her assistance in securing a replacement.

RESIGNATION LETTER
(Production Assistant)

---

178 Green Street
Pittsburgh, PA 15222
(412) 555-5555

August 4, 20--

Pat Cummings
Internship Coordinator
Any Television Coordinator
1140 Main Street
Allentown, PA 18101

Dear Mr. Cummings:

    With this letter, I would like to offer notice of the termination of my production assistantship. As I am preparing to return to school, August 18 will be my last day of employment.

    My experience at Any Television Station has been both educational and enjoyable. I know that the production work I have been involved in will continue to benefit me in the future.

    Thank you for affording me this experience. I am grateful to have contributed to Any Television Station in return for the skills and knowledge I have gained.

Yours truly,

Chris Smith

▶ Employee immediately specifies last date of employment.

▶ Letter briefly describes reason for departure.

RESIGNATION LETTER
(Speech Pathologist)

178 Green Street
Santa Fe, NM 87504
(505) 555-5555

July 3, 20--

Pat Cummings
Principal
Any School
1140 Main Street
Deming, NM 87199

Dear Ms. Cummings:

I am writing to inform you of my resignation, effective July 15. Although I have enjoyed my position as a Speech Pathologist at Any School, I have accepted another position where I feel my diverse skills will be more fully utilized.

I want to thank you for the wonderful experience I had here. Both the staff and the students were great to work with. I wish you much luck in the approaching academic year.

Sincerely,

Chris Smith

▶ Tone is both polite and somewhat formal.   ▶ In a rejection letter, stating reason for departure is optional.

RESIGNATION LETTER
(Transaction Processing Supervisor)

178 Green Street
St. Louis, MO 63090
(314) 555-5555

December 12, 20--

Pat Cummings
Operations Manager
Any Corporation
1140 Main Street
St. Louis, MO 63102

Dear Mr. Cummings:

Please accept this as formal notification of my resignation from Any Corporation. I am fully prepared to offer the customary two weeks notice. My last day of employment with you will therefore be December 29.

While I have found my experience at Any Corporation to be very rewarding, I have accepted another position which I feel is better suited to my career goals. In my current role as Supervisor of Transaction Processing, I have successfully restructured processing procedure, increased profits, and supervised a sizeable staff. I am ready to move forward, confident of the superior skills I have acquired under your competent management.

Thank you for your confidence in my abilities. I hope I have succeeded in contributing to your long-term goals.

Sincerely,

Chris Smith

▶ Letter's purpose is immediately stated.

▶ Resignation letters are generally short and to the point.

RESIGNATION LETTER
(Vice-President, Sales)

178 Green Street
Falls Church, VA 22043
(703) 555-5555

August 22, 20--

Pat Cummings
President
Any Company
1140 Main Street
Alexandria, VA 22312

Dear Ms. Cummings:

I have enjoyed serving as Vice-President of Sales, but I have received an offer from another pharmaceutical company that I feel is better suited to my career objectives. Regrettably, I submit this letter as notice of my resignation.

My last day will be September 6. If I can be of any assistance in recommending potential candidates for my position, I would be more than happy to help.

I wish you the best of luck and future success.

Sincerely,

Chris Smith

▶ Employee offers his/her assistance in securing a replacement.

▶ Employee expresses regret for departure.

CHAPTER 34

ACCEPTANCE LETTER

Even if you've been verbally offered the position of your choice, remember that no hiring decision is final until it is in writing. Confirm your acceptance of a job offer with a brief, but gracious letter. Express thanks for the organization's decision and briefly describe your enthusiasm for the new position. You may also use this opportunity to confirm terms of your agreement, including start date, salary, and benefits. In addition to solidifying the details, an acceptance letter shows you recognize the importance of good manners. Ken O. sent a polite thank-you letter the day after receiving an employment offer from A&R Mitchell Design Company. When he began work three weeks later, his employer remembered that letter and Ken started off his new association on the right foot.

ACCEPTANCE LETTER
(Accountant)

178 Green Street
Cedar City, UT 84720
(801) 555-5555

December 4, 20--

Pat Cummings
Account Manager
Any Corporation
1140 Main Street
Salt Lake City, UT 84110

Dear Mr. Cummings:

Please receive this letter as my formal acceptance of your employment offer. I am very excited about joining the ranks at Any Corporation, and I hope to quickly make a contribution to your qualified accounting staff.

Yesterday, I submitted a formal resignation notice to my current employer, and have arranged a start date of December 9. I will contact you later this week to confirm that date and to provide any additional information you might need.

In the interim, be assured of my enthusiasm about beginning a new phase of my career with Any Corporation. I look forward to working with you.

Sincerely,

Chris Smith

▶ Candidate confirms termination of previous employment.

▶ Candidate expresses confidence in his/her ability to fulfill employer's expectations.

ACCEPTANCE LETTER
(Benefits Administrator)

178 Green Street
Weeping Water, NE 68463
(402) 555-5555

May 22, 20--

Pat Cummings
Human Resources Director
Any Corporation
1140 Main Street
Chicago, IL 60605

Dear Ms. Cummings:

    I would like to express my enthusiam for my new position as Benefits Administrator. This is an exciting opportunity, and I am eager to join your ranks.

    I have turned in my resignation to my present employer, and I will begin working for you three weeks from today (Monday, June 18). During the interim, I will remain in contact with both you and Rick Starchon in order to ensure that my initiation is a smooth one.

    Again, thank you for your confidence and support. I look forward to fulfilling your expectations.

Sincerely,

Chris Smith
cc: Rick Starchon

▶ Letter cites specific start date.

▶ In closing, candidate suggests follow-up contact to finalize terms of agreement.

ACCEPTANCE LETTER
(Contractor)

178 Green Street
Mayville, WI 53050
(414) 555-5555

May 1, 20--

Pat Cummings
Principal Architect
Any Corporation
1140 Main Street
Columbia, SC 29208

Dear Mr. Cummings:

I am pleased to accept the offer to assist you on the Glendale Shopping Complex project. The proposal you gave me sounds very exciting, and I am excited about being given the chance to add my expertise to such a challenging endeavor.

As you know, I am in the process of securing housing to facilitate my move to Columbia. I expect to be settled in your area by the end of the month, in plenty of time to start work in mid-June. Should this arrangement present a conflict, please let me know.

I will keep in touch as my start date nears. Thank you again for your kind offer.

Sincerely,

Chris Smith

▶ Candidate invites employer to inquire about additional information.

▶ Candidate accepts terms of employment offer.

ACCEPTANCE LETTER
(Customer Service Representative)

178 Green Street
South Pasadena, CA 91030
(213) 555-5555

April 1, 20--

Pat Cummings
Customer Service Manager
Any Corporation
1140 Main Street
Los Angeles, CA 90010

Dear Ms. Cummings:

    I would like to thank you and Donald Grasier for offering me the position of Customer Service Representative during our meeting on Friday. As you suggested, I took the weekend to consider your offer, and am pleased to accept its terms.

    This morning I gave notice to my current employer and should be able to begin work at Any Corporation on Monday, April 17. Please let me know if there are any papers we need to go over before my start date.

    Thank you again for providing me with this opportunity. I am very excited to join your sales team!

Sincerely,

Chris Smith
cc: Donald Grasier

▶ Letter includes reference to all involved in hiring process.

▶ Candidate expresses willingness to complete necessary preparations before start date.

ACCEPTANCE LETTER
(Editorial Assistant)

178 Green Street
Halifax, MA 02338

July 6, 20--

Pat Cummings
Editor
Any Publishing Company
1140 Main Street
Port Chester, NY 10573

Dear Mr. Cummings:

As per our telephone conversation, I would like to confirm my acceptance of your employment offer. This position as Editorial Assistant provides exactly the kind of experience I hoped to find. I feel confident that I can make a significant contribution to Any Publishing Company, and I am grateful for the opportunity you have given me.

As we discussed, I will report to work at 8:00 A.M. on Monday, July 17. I will be moving to New York on July 11. Until then, I can be reached in Massachusetts at (617) 555-5555. Again, I appreciate your confidence in me and look forward to beginning work.

Sincerely,

Chris Smith

▶ Candidate provides any additional information needed before start date.

▶ Candidate reiterates terms of agreement previously discussed.

ACCEPTANCE LETTER
(Geographer)

178 Green Street
St. Paul, MN 55104
(612) 555-5555

May 12, 20--

Pat Cummings
Hiring Coordinator
Any Government Agency
1140 Main Street
Minneapolis, MN 55413

Dear Ms. Cummings:

I am grateful for the opportunity to be part of such an esteemed department in the agency. I look forward to assuming my post as Geographer, and I am happy to accept the terms of our agreement.

As discussed, my graduation date is set for May 31, and I will be available to begin the following Monday, June 5. I will contact your offices early next week to schedule my training session.

Again, thank you. I am very excited to begin.

Sincerely,

Chris Smith

▶ In closing, candidate suggests follow-up contact to finalize terms of agreement.

▶ Candidate reiterates terms of agreement previously discussed.

ACCEPTANCE LETTER
(Group Leader)

178 Green Street
Simons Island, GA 31522
(912) 555-555

November 27, 20--

Pat Cummings
Program Director
Any Treatment Center
1140 Main Street
Moultire, GA 31776

Dear Mr. Cummings:

    It is with great expectation that I accept your offer of employment with Any Treatment Center. The prospect of working as a Group Leader at such a progressive and reputable center is very exciting to me.

    The terms of your invitation are very generous, and I will immediately make plans to facilitate a start date within the next two weeks. As requested, I will call your office on Friday to finalize arrangements.

    Thank you very much for your trust in my capabilities, Mr. Cummings. I am very eager to begin training and prove my worth.

Sincerely,

Chris Smith

▶ Candidate suggests time frame for follow-up contact.

▶ Letter expresses candidate's enthusiasm for new position.

ACCEPTANCE LETTER
(Statistician)

178 Green Street
Kingston, RI 02881
(401) 555-5555

February 25, 20--

Pat Cummings
Chief Statistician
Any Corporation
1140 Main Street
Pawtucket, RI 02862

Dear Ms. Cummings:

I received your letter, and I am very pleased to accept your offer of employment as a Statistician at Any Corporation. I appreciate your trust in my skills, and will make every effort to contribute to your team.

I have given notice of my resignation at my current employer and intend to start at Any Corporation on Monday, March 13. As per your request, I have scheduled a physical exam for this week, and will submit the appropriate materials on my first day of work.

I am very excited to begin working with you and your statistical staff.

Sincerely,

Chris Smith

▶ Candidate confirms termination of previous employment.

▶ Candidate expresses willingness to complete necessary preparations before start date.

ACCEPTANCE LETTER
(Underwriter)

178 Green Street
Batavia, IL 60510
(708) 555-5555

October 16, 20--

Pat Cummings
General Manager
Any Insurance Agency
1140 Main Street
Decatur, IL 62526

Dear Mr. Cummings:

I received your letter dated October 13, and I am pleased to accept your employment offer. I am very excited to begin work as an Underwriter for such a prestigious organization.

I would like to confirm my start date of October 30. I have already given notice to my current employer, and expect a smooth transition to Any Insurance Agency.

Should you require any additional information, please do not hesitate to contact me. Once again, I would like to thank you and Frank Russo for your positive response to my candidacy.

Sincerely,

Chris Smith
cc: Frank Russo

▶ Candidate refers to favorable aspect of new environment.

▶ Letter includes reference to all involved in hiring process.

INDEX